Social Media
a critical introduction

Christian Fuchs

Los Angeles | London | New Delhi
Singapore | Washington DC

Los Angeles | London | New Delhi
Singapore | Washington DC

SAGE Publications Ltd
1 Oliver's Yard
55 City Road
London EC1Y 1SP

SAGE Publications Inc.
2455 Teller Road
Thousand Oaks, California 91320

SAGE Publications India Pvt Ltd
B 1/I 1 Mohan Cooperative Industrial Area
Mathura Road
New Delhi 110 044

SAGE Publications Asia-Pacific Pte Ltd
3 Church Street
#10-04 Samsung Hub
Singapore 049483

Editor: Mila Steele
Editorial assistant: James Piper
Production editor: Imogen Roome
Proofreader: Leigh C. Timmins
Indexer: Martin Hargreaves
Marketing manager: Michael Ainsley
Cover design: Jennifer Crisp
Typeset by: C&M Digitals (P) Ltd, Chennai, India
Printed in Great Britain by
Ashford Colour Press Ltd

Library of Congress Control Number: 2013939264

British Library Cataloguing in Publication data

A catalogue record for this book is available from
the British Library.

MIX
Paper from
responsible sources
FSC
www.fsc.org   FSC® C011748

ISBN 978-1-4462-5730-2
ISBN 978-1-4462-5731-9 (pbk)

Social Media

Contents

1

What is a Critical Introduction to Social Media?

Key questions

- What is social about social media?
- What does it mean to think critically?
- What is Critical Theory and why is it relevant?
- How can we approach Critical Theory?

Key concepts

Social media
Critical theory

Marxist theory
Critical political economy

Overview

What is social about social media? What are the implications of social media platforms such as Facebook, Google, YouTube Wikipedia, Twitter, for power, the economy and politics? This book gives a critical introduction to studying social media. It engages the reader with the concepts needed for critically understanding the world of social media with questions such as:

- Chapter 2: What is social about social media?
- Chapter 3: How meaningful is the notion of participatory culture for thinking about social media?

- Chapter 4: How useful are the concepts of communication power and mass self-communication in the network society for thinking about social media?
- Chapter 5: How does the business of social media work?
- Chapter 6: What is good and bad about Google, the world's leading Internet platform and search engine?
- Chapter 7: What is the role of privacy and surveillance on Facebook, the world's most successful social networking site?
- Chapter 8: Has Twitter brought about a new form of politics and democracy and a revitalization of the political public sphere?
- Chapter 9: What are the potentials of WikiLeaks, the world's best-known online watchdog, for making power transparent?
- Chapter 10: What forms and principles of collaborative knowledge production are characteristic for Wikipedia, the world's most widely accessed wiki-based online encyclopaedia?
- Chapter 11: How can we achieve social media that serve the purposes of a just and fair world, in which we control society and communicate in common?

This book introduces a theoretical framework for critically understanding social media that is used for discussing social media platforms in the context of specific topics: being social (Chapter 2), participatory culture (Chapter 3), communication and media power (Chapter 4), political economy (Chapter 5), political ethics (Chapter 6), surveillance and privacy (Chapter 7), democracy and the public sphere (Chapter 8), power and transparency (Chapter 9), collaborative work (Chapter 10), the commons (Chapter 11).

Social Media and the Arab Spring

2011 was a year of protests, revolutions and political change. It was a year where people all over the world tried to make their dreams of a different society reality. Wael Ghonim is the administrator of the Facebook page "We are all Khaled Said". He says that this page and other social media were crucial for the Egyptian revolution: "I always said that if you want to liberate a society [. . .] if you want to have a free society. [. . .] This is Revolution 2.0. [. . .] Everyone is contributing to the content".[1] Technology analyst Evgeny Morozov, in contrast to Ghonim, says that social media do not bring about revolutions: the talk of Twitter and Facebook revolutions is "a naive belief in the emancipatory nature of online communication that rests on a stubborn refusal to acknowledge its downside" (Morozov 2010, xiii). Pointing, clicking, uploading, liking and befriending on Facebook would be "slacktivism" – "feel-good online activism that has zero political or social impact. It gives those who participate in 'slacktivist' campaigns an illusion of having a meaningful impact on the world without demanding anything more than joining a Facebook group" (Morozov 2009). For Morozov (2013, 127), Ghonim is "a man who lives and breathes Internet-centrism" – an ideology that reduces societal change to the Internet.

---

1 http://technorati.com/politics/article/revolution-20-wael-ghonim-thanks-mark, accessed on July 2, 2013.

Social Media and the Occupy Movement

2011 was also the year in which various Occupy movements emerged in North America, Greece, Spain, the United Kingdom and other countries. One of their protest tactics is to build protest camps in public squares that are centres of gravity for discussions, events and protest activities. Being asked about the advantages of Occupy's use of social media, respondents in the OccupyMedia! Survey[2] said that they allow them to reach a broad public and to protect themselves from the police (for the detailed results see: Fuchs 2013):

- "As much as I wish that occupy would keep away from a media such as Facebook it got the advantage that it can reach out to lots of people that [. . .] [are] otherwise hard to reach out to" (#20).
- "All of these social media [. . .] Facebook, Twitter etc. helps spread the word but I think the biggest achievement is Livestream: those of us who watch or participate in change can inform other streamers of actions, police or protest moving from one place [. . .] to another. That saved many streamers from getting hurt or less arrests" (#36).

At the same time, the respondents identified risks of the use of commercial social media:

- "Facebook is generally exploitative, and controls the output of Facebook posts, the frequency they are seen by other people. It's a disaster and we shouldn't use it at all. But we still do" (#28).
- "There have been occasions where the police seemed to have knowledge that was only shared in a private group and/or text messages and face-to-face" (#55).
- "Events for protests that were created on Facebook, but not organized IRL [in real life]. Many 'participants' in calls for protests on Facebook, but at least 70% of them [don't] [. . .] show up at the actual demonstration" (#74).
- "Twitter has been willing to turn over protestors' tweets to authorities which is a big concern" (#84).
- "Censorship of content by YouTube and email deletions on Gmail" (#103).
- "Yes, my Twitter account was subpoena'd, for tweeting a hashtag. The supboena was dropped in court" (#238).
- "Facebook = Tracebook" (#203).

Unpaid Work for the Huffington Post

The Huffington Post (HP) is the most popular news blog in the world. Arianna Huffington started it in 2005. It has been based on the contributions of many unpaid voluntary bloggers (Fuchs 2014). In 2011, AOL bought the Huffington Post for

---

2 The data collection for the OccupyMedia! Survey took place from November 6, 2012 until February 20, 2013. I conducted the research as an online survey. Its aim was to find out more about how Occupy activists use social media and what opportunities and risks of social media they see. The survey resulted in a dataset with $N = 429$ respondents.

US$315 million and turned it into a profit-oriented business. The writer Jonathan Tasini, who had contributed to the HP, filed a $105-million class action suit against HP, arguing that it unjustly enriched itself from its bloggers' unpaid contributions when it was turned into a business and acquired by AOL. Tasini stated: "In my view, the Huffington Post's bloggers have essentially been turned into modern-day slaves on Arianna Huffington's plantation. [. . .] She wants to pocket the tens of millions of dollars she reaped from the hard work of those bloggers."[3]

What is the role and potential of social media in protests and revolution? Is social media use a form of clicktivism and slacktivism that soothes the conscience of concerned middle-class people who do not want to take risks? Is it a powerful tool of protest? What is the role of commercial interests, the state and politics in social media? Do activists and citizen journalists run the risk of being monitored and surveilled by the police and exploited by social media companies that turn the voluntary work of users into money? And if this is the case, then what are the alternatives?

In order to answer such questions, we need to study social media critically. But what is social media? And what is critical thinking?

1.1. What is Social about Social Media?

Questions that many people immediately ask when one employs the term "social media" are: What is social about social media? Are not all media social? These questions have to do with another question: What does it mean to be social?

Information and Cognition

Are human beings always social or only if they interact with others? In sociological theory, there are different concepts of the social (see Chapter 2). Some say that all media are social because they are part of society and aspects of society are present in the technological artefacts we use. This means that if you sit alone in front of your computer, type a document in your word processor and are not connected to the Internet, your activities are perfectly social: the ideas you think and write up refer to ideas of other people and what is happening in society; the word processor has certain features and functions that were all designed by humans for certain reasons and under specific working conditions. So cognition is a social activity. The computer you use may have been assembled in China and the raw materials out of which its components were made may come from mines in Africa. You cannot see all the labour that goes into the computer, but nonetheless it is a tool that was created in society by humans who experience certain working conditions. If we employ this broad understanding of sociality, then not just Facebook is social, but also television, the radio, the telegraph, posters, books, wall paintings and all other forms of information.

---

3 www.forbes.com/sites/jeffbercovici/2011/04/12/aol-huffpo-suit-seeks-105m-this-is-about-justice/, accessed on July 2, 2013.

Communication

Other people say that not all media are social, but only those that support communication between humans. Communication is a reciprocal process between at least two
humans, in which symbols are exchanged and all interaction partners give meaning
to these symbols. Computer-mediated communication did not start with Facebook
and Twitter: Ray Tomlinson sent the first Internet email from one computer to the
other in 1971.[4] If we understand social activity to mean communication or symbolic
interaction, then not all media use is social. Based on this understanding, it is not
social if you write a document alone, but it is social to send an email or chat with a
friend on Facebook. Communication is a basic feature of all societies and all human
activity. We cannot live and survive without communication, just like we cannot survive without food and water. Communication takes place routinely in everyday life.

Community

Some communications that take place repeatedly result in something more
than just social relationships – they involve feelings of belonging together or
friendship. Communication turns this form of the social into community. A
certain share of the communications on Facebook is part of communities of
personal friends, political activists, hobby or fan groups. But online communities are not new; they existed already in bulletin board systems such as the
WELL (Whole Earth 'Lectronic Link) in the 1980s.

Collaboration and Co-operative Work

A fourth form of sociality is collaboration or co-operative work. The research area
of computer-supported co-operative work (CSCW) was founded in the 1980s and
deals with how computers enable human co-operation. Collaborative work, as
for example the co-operative editing of articles performed on Wikipedia or the
joint writing of a document on Google Docs, is not new in computing, although
the popularity of Wikipedia and wiki platforms such as Mediawiki, PBWorks,
Wikispaces is a more recent development. CSCW was already the subject of academic discussions in the 1980s when a conference series started with the first
ACM Conference on CSCW that took place in December 1986 in Austin, Texas. The
concept of the wiki is also not new: the first wiki technology (the WikiWikiWeb)
was introduced by Ward Cunningham in 1995.

Information, Communication, Collaboration and Community are Forms of Sociality but What is Now Social about Facebook?

There are different forms of the social, such as information, communication,
communities and collaboration. When we talk about "social media", we have

---

4 See http://openmap.bbn.com/~tomlinso/ray/firstemailframe.html and http://openmap.bbn.com/~tomlinso/
ray/ka10.html, accessed on July 2, 2013.

to be careful to specify which meaning of the term "social" we are employing. Therefore, studying social media is in need of social theory and social philosophy. These tools of thought allow us to come to grips with the basic meaning of terms such as sociality, media, society, power, democracy, participation, culture, labour, communication, information, the public sphere, the private realm, etc. that are often employed when discussing social media, but often poorly understood.

All computing systems, and therefore all web applications, as well as all forms of media can be considered as social because they store and transmit human knowledge that originates in social relations in society. They are objectifications of society and human social relations. Whenever a human uses a computing system or a medium (also if s/he is alone in a room), s/he cognizes based on objectified knowledge that is the outcome of social relations. But not all computing systems and web applications support direct communication between humans, in which at least two humans mutually exchange symbols that are interpreted as being meaningful. Amazon mainly provides information about books and other goods one can buy; it is not primarily a tool of communication, but rather a tool of information, whereas Facebook has in-built communication features that are frequently used (mail system, walls for comments, forums, etc.).

Social media is a complex term with multi-layered meanings. Facebook contains a lot of content (information) and is a tool for communication and for the maintenance creation of communities. It is only to a minor degree a tool for collaborative work, but involves at least three types of sociality: cognition, communication and community. Chapter 2 focuses more in depth on the concept of social media.

Understanding social media critically means, among other things, to engage with the different forms of sociality on the Internet in the context of society. If one compares the most frequently accessed websites in 2013 to the ones that were popular in 2000, then one sees that the most accessed sites in 2000 were MSN, Yahoo, Excite, AOL, Microsoft, Daum, eBay and Altavista,[5] whereas in 2013 the most accessed websites in the world include Google, Facebook, YouTube, Yahoo!, Baidu, Wikipedia, Windows Live, QQ, Amazon and Twitter, Blogspot, LinkedIn, Wordpress.[6] The difference is that these platforms now include social networking sites (Facebook, LinkedIn), video sharing sites (YouTube), blogs (Blogspot, Wordpress), wikis (Wikipedia) and microblogs (Twitter, Weibo). There are relatively new companies in the Internet business that did not exist in 2000. What makes sites like Facebook distinct is that they are integrated platforms that combine many media and information and communication technologies, such as webpages, webmail, digital image, digital video, discussion group, guest book, connection list, or search engine. Many of these technologies are social network tools themselves. Social networking sites, sharing sites for user-generated content, blogs, microblogs and wikis, just like all other

5 According to alexa.com, version from August 15, 2000, archived on http://web.archive.org/web/200008150 52659/, www.alexaresearch.com/clientdir/web_reports/top_websites_nonclient.cfm, accessed on July 2, 2013.
6 According to alexa.com, version from February 25, 2013.

media, are social in the broad understanding of the term as information. Some of them support communication, some collaborative work, content sharing or community-building. These latter three forms of sociality have, due to the rise of platforms like Facebook, LinkedIn, Wikipedia or YouTube, become more important on the World Wide Web (WWW).

The discussion shows that understanding social media requires asking and engaging with a lot of theoretical questions. This book invites the reader to engage with theory and philosophy for understanding contemporary media. Social theory not only allows us to understand the meaning of concepts, it also allows us to ask important questions about the world and it can be fun to theorize and to discuss theories with others. And the best questions we can ask are critical ones. But what does critical thinking mean? And why does it matter?

1.2. What is Critical Thinking and Why Does it Matter?

When discussing the question "What does it mean to be critical?" with academic colleagues, many have the immediate reaction: we are all critical because we ask critical questions and criticize the work of our academic colleagues. Scholars who characterize themselves as critical thinkers or critical theorists often question these claims. They emphasize the term "critical" and the need for being critical in order to stress that in their view not everyone is critical and that a lot of thought (academic or not) is uncritical. Their basic argument is that not all questions really matter to the same extent for society and that those whom they call uncritical or administrative researchers often focus on questions and research that is irrelevant, or even harmful, for improving society in such a way that all can benefit. They are concerned with questions of power.

Power

Power is a complex concept, discussed in more detail in Chapter 4, that focuses on communication power. Power has to do with who controls society, who is taking important decisions, who owns basic resources, who is considered as being influential, who has the reputation to influence and change society, who is an opinion maker, or who defines dominant norms, rules and values. The question "Who is in power?" immediately begets the question "And who lacks the capacity to influence and change things?". Power asymmetries mean that there are groups of people who benefit in society at the expense of others, by using them for their own ends and deriving advantages that do not benefit society as a whole or those who are being used.

It makes a difference whether one asks questions about society with a concern for power or not. Let's come back to the topic of social media. One can ask a lot of questions that ignore the topic of power. For example:

- Who uses social media?
- For what purposes are social media used?
- Why are they used?
- About what do people communicate on social media?
- What are the most popular social media?
- How can politicians and parties best use social media for obtaining more votes in the next elections?
- How can companies use social media for improving their advertisements and public relations so that they make more profits?
- How much average profit does one click on a targeted ad that is presented on Facebook or Google bring a company?
- How can a company make profit by crowdsourcing work to users and employing free and open source software?

Such questions are not uncommon, but rather quite typical. Yet they include two problems. First, many of them ignore the topic of power. They do not ask the questions who benefits and who has disadvantages from the use of social media, the Internet and ICTs (information and communication technologies) and how the benefits of some are based on the disadvantages of others. Second, such questions are based on a particularistic logic: they are concerned with how certain groups, especially companies and politicians, can benefit from social media and ignore the question of how this use benefits or harms others and society at large. So uncritical questions ask, for example, how *companies* can benefit from social media, but do not discuss the working conditions in these companies – the wealth gap between the well-off, managers and shareholders, on the one hand, and the large number of the unemployed, the homeless and precarious workers on the other hand, and the rising inequality in the world.

Let's go back to the three examples of social media in the Arab Spring, the Occupy movement and the Huffington Post. What does it mean to ask critical questions in the context of these examples?

Asking Critical Questions about Social Media and the Arab Spring

- Which power structures are underlying contemporary revolutions and protests?
- How do they influence the use of social media?
- What are the realities, opportunities and risks of social movements' social media use?
- Does the corporate character of platforms like Facebook, Twitter and YouTube negatively impact social movements' use?
- If so, how?

- How do social movements try to establish and use alternative, non-profit and non-commercial social media? What are the advantages and potentials of such platforms in contrast to for-profit platforms?
- Which problems and limits do such alternative platforms face in capitalist society, in which the control of resources (money, time, attention, influence, etc.) is asymmetrically distributed?
- Is there a risk that governments monitor social movements' social media use and use the obtained data for repressing, torturing or blackmailing activists?
- Which forms of economic and political censorship of social media are there, how do they work and what needs to be done to fight against them?

Asking Critical Questions about Social Media and the Occupy Movement

- What kind of movement is Occupy and how does it relate to the power structures of contemporary society?
- What are the realities, opportunities and risks of Occupy's social media use?
- Which potentials for creating a public sphere in protests does the use of livestreams and alternative social media have in protests?
- How do governments try to monitor the social media use of activists and why is this problematic?
- How can activists best handle the contradiction between increased public visibility and increased police surveillance that shapes Occupy's social media use best?
- What is activists' perceived role of social media in the Occupy movement?
- How do they assess the empowering and limiting aspects of social media?
- Which advantages and disadvantages do Occupy activists see in relation to the movements' use of commercial digital media and alternative, non-commercial, non-profit digital media?

Asking Critical Questions about Unpaid Work for the Huffington Post

- What is a commodity and and what is the process by which something is turned into a commodity (=commodification)?
- How does commodification work on social media such as the Huffington Post?
- What is the role of advertising in these models? What is the role of users' activities in these models?
- Why is commodification in general, and on social media in particular, problematic?

- What are the negative implications of crowdsourcing and targeted advertising?
- What does exploitation of labour mean?
- In what way is the labour of users on social media exploited?
- How can the use of Facebook be exploited labour even though I am not paid for it, I do it in my free time and I find that it is a fun activity that is helpful in my everyday life?
- How can Facebook use be labour even though it is so different from working in a coal mine and feels more like singing a song with friends at a campfire?
- Can something be exploitation even though it does not feel like exploitation and is fun? Do users actually think about corporate social media use as labour?
- Do they see any problems? If so, what problems? If not, why not?
- How do trade unions, data protection agencies, privacy advocates, consumer protection groups and social movements react to the existence of this digital labour?
- Are there any alternatives to commercial social media? What are the opportunities and limitations of alternative social media?

The list of questions is exemplary and far from complete. It shows that many critical questions can be asked about social media and need to be asked. Thinking critically about society and the media is concerned with creating structures of society and the media where everyone can benefit.

1.3. What is Critical Theory?

Critical theory is a specific form of critical thinking. Why is it relevant for understanding computer technologies?

The history of communication and transport technologies is not a progressive success story. Although many people today benefit in mutual ways from using books, telephones, trains, cars, television, radio, computers, the Internet, or mobile phones, the history of these technologies is deeply embedded into the history of capitalism, colonialism, warfare, exploitation and inequality. Winseck and Pike (2007) show, with the example of the global expansion of cable and wireless companies (such as, for example, Western Union, Commercial Cable Company, Atlantic Telegraph Company or Marconi) in the years 1860–1930, that there was a distinct connection between communication, globalization and capitalism. Edwin Black (2001) has shown in his book *IBM and the Holocaust* that by selling punch card systems to the Nazis, International Business Machines (IBM) assisted them in their attempt to extinguish the Jews, ethnic minorities, communists, socialists, gay people, the handicapped and others. The Nazis used these systems for numbering the victims, storing and processing where they should be brought, what should happen to them, and for organizing their transport to extermination camps such as Auschwitz, Bergen-Belsen, Buchenwald, Dachau, Majdanek, Mauthausen, Ravensbrück or Sachsenhausen. IBM made an international business out of mass murder (*I-B-M*) by accumulating profits from selling data storage and processing machines to the Nazis. The punch cards covered information on where a victim would be deported, the type of victim he/she was (Jew, homosexual, deserter, prisoner of war, etc.), and his/her status. Code status 6 was "Sonderbehandlung" (special treatment), which meant death in the gas chamber. Black has shown that the system was delivered and maintained by IBM and that IBM New York and the German Nazi state made rental contracts. Black (2001, 9) says that there was a "conscious involvement – directly and through its subsidiaries –" of IBM "in the Holocaust, as well as [...] in the Nazi war machine that murdered millions of others throughout Europe". The computer and the Internet have their origins in the mili-tary-industrial complex and were later commercialized. They both first served the interest of war before companies discovered the profitability of these technologies. The examples show that corporate, military or state interests often stand above the communicative interest of humans.

This book is based on a concern for human interests and for overcoming the global problems of society. We live in turbulent times that are shaped by world-wide inequality, global economic crisis, global ecological crisis, war and ter-rorism, high unemployment, precarious living and working conditions, rising poverty levels, etc. Can all benefit in this situation from social media? Or is it likely that only some benefit at the expense of others? In this book, I ask ques-tions about power and (in)equality in contemporary society. I want to stress that it is important to be concerned about alleviating inequality and creating a society of equals, in which all benefit and lead a good life. The book is based on the nor-mative assumption that we need a society and social media that benefit not just some of us, but all of us. This universal concern makes this book a critical book. Therefore it is called "Social Media: A Critical Theory".

Critical theory is especially connected to one name: Karl Marx.

You Want me to Read Karl Marx? Are You Crazy? Why Should I Do That?

Karl Marx does not need much introduction. He was a thorough theorist and fierce critic of capitalism, a public intellectual, a critical journalist, a polemicist, a philosopher, economist, sociologist, political scientist, historian, Hegelian, author (with Friedrich Engels) of the *Communist Manifesto* (1848) and *Capital* (1867, 1885, 1894), a leader of the Communist League and the International Workingmen's Association and one of the most influential political thinkers in the nineteenth, twentieth and twenty-first centuries.

But wasn't Marx responsible for the horrors of Stalin and the Soviet Union? Marx did not live in the 1930s, when Stalin organized show trials and killed his opponents. So he cannot really be blamed for what happened more than 50 years after his death. Furthermore, in many of his writings Marx was deeply concerned with humanism and a democratic form of socialism, whereas Stalin and his followers were arguably not (for a thorough discussion of why prejudices against Marx are incorrect, see Eagleton 2011).

The capitalist crisis that started in 2008 has made clear that there are huge gaps between the rich and the poor, owners and non-owners of capital and that there are big problems of capitalism. The Occupy movement has made class an important topic. Occupy Wall Street argues that there is a "corrosive power of major banks and multinational corporations over the democratic process" and that "the role of Wall Street in creating an economic collapse [. . .] has caused the greatest recession in generations".[7] Occupy London defines itself as "part of the global social movement that has brought together concerned citizens from across the world against this injustice and to fight for a sustainable economy that puts people and the environment we live in before corporate profits. [. . .] Ordinary people – families, small businesses and communities – are being forced to pay for a crisis they didn't cause".[8]

Marx analyzed how class, capitalism, crisis and power work and what the potentials of struggles for a better world are. Occupy and the reality of capitalism make Marx's themes very topical. The engagement with Marx can help us to better understand the situation we are in today, the problems society is facing and how struggles for a better future can be organized.

But isn't Marx a nineteenth-century thinker? Why should I read him if I want to understand social media? Obviously, Marx did not use Facebook. So why should I care about his works today?

So, You Tell Me that Marx Invented the Internet?

Some scholars have said that Marx never commented on networked media (McLuhan 2001, 41). But Marx discussed the implications of the telegraph for the globalization of trade, production and society, was one of the first philosophers and sociologists of technology in modern society, anticipated the role of knowledge labour and the rise of an information society and was himself a critical journalist. This shows that somebody who cares about the analysis of media and communication has many reasons to engage with Marx. Marx stressed the importance of the concept of the social: he highlighted that phenomena in society (such as money or markets and, today, the Internet, Facebook, Twitter, etc.) do not simply exist, but are the outcome of social relations between human beings. They do not exist automatically and by necessity because humans can change society. Therefore, society and the media are open for change and contain the possibility of a better future. If we want to understand what is social about social media, then reading Marx can help us a lot.

In his work the *Grundrisse*, Marx described a global information network, in which "everyone attempts to inform himself" about others and "connections are introduced" (Marx 1857/1858, 161). Such a description not only sounds like an anticipation of the concept of the Internet, it is also an indication that Marx's thought is relevant for Media/Communication Studies and the study of the Internet and social media. This passage in the *Grundrisse* is an indication that

---

7 www.occupywallst.org/about/, accessed on July 2, 2013.
8 www.occupylondon.org.uk/about/about-occupy-london-2, accessed on July 2, 2013.

although the Internet as technology was a product of the Cold War and Californian counter-culture, Marx already anticipated its concept in the nineteenth century – *Karl Marx invented the Internet!*

How Can One Define Critical Theory?

Ben Agger (2006, 4f) argues that critical social theory is based on seven foundations:

- It is a critique of positivism and of the assumption that theory is value free.
- It argues for the possibility of a better future without domination and exploitation.
- It sees domination as a structural phenomenon.
- It shows how humans, who live in structures of domination, tend to reproduce these structures in false consciousness.
- It is interested in everyday life such as the workplace and the family.
- It conceives structure and agency as dialectical.
- It sees liberation as a process that must be accomplished by the oppressed and exploited themselves.

Relating these aspects to Marx's works, we can identify six dimensions of a critical theory:

1. Critical ethics.
2. Critique of domination and exploitation.
3. Dialectical reason.
4. Struggles and political practice.
5. Ideology critique.
6. Critique of the political economy.

1. Critical Theory has a Normative Dimension

Criticism "measures individual existence against essence" (Marx 1997, 61f). This means that critical theory is normative and realistic, it argues that it is possible to logically provide reasonably grounded arguments about what a good society is, that the good society relates to conditions that all humans require to survive (the essence of humans and society), and that we can judge existing societies according to the extent they provide or fail to provide/humane conditions.

2. Critical Theory is a Critique of Domination and Exploitation

Critical theory questions all thought and practices that justify or uphold domination and exploitation. Domination means that one group benefits at the expense of others and has the means of violence at hand that they can use for upholding the situation where the one benefits at the expense of others. Exploitation is a specific form of domination, in which one group controls property and has the means to force others to work so that they produce goods or property that they do not own themselves, but that the owning class controls.

An example is that a slave-owner owns a slave as property and owns all products that the slave creates; it even allows killing her/him if s/he refuses to work. A somewhat different example is that Facebook Inc. is a company controlled by private shareholders who own the Facebook platform. Facebook's users create data whenever they are online that refers to their profiles and online behaviour. This data is sold to Facebook's advertising clients who are enabled to present targeted advertisements on users' profiles. Without Facebook users, there would be no profit. So, one can say that users create the monetary value and profit of Facebook. But they do not own this profit, which is rather controlled by Facebook's shareholders. So, also, Facebook users are exploited.

Marx formulated the categoric imperative of critical theory "to overthrow all conditions in which man is a degraded, enslaved, neglected, contemptible being" (Marx 1997, 257f). Critical theory wants to show that a good life for all is possible and that domination and exploitation alienate humans from achieving such a society. Marx therefore identifies the "task of philosophy [. . .] to unmask human self-alienation" (Marx 1997, 251). In deconstructing alienation, domination and exploitation, critical theory also makes demands for a self-determined, participatory and just democracy. Participatory democracy is a society in which all decisions are made by those who are concerned by them and all organizations (workplaces, schools, cities, politics, etc.) are controlled by those who are affected by them. Such a society is not only a grassroots political democracy, i.e. a society controlled by all people, but also an economic democracy, in which producers control the production process and the means and outcomes of production. Critical theory wants to make the world conscious of its own possibilities. The "world has long dreamed of something of which it only has to become conscious in order to possess it in actuality" (Marx 1997, 214).

3. Critical Theory Uses Dialectical Reasoning as a Method of Analysis

Dialectical reasoning is a philosophical method for understanding the world. The dialectical method identifies contradictions. Contradictions are "the source of all dialectics" (Marx 1867, 744). Dialectics tries to show that and how contemporary society and its moments are shaped by contradictions. A contradiction is a tension between two poles that require each other to exist, but have opposing qualities. Basic contradictions are, for example, those between being and nothingness and life and death: all things have a beginning and an end. The end of one thing gives rise to a new thing. So, for example, the music industry's trial against the Napster filesharing platform resulted in the end of Napster, but not in the end of the filesharing technology, as the rise of related technologies such as Kazaa, BitTorrent and the PirateBay platform showed.

Contradictions result in the circumstance that society is dynamic and that capitalism assures the continuity of domination and exploitation by changing the way these phenomena are organized. Dialectics "regards every historically developed form as being in a fluid state, in motion, and therefore grasps its transient aspects as well" (Marx 1867, 103). The "movement of capitalist society is full of contradictions" (Marx 1867, 103). In a contradiction, one pole of the dialectic can only exist because the opposing pole exists: they require and exclude each other at the same time. In a dominative society (such as capitalism), contradictions cause problems and are to a certain extent also the seeds for overcoming these problems. They have positive potentials and negative realities at the same time.

Marx analyzed capitalism's contradictions, for example: the contradictions between non-owners/owners, the poor/the rich, misery/wealth, workers/capitalists, use value/exchange value, concrete labour/abstract labour, the simple form of value/the relative and expanded form of value, social relations of humans/relations of things, the fetish of commodities and money/fetishistic thinking, the circulation of commodities/the circulation of money, commodities/money, labour power/wages, subject/object, labour process/valorization process, subject of labour (labour power, worker)/the object of labour (the means of production), variable capital/constant capital, surplus labour/surplus product, necessary labour time/surplus labour time, single worker/co-operation, single company/industry sector, single capital/competing capitals, production/consumption, productive forces/relations of production.

The tension between opposing poles can be resolved in a process that Hegel and Marx called "sublation" and "negation of the negation". Sublation is a difficult concept that helps us to understand how change happens. For example, it can be used for explaining what is new and old about the contemporary form of social media. The German philosopher Georg Wilhelm Friedrich Hegel first introduced this concept. It is difficult because its meaning is not intuitively clear. This has to do with the fact that the term comes from the German word *Aufhebung*, which cannot be directly translated to English. It has three meanings: (a) to eliminate, (b) to preserve and (c) to lift up. Hegel used this notion as a language game in order to express that change of something means that (a) the current state is eliminated, (b) some aspects of the old state are preserved in the new state and (c) a new quality emerges in the new state. Marx applied the concept of sublation to society in order to explain how it changes.

Take the example of Facebook. It is a sublation of earlier Internet platforms: (a) It eliminated the dominance of other Internet technologies, such as, for example, guest books on websites. Nowadays it is much more common that users write on the walls of their Facebook friends. But (b) the guest book has also been preserved on Facebook: the wall is a kind of guest book. And (c) Facebook is more than just a guest book for commenting; it also includes features such as email, photo and video sharing, discussion forums, fan pages and the friends list.

Marx was concerned with dialectical relations in society. So, for example, there is a dialectical relation between labour power and wages: labour power is the capacity to work; work is the transformation of nature by human activity so that goods emerge. In capitalism, a lot of labour power is organized as wage labour. So wages exist only in relation to labour power (for paying labour power), and capitalism forces workers to earn wages in order to have money for buying goods. Labour and wages cannot exist without one another in capitalism. Workers, however, do not have the power to determine their wages. Marx (1867) argued that the power of the owners of firms that employ workers results in the circumstance that they only pay parts of the work the labour performs, only a certain number of hours a day, whereas the other part is unpaid. The work that is performed unpaid is called surplus labour and the unpaid work time (measured in hours) surplus value. Surplus labour is a specific form of labour that emerges from the relation of labour power and wages in capitalism. The production of surplus value is the source of profit. For example, if workers in a company produce goods that are sold for €10 000, but their wages are only €5000, then there is an unpaid surplus labour that has produced a profit/surplus of €5000. Marx considers the unpaid production of surplus by workers and the appropriation of this value by capitalists to be the main scandal and injustice of capitalism. He therefore argues that there is a class relation (contradictory interests) between workers and capitalists.

Capitalism's class relation is another dialectical contradiction. Marx says that its sublation is not possible within capitalism, but requires to overcome this type of society and to build a new society. We will come back to the concept of surplus value in Chapter 5.

There are contradictions in capitalism that are persistent and not frequently sublated. They are at the heart of human misery in capitalism. Their sublation can only be achieved by political struggle and means the end of capitalism. These are especially the antagonisms between productive forces/relations of production, owners/non-owners, the poor/the rich, misery/wealth, workers/ capitalists, dominated groups/oppressors. The contradiction between productive forces and relations of production is partly sublated in crisis situations, but reconstitutes itself right in the crisis. Its true sublation can only be achieved by the overthrow of capitalism. If, in capitalism, an important contradiction is the one between the owning class that exploits the non-owning class, then the goal of critical theory is the representation of the interest of oppressed and exploited groups and the overcoming of class society. "It can only represent a class whose historical task is the overthrow of the capitalist mode of production and the final abolition of all classes – the proletariat" (Marx 1867, 98).

In formulating a critique of exploitation and domination, critical theory develops "new principles for the world out of the principles of the world" (Marx 1997, 214). Dialectical thinking argues that the foundations of a classless society develop already within capitalism; that capitalism, on the one hand, produces new forms of co-operation that are, on the other hand, within class relations, forms of exploitation and domination. In capitalism, the forces of production are at the same time destructive forces.

4. Critical Theory is Connected to Struggles for a Just and Fair Society – It is an Intellectual Dimension of Struggle

Critical theory provides a "self-understanding [. . .] of the age concerning its struggle and wishes" (Marx 1997, 315), it can "show the world why it actually struggles" and is "taking sides [. . .] with actual struggles" (Marx 1997, 214). This means that critical theory can help to explain the causes, conditions, potentials and limits of struggles. Critical theory rejects the argument that academia and science should and can be value-free. It rather argues that political worldviews shape all thought and theories. There are deeply political reasons why a person is interested in a certain topic, aligns himself/herself with a certain school of thought, develops a particular theory and not another one, refers to certain authors and not others because modern society is shaped by conflicts of interests, and therefore, in surviving and asserting themselves, scholars have to make choices, enter strategic alliances and defend their positions against others. Critical theory holds not only that theory is always political, but also that critical theory should develop analyses of society that struggle against interests and ideas that justify domination and exploitation.

5. Ideology Critique: Critical Theory is a Critique of Ideology

Ideologies are practices and modes of thought that present aspects of human existence that are historical and changeable as eternal and unchangeable. It is possible, for example, to claim that there is no alternative to Facebook and that the organizational model of Facebook, which uses targeted advertising, is the only possible form of a social networking site. Facebook is so dominant and has more than a billion users. Many of its users have several hundred contacts. It is difficult to imagine that there could be an alternative to Facebook because we are afraid to lose the possibility of communication with these contacts. But what if one could import all these contacts to another platform that does not have complex privacy policies, does not use targeted advertising and where all Facebook contacts are available? Ideologies claim that things cannot be changed, have always been or need to be the way they are now. Marx, in contrast, argued that everything in society is social, which also means that it can be changed by humans and that all things have a beginning and an end.

Ideology critique wants to remind us that everything that exists in society is created by humans in social relationships and that social relationships can be changed. It wants to bring "problems into the self-conscious human form" (Marx 1997, 214), which means that it wants to make humans conscious of the problems they are facing in society and the causes of these problems. Arguments like "there is no alternative to capitalism, neoliberalism, competition, egoism, racism, etc. because man is egoistic, competitive, etc." forget about the social character of society and create the impression that the results of social activity are unchangeable things. Critical theory provides an "analysis of the mystical consciousness that is unclear about itself" (Marx 1997, 214).

6. Critical Theory is a Critique of the Political Economy

Critical theory analyzes how capital accumulation, surplus value exploitation and the transformation of aspects of society into commodities (commodification) work and what the contradictions of the capitalist mode of production are. A commodity is a good that is exchanged with other goods in a certain quantitative relationship: x amount of commodity A = y amount of commodity B. "In the critique of political economy, therefore, we shall examine the basic categories, uncover the contradiction introduced by the free-trade system, and bring out the consequences of both sides of the contradiction" (Engels 1843/1844, 175). Critical political economy is concerned with how resources are produced, distributed and consumed and which power relations shape these resources. These resources can be physical productions, such as a car, but also non-physical goods, such as information. The information uploaded to Facebook is produced by users, but not owned and controlled by them: Facebook obtains the right to sell data about the uploaded information and your usage behaviour to other companies. It controls the profits derived from this process. Also, attention has its own political economy on the Internet: not everyone has the same power to be heard, seen and read on social media. Powerful actors such as, for example, CNN or *The New York Times* have much more visibility than a single political blogger. George Orwell was describing an animal kingdom, in which some animals are "more equal than others" (Orwell 1945, 85). On capitalist social media such as Google, Facebook, Twitter and YouTube, some users are more equal than others – which means that there is inequality.

1.4. Critical Theory Approaches

The Frankfurt School – Not a Sausage, but a Critical Theory

The Frankfurt School is a tradition of critical thinking that has its origins in the works of scholars like Herbert Marcuse, Max Horkheimer and Theodor W. Adorno (for introductions see Held 1980, Wiggershaus 1995). All six dimensions of Marx's theory can be found in the Frankfurt School's understanding of critique and can be exemplified by studying Marcuse's (1988, 134–158) essay "Philosophy and Critical Theory", Horkheimer's (2002, 188–252) essay "Traditional and Critical Theory", Marcuse's (1988, 43–87) article "The Concept of Essence" and the section "The Foundations of the Dialectical Theory of Society" in Marcuse's book *Reason and Revolution* (1941, 258–322). These texts are apt because they describe the fundamentals of how the thinkers of the Frankfurt School thought one should study society.

Critical theory is *ethical*. It has a "concern with human happiness" (Marcuse 1988, 135). It is a *critique of domination and exploitation*. It holds that "man can be more than a manipulable subject in the production process of class society" (Marcuse 1988, 153). The goal of critical theory is the transformation of society as a whole (Horkheimer 2002, 219) so that a "society without injustice" (221) emerges. Like Marx, critical theory makes use of *dialectical reason*. It argues that concepts that describe the existence of capitalism (profit, surplus value, worker, capital, commodity, etc.) are dialectical because they "transcend the given social reality in the direction of another historical structure which is present as a tendency in the given reality" (Marcuse 1988, 86). Critical theory wants to advance *struggles and political practice*. "The materialist protest and materialist critique originated in the struggle of oppressed groups for better living conditions and remain permanently associated with the actual process of this struggle" (Marcuse 1988, 141). It advances a *critique of ideology* by trying to show that capitalism's central phenomena in many presentations of reality "do not immediately appear to men as what they are 'in reality', but in masked, 'perverted' form" (Marcuse 1988, 70). Critical theory bases its ideas on Marx's *critique of the political economy* (Horkheimer 2002, 244).

Jürgen Habermas built his approach on the classical Frankfurt School and at the same time worked out the concept of communicative rationality, by which he went beyond the classical tradition. Habermas (1984, 285f) distinguishes between instrumental (non-social, success-oriented), strategic (social, success-oriented) and communicative action (social, oriented on understanding). Habermas (1971, 53) conceives instrumental action and communicative action as the two fundamental aspects of social praxis.

Communication is certainly an important aspect of a society free of dominations. It is, however, in capitalism also a form of interaction, in which ideology is, with the help of the mass media, made available to dominated groups. Communication is not automatically progressive. Habermas differentiates instrumental/strategic reason and communicative reason, whereas Horkheimer draws a distinction between instrumental reason and critical reason (Horkheimer 1947) and, based on it, between traditional and critical theory (Horkheimer 2002). Habermas splits off communication from instrumentality and thereby neglects that, in capitalism, the dominant system uses communication just like technology, the media, ideology or labour as an instrument for defending its rule. Communication is not pure and left untouched by structures of domination; it is antagonistically entangled into them. For Horkheimer (based on Marx), critical theory's goal is man's "emancipation from slavery" (Horkheimer 2002, 249) and "the happiness of all individuals" (248). Horkheimer has in mind the emancipation of communication just like the emancipation of work, decision-making and everyday life. His notion of critical rationality is larger than Habermas' notion of communicative rationality which risks becoming soaked up by non-critical approaches that use Habermas' stress on communication for instrumental purposes. The concept of communication can be critical, but is not necessarily critical, whereas the concept of a critique of exploitation and domination is necessarily critical.

Critical Political Economy of Media and Communication – Studying the Media and Communication Critically

Dwayne Winseck (2011) provides a map of the landscape of Political Economy research in Media and Communication Studies by identifying four approaches and speaking of Political Economies of Media:

- Neoclassical Political Economy of the Media,
- Radical Political Economy of the Media,
- Schumpeterian Institutional Political Economy of the Media,
- The Cultural Industries School.

In his seminal introduction to the field, Vincent Mosco defines the Political Economy of Communication as the "study of the social relations, particularly the power relations, that mutually constitute the production, distribution, and consumption of resources, including communication resources" (Mosco 2009, 2). Marxian Political Economy of Communication decentres the media by "placing in the foreground the analysis of capitalism, including the development of the forces and relations of production, commodification and the production of surplus value, social class divisions and struggles, contradictions and oppositional movements" (Mosco 2009, 94). Graham Murdock and Peter Golding (2005) argue that the Critical Political Economy of Communications analyzes "the interplay between the symbolic and the economic dimensions of public communications" (60) and "how the making and taking of meaning is shaped at every level by the structured asymmetries in social relations" (62). A critical political economy of social media is particularly interested in the power relations that govern the production, distribution and use of information of platforms like Facebook.

The following terms have been used for naming this field: Political Economy of Communication (Mosco 2009), Political Economy of Communications (Wasko 2004; Wasko, Murdock and Sousa 2011), Political Economy of Culture (Calabrese and Sparks 2004), Political Economy of Information (Garnham 2011; Mosco and Wasko 1988), Political Economy of Mass Communication (Garnham 1990) and Political Economy of the Media (Golding and Murdock 1997b; McChesney 2008). All of these approaches refer mainly to Winseck's second approach.

The Critical Political Economy of Communication studies media communication in the context of power relations and the totality of social relations and is committed to moral philosophy and social praxis (Mosco 2009, 2–5). It is holistic, historical, cares about the public good and engages with moral questions of justice and equity (Murdock and Golding 2005, 61). Golding and Murdock (1997a) mention five characteristics of the Critical Political Economy of the Media:

- holism,
- historicity,
- realist and materialist epistemology,
- moral and philosophical foundations,
- a focus of the analysis on cultural distribution and on the distribution between the private and public control of communications.

Important topics of the Critical Political Economy of Communication include media activism; media and social movements; the commodification of media content, audiences and communication labour; capital accumulation models of the media; media and the public sphere; communication and space-time; the concentration of corporate power in the communication industry; the media and globalization; the media and imperialism; the media and capitalism; media policies and state regulation of the media; communication and social class, gender, race; hegemony; the history of communication industries; media commercialization; media homogenization/diversification/multiplication/integration; media and advertising, media power (Garnham 1990, 1995/1998, 2000; Hardy 2010; Mosco 2009; Wasco 2004).

Dallas Smythe (1981, xvi–xviii) identified eight core aspects of a Marxist political economy of communications: materiality, monopoly capitalism, audience commodification and advertising, media communication as part of the base of capitalism, labour power, critique of technological determinism, consciousness, arts and learning.

Critical Political Economy and the Frankfurt School are Two Critical Theories but Do We Really Need Two of Them?

There are connections between Critical Political Economy and the Frankfurt School's stress on ideology. For Murdock and Golding (1974, 4), the media are organizations that "produce and distribute commodities", are the means for distributing advertisements, and they also have an "ideological dimension" by disseminating "ideas about economic and political structures". The approaches of the Frankfurt School and of the Critique of the Political Economy of Media and Communication should be understood as being complementary. There has been a stronger focus on ideology critique in the Frankfurt School approach for historical reasons. For Horkheimer and Adorno (2002), the rise of German fascism, the Stalinist praxis and American consumer capitalism showed the defeat of the revolutionary potentials of the working class (Habermas 1984, 366f). They wanted to explain why the revolutionary German working class followed Hitler, which brought up their interest in the analysis of the authoritarian personality and media propaganda. The Anglo-American approach of the Political Economy of the Media and Communication was developed by people like Dallas Smythe and Herbert Schiller in countries that did not experience fascism, which might be one of the factors that explain the differences in emphasis on ideology and capital accumulation. Whereas North American capitalism was based on pure liberal ideology and a strong consumer culture, German capitalism after 1945 was built on the legacy of National Socialism and a strong persistence of authoritarian thinking.

Horkheimer's (1947) notion of instrumental reason and Marcuse's (1964) notion of technological rationality open up connections between the two approaches. Horkheimer and Marcuse stressed that in capitalism there is a tendency that freedom of action is replaced by instrumental decision-making on the part of capital and the state so that the individual is expected to only react and not to act. The two concepts are grounded in Georg Lukács' (1923/1972) notion of reification, which is a reformulation of Marx's (1867) concept of fetishism. Reification means "that a relation between people takes on the character of a thing and thus acquires 'phantom objectivity', an autonomy that seems so strictly rational and all-embracing as to conceal every trace of its fundamental nature: the relation between people" (Lukács 1923/1972, 83).

Capitalist media are modes of reification in a double sense. First, they reduce humans to the status of consumers of advertisements and commodities. Second, culture is, in capitalism, to a large degree connected to the commodity form: there are cultural commodities that are bought by consumers and audience commodities that the media consumers become themselves by being sold as an audience to the capitalist media's advertising clients (see the debate about audience commodification: Murdock 1978; Smythe 1977). Third, in order to reproduce its existence, capitalism has to present itself as the best possible (or only possible) system and makes use of the media in order to try to keep this message (in all its differentiated forms) hegemonic. The first and the second dimension constitute the economic dimension of instrumental reason, the third dimension the ideological form of instrumental reason. Capitalist media are necessarily a means of advertising and commodification and spaces of ideology. Advertisement and cultural commodification make humans an instrument for economic profit accumulation. Ideology aims at instilling the belief in the system of capital and commodities into humans' subjectivity. The goal is that human thoughts and actions do not go beyond capitalism, do not question and revolt against this system and thereby play the role of instruments for the perpetuation of capitalism. It is of course an important question to what extent ideology is always successful and to what degree it is questioned and resisted, but the crucial aspect about ideology is that it encompasses strategies and attempts to make human subjects instrumental in the reproduction of domination and exploitation.

A critical theory of media and technology analyzes "society as a terrain of domination and resistance and engages in critique of domination and of the ways that media culture engages in reproducing relationships of domination and oppression" (Kellner 1995, 4). It is "informed by a critique of domination and a theory of liberation" (Kellner 1989, 1; see also Feenberg 2002; Kellner 2009).

Critical Theory and Critique of the Political Economy of Social Media

Frankfurt School Critical Theory and the Critical Political Economy of Media/Communication have both developed critiques of the role of media communication in exploitation, as means of ideology and potential means of liberation and struggle. Both traditions are valuable, important and complementary approaches for studying social media critically. The approach presented in this book is methodologically grounded in a combination of Frankfurt School Critical Theory and the Critique of the Political Economy of Media/Communication/Information/Culture (for this approach see also Fuchs 2009a, 2011b).

Marx developed a Critique of the Political Economy of Capitalism, which means that his approach is:

(a)   an analysis and critique of capitalism,
(b)   a critique of liberal ideology, thought and academia,
(c)   transformative practice.

The globalization of capitalism, its new global crisis, the new imperialism and the role of knowledge and communication in capitalism (anticipated by Marx's notions of the means of communication and the General Intellect) have resulted in a renewed interest in Marx that should also be practised in Media and Communication Studies (Fuchs 2011b). To a certain extent, the German tradition of the Critique of the Political Economy of Communication has engaged with Marx and connected these works to the analysis of the role of communication in capitalism (see, for example, Holzer 1973, 1994; Knoche 2005). The problem is that these approaches have, due to limited language capacities and limited resources, hardly been translated into English, which has left their impact limited to national levels and has resulted in a lack of international diffusion. Horst Holzer (1994) spoke of Marxian analysis as the forgotten theory of communication in the German world (Holzer 1994).

Holzer (1973, 131, 1994, 202ff) and Manfred Knoche (2005) distinguish four functions of the media in capitalism that are relevant for the Marxist Critique of the Political Economy of the Media and Communication:

1. Capital accumulation in the media industry.
2. Advertising, public relations and sales promotion for other industries.
3. Legitimization of domination and ideological manipulation.
4. Reproduction, regeneration, and qualification of labour power.

Holzer and Knoche have provided a good framework that is, however, too structuralistic and tends to lack the aspect of struggles.

A more complete task for a Critical Theory and Critique of the Political Economy of Communication, Culture, Information and the Media is to focus on the critique and analysis of the role of communication, culture, information and the media in capitalism in the context of:

- processes of capital accumulation (including the analysis of capital, markets, commodity logic, competition, exchange value, the antagonisms of the mode of production, productive forces, crises, advertising, etc.),
- class relations (with a focus on work, labour, the mode of the exploitation of surplus value, etc.),
- domination in general,
- ideology (both in academia and everyday life)

as well as the analysis of and engagement in:

- struggles against the dominant order, which includes the analysis and advancement of
- social movement struggles and
- social movement media that
- aim at the establishment of a democratic socialist society that is based on communication commons as part of structures of commonly-owned means of production (Fuchs 2011b).

The approach thereby realizes that in capitalism all forms of domination are connected to forms of exploitation (Fuchs 2008a, 2011b).

Based on the methodological combination of Critical Theory and Critique of the Political Economy with a special interest in Karl Marx's works and dialectical philosophy, this book presents a critical theory of social media, which means that it outlines the predominant forms of capital accumulation of social media, the class relations and modes of surplus value exploitation underlying these capital accumulation models, and analyzes the ideologies underlying capitalist social media and the potentials and limits for alternative social media and struggles for a just society that enables commons-based digital media.

"Philosophy is preserved in science as critique" (Habermas 1971, 63). If we want to conduct a critical analysis of social media, then we require a critical philosophy as a foundation. The tradition that goes back to Hegel and Marx is the most suitable critical philosophy tradition for such a project. Dialectical philosophy can provide a strong philosophical and theoretical grounding of Critical Media and Communication Studies (Fuchs 2011b, chapters 2 and 3). It is well suited for helping to bridge gaps in the field of Critical Media and Communication Studies (between the focus on structure and agency, subject and object, reason and experience, technology and society, economy and culture, pessimism and optimism, risks and opportunities, work and pleasure/joy, alienation and self-actualization, etc.) and for avoiding one-sided approaches.

Critical theory "never simply aims at an increase of knowledge as such" (Horkheimer 2002, 249). The task of this book is therefore not simply to produce new knowledge about social media, but to enable critical insights into the potentials and limits of social media that can enter into struggles for a just society. Critical theory wants to bring "to consciousness potentialities that have emerged within the maturing historical situation" (Marcuse 1988, 158). It analyzes "the tension between potentiality and actuality, between what man and things could be and what they are in fact, [since this] is one of the dynamic focal points of this theory of society" (Marcuse 1988, 69). This book analyzes the actuality of social media in contemporary capitalism and the potentials and limits for overcoming the corporate character of social media and for establishing a truly participatory Internet within the context of a participatory democracy.

Economic theory becomes critical theory by the insight that capitalism's "natural objectivity is mere semblance" and that it "is a specific historical form of existence that man has given himself" (Marcuse 1941, 281). This book wants to contribute to the insight that the capitalist character of social media, i.e. their grounding in profit logic, commodity logic, (targeted) advertising and exploited labour is not a necessity, but a historical consequence of the commercial and capitalist organization of the Internet. Deconstructing the semblance of the necessity of corporate social media wants to contribute to the formation of consciousness about and struggles for a public, commons-based Internet.

RECOMMENDED READINGS AND EXERCISES

If you want to understand social media in a critical manner, it makes sense to start with foundational readings in critical theory. Therefore readings recommended in this section include works by Karl Marx, Herbert Marcuse, Max Horkheimer, Theodor W. Adorno and a debate between Adorno and Karl Popper on what the notion of the critical means in the social sciences. Three more readings (by Nicholas Garnham and Lawrence Grossberg) focus on a foundational debate about what it means to study the media and culture critically.

Marx, Karl. 1843. Toward the critique of Hegel's philosophy of law: Introduction. In *Writings of the young Marx on philosophy and society*, 249–265. Indianapolis, IN: Hackett.

In this famous work Marx introduces his concept of ideology and argues that religion is the "opium of the people". Ask yourself:

- What does Marx mean by ideology? What are its characteristics?

- Give some examples of ideologies.

- What are important ideologies today?

- Where have social media merged with ideologies? Provide some examples. What exactly is the content of these ideologies? What claims are they making? What does reality look like and how can you determine what reality looks like in contrast to the claims made by social media ideologies? Search for examples and discuss them.

Marx, Karl. 1844. *Economic and philosophic manuscripts of 1844*. Mineola, NY: Dover.

This is one of Marx's earliest works on labour, capital, private property, estranged/alienated labour and communism. It is generally considered as his most important work for grounding a humanist critical theory that wants to create a society in which all humans live a good life. Questions for discussion and consideration:

- What is, for Marx, the most fundamental problem of capitalism?

- What does Marx mean by alienation (note: a synonymous term is estrangement)?

- How does Marx understand the term "communism"?

- How can Marx's concepts of capitalism, labour, alienation (and alternatives) be used for understanding social media critically?

Marcuse, Herbert. 1932. New sources on the foundation of historical materialism. In *Heideggerian Marxism*, 86–121. Lincoln, NE: University of Nebraska Press.

Although written in 1844, Marx's *Economic and philosophical manuscripts* were only published in 1932 (in German, later in English and other languages). Marcuse's text is one of the first reviews. It helps you to better understand Marx's philosophical text. Read first Marcuse and then Marx. Discuss in groups and compare the results:

- What do Marx and Marcuse (based on Hegel) mean by the essence of a thing? Try to give some examples of the essence of something.

- What is the difference between the essence and the existence of something in society? Try to give some examples.

- What is the essence of social media? What is the existence of social media? Is there a difference between the essence and the existence of social media?

Horkheimer, Max. 1937. Traditional and critical theory. In *Critical theory: Selected essays*, 188–243. New York: Continuum.

Marcuse, Herbert. 1937. Philosophy and critical theory. In *Negations: Essays in Critical Theory*, 134–158. Boston, MA: Beacon Press.

These two articles were subsequently published and are two foundational texts of the Frankfurt School. They try to explain what Critical Theory is. Exercises:

- Every person in the classroom writes down how s/he defines "being critical". Compare the answers and make a list of which elements of criticism were identified.

- Discuss in groups and compare the results: How do Horkheimer and Marcuse define critical theory? What are the important elements of critical theory?

- Compare your own definitions of critique in the initial exercise to Horkheimer's and Marcuse's understandings. Argue what commonalities and differences there are.

- Discuss: What are purposes and tasks of a critical theory of the Internet and social media?

Marcuse, Herbert. 1941. The foundations of the dialectical theory of society. In *Reason and revolution: Hegel and the rise of social theory*, 258–322. Amherst, NY: Humanity Books.

In this chapter, Marcuse discusses how Marx used Hegel's dialectical philosophy for constructing a dialectical theory of society. Discuss in groups and compare the results:

- What is dialectical philosophy? Try to give some examples of dialectical philosophy.

- What is, for Marx, a dialectical theory of society? Try to find some examples of dialectical relationships and dialectical development in contemporary society.

- What are basic assumptions of a dialectical theory of the Internet and social media? Try to formulate a general concept and to give some examples.

Adorno, Theodor W., Hans Albert, Ralf Dahrendorf, Jürgen Habermas, Harald Pilot and Karl R. Popper. 1976. *The positivist dispute in German sociology*, 1–122, 288–296. London: Heinemann.

The positivist dispute was a debate in German sociology in the early 1960s about what it means to be critical. The main participants were Theodor W. Adorno and Karl Popper. Jürgen Habermas and others also contributed to the debate. Ask yourself:

- How does Popper define critique? What are basic elements of his understanding?

- How does Adorno define critique? What are basic elements of his understanding?

- On which aspects do Popper and Adorno agree and disagree?

- Which elements are needed for a critical theory of the Internet and social media? What are basic assumptions of such a theory if it is based on Adorno? What are its basic assumptions if it is based on Popper?

Garnham, Nicholas. 1995a. Political Economy and Cultural Studies: Reconciliation or divorce? *Critical Studies in Mass Communication* 12 (1): 62–71.

Grossberg, Lawrence. 1995. Cultural Studies vs. Political Economy. *Critical Studies in Mass Communication* 12 (1): 72–81.

Garnham, Nicholas. 1995b. Reply to Grossberg and Carey. *Critical Studies in Mass Communication* 12 (1): 95–100.

Critical Political Economy and Cultural Studies are two important approaches for studying media and communication. They have both to a certain degree been inspired by Marx's works. In 1995 Nicholas Garnham, a major political economist of the media, and Lawrence Grossberg, an important Cultural Studies scholar, had a now famous debate about the relationship of Political Economy and celebratory Cultural Studies. The debate focuses on the role of class, gender, race, production, consumption, work, leisure, ethics and politics for studying the media and shows profound disagreements between the two scholars.

- Discuss the major points of disagreement between Garnham and Grossberg. Make a systematic and ordered list of arguments that show Garnham's argument on the one hand and Grossberg's opposing argument on the other hand. Give a name to each topic of discussion and think about how these topics are related.

- Try to form your own opinion on this debate. Discuss your views first in groups and compare the results of the group discussions.

Think about whether, and how, the two different positions that Garnham and Grossberg take play a role in studying social media and the Internet today.

I
FOUNDATIONS

1
FOUNDATIONS

2

What is Social Media?

Key questions

- What does it mean to besocial?
- What kinds of social theories exist?
- How can social theory help us to understand what is social about social media?
- How social is the web?

Key concepts

Internet
Social media
Web 1.0
Web 2.0
Web 3.0
Émil Durkheim's notion of social facts

Max Weber's notions of social
    action and social relations
Ferdinand Tönnies' concept of
    community
Karl Marx's concept of co-operative
    work

Overview

This chapter introduces how one can think about social media. You will engage with the question: What is social about social media? One of the first reactions that many people have when hearing the term "social media" is to ask: "Aren't all media social?" This depends on how one conceives the social. In order to understand the meanings of this term, we need to go into sociological theory. This chapter presents some concepts of what it can mean to be social and discusses the implications of these concepts for understanding social media.

Mainly, sociological theory has asked the question of what it means to be social. Answering it therefore requires engagement with sociological theory. Specifically, I will introduce Durkheim's, Weber's, Marx's and Tönnies' concepts of sociality and apply them to providing an explanation of the social media concept.

Section 2.1 discusses the question of what new social media are and provides some basic features and criticisms of the terms "web 2.0" and "social media". In section 2.2, you can read different definitions of social media. I point out that we need social theory to understand what is social about social media. For this task, some sociological theory concepts are introduced that allow us to better understand the sociality of social media. I introduce the four concepts developed by social theorists. Émile Durkheim (1858–1917) was a French sociologist who developed the concept of social facts. Max Weber (1864–1920) was a German sociologist who worked out a theory of social action and social relations. Karl Marx (1818–1883) was a social theorist who established a critical theory of capitalism. Collaborative work is one of this theory's concepts. Ferdinand Tönnies (1855–1936) was a German sociologist who is most well known for his theory of community. Section 2.3 discusses how the concepts of these four thinkers can be used in constructing a model of social media. It also examines how one can empirically study the continuities and changes of the WWW.

2.1. Web 2.0 and Social Media

Web 2.0

The terms "social media" and "web 2.0" have in the past years become popular for describing types of World Wide Web (WWW) application, such as blogs, microblogs like Twitter, social networking sites, or video/image/file sharing platforms or wikis. As the word "social" features prominently in the term "social media", the question arises: What is social about social media?

The term "web 2.0" was coined in 2005 by Tim O'Reilly (2005a, 2005b), the founder of the publishing house O'Reilly Media, which focuses on the area of computer technology. O'Reilly (2005a) lists the following as the main characteristics of web 2.0: radical decentralization, radical trust, participation instead of publishing, users as contributors, rich user experience, the long tail, the web as platform, control of one's own data, remixing data, collective intelligence, attitudes, better software by more users, play, undetermined user behaviour. He provides the following more formal definition:

> Web 2.0 is the network as platform, spanning all connected devices; Web 2.0 applications are those that make the most of the intrinsic advantages of that platform: delivering software as a continually-updated service that gets better the more people use it, consuming and remixing data from multiple sources, including individual users, while providing their own data and services in a form that allows remixing by others, creating network effects through an "architecture of participation", and going beyond the page metaphor of Web 1.0 to deliver rich user experiences. (O'Reilly 2005b)

O'Reilly creates the impression that the WWW, featuring BitTorrent, blogs, Flickr, Google, tagging, Wikipedia, etc., was in 2005 radically new and different from the earlier web (1.0). O'Reilly (2005a) consequently spoke of web 2.0 as a "new platform" that features "new applications".

In 2000, a crisis of the Internet economy emerged. The inflow of financial capital had driven up the market values of many Internet companies, but profits could not hold up with the promises of high market values. The result was a financial bubble (the so-called dot.com bubble) that burst in 2000, resulting in many start-up Internet companies going bankrupt. They were mainly based on venture capital financial investments and the hope of delivering profits in the future, and this resulted in a gap between share values and accumulated profits. The talk about the novelty of "web 2.0" and social media fits well into the post-crisis situation, in which investors had to be convinced to invest into new Internet start-up companies, which was difficult after the 2000 crisis. The ideology that web 2.0 is something new and different and that it has new economic and democratic potentials helped to convince investors. Web 2.0 and social media were therefore born in the situation of capitalist crisis as ideologies aimed at overcoming the crisis and establishing new spheres and models of capital accumulation for the corporate Internet economy. The talk about novelty was aimed at attracting novel capital investments.

Although Tim O'Reilly surely thinks that "web 2.0" denotes actual changes, he says that the crucial fact about it is that users, as a collective intelligence, co-create the value of platforms like Google, Amazon, Wikipedia or Craigslist in a "community of connected users" (O'Reilly and Battelle 2009, 1). He admits that the term was mainly created for identifying the need of new economic strategies for Internet companies after the "dot-com" crisis, in which the bursting of financial bubbles caused the collapse of many Internet companies. So he states in a paper published five years after the invention of the term "web 2.0" that this nomenclature was "a statement about the second coming of the Web after the dotcom bust". He was speaking at a conference that was "designed to restore confidence in an industry that had lost its way after the dotcom bust" (ibid.).

Critiques of Web 2.0 and Social Media Optimism

Critiques of web 2.0/social media optimism have, for example, stressed the following points:

- Online advertising is a mechanism by which corporations exploit Internet users who form an Internet prosumer/produser commodity and are part of a surplus-value generating class that produces the commons of society that are exploited by capital (Fuchs 2008a, 2010c).
- Web 2.0 is based on the exploitation of free labour (Terranova 2004).
- Most Internet users are part of a creative precarious underclass that needs economic models that assist them in making a living from their work (Lovink 2008).

- Blogging is mainly a self-centred, nihilistic, cynical activity (Lovink 2008).
- The Internet economy is dominated by corporate media chains (Stanyer 2009).
- Web 2.0 is contradictory and therefore also serves dominative interests (Cammaerts 2008).
- Web 2.0 optimism is uncritical and an ideology that serves corporate interests (Fuchs 2008a; Van Dijck and Nieborg 2009).
- Web 2.0 is a marketing ideology (Scholz 2008).
- The notion of sharing is used by Facebook and other corporate social media for mystifying the logic of profit, advertising and commerce that is at the heart of their operation (John 2013).
- Web 2.0 users are more passive users than active creators (Van Dijck 2009).
- Web 2.0 discourse advances a minimalist notion of participation (Carpentier and De Cleen 2008).
- Web 2.0 discourse is technological fetishism that advances post-politics and depoliticization in communicative capitalism (Dean 2005, 2010).
- Social media optimism is based on the techno-deterministic ideologies of cyber-utopianism and Internet-centrism (Morozov 2011) that only postulate advantages for businesses and society without taking into account the realities of exploitation and the contradictions of capitalism (Freedman 2012; Fuchs 2011b, chapter 7).
- Corporations appropriate blogs and web 2.0 in the form of corporate blogs, advertising blogs, spam blogs and fake blogs (Deuze 2008).
- José van Dijck (2013, 11) argues that social media automate the social by engineering and manipulating social connections. It would make "sociality technical" (Van Dijck 2013, 12). Douglas Rushkoff (2010, 158) says that as a result "we are optimizing humans for machinery". "These days the social is a feature. It is no longer a problem (as in the nineteenth and twentieth centuries when the Social Problem predominated) or a sector in society provided for deviant, sick, and elderly people. Until recently, employing an amoral definition of the social was unthinkable" (Lovink 2011, 6).

How New are Social Media?

Matthew Allen (2012) and Trebor Scholz (2008) argue that social media applications are not new and that their origins can be traced back to years earlier than 2005. Blogs were already around at the end of the 1990s, the wiki technology was suggested by Ward Cunningham in 1994 and first released in 1995, social networking sites already existed in 1995 (Classmates) and in 1997 (Sixdegrees), Google was founded in 1999. The discourse of ever newer versions would allow "products to claim to be new" (Allen 2012, 264), but at the same time also sustain "continuity and promise an easy transition from what came before" (ibid.). Versions would be ways of encouraging consumption.

When talking about novelty, one has to be clear whether one talks about the novelty of technology, usage patterns or power relations.

Allen and Scholz argue that the technologies that constitute "social media"/"web 2.0" are not new. However, on the level of usage, these technologies were not popular in the 1990s and have become popular rather recently. On the level of the power relations of the Internet, it is just as unlikely that nothing changes at all as it is unlikely that there is radical change, because at a certain level of its organization capitalism requires change and novelty in order to stay the same (system of surplus value exploitation and capital accumulation) and continue to exist.

2.2. The Need of Social Theory for Understanding Social Media

Definitions of Web 2.0 and Social Media

Michael Mandiberg argues that the notion of "social media" has been associated with multiple concepts: "the corporate media favorite 'user-generated content', Henry Jenkin's media-industries-focused 'convergence culture', Jay Rosen's 'the people formerly known as the audience', the politically infused 'participatory media', Yochai Benkler's process-oriented 'peer-production', and Tim O'Reilly's computer-programming-oriented 'Web 2.0'" (Mandiberg 2012, 2).

Here are some example definitions of web 2.0 and social media that can be found in the research literature:

- Social media and social software are tools that "increase our ability to share, to co-operate, with one another, and to take collective action, all outside the framework of traditional institutional institutions and organizations" (Shirky 2008, 20f).

- The novelty of social media would be "the scale at which people who never had access to broadcast media are now doing so on an everyday basis and the conscious strategic appropriation of media tools in this process. Home videos were once viewed by only a few unless selected by curators of TV shows like America's *Funniest Home Videos*. Today, anyone equipped with a smartphone and an internet connection can post their footage on YouTube. What's posted online is not necessarily visible to everyone, but when people choose to share content in 'spreadable' media (Jenkins, Ford, & Green, forthcoming (2013)) – home videos like 'Charlie Bit Me' appear to 'go viral', quickly garnering millions of hits" (Baym and boyd 2012, 321).

- "Social media is the latest buzzword in a long line of buzzwords. It is often used to describe the collection of software that enables individuals and communities to gather, communicate, share, and in some cases collaborate or play. In tech circles, social media has replaced the earlier fave 'social software'. Academics still tend to prefer terms like 'computer-mediated communication' or 'computer-supported co-operative work' to describe the practices that emerge from these tools and the old skool academics might even categorize these tools as 'groupwork' tools. Social media is driven by another buzzword: 'user-generated content' or content that is contributed by participants rather than editors" (boyd 2009).

- Van Dijck: "The very word 'social' associated with media implies that platforms are user centered and that they facilitate communal activities, just as the term 'participatory' emphasizes human collaboration. Indeed, social media can be seen as online facilitators or enhancers of *human* networks – webs of people that promote connectedness as a social value" (Van Dijck 2013, 11). "As a result of the interconnection of platforms, a new infrastructure emerged: an ecosystem of connective media with a few large and many small players. The transformation from networked communication to 'platformed' sociality, and from a participatory culture to a culture of connectivity took place in a relatively short time span of ten years" (Van Dijck 2013, 4).

- "Social media indicate a shift from HTML-based linking practices of the open web to liking and recommendation, which happen inside closed systems. Web 2.0 has three distinguishing features: it is easy to use, it facilitates sociality, and it provides users with free publishing and production platforms that allow them to upload content in any form, be it pictures, videos, or text" (Lovink 2011, 5).

- "Since at least 2004, the internet, and more specifically the web, has witnessed a notorious and controversial shift away from the model of the static web page towards a social web or Web 2.0 model where the possibilities of users to interact with the web have multiplied. It has become much easier for a layperson to publish and share texts, images and sounds. A new topology of distribution of information has emerged, based in 'real' social networks, but also enhanced by casual and algorithmic connections" (Terranova and Donovan 2013, 297).

- "In the first decade or so of the Web's existence (from the 1990s to the early or mid-200s), websites tended to be like separate gardens. [. . .] Web 2.0 is like a collective allotment. Instead of in individuals tending their own gardens, they come together to work collaboratively in a shared space. [. . .] At the heart of Web 2.0 is the idea that online sites and services become more powerful the more they *embrace* this network of potential collaborators" (Gauntlett 2011, 4f). It is characterized by the emergence of a "'making and doing' culture" (Gauntlett 2011, 11) and by "making and sharing our own *media* culture – I mean, via lo-fi YouTube videos, eccentric blogs, and homemade websites, rather than by having to take over the traditional media of television stations and printing presses" (Gauntlett 2011, 18). Making things online and offline would connect things together and involve "a social dimension and connect us with other people", the social and physical world (Gauntlett 2011, 3).

- Social media tools feature "the elements of profile, contacts and interaction with those contacts", "blur the distinction between personal communication and the broadcast model of messages sent to nobody in particular" (Meikle and Young 2012, 61). Social media "manifest a convergence between personal communication (to be shared one-to-one) and public media (to be shared with nobody in particular)" (Meikle and Young 2012, 68).

These approaches discussed above describe various forms of online sociality: collective action, communication, communities, connecting/networking, co-operation/collaboration, the creative making of user-generated content, playing, sharing. They show that defining social media requires an understanding of sociality: What does it mean to be and act in a social way? What is the social all about? There are different answers to these questions. The field concerned with these kinds of questions is called social theory. It is a subfield of sociology. To provide answers, we therefore have to enter the research field of social theory.

Media and Social Theory

Media are not technologies, but techno-social systems. They have a technological level of artefacts that enable and constrain a social level of human activities that create knowledge that is produced, diffused and consumed with the help of the artefacts of the technological level. There is a recursive dynamic relation between the technological and the social level of the media. Media are based on what Anthony Giddens (1984) calls the duality of structure and agency (see Figure 2.1, Fuchs 2003): "According to the notion of the duality of structure, the structural properties of social systems are both medium and outcome of the practices they recursively organise" (25) and they both enable and constrain actions (26). Media are techno-social systems, in which information and communication technologies enable and constrain human activities that create knowledge that is produced, distributed and consumed with the help of technologies in a dynamic and reflexive process that connects technological structures and human agency.

The Internet consists of both a technological infrastructure and (inter)acting humans. It is not a network of computer networks, but a network that interconnects social networks and technological networks of computer networks (see Figure 2.2). The technical network structure (a global computer network of computer networks based on the TCP/IP (Transmission Control Protocol/Internet Protocol) protocol, a model that is used for defining how data is formatted, transmitted and received on the Internet) is the medium for and outcome of human agency. It enables and constrains human activity and thinking and is the result of productive social communication and co-operation processes. The technological structure/part of the Internet enables and constrains human behaviour and is itself produced and permanently reproduced by the human communicative part of the Internet. The Internet consists of a technological system and a social subsystem that both have a networked character. Together these two parts form a techno-social system. The technological structure is a network that produces and reproduces human actions and social networks and is itself produced and reproduced by such practices.

If we want to answer the question what is social about social media and the Internet, then we are dealing with the level of human agency. We can distinguish different forms of sociality at this level. They correspond to the

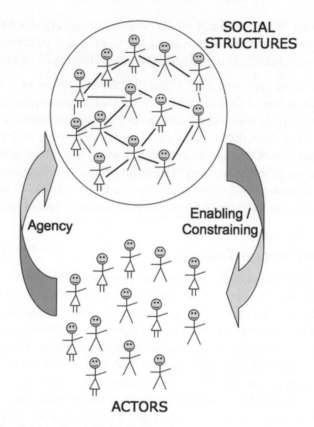

Figure 2.1   The dialectic of structure and agency

three most important classical positions in social theory, the ones defined by Émile Durkheim, Max Weber and Karl Marx (Elliott 2009, 6f).

Émile Durkheim: The Social as Social Facts

The first understanding of sociality is based on Émile Durkheim's notion of the *social* – social facts:

> A social fact is every way of acting, fixed or not, capable of exercising on the individual an external constraint; or again, every way of acting which is general throughout a given society, while at the same time existing in its own right independent of its individual manifestations. (Durkheim 1982, 59)

All media and all software are social in the sense that they are products of social processes. Humans in social relations produce them. They objectify knowledge that is produced in society, applied and used in social systems. Applying Durkheim's idea of social facts to computing means that all software applications and media are social because social structures are fixed and objectified in them. These structures are present even if a user sits in front of a screen alone and browses

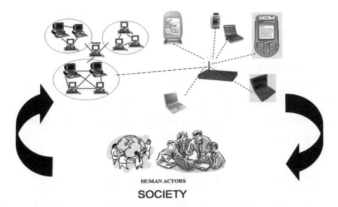

HUMAN ACTORS
SOCIETY

Figure 2.2 The Internet as duality of technological computer networks and social networks of humans

information on the World Wide Web because, according to Durkheim, they have an existence of their own, independent of individual manifestations. Web technologies therefore are social facts.

Max Weber: The Social as Social Relations

The second understanding of sociality is based on Max Weber. His central categories of sociology are *social action* and *social relations*: "Action is 'social' insofar as its subjective meaning takes account of the behavior of others and is thereby oriented in its course" (Weber 1978, 4). "The term 'social relationship' will be used to denote the behaviour of a plurality of actors insofar as, in its meaningful content, the action of each takes account of that of the others and is oriented in these terms" (Weber 1978, 26). These categories are relevant for the discussion because they allow a distinction between *individual* and *social activities*:

> Not every kind of action, even of overt action, is "social" in the sense of the present discussion. Overt action is not social if it is oriented solely to the behavior of inanimate objects. For example, religious behavior is not social if it is simply a matter of contemplation or of solitary prayer. [. . .] Not every type of contact of human beings has a social character; this is rather confined to cases where the actor's behavior is meaningfully oriented to that of others. (Weber 1978, 22f)

Weber stresses that in order to constitute a social relation, behaviour needs to be a meaningful symbolic interaction between human actors.

Ferdinand Tönnies: The Social as Community

The notions of community and co-operation, as elaborated by Tönnies and Marx, are the foundation for a third understanding of the social as collaboration. Ferdinand Tönnies conceives co-operation in the form of "sociality as community". He argues that "the very existence of *Gemeinschaft* [community] rests in the consciousness of belonging together and the affirmation of the condition of mutual dependence" (Tönnies 1988, 69), whereas *Gesellschaft* (society) for him is a concept in which "reference is only to the objective fact of a unity based on common traits and activities and other external phenomena" (Tönnies 1988, 67). Communities would have to work within a harmonious consensus of wills, folkways, belief, mores, the family, the village, kinship, inherited status, agriculture, morality, essential will and togetherness. Communities are about feelings of togetherness and values.

Karl Marx: The Social as Co-operative Work

Marx discusses community and collaborative aspects of society with the help of the notion of co-operative work. Marx and Engels argued that co-operation is the essence of society. In capitalism, it has become subsumed under capital so that it is alienated labour, and can only be fully developed in a free society. For Marx and Engels, co-operation is the essence of the social:

> By social we understand the co-operation of several individuals, no matter under what conditions, in what manner and to what end. It follows from this that a certain mode of production, or industrial stage, is always combined with a certain mode of co-operation, or social stage, and this mode of co-operation is itself a "productive force". (Marx and Engels 1846, 50)

Co-operation is a foundation of human existence:

> By the co-operation of hands, organs of speech, and brain, not only in each individual, but also in society, human beings became capable of executing more and more complicated operations, and of setting themselves, and achieving, higher and higher aims. (Engels 1886, 288)

But co-operation is also the foundation of capitalism: "A large number of workers working together, at the same time, in one place (or, if you like, in the same field of labour), in order to produce the same sort of commodity under the command of the same capitalist, constitutes the starting-point of capitalist production" (Marx 1867, 439).

Marx argues that capitalists exploit the collective labour of many workers by appropriating surplus value. Co-operation would therefore turn, under capitalist conditions, into alienated labour. This antagonism between the co-operative character of production and private appropriation that is advanced by the capitalist development of the productive forces is a factor that constitutes crises of capitalism and points towards and anticipates a co-operative society:

> The contradiction between the general social power into which capital has developed and the private power of the individual capitalists over these social conditions of production develops ever more blatantly, while this development also contains the solution to this situation, in

that it simultaneously raises the conditions of production into general,
communal, social conditions. (Marx 1894, 373)

A fully developed and true humanity is, for Marx, only possible if man "really brings
out all his *species*-powers – something which in turn is only possible through the co-
operative action of all of mankind" (Marx 1844, 177). For Marx, a co-operative society is the realization of the co-operative essence of humans and society. Hence he
speaks based on the Hegelian concept of truth (i.e. the correspondence of essence
and existence, the way things should be and the way they are) of the "reintegra-
tion or return of man to himself, the transcendence of human self-estrangement",
"the real *appropriation* of the *human* essence by and for man", "the complete return
of man to himself as a *social* (i.e., human) being" (Marx 1844, 135). Marx (1875)
speaks of such transformed conditions as the co-operative society.

The basic idea underlying Marx's notion of co-operation is that many human
beings work together in order to produce goods that satisfy human needs and
that, hence, also the ownership of the means of production should be co-operative. It is interesting that Marx already had a vision of a globally networked information system. Of course he did not speak of the Internet in the mid-nineteenth
century, but he anticipated the underlying idea: Marx stresses that the globalization of production and circulation necessitates institutions that allow capitalists
to inform themselves on the complex conditions of competition:

> Since, "if you please," the autonomization of the world market (in which
> the activity of each individual is included), increases with the develop-
> ment of monetary relations (exchange value) and vice versa, since the
> general bond and all-round interdependence in production and con-
> sumption increase together with the independence and indifference of
> the consumers and producers to one another; since this contradiction
> leads to crises, etc., hence, together with the development of this aliena-
> tion, and on the same basis, efforts are made to overcome it: institutions
> emerge whereby each individual can acquire information about the
> activity of all others and attempt to adjust his own accordingly, e.g. lists of
> current prices, rates of exchange, interconnections between those active
> in commerce through the mails, telegraphs etc. (the means of communi-
> cation of course grow at the same time). (This means that, although the
> total supply and demand is independent of the actions of each individual,
> everyone attempts to inform himself about them, and this knowledge
> then reacts back in practice on the total supply and demand. Although on
> the given standpoint, alienation is not overcome by these means, never-
> theless relations and connections are introduced thereby which include
> the possibility of suspending the old standpoint.) (The possibility of
> general statistics, etc.) (Marx 1857/1858, 160–161)

Although Marx here speaks of lists, letters and the telegraph, it is remark-
able that he saw the possibility of a global information network in which

"everyone attempts to inform himself" on others and "connections are introduced". Today the Internet is such a global system of information and communication, which represents a symbolic and communicative level of mechanisms
of competition, but also poses new opportunities for "suspending the old standpoint".

Tönnies' and Marx's notions of the social have in common the idea that
humans work together in order to produce new qualities of society (non-
physical ones, i.e. shared feelings, in the case of Tönnies and material ones,
economic goods, in the case of Marx).

2.3. Explaining Social Media with Durkheim, Weber, Marx and Tönnies

A Model of Human Sociality

The three notions of sociality (Durkheim's social facts, Weber's social actions/
relations, Marx's and Tönnies' co-operation) can be integrated into a model of
human social activity. It is based on the assumption that knowledge is a threefold
dynamic process of cognition, communication and co-operation (Hofkirchner
2013[1]). Cognition is the necessary prerequisite for communication and the
precondition for the emergence of co-operation. Or in other words: in order to
co-operate you need to communicate and in order to communicate you need to
cognize. Cognition involves the knowledge processes of a single individual. They
are social in the Durkheimian sense because the existence of humans in society
and therefore social relations shape human knowledge. Humans can only exist
by entering into social relations with other humans. They exchange symbols in
these relations – they communicate. This level corresponds to Weber's notion of
social relations. A human being externalizes parts of its knowledge in every social
relation. As a result, this knowledge influences others, who change part of their
knowledge structures and, as a response, externalize parts of their own knowledge, which results in the differentiation of the first individual's knowledge. A
certain number of communications is not just sporadic, but continuous over time
and space. In such cases, there is the potential that communication results in co-
operation, the shared production of new qualities, new social systems, or new
communities with feelings of belonging together. This is the level of co-operative
labour and community. It is based on the theories of Marx and Tönnies.

Information (cognition), communication and co-operation are three nested and
integrated modes of sociality (Hofkirchner 2013). Every medium can be social in
one or more of these senses. All media are information technologies. They provide
information to humans. This information enters into the human realm of knowledge as social facts that shape thinking. Information media are, for example, books,
newspapers, journals, posters, leaflets, films, television, radio, CDs, DVDs. Some

---

1 See also Fuchs and Hofkirchner 2005; Hofkirchner 2002.

media are also media of communication – they enable the recursive exchange of information between humans in social relations. Examples are letters in love relations, the telegraph and the telephone. Brecht (1932/2000), Enzensberger (1970/1997) and Smythe (in his essay "After bicycles? What?"; Smythe 1994, 230–244) have discussed the possibility that broadcasting technologies are transformed from information into communication technologies.

Networked computer technologies are technologies that enable cognition, communication and co-operation. The classical notion of the medium was confined to the social activities of cognition and communication, whereas the classical notion of technology was confined to the area of labour and production with the help of machines (such as the conveyor belt). The rise of computer technology and computer networks (such as the Internet) has enabled the convergence of media and machines – the computer supports cognition, communication and co-operative labour (production); it is a classical medium and a classical machine at the same time. Furthermore, it has enabled the convergence of production, distribution (communication) and consumption of information – you use only one tool, the networked computer, for these three processes. In contrast to other media (like the press, broadcasting, the telegraph, the telephone), computer networks are not only media of information and communication, but also enable the co-operative production of information.

In discussions about the novelty, discontinuities and continuities of the contemporary WWW, one can find a lot of confusion about which notion of sociality one actually talks about. It is, furthermore, often unreflective if one talks about continuity and changes of the technological level or the level of social relations. The latter is also the level of power relations in society, i.e. the level at which in heteronomous societies certain groups and individuals try to make use of resource advantages, violence and means of coercion (physical violence, psychological violence, ideology) in order to derive benefits at the expense of others. When talking about changes of media or the Internet, one should always specify which level of analysis (technology, power relations) and which dimension of sociality one is referring to. The question of whether the Internet and the WWW have changed in the past x number of years always depends on the level of analysis, the granularity of analysis and the employed understanding/dimension of sociality. Different assumptions about the novelty or oldness, the discontinuity and continuity of the media, the Internet and the WWW are based on different definitions of the social, different levels of analysis and different levels of granularity of the analysis. Most of these discussions are very superficial and lack an understanding of social theory and philosophy.

One hypothesis of this book is that in order to maintain the inequality of the power relations of capitalism and capital accumulation, capitalism needs to change its productive forces, which includes the change of its informational productive forces. Therefore the technological and informational structures of the Internet have to a certain degree changed in order to guarantee the continuity of commodity culture, exploitation, surplus value generation and capital accumulation. The changes of the media and the Internet are shaped by complex, dialectical and contradictory continuities and discontinuities.

Web 1.0, Web 2.0, Web 3.0

If the web (WWW) is defined as a techno-social system that comprises the social processes of cognition, communication and co-operation, then the whole web is social in the Durkheimian sense because it is a social fact. Parts of it are communicative in the Weberian sense, while it is the community-building and collaborative part of the web that is social only in the most concrete sense of Tönnies and Marx. The part of the web that deals with cognition is exclusively Durkheimian without being Weberian, let alone Tönniesian–Marxian. The part that is about communication is Weberian and Durkheimian. And only the third, co-operative, part has all three meanings. Based on this distinction we can say that web 1.0 is a computer-based networked system of human cognition, web 2.0 a computer-based networked system of human communication, web 3.0 a computer-based networked system of human co-operation (Fuchs 2008a; Fuchs et al. 2010). Table 2.1 gives an overview of the application of the different concepts of sociality to the WWW. The distinction between the three dimensions of sociality is not an evolutionary or historical one, but rather a logical one. The use of the discourse of versions expresses the dialectical-logical connection of the three modes of sociality:

- Communication is based on and requires cognition, but is more than and different from cognition.
- Co-operation is based on and requires communication, but is more than and different from communication.
- Communication is a Hegelian dialectical *Aufhebung* (sublation) of cognition, co-operation is a dialectical *Aufhebung* of communication. *Aufhebung* means a relation between entities, in which one entity is preserved in the other and the other entity has an additional quality that is different from the first one (for a detailed discussion see Fuchs 2011b, Chapters 2.4 and 3.3). This difference also eliminates the first entity within the second, the preservation of qualities is at the same time an elimination – the two entities are different.

One, two or all three forms of sociality can (at a certain point of analysis) to a certain degree shape the WWW or any other medium. The task of empirical studies that are based on theoretical conceptions of the social is to analyze the presence or absence and the degree of presence of the three types of sociality in a certain medium.

The three forms of sociality (cognition, communication, co-operation) are encapsulated into each other. Each layer forms the foundation for the next one, which has new qualities. Figure 2.3 visualizes the encapsulation of the three dimensions of sociality on the WWW.

It is unlikely that the web (understood as a techo-social system that is based on the interaction of technological computer networks and social networks of power) has not changed in the years since 2000 because capital has reorganized itself as a result of the capitalist crisis in 2000 so that it can survive and find new spheres of accumulation. It is also unlikely that the web is something completely new because, as we have seen, the Internet is a complex techno-social system

Table 2.1 Different understandings of sociality on the web

	Approach	Sociological theory	Meaning of sociality on the WWW
1	Structural Theories	*Émile Durkheim*: Social facts as fixed and objectified social structures that constantly condition social behaviour.	All computers, the Internet and all WWW platforms are social because they are structures that objectify human interests, understandings, goals and intentions, have certain functions in society and effect social behaviour.
2	Social Action Theories	*Max Weber*: Social behaviour as reciprocal symbolic interaction.	Only WWW platforms that enable communication over spatio-temporal distances are social.
3	Theories of Social Co-operation	*Ferdinand Tönnies*: Community as social systems that are based on feelings of togetherness, mutual dependence, and values.	Web platforms that enable the social networking of people, bring people together and mediate feelings of virtual togetherness are social.
		Karl Marx: The social as the co-operation of many humans that results in collective goods that should be owned co-operatively.	Web platforms that enable the collaborative production of digital knowledge are social.
4	Dialectic of Structure and Agency		The Web as a dynamic threefold system of human cognition, communication and co-operation.
	Émile Durkheim: cognition as social due to conditioning external social facts	Web 1.0 as a system of human cognition.	
	Max Weber: communicative action	Web 2.0 as a system of human communication.	
	Ferdinand Tönnies, Karl Marx: community-building and collaborative production as forms of co-operation	Web 3.0 as a system of human co-operation.	

with different levels of organization and sociality that have different speeds and depths of change within capitalism.

Empirically Studying Changes of the Web

If and how the web has changed needs to be studied empirically. Such empirical research should be based on theoretical models. I want to give an example for testing the continuity and discontinuity of the WWW. We want to find out to which degree cognition, communication and co-operation, the three modes of sociality, were featured in the dominant platforms that made up the technical

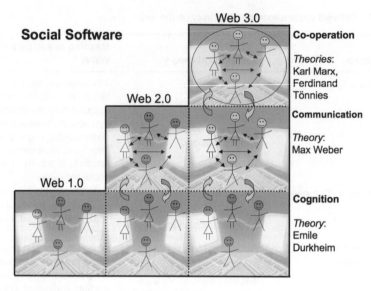

Figure 2.3   Three dimensions of the web's sociality

structures of the WWW in the USA in 1998 and 2011. The statistics are based on the number of unique users in one month of analysis. According to the claims made by O'Reilly (2005a, 2005b), 2002 was a year in the era of 1998, and 2013 one in the era of web 2.0. By conducting a statistical analysis, we can analyze the continuities and discontinuities of the technical structures of the WWW. Table 2.2 shows the results.

The analysis shows that there are continuities and discontinuities in the development of the dominant platforms of WWW in the USA if one compares the years 2002 and 2013. In 2002, there were 20 information functions, 13 communication functions and one co-operation function available on the top 20 websites. In 2013, there are 20 information functions, 16 communication functions and four co-operation functions on the top 20 websites. The number of websites that are oriented towards pure cognitive tasks (like search engines) has decreased from seven in 2002 to four in 2013. In 2013, the number of websites that also have communicative or co-operative features is larger than the one of the pure information sites (four). This shows that the technological foundations for communicative and co-operative sociality have increased quantitatively. The quantitative increase of collaborative features from one to six has to do with the rise of Facebook, Google+, Wikipedia and LinkedIn: collaborative information production with the help of wikis and collaborative software (Wikipedia, Google Docs) and social networking sites oriented towards community-building (Facebook, Google+, LinkedIn). There are continuities and discontinuities in the development of the WWW in the period 2002–2013. The changes concern the rising importance of co-operative sociality. This change is significant, but not dramatic. One novelty is the rise of social networking sites (Facebook, LinkedIn, Google+, MySpace, etc.). Another change is the emergence of blogs (Wordpress, Blogger/Blogpost, Huffington Post), microblogs (Twitter) and file-sharing

Table 2.2 Information functions of the top 20 websites

December 9, 2002 (three-month page ranking based on page views and page reach)			February 26, 2013 (one-month page ranking based on average daily visitors and page views)		
Rank	Website	Primary information functions	Rank	Website	Primary information functions
1	yahoo.com	cogn, comm	1	google.com	cogn, comm, coop
2	msn.com	cogn, comm	2	facebook.com	cogn, comm, coop
3	daum.net	cogn, comm	3	youtube.com	cogn, comm
4	naver.com	cogn, comm	4	yahoo.com	cogn, comm
5	google.com[1]	cogn	5	baidu.com	cogn, comm
6	yahoo.co.jp	cogn, comm	6	wikipedia.org	cogn, comm, coop
7	passport.net	cogn	7	live.com	cogn, comm
8	ebay.com	cogn	8	qq.com	cogn, comm
9	microsoft.com	cogn	9	amazon.com	cogn
10	bugsmusic.co.kr	cogn	10	twitter.com	cogn, comm
11	sayclub.com	cogn, comm	11	blogspot.com	cogn, comm
12	sina.com.cn	cogn, comm	12	linkedin.com	cogn, comm, coop
13	netmarble.net	cogn, comm, coop	13	google.co.in	cogn, comm, coop
14	amazon.com	cogn	14	taobao.com	cogn
15	nate.com	cogn, comm	15	yahoo.co.jp	cogn, comm
16	go.com	cogn	16	bing.com	cogn
17	sohu.com	cogn, comm	17	msn.com	cogn, comm
18	163.com	cogn, comm	18	google.co.jp	cogn, comm, coop
19	hotmail.com	cogn, comm	19	ebay.com	cogn
20	aol.com	cogn, comm	20	yandex.ru	cogn, comm
		cogn: 20 comm: 13 coop: 1			cogn: 20 comm: 16 coop: 4

Data source: alexa.com.
[1]Google's main communicative feature, the email service gMail, was launched in 2004.

websites (YouTube), which have increased the possibilities of communication and information sharing in the top 20 US websites. Google has broadened its functions: it started as a pure search engine (in 1999), introduced communication features in 2007 (gMail) and its own social networking site platform (Google+) in June 2011.

The statistics indicate that the rise of co-operative sociality supported by social networking sites and wikis, and the differentiation of cognitive and communicative sociality (the emergence of file-sharing sites and blogs, including microblogs like Twitter), have to a certain degree changed the technical structures of the WWW in order to enable new models of capital accumulation and the maintenance of the capitalist character of the WWW. Another significant change is the rise of the search engine Google, which has pioneered the web capital accumulation models by introducing targeted advertising that is personalized to the interests of users and monitors their online behaviour and personal interests on the Internet. The change of the technical structures of the WWW has enabled the continuity of the logic of capital accumulation on the Internet after the dot.com bubble. Wikipedia, which is a non-profit and non-commercial platform funded by user donations, has entered the scene. It is the only successful WWW platform thus far that is not based on a capital accumulation model.

2.4. Conclusion

Analyzing continuities and discontinuities of the web requires social theory foundations. The WWW is not social in a simple sense, but to certain degrees on certain levels of analysis that are grounded in sociological conceptions of sociality. If one compares WWW use in the late 1990s to the end of the first decade of the second millennium, one finds the use patterns of the WWW are shaped by continuities and discontinuities. Information is continuously present, communication has been transformed, web technologies of co-operation have become more frequently used and important, but are certainly not dominant. The web is neither purely old nor purely new; it is a complex techno-social system embedded into power structures of capitalism that has to change to a certain extent at certain levels in order to enable the continuity of Internet-based capital accumulation.

   This chapter dealt with the question: What is social media? Its main results are as follows:

- Dealing with the question "What is social media?" requires an understanding of what the social is all about. It is, in this respect, helpful to look at social theory for engaging with concepts of sociality in society. Relevant concepts of sociality include social facts (Émile Durkheim), social relations/ social action (Max Weber), co-operative labour (Karl Marx) and community (Ferdinand Tönnies).

- Claims about the novelty and opportunities of "web 2.0" and "social media" like blogs, social networking sites, wikis, microblogs or content-sharing sites originated in the context of the dot.com crisis of the Internet economy and the resulting search for new business models and narratives that convince investors and users to support new platforms. The ideology of novelty intends to attract investors and users.

- Most social media technologies originated before 2005, when Tim O'Reilly established the concept of web 2.0. Wikis, blogs, social networking sites, microblogs and content-sharing sites have, however, become really popular since the middle of the first decade of the second millennium. It is both unlikely that in the years 2000–2010 the WWW has not changed at all and unlikely that it has radically changed. The capitalist Internet economy needs to change and innovate in order to guarantee the continuity of capital accumulation.

- The two concepts of participation and power have been used for characterizing social media (participatory culture, power and counter-power of mass self-communication). Class is another concept that is particularly suited. Great care should be taken to avoid techno-deterministic thinking, techno-centrism, techno-optimism, techno-pessimism and naturalization of domination in conceptualizing qualities of social media. Engaging with social theory, the history of concepts and the philosophical groundings of the Internet can provide help for developing concepts that describe structure, agency and dynamics of social media.

- Media are techno-social systems in which technological structures interact with social relations and human activities in complex ways. Power structures shape the media and the social relations of the media. When analyzing social media, one should be clear about and should explicate the level of analysis.

RECOMMENDED READINGS AND EXERCISES

Making sense of social media requires a theoretical understanding of what it means to be social. Sociological theory offers different concepts of the social. The following suggested readings introduce you to various concepts of the social by thinkers such as Émile Durkheim, Max Weber, Ferdinand Tönnies and Karl Marx.

Durkheim, Émile. 1895. The rules of sociological method. In *Classical sociological theory*, ed. Craig Calhoun, Joseph Gerteis, James Moody, Steven Pfaff and Indermohan Virk, 139–157. Malden, MA: Blackwell.

In "The rules of sociological method", Émile Durkheim introduces some basic foundations of a functionalist social theory, such as the notion of social facts. Discuss in groups and compare your results:

- What is a social fact?

- Make a list of economic, political and cultural examples of social facts that can be found in contemporary society.

- Each group can choose one web platform (such as Google, Yahoo, Facebook, Twitter, Weibo, Wikipedia, etc.). Think in your group about how this platform works and what kind of activities it supports. Make a list of social facts that can be found on the platform.

Weber, Max. 1914. Basic sociological terms. In *Classical sociological theory*, ed. Craig Calhoun, Joseph Gerteis, James Moody, Steven Pfaff and Indermohan Virk, 139–157. Malden, MA: Blackwell.

In "Basic sociological terms", Max Weber introduces foundational categories of a sociological action theory, such as action, social action and social relations. Discuss in groups and compare your results:

- How does Max Weber define social action?

- Make a list of examples of online activities that correspond to Weber's theory of the social and non-social. Compare how Durkheim would characterize the sociality of these platforms.

- Try to find examples of the four types of social action that Weber identifies.

- Try to find examples of four types of online social action according to Weber.

Tönnies, Ferdinand. 2001. *Community and civil society*, 17–51. Cambridge: Cambridge University Press.

Rheingold, Howard. 2000. *The virtual community: Homesteading on the electronic frontier*. Cambridge, MA: MIT Press. Chapter 11: Rethinking virtual communities.

Ferdinand Tönnies first published *Community and Civil Society* in 1887. In this work, he draws a distinction between *Gemeinschaft* (community) and *Gesellschaft* (society). It is interesting to read this text in combination with Howard Rheingold's *The Virtual Community*, where he discusses the logic of community in the age of the Internet and how it is limited by the logic of commodities that Tönnies considered specific for what he termed society. Discuss in groups and compare your results:

- Identify basic characteristics of a community according to Ferdinand Tönnies. Construct a list of features of a community.

- Try to identify different groups that you are in contact with on Facebook or another social networking site. Which of these groups are communities according to Tönnies, which are not, and why? Try to test the applicability of all community features that you have identified.

- What are, according to Howard Rheingold, the basic features of a virtual community? In which respects is Facebook a virtual community, and in which respects not? What does Howard Rheingold mean by "commodification of community"? Having read his chapter, how do you think he assesses Facebook?

- Additional exercise: Organize a conversation with Howard Rheingold or another well-known Internet scholar about what s/he sees as the positive and negative features of social media.

Marx, Karl. 1867. *Capital. Volume I*. London: Penguin. Chapter 13: Co-operation.

Capital. Volume I is one of the most influential books in economic thought. It contains a chapter that discusses the phenomenon of collaborative work and its role in the modern economy. Discuss in groups and compare your results:

- Try to give a definition of what co-operation and collaborative work are (this requires that you also define the concept of "work").

- How does Marx see the role of co-operation in capitalism?

- How does co-operation work on Wikipedia? Try to identify commonalities and differences between the co-operation brought about by capitalism that Marx describes and co-operation on Wikipedia. What are the differences and commonalities?

3

Social Media as Participatory Culture

Key questions

- What is participatory culture? How have different scholars attempted to define it?
- How have scholars understood participatory culture within the realm of socialmedia?
- What do scholars mean by 'participatory democracy'?
- Are contemporary social media truly participatory?

Key concepts

Henry Jenkins's notions of
  participatory culture and
  spreadable media

Participatory culture as ideology
Participatory democracy
Digital labour

Overview

Participatory culture is a term that is often used for designating the involvement of users, audiences, consumers and fans in the creation of culture and content. Examples are the joint editing of an article on Wikipedia, the uploading of images to Flickr or Facebook, the uploading of videos to YouTube and the creation of short messages on Twitter or Weibo.

The participatory culture model is often opposed to the mass media and broadcasting model typical of newspapers, radio and television, where there is one sender and many recipients. Some scholars argue that culture and society become more democratic because users and audiences are enabled to produce culture themselves and to not just listen or watch without actively making and creating culture:

- The Internet analyst Clay Shirky (2011a, 27) has argued that social media result in "the wiring of humanity" and let "us treat free time as a shared global resource, and lets us design new kinds of participation and sharing that take advantage of that resource".
- The Australian scholar Axel Bruns argues that produsage, the combination of production and use, is characteristic of social media. As the result of social media he envisions a "produsage-based, participatory culture" (Bruns 2008, 256) and "a produsage-based democratic model" (372).
- Similarly, the business consultants Don Tapscott and Anthony Williams (2007, 15) argue that social media result in the emergence of "a new economic democracy […] in which we all have a lead role".

All three statements have in common that they highlight positive aspects of social media and point out that these media are possible to make culture and society more democratic. This chapter critically questions these claims. Section 3.1 discusses the notion of participatory culture, section 3.2 deals with Henry Jenkins' focus on fan culture, section 3.3 addresses his discussion of social media, and section 3.4 looks at how he sees the so-called digital labour debate, i.e. the role of unpaid user activities in value-generation.

3.1. The Notions of Participation and Participatory Culture

Social Media as Spreadable Media

For Henry Jenkins, the main characteristic of "social media"/"web 2.0" is that they are spreadable media (Jenkins, Li, Krauskopf and Green 2009): "Consumers play an active role in 'spreading' content [. . .] Consumers in this model are [. . .] grassroots advocates for materials which are personally and socially meaningful to them" (Jenkins et al. 2009, part 2). Spreadable media are based on the logic "if it doesn't spread, it's dead" (Jenkins, Ford and Green 2013, 1) and involve audiences that "actively" shape "media flows" (2) so that culture becomes "far more participatory" (1). Sharing, co-creation, remixing, reuse and adaption of content on Facebook, YouTube and other online platforms are, for Jenkins, a manifestation of a gift economy.

He argues that spreadable media "empower" consumers and "make them an integral part" of a commodity's success (Jenkins et al. 2009, part 8). The "longer term" benefits would include the expansion of "the range of potential markets for a brand" and the intensification of "consumer loyalty by increasing emotional attachment to the brand or media franchise" (Jenkins et al. 2009, part 8).

Jenkins, Ford and Green (2013, xii) argue that they "accept as a starting point that the constructs of capitalism will greatly shape the creation and circulation of most media texts for the foreseeable future" and that those companies that "listen to [. . .] their audiences" will strive. They accept the logic of capitalism in a time of crisis, where trust in corporations is low and capitalism has shown that it organizes society necessarily in such a way that exploitation, misery and precariousness are a necessary reality for a certain share of people.

When Pepsi launched a marketing campaign in 2007, which allowed consumers to design the look of a Pepsi can that was featured on 500 million Pepsi cans around the United States, the task was not, as frequently claimed by management gurus, to create "a new economic democracy [. . .] in which we all have a lead role" (Tapscott and Williams 2007, 15; for a critique of this approach, see Fuchs 2008b), but to outsource design work and thereby surplus value-generation cheaply to consumers and to ideologically bind the emotions of the consumers to the brand so that more Pepsi could be sold and more profit be made. The Convergence Culture Consortium that includes GSD&M Advertising, MTV Networking and Turner Broadcasting funded Jenkins' study of spreadable media.

Participatory Culture

For Jenkins, social media are also an expression of participatory culture. Jenkins defines participatory culture as culture "in which fans and other consumers are invited to actively participate in the creation and circulation of new content" (Jenkins 2008, 331). It also involves "participants who interact with each other" (Jenkins 2008, 3). Participation involves, for Jenkins, "new forms of participation and collaboration" (Jenkins 2008, 256). Jenkins points out, based on Pierre Lévy (1997), that those who engage in "participatory culture" pool resources and combine skills so that collective intelligence emerges as "an alternative source of media power" (Jenkins 2008, 4).

Jenkins defines participatory as a culture with:

1. relatively low barriers to artistic expression and civic engagement,
2. strong support for creating and sharing creations with others,
3. some type of informal mentorship whereby what is known by the most experienced is passed along to novices,
4. members who believe that their contributions matter, and
5. members who feel some degree of social connection with one another (at the least, they care what other people think about what they have created). (Jenkins, Purushotma, Weigel, Clinton and Robison 2009, 5f)

Participatory Democracy

Jenkins has argued that increasingly "the Web has become a site of consumer participation" (Jenkins 2008, 137). A problem of concepts like "participatory culture" is that participation is a political science term that is strongly connected to participatory democracy theory and authors like Crawford Macpherson (1973) and Carole Pateman (1970). An article by Staughton Lynd (1965) that describes the grassroots organization model of the Students for a Democratic Society (SDS) made the earliest use of the term "participatory democracy" that I could trace in the literature. One should avoid a vulgar use of the term "participation". Internet Studies should relate the usage of the term to participatory democracy theory, in which it has the following dimensions (Fuchs 2011b, chapter 7):

1. The intensification and extension of democracy as grassroots democracy to all realms of society.

2. The maximization of human capacities (Macpherson (1973): human developmental powers) so that humans become well-rounded individuals.

3. Extractive power as impediment for participatory democracy:

   Macpherson (1973) argues that capitalism is based on an exploitation of human powers that limits the development of human capacities. The modern economy "by its very nature compels a continual net transfer of part of the power of some men to others [for the benefit and the enjoyment of the others], thus diminishing rather than maximizing the equal individual freedom to use and develop one's natural capacities". (Macpherson 1973, 10f)

4. Participatory decision-making.

5. Participatory economy: a participatory economy requires a "change in the terms of access to capital in the direction of more nearly equal access" (Macpherson 1973, 71) and "a change to more nearly equal access to the means of labour" (73). In a participatory society, extractive power is reduced to zero (74). A democratic economy involves "the democratising of industrial authority structures, abolishing the permanent distinction between 'managers' and 'men'" (Pateman 1970, 43).

6. Technological productivity as material foundation of participatory democracy.

7. Participation as education in participation.

8. Pseudo-participation as ideology.

Ignoring Ownership, Capitalism and Class: Cultural and Political Reductionism

For Jenkins, participation means that humans meet on the net, form collectives, create and share content. He has a culturalistic understanding of participation and ignores the notion of participatory democracy, a term which has political, political economic and cultural dimensions. Jenkins' definition and use of the term "participatory culture" ignores aspects of participatory democracy; it ignores questions about the ownership of platforms/companies, collective decision-making, profit, class and the distribution of material benefits. Jenkins, Purushotma, Weigel, Clinton and Robison (2009, 9) mention community membership, production, collaboration and sharing as activities in participatory cultures, whereas ownership is not mentioned. The 11 skills listed as characteristics for literacy in participatory culture do not include critical thinking, but rather activities that can all work well in a company context (collective intelligence, networking, multitasking, etc.; Jenkins, Purushotma, Weigel, Clinton and Robison 2009, xiv). Corporate platforms owned by Facebook, Google and other large companies strongly mediate the cultural expressions of Internet users. Neither the users nor the waged employees of Facebook, Google and others determine the business decisions of these companies. They do not "participate" in economic decision-making, but are excluded from it.

Jenkins' concept of participation is not theoretically grounded. Also, Nico Carpentier (2011), who advances a more nuanced approach that is grounded in political theory, ignores ownership aspects of the participation concept. He conceives participation as "equal power relations in decision-making processes" (Carpentier 2011, 69) and media participation as co-decision-making in the contexts of media technology, content, people and organizations (130). This notion of media participation is explicitly a political concept (354), focusing on involvement in media decision-making (355) and avoiding a broad definition of participation (69). Carpentier does not include aspects of media ownership, neither does he consider ownership questions as questions relating to participation. In contrast to Crawford MacPherson, Carpentier ignores the level of political economy of participation and reduces participation to the political level. The problem of Carpentier's political reductionistic concept of (media) participation is that it implies that full "participation" can be achieved without letting people participate in the ownership of the organizations in which they work, as long as they are involved in decision-making. The topic of inequality of ownership and wealth is ignored and declared to be secondary or unimportant. A truly participatory media democracy must also be an ownership democracy (Fuchs 2014, 2011b). Carpentier, although being theoretically versed and well read, just like Jenkins, ends up with a reductionistic concept of media participation. Reductionism means that a certain aspect of the world is explained based on one specific dimension, although other dimensions also matter. In the social sciences, liberal and conservative scholars have often claimed that Marxism reduces explanations of society to the economy. At the same time, the same scholars often ignore aspects of class and capitalism and thereby reduce explanations of society either to politics (politicism, political reductionism) or culture (culturalism).

Jenkins, Ford and Green (2013, 193) argue that participatory culture is relative and that we "do not and may never live in a society where every member is able to fully participate". This passage essentializes exclusion, as if it were a natural feature of every type of society. Essentialism is a form of argumentation that does not see phenomena as historical, which means that they have a beginning and an end and can be changed by human action. These phenomena (such as money, capital, domination, violence, egoism, competition, etc.) are declared to exist necessarily and forever. Karl Marx (1867) has termed this form of argumentation "fetish thinking": certain phenomena are treated like being things and the fact that they are social circumstances that can be changed by humans is ignored.

Participation means that humans have the right and reality to be part of decisions and to govern and control the structures that affect them. Rights are always universal and not particularistic. For example, if human rights are only valid for some people but not others, then they are no rights at all. Similarly, participation is a universal political demand, not a relative category. Otherwise one could say that a dictatorship is a participatory democracy because a ruling elite is "participating", which is, however, only a relatively small part of the population.

When Jenkins writes about political goals, he remains rather vague with formulations such as the demand for "corporate responsibility" (Jenkins 2008, 259) or "a much greater diversity of opinion" (Jenkins 2008, 250; see also 268). He says it is important for "pressuring companies to change the products they are creating and the ways they relate to their consumers" (Jenkins 2008, 261), that there is an "alarming concentration of the ownership of mainstream commercial media" (Jenkins 2008, 18) and that "concentration is bad" (Jenkins 2008, 259). The basic question is whether capitalist organizations can ever be responsible, given that they must necessarily be interested in reducing wage and investment costs in order to increase profits if they want to survive in the competition process. The notion of diverse opinion remains empty if one does not consider the question of whether a fascist opinion is equally desirable and valuable as a democratic socialist opinion. Capitalism is based on the need to increase productivity for increasing profits. But productivity and competitive advantages tend to be asymmetrically distributed. As a result, competition tends to turn into monopolies and capital concentration. Media and other concentration is not just something that is bad, but rather a structural feature of capitalism.

White Boys with "Participatory" Toys

Internet culture is not separate from political economy, but is to a large extent organized, controlled and owned by companies (platforms like Wikipedia are non-corporate models that are different from the dominant corporate social media model). Social media culture is a culture industry. Jenkins' notion of "participatory culture" is mainly about expressions, engagement, creation, sharing, experience, contributions and feelings and not so much about how these practices are enabled by and antagonistically entangled into capital accumulation. Jenkins tends to advance a reductionistic understanding of culture that ignores contemporary culture's political economy. Furthermore, he reduces the notion of participation to a cultural dimension, ignoring the broad notion of participatory democracy and its implications for the Internet. An Internet that is dominated by corporations that accumulate capital by exploiting and commodifying users can in the theory of participatory democracy never be participatory, and the cultural expressions on it cannot be an expression of participation.

Important goals for Jenkins seem to be that companies establish "stronger connections with their constituencies and consumers" (Jenkins 2008, 22), a "collective bargaining structure" (Jenkins 2008, 63) between fans and companies, brand communities that "empower" consumers to "assert their own demand on the company" (Jenkins 2008, 80), "experiments in consumer-generated content" that "have an influence on the mass media companies" (Jenkins 2008, 172), and cultural entrepreneurs that give "their consumers greater opportunities to shape the content and participate in its distribution" (Jenkins 2008, 268). Jenkins is deeply concerned with the question of whether consumers will be able to shape the content of cultural commodities according to their desires by engaging as active and creative prosumers in "participatory culture".

Jenkins' writings read much like a celebration of participatory culture as a structure that allows consumers "to participate in the production and distribution of cultural goods" (Jenkins 2008, 137) that does not much engage with or analyze the downsides of the Internet, such as the economic crisis; the exploitation of users; concerns about privacy violations and surveillance; e-waste (Maxwell and Miller 2014); the exploitation of miners who often extract the minerals needed for the production of laptops, computers and other hardware under slave-like working conditions (this topic is also called "conflict minerals" because of the wars and interest conflicts that often underlie these working conditions); and the exploitation of hardware manufacturers who often are overworked, underpaid and conduct their jobs in toxic workplaces (Fuchs 2014). Participatory democracy is a demand that speaks against such problems, whereas participatory culture is a rather harmless concept mainly created by white boys with toys who love their toys.

3.2. Online Fan Culture and Politics

Fan Culture as Politics?

Henry Jenkins sees fan communities in general, and online fan communities in particular, as "preparing the way for a more meaningful public culture" (Jenkins 2008, 239). He tends to idealize the political potentials of fan communities and cannot explain why these communities should make fans more interested and active in politics. From the circumstances that "fans are viewers who speak back to the networks and the producers" and that they "know how to organize to lobby on behalf of endangered series" (Jenkins 1992, 284), it does not follow that fans have an interest in protesting against racism, neoliberalism, wage cuts, the privatization of education or welfare, lay-offs in the companies, etc. Toby Miller asks in this context, can "fans be said to engage with labour exploitation, patriarchy, racism, and neo-imperialism, or in some specifiable way make a difference to politics beyond their own selves, when they interpret texts unusually or chat about romantic frustrations?" (Miller 2008, 220).

Henry Jenkins mistakenly assumes an automatic connection with fandom in popular culture and political protest. He also mistakes politics with popular culture and sees politics taking place largely as micro politics within popular culture (as the struggle of fans to make the culture industry respect their ideas in the design of plots). The protestors who brought about a revolution in Egypt in 2011 to a certain extent also made use of media (like Facebook, Twitter and mobile phones) for forming communities – not fan communities, but rather a political community engaging in street protests, strikes, blockades, and the struggle against a regime. Their political practices have shown how a revolution works and that revolution is possible today. The revolution was not caused by social media, but only supported by them. Fan communities played no significant role in this process. Many passages of Jenkins' books (for example, Jenkins 2006, 10f) convey the impression that he wants to get rid of the heritage of Critical Studies having to be political in an analysis and that he feels the desire to engage purely with the fun of popular culture. But if academics do not engage with popular culture for political reasons (to establish a just society), what is really the goal and justification for it?

Henry Jenkins (2008, 12) says that he is "not simply a consumer of many of these media products; I am also an active fan". He says that his living room is full of various media players and recorders, "a huge mound of videotapes, DVDs and CDs, game cartridges and controllers" (Jenkins 2008, 15). Fandom as such is not a problem, if the researcher, who is also a fan of his object of study, manages to maintain critical reflexivity. I am a fan of *The Simpsons*, Monty Python, 3WK Underground Radio or bands such as Mogwai, Radiohead and The Fall, but I do not think that it is political to watch these programmes or listen to these bands. In a lot of contemporary works on popular culture, one gets the impression that scholars want to rationalize their own fandom and their love for commodity culture by trying to identify progressive political aspects of the consumption and logic of cultural commodities. Because they like spending their work time and free time consuming popular culture, they tend to justify this behaviour as a form of political resistance. There is then no need to engage in, or support, the more risky activities of political movements because popular culture is declared to be a political movement itself. Most intellectuals are probably fond of some type of popular culture, but it makes a difference whether one sees and celebrates this fondness as an act of resistance or not.

Is Online Fascism Participatory Culture?

Cultural communities are not automatically politically progressive. An example is that document.no and an accompanying Facebook group are gathering places for Norwegian right-wing extremists, who oppose immigration to Norway and argue for advancing Islamophobia and the idea of cultural purity. The fascist terrorist Anders Behring Breivik, who killed 77 people in the Norwegian terror attacks on July 22, 2011, was one of the active members of this community. Jenkins does not much discuss the negative potentials and realities of online communities and cultural communities.

www.ultras.ws is a discussion forum of the Ultras soccer fan movement. One can find anti-Semitic and racist jokes in the forum, and in a survey conducted in the forum 56% said that it is no problem if fans shout "Jews" for characterizing opposing teams.[1] The following joke is typical and no exception, but rather the rule,

---

1 www.ultras.ws/umfrage-juden-jena-rufe-und-die-strafe-t4414.html, accessed on August 1, 2011.

in this forum:[2] "How do you get 30 Jews into a Trabi [=a small car common in East Germany under Soviet times]? Two in the front, three in the back and the rest in the ashtray." The concept of participatory culture has a focus on "community involvement" (Jenkins, Purushotma, Weigel, Clinton and Robison 2009, 6). However, it idealizes community and fan culture as progressive and ignores the fact that the collective intelligence and activity of cultural communities and fandom can easily turn into a fascist mob, especially in situations of capitalist crisis that are prone to advance the growth and radicalization of right-wing extremism.

Jenkins has, thus far, mostly analyzed the fan communities he likes and rather neglected those that have fascist potentials. Fascist communities do not seem to fit his concept of fandom and communities. Jenkins (1992, 290) says that fans are not necessarily progressive, but that they have the potential to be active (293) and that they "find the ability to question and rework the ideologies that dominate the mass culture" (290). There is no doubt also that hooligan soccer fan groups are active (they actively inflict violence against other fans and immigrants, make active plans to harass, threaten or kill them, etc.), but activity and creativity of fans is not necessarily, as assumed by Jenkins in his deterministic and reductionistic logic of argumentation, a questioning of ideologies; it can just as likely be a reproduction of dominant ideologies (like racism). Although Jenkins assures his readers in single sentences that fans are not always progressive, the structure of his examples and other formulations advance exactly the conclusion that they are progressive.

3.3. Social Media and Participatory Culture

Social Media Capitalism

Although Henry Jenkins is to a certain extent aware that corporations exert greater power than consumers (Jenkins 2008, 3, 175), he focuses the reader's attention in most of his books on the presentation of hundreds of examples that want to assert to the reader that contemporary media empower consumers because they enable production processes and that consumers successfully resist corporatism. He conceives media prosumption as inherently participatory. Jenkins argues that increasingly "the Web has become a site of consumer participation" (Jenkins 2008, 137) and hardly gives any examples of corporate domination in culture or on the Internet. Therefore, the notion of participatory culture takes on a reified character in his works.

Jenkins argues that participatory culture advances cultural diversity (Jenkins 2008, 268), but overlooks that not all voices have the same power and that produced content and voices are frequently marginalized because visibility is a central resource in contemporary culture that powerful actors, such as media corporations, can buy. Jenkins assumes that diversity is the linear result of prosumption.

Jenkins simply constructs a dualistic "both . . . and" argument based on the logic that "Web 2.0 is both . . . and . . . ": both pleasure and exploitation, both a space of

---

2 www.ultras.ws/viewtopic.php?p=483232, accessed on July 29, 2013.

participation and a space of commodification. Convergence is "both a top-down corporate-driven process and a bottom-up consumer-driven process. Corporate convergence coexists with grassroots convergence" (Jenkins 2008, 18). He wants to focus on the aspects of pleasure and creativity and to leave the topic of exploitation to others and does not, thereby, grasp the dialectics at work and the relations of dominance we find on web 2.0. The question is not only what phenomena we find on social media, but how they are related and to what extent and degree they are present. There is no doubt that web 2.0 users are creative when they generate and diffuse user-generated content. But the question is also how many web 2.0 users are active and what degree of activity and creativity their practices have. So, for example, in Sweden, one of the world's most advanced information societies, only 6% of Internet users write blog postings occasionally and only 1% do so on a daily basis (Findahl 2012). Scholars like Jenkins tend to overstate the creativity and activity of users on the web. Creativity is a force that enables Internet prosumer commodification, the commodification and exploitation of the users' activities and the data they generate. Creativity is not outside or alongside exploitation on web 2.0; it is its very foundation.

YouTube

Jenkins (2008, 274) argues that YouTube is a site "for the production and distribution of grassroots media" and that on YouTube "participation occurs at three distinct levels [. . .] – those of production, selection, and distribution" (Jenkins 2008, 275), without considering the fact that YouTube is owned by Google and that the revenues that are accumulated with online advertising on YouTube do not belong to the immediate content producers, but to the shareholders of Google. Jenkins here neglects ownership as a central aspect of participation. The most popular YouTube videos stem from global multimedia corporations like Universal, Sony and Walt Disney (see Table 5.1 in Chapter 5). Google and Facebook are based on targeted advertising models and a commercial culture, which results in huge profits for these companies. Politics on YouTube, Twitter and Facebook are possible, but are minority issues – the predominant focus of users is on non-political entertainment. Web 2.0 corporations and the usage they enable are not an expression of participatory democracy. As long as corporations dominate the Internet, it will not be participatory. The participatory Internet can only be found in those areas that resist corporate domination and where activists and users engage in building and reproducing non-commercial, non-profit Internet projects like Wikipedia or Diaspora. Jenkins (and many others) continuously ignores questions of who owns, controls and materially benefits from corporate social media.

Jenkins is aware of the topic of the exploitation of digital labour on the Internet (Green and Jenkins 2009; Jenkins 2009). He concludes, however, that the problem is that "YouTube pushes up content which receives support from other users" (Jenkins 2009, 124), which is only part of the truth and ignores the fact that large corporate media companies' content is so popular because they have resource advantages in attaining recognition and attention over everyday users.

Jenkins concludes that "a more collaborative approach" is needed that is based on a "negotiation of the implicit social contract between media producers and con-sumers, balancing the commodity and cultural status of creative goods" (Green and Jenkins 2009, 222). This view ignores the contradictory and crisis character of capitalism. The history of capitalism is a history of the colonization of societies and human spaces in order to create new spaces of commodification and capital accumulation and is a history of the crisis of capitalism. There can be no long-term peace between capital and consumers/workers/prosumers because the first has an inherent interest in exploiting the latter and accumulation leads to crisis, which is the ultimate disruption of temporary class compromises. Also, the welfare-oriented model of Fordist capitalism was ended by the world economic crisis in the 1970s, which shows that capitalism is inherently crisis-ridden.

Blogs

In the corporate social media sphere, attention is unequally distributed: big companies, celebrities and well-known political actors enjoy attention advan-tages and the most active prosumers come from the young, educated middle-class. Jenkins (2008, 227) celebrates blogs as a "means for their participants to express their distrust of the news media and their discontent with politics as usual", "potentially increasing cultural diversity and lowering barriers in cultural participation", "expanding the range of perspectives", as "grassroots intermediaries" that ensure "that everyone has a chance to be heard" (Jenkins 2006, 180f). He forgets the lack of visibility in the public sphere of most politi-cal blogs. Political blogs have hardly been able to reach the large numbers of readers of the websites of big corporate newsmakers like CNN and *The New York Times*. Statistics of the most frequently accessed web platforms (alexa. com, measured by a combined index of average daily visitors and page views over the past month, accessed on February 28, 2013) show that popular political blogs tend to get much less visibility and attention than mainstream news websites. Political blogs do not rank under the top 1000. Examples are: Daily Kos (#3211), NewsBusters (#4838), Raw Story (#5105), Talking Points Memo (#5128), Hot Air (#5293), ThinkProgress (#5467), Mediaite =(#5981), LewRockwell (#8597), Redstate (#16353), Common Dreams (#17567), Crooks and Liars (#20372), Power Line (#21329), Wonkette (#30087), AmericaBlog (#41220), Andrew Sullivan's Daily Dish (#68132), Little Green Footballs (#73382), Eschaton (#104454), Liberal Conspiracy (#229574), Labourlist (#299278), Left Food Forward (#404020) and My DD (#540384). In contrast, popular mainstream news sites achieve top rankings: BBC Online (#54), CNN (#80), *The New York Times* (#120), *Daily Mail* (#125), *Der Spiegel* (#222), Indiatimes (#127), *The Guardian* (#197). This inequality shows that visibility and popularity on the web are stratified.

The political economy of online attention tends to privilege large media companies that have established brands and control a lot of resources. The Huffington Post (#92) started in 2005 as a blog project, acquired venture capital investment and so became a relatively popular site. It was purchased by AOL in February 2011 and thereby became part of the mainstream media market. Its business model is targeted advertising. The example shows that alternative online media can easily become commodified and transformed into capitalist businesses.

One can now argue that political blogs still gather a lot of attention and as a total phenomenon have a lot of readers. The advantage of a site like *The New York Times* is that it attracts the attention of a high number of people who all have the same information as a basis for discussion and opinion-formation. This does not mean that the information published in the mainstream media is superior and unproblematic. To the contrary, it is often more one-dimensional and distorted than the information on political blogs. But gathering a large number of people on one site is a power in itself, whereas gathering some people on many dispersed sites fragments the public, results in "a huge number of isolated issue publics" (Habermas 2006, 423) and risks "cultural relativism" that neglects that democracy is in need of "some common normative dimensions" and "more generalized media" (Garnham 1992, 369).

3.4. Henry Jenkins and Digital Labour

The digital labour debate is a discourse that has emerged in Critical Media and Communication Studies with the rise of social media (see Arvidsson and Colleoni 2012; Fuchs 2010c, 2012c, as well as the contributions in Burston, Dyer-Witheford and Hearn 2010; Scholz 2013). It focuses on the analysis of unpaid user labour and other forms of labour (such as slave labour in Africa, highly exploited ICT manufacturing work) that are necessary for capital accumulation in the ICT industries. In this debate, the works of Dallas Smythe (1977, 1981/2006) have gained new significance (for a detailed discussion, see Fuchs 2012a). Smythe argued that audiences of advertising-financed newspapers, TV and radio stations work when giving attention to these media (audience labour) and produce themselves as a commodity (the audience commodity) that is sold to advertisers. In the book *Spreadable Media: Creating Value and Meaning in a Networked Culture* (Jenkins, Ford and Green 2013), Henry Jenkins and his colleagues engage with some of the arguments in the digital labour debate.

Dallas Smythe, Digital Labour and Henry Jenkins

Jenkins, Ford and Green (2013, 127) discuss Smythe's approach and comment that "companies are often profiting from this audience labor, but it's crucial not to paint this wholly as exploitation, denying the many ways audience members benefit from willing participation in such arrangements". They argue against representatives of the digital labour discourse that "free labour may be meaningful and rewarding" (57). The authors make the argument that users are not purely motivated by financial returns (58f), but by the desire to "share with a larger audience", the "pride in their accomplishments" and the "desire for dialogue" (59).

Jenkins, Ford and Green insinuate that representatives of digital labour theory assume that the money logic drives users, which they definitely do not. The three authors miss the point that the profit orientation is inherent in capitalism, not in users or audiences, who are confronted with the commodity form in their everyday lives. Audience work would be engaged, not exploited (60), and would be "labor[s] of love" (61). It would have much to do with worth, i.e. "sentimental investment" (71).

There is no doubt that users are motivated by social and communicative needs and desires to use social media. But the fact that they love these activities does not make them less exploited. Jenkins' argument follows the logic "if users like it, then it is no problem". That work is and feels like play does not mean that it is more or less exploited, but rather that the structures of work are changing. Exploitation is measured as the degree of unpaid labour from which companies benefit at the expense of labour. If exploitation does not feel like exploitation, then this does not mean that it does not exist. It is exploitation even if users like it. User labour is objectively exploited and, to a certain degree, at the same time enjoyed by the users. This does not diminish the degree of exploitation, but rather shows the contradictions of culture in capitalism. In Jenkins' terminology one can say that social media corporations capitalize on users' desire for social, intellectual and cultural worth in order to exploit their labour and make them create monetary value. In Jenkins' account, cultural worth is seen as legitimatization of exploitation: it is perfectly fine for him that users are exploited if they feel they are appreciated by other users and companies.

Jenkins and his colleagues argue that Smythe and the digital labour approach overlook that audience members benefit from corporate web 2.0. But they overlook in this critique that money has a central importance in capitalism because it is a general equivalent of exchange: it is the only commodity that can be exchanged against all other commodities. It is the universal commodity and is therefore of specific relevance. One can directly buy food, games, computers, phones, etc. with money. One can, at most, gain such goods indirectly by making use of reputation and social connections. Money is a privileged medium for achieving objectives in capitalism, which is why capitalism is an economy that is based on instrumental reason.

Social Media and Fans, Fans, Fans – Did Occupy, the Arab Spring and WikiLeaks Never Happen?

Jenkins, Ford and Green's (2013, 29) book *Spreadable Media* mainly uses examples from fan culture because "fan groups have often been innovators in using participatory platforms". Reading this book, one gets the impression that the world is only inhabited by fans, as if the Arab Spring, WikiLeaks, Anonymous, the Occupy movement and the widespread protests and revolutions in the world during 2011 never happened. One wonders why Henry Jenkins advances a new form of elitism that privileges fans and disregards activists and citizens. The book, for example, discusses the online platform 4chan, but ignores the political hacking of Anonymous that was born on 4chan.

3.5. Conclusion

Jenkins' work stands in the celebratory Cultural Studies tradition that focuses on worshipping TV audiences (and other audiences) as "rebelling" and constantly "resisting" in order to consume ever more. Jenkins (2008, 259) opposes the approaches of political economists like Noam Chomsky and Robert McChesney because their "politics of critical pessimism is found on a politics of victimization", whereas his own "politics of critical utopianism is founded on a notion of empowerment". It is incorrect to characterize the Critical Political Economy approach as disempowering because it frequently stresses the potential of political movements and their media use for bringing about transformation. Jenkins is a utopian thinker in respect to the circumstance that he sees resistance of consumers necessarily and almost always at work in popular culture and ignores aspects of exploitation and ideology, but due to this approach he is certainly not a critical utopian, but only a utopian. Critical Theory and Critical Political Economy do not, as claimed by Jenkins (1992, 291), read "the audiences from the structures of the text or in terms of the forms of consumption generated by the institutions of production and marketing", they are rather in contrast to Jenkins and other Cultural Studies scholars concerned about the phenomena of exploitation (of workers and audiences) and class inequality that are implicated by the commodity form of culture. They see deep inequalities at the heart of the commodity form and therefore question the logic of commodification and capital accumulation.

Media and Communication Studies should forget about the vulgar and reductionistic notion of participation (simply meaning that users create, curate, circulate or critique content) and focus on rediscovering the political notion of participation by engaging with participatory democracy theory. There was a time when Cultural Studies scholars were claiming about others that they are economic reductionists. Today, it has become overtly clear – and Jenkins' work is the best expression of this circumstance – that cultural reductionism has gone too far, that the cultural turn away from Critical Political Economy was an error and that Media and Communication Studies needs to rediscover concepts like class and participatory democracy.

We can summarize the main results of this chapter as follows:

- Henry Jenkins reduces the notion of participation to a cultural dimension, ignoring the broad notion of participatory democracy and its implications for the Internet. An Internet that is dominated by corporations that accumulate capital by exploiting and commodifying users can never, in the theory of participatory democracy, be participatory and the cultural expressions of it cannot be expressions of participation. Jenkins especially neglects ownership as an aspect of participation and does not give attention to aspects of class and capitalism.

- Jenkins mistakenly assumes an automatic connection of fandom in popular culture and political protest. He also mistakes politics with popular culture and sees politics taking place largely as micro politics within popular culture (as the struggle of fans for making the culture industry respect their ideas in the design of plots).
- Jenkins' account of participatory culture and social media as producers of participatory culture is a form of cultural reductionism and determinism that neglects structural constraints of human behaviour and the dialectic of structure and agency.
- In his arguments, Jenkins misses the central economic relevance of money in the economy and argues that the exploitation of users' digital labour is not really a problem if they have social benefits from platform usage.

RECOMMENDED READINGS AND EXERCISES

Engaging with different texts is a good approach for understanding the topic of participatory culture. The suggested readings include works on participatory culture by Henry Jenkins and political theorists such as Carole Pateman and Crawford Macpherson, who engage with the notion of participatory democracy. Contrasting these texts allows us to work out different understandings of the notion of participation.

Jenkins, Henry. 2008. *Convergence culture*. New York: New York University Press. Introduction: Workshop at the altar of convergence: A new paradigm for understanding media change. Chapter 4: Quentin Tarantino's Star Wars? Grassroots creativity meets the media industry. Chapter 5: Why Heather can write: Media literacy and the Harry Potter wars. Conclusion: Democratizing television? The politics of participation.

Green, Joshua and Henry Jenkins. 2009. The moral economy of web 2.0: Audience research and convergence culture. In *Media industries: History, theory, and method*, ed. Jennifer Holt and Alisa Perren, 213–225. Malden, MA: Wiley-Blackwell.

Jenkins, Henry. 2009. What happened before YouTube. In *YouTube*, ed. Jean Burgess and Joshua Green, 109–125. Cambridge: Polity Press.

These readings give an introduction to Henry Jenkins' notion of participatory culture. Discuss in groups:

- First, make a list of the characteristics of Henry Jenkins' concept of participatory culture. Make the list systematic by introducing dimensions of participatory culture.

- Think about how to define the concept of culture and which aspects and dimensions it has. Go back to your list of characteristics of participatory culture and try to make it theoretically systematic by mapping the dimensions of culture you identified and the characteristics of participatory culture. Try to avoid overlapping categories/dimensions.

- Together, look at those passages and articles/chapters that mention social media/web 2.0 platforms. Use your typology/list of characteristics of participatory culture to identify what Jenkins sees as characteristics of participatory web culture.

Pateman, Carole. 1970. *Participation and democratic theory*. Cambridge: Cambridge University Press. Chapter IV: "Participation" and "democracy" in industry. Chapter VI: Conclusion.

Macpherson, Crawford Brough. 1973. *Democratic theory*. Oxford: Oxford University Press. Chapter I: The maximization of democracy. Chapter II: Democratic theory: Ontology and technology. Chapter III: Problems of a non-market theory of democracy.

Held, David. 2006. *Models of democracy* (3rd edition), 209–216. Cambridge: Polity Press.

Pateman, Carole. 2012. Participatory democracy revisited. *Perspectives on Politics* 10 (1): 7–19.

Crawford Brough Macpherson and Carole Pateman are two of the most important political thinkers who have written on the concept of participatory democracy. Their books *Democratic Theory* and *Participation and Democratic Theory* are classical works in political theory. David Held's reading is a supplementary text for better understanding the term "participatory democracy".

- Make a list of characteristics of the concept of participatory democracy, as introduced by Pateman and Macpherson. Try to make the list systematic by identifying dimensions of democracy, and avoid overlapping dimensions.

- Discuss where examples of participatory democracy can be found and in which respect these examples have the characteristics of participatory democracy that you identified. Are there examples for participatory democracy on the Internet?

- Try to think about what the Internet and social media would look like in a participatory democracy. What changes to the society, the current Internet and current social media are needed in order to establish a participatory democracy and a participatory Internet/web? Compare such a concept of a participatory Internet to Henry Jenkins' concept of participatory culture.

- Conduct a search for reviews of Henry Jenkins' books in databases such as Social Sciences Citation Index, Communication and Mass Media Complete, Scopus, Sociological Abstracts, Google Scholar, etc. Distribute all the reviews you found among those participating in the exercise. After reading the reviews, construct a systematic and ordered list of points of criticism of his works. Discuss these points in class.

- Search in Jenkins' books and articles to see if he refers to the authors who criticized him and, if so, how he responds to their criticism. If you find such responses, discuss them in class.

Social Media and Communication Power

Key questions

- What is power? What is counter-power?
- How does power relate to communication?
- How has social media influenced our conception of communication power?
- What has been the role of social media-communication power in the Arab spring and the Occupy movement?

Key concepts

Power
Counter-power

Manuel Castells' concept of mass
self-communication
Communication power

Overview

Power is a key concept in political theory, but it has been defined in different ways. Max Weber says that it is the "chance of a man or a number of men to realize their own will in a social action even against the resistance of others who are participating in the action" (Weber 1978, 926). For Jürgen Habermas, power has to do with the realization of collective goals, means of coercion, symbols of power and status, decision-making authorities, disadvantages, power of definition, counter-power, organization, and legitimation (Habermas 1984, 1987). Niklas Luhmann (2000, 39) sees power as the achievement of inducing someone to act in a certain way when he wouldn't act that way normally and only does so due to the threat of possible sanctions. For these authors, power has to do with the capacity of one group to use means of coercion against others so that it asserts its will and interests.

Michel Foucault argued that such a definition of power ignores the fact that power is not only located in powerful bodies such as the state or companies: "We must cease once and for all to describe the effects of power in negative terms: it 'excludes,' it 'represses,' it 'censors,' it 'abstracts,' it 'masks,' it 'conceals.' In fact, power produces, it produces reality, it produces domains of objects and rituals of truth. The individual and the knowledge that may be gained of him belong to this production" (Foucault 1977, 250). He said that "there are no relations of power without resistance" (Foucault 1980, 142).

Anthony Giddens defines power as "'transformative capacity', the capability to intervene in a given set of events so as in some way to alter them" (Giddens 1985, 7), as the "capability to effectively decide about courses of events, even where others might contest such decisions" (ibid.: 9). So, for Giddens, as opposed to Weber, Habermas and Luhmann, power is a general concept – the capacity of humans to act and to thereby transform society.

No matter which of these definitions one follows, it is clear that power has to do with the question of who can influence what society looks like and who controls the means that allow such influence. In the information society, communication and communication technologies have become ubiquitous in everyday life and society. The question is therefore how power has been transformed in an information society and what communication power is.

Manuel Castells is one of the most cited authors in the social sciences and media/communication studies. This chapter focuses on Castells' approach and his concept of communication power in the context of social media. Manuel Castells worked for a long time in urban sociology and with the rise of the World Wide Web became a leading Internet researcher. He is Professor of Sociology at the Open University of Catalonia in Barcelona, where he also directs the Internet Interdisciplinary Institute (IN3). He is also Professor of Communication Technology and Society at the University of Southern California's Annenberg School of Communication.

In his approach, Manuel Castells stresses the role of the Internet and social media in what he terms the network society. He has in this context worked out the concepts of communication power and mass self-communication. For Manuel Castells, social media communication is mass self-communication. He argues that the emergence of this type of communication has resulted in profound shifts in the power structures of society. In this chapter, I present, discuss and critically analyze the theoretical foundations of Castells' approach.

We will discuss the role of social theory in Castells' approach (in section 4.1), the concept of communication power (4.2), communication power on social media (4.3) and communication power in the Arab Spring and the Occupy movement (4.4).

4.1. Social Theory in the Information Age

What is Social Theory?

My experience is that if one asks Internet and social media researchers what social theories they use, some of them will answer: Manuel Castells' theory. But what is social theory? Social theory is the systematic development and connection of "concepts with which to grasp social life, with identifying patterns in social relations and social action, with producing explanations for both specific features of life in society and changes in overall forms of society" (Calhoun et al. 2007, 3). It is an endeavour to understand events, institutions and trends in society, the connections between events, institutions and trends and the connection of personal life to society (Calhoun et al. 2007, 4). It is also concerned with "the nature of human action", interaction and institutions (Giddens 1984, xvii), the human being, human doing and the reproduction and transformation of society (xx). Philosophical debates and philosophical reasoning are important tools for social theory (Giddens 1984, xvii).

Sociology and social theory have their roots in philosophy (Adorno 2000, 176, 2002, 8, 54). Tasks of (critical) social theory include to point out and make people aware of unrealized potentials of society, to point out possibilities of action in contemporary society, to ask new and different questions about the present order of society (Calhoun 1995, 7f), to strengthen the imagination of people about what a better society could look like, to point out and make people aware of contemporary problems of society that limit the realization of society's possibilities, to provide narratives about which society we live in and the main characteristics of this society so that discussions about the character and problems of contemporary society are enabled, and to analyze the relation between appearance (that which is/exists) and essence (that which should be) (Adorno 2002, 25).

Given the role of social philosophy in social theory and its role of providing guidance about questions that focus on which society we live in, it is important that each theory justifies why a certain concept is employed in a certain way and not in another way. This requires engagement with other theories and arguments relating to these theories. Castells only provides his own definitions without providing reasons why these definitions are superior to others.

Castells: Social Theorist of the Internet in the Information Society?

Castells' approach deals with life and communication in what he calls the "network society". He is author of the trilogy, *The Information Age* (Castells 2000, 2004, 2010b), which was followed up by *Communication Power* (Castells 2009). Castells says that the Information Age "does not present a formal, systematic theory of society, it proposes new concepts and a new theoretical perspective to understand the trends that characterize the structure and dynamics of our societies in the world of the twenty-first century" (Castells 2010b, xix). So Castells does see his approach as a social theory. A social theory of the Internet in society needs to start by providing an understanding of questions like: What is society? How is a society made up? How does social transformation work in society? What is the role of structures and agency in society? What is the relationship of the human individual and society? It can then move on to applying these questions first to modern society and then to contemporary society in order to have theoretical knowledge at hand that allows understanding, conceptualizing, and criticizing the role of the Internet in contemporary society (see Fuchs 2008a). Castells mainly presents a history of the Internet and its context, whereas his work lacks a theory of society and a theory of modern society. He provides a brief, 13-page conceptual framework in the prologue of *The Information Age* (Castells 2010b, 5–18) that describes the relationship of technology and society as consisting of structures of production (modes of production, modes of development), experience and power. It is, however, unclear if Castells here talks about society in general or specific societies because he talks about class relationships as part of production (Castells 2010b, 15f). Class is certainly an aspect of modern society, but, as Marx knew when talking about classless societies, is not necessarily present in all societies.

The task of *Communication Power* is to "advance the construction of a grounded theory of power in the network society" (Castells 2009, 5). Castells does not want to place himself in theoretical debates (he bases his approach on "a selective reading of power theories" (Castells 2009, 6)), does not want to write books about books (Castells 2009, 6, 2010b, 25), and thinks that social theory books are contributing to the deforestation of the planet (Castells 2009, 6), which is just another way of saying that they are unimportant and not worth the paper they are printed on.

Lacking grounding in social theory, Castells cannot explain why he uses a certain definition of power, globalization, social movements, etc., and why he thinks we live in a network society rather than a post-industrial society, capitalist society, new capitalist Empire/imperialism, finance capitalism, knowledge society, etc. It is simplistic to give single definitions and not to engage with the history of concepts. An approach is only adequately grounded if it can logically justify why it uses concepts in a certain way and not in another. Understanding contemporary society requires engaging with social philosophy and the history of conceptualizing society in order to be meaningful. Castells' aversion to social theory discourses makes him fall short of providing a grounded and justified approach. His approach is neither a social theory nor adequately theoretically grounded, but rather an arbitrary and unsystematic form of conceptualizing and a collection of observations.

4.2. Communication Power in the Network Society

Castells on Power: An Essential Feature of All Societies?

Castells (2009, 43–47, 418–420) introduces four kinds of power in the network society: networking power, network power, networked power, network-making power. Inspired by Max Weber, he defines power as "the relational capacity that enables a social actor to influence asymmetrically the decisions of other social actor(s) in ways that favor the empowered actor's will, interests, and values" (Castells 2009, 10). Power is associated with coercion, domination, violence or potential violence, and asymmetry. He refers to the power concepts of Foucault, Weber and Habermas, and argues that he builds on Giddens' structuration theory. However, Giddens conceives power in a completely different way, a way that is neither mentioned nor discussed by Castells. For Giddens, power is "'transformative capacity', the capability to intervene in a given set of events so as in some way to alter them" (Giddens 1985, 7), the "capability to effectively decide about courses of events, even where others might contest such decisions" (Giddens 1985, 9). Power is, for Giddens, characteristic of all social relationships; it "is routinely involved in the instantiation of social practices" and is "operating in and through human action" (Giddens 1981, 49f).

In Giddens' structuration theory, power is not necessarily coercive, violent and asymmetrically distributed. Therefore, it becomes possible to conceive and analyze situations and social systems in which power is more symmetrically distributed, for example situations and systems of participatory democracy. Power understood as transformative capacity seems indeed to be a fundamental aspect of all societies. This also means that there is a huge difference between Castells' approach and Giddens' structuration theory, which is not problematic as such, but should also be explicated, especially because Castells (2009, 14) says that he builds on Giddens' structuration theory, which, in my opinion, he does not. The problem with Castells' notion of power is that he sees coercive, violent, dominative power relationships as "the foundational relations of society throughout history, geography, and cultures" (Castells 2009, 9). Such power is for him "the most fundamental process in society" (Castells 2009, 10). Furthermore, Castells (2009, 13) dismisses the "naïve image of a reconciled human community, a normative utopia that is belied by historical observation".

Is it really likely that all history of humankind and all social situations and systems in which we live are always and necessarily shaped by power struggles, coercion, violence and domination? Relationships of love, intimacy and affection are in modern society unfortunately often characterized by violence and coercion and are therefore frequently (in Castells' terms) power relationships. But isn't love a prototypical phenomenon, where many people experience feelings and actions that negate violence, domination and coercion? Isn't the phenomenon of altruism in love and civil society the practical falsification of the claim that coercive power is the most fundamental process in society? My claim is that not coercive power, but co-operation is the most fundamental process in society (Fuchs 2008a, 31–34, 40–58), and that it is indeed possible to create social systems without coercive power (in Castells' terms) and with a symmetric distribution of power (in Giddens' terminology). If one is conceiving of power as violent coercion, then one naturalizes and fetishizes coercion and violent struggles as necessary and therefore not historical qualities of society. The problematic ideological-theoretical implication is that in the final instance war must exist in all societies and a state of peace is dismissed and considered as being categorically impossible. Castells surely does not share this implication, as his analysis of communication power in the Iraq war shows (Castells 2009).

Power and Technocratic Language

One problem regarding Castells' (2009) book is that he tends to use rather technocratic language for describing networks and communication power – social networks, technological networks and techno-social networks are all described with the same categories and metaphors that originate in computer science and computer technology: program, meta-programmers, switches, switchers, configuration, inter-operability, protocols, network standards, network components, kernel, program code, etc. I have no doubt that Manuel Castells does not intend to conflate the difference between social and technological networks. He has argued in the past, for example, that social networks are a "networking form of social organization" and that information technology is the "material basis" for the "pervasive expansion" of social networks (Castells 2010b, 500).

But even if the terminology that Manuel Castells now tends to employ is only understood in a metaphorical sense, it is a problem that he describes society and social systems in technological and computational terms so that the *differentia specifica* of society in comparison to computers and computer networks – that society is based on humans, reflexive and self-conscious beings that have cultural norms, anticipative thinking, and a certain freedom of action that computers do not have – gets lost. It is no surprise that, based on the frequent employment of such metaphors, Castells (2009, 45) considers Bruno Latour's actor network theory as brilliant. It is important that one distinguishes the qualities of social networks from the qualities of technological networks and identifies the emergent qualities of techno-social networks such as the Internet (Fuchs 2008a, 121–147).

Castells acknowledges that there is a "parallel with software language" (Castells 2009, 48), in his terminology, but he does not give reasons why he uses these parallels and why he thinks such parallels are useful. Obviously society is shaped by computers, but it is not a computer itself, so there is, in my opinion, simply no need for such a terminological conflationism. Computer metaphors of society can, just like biological metaphors of society, become dangerous under certain circumstances so, in my opinion, it is best not to start to categorically conflate the qualitative difference between society and technology. Technology is part of society and society creates, produces and reproduces technology. Society is more than just technology and has emergent qualities that stem from the synergetical interactions of human beings. Technology is one of many results of the productive societal interactions of human beings. It therefore has qualities that are, on the one hand, specifically societal, but on the other hand, different from the qualities of other products of society. It is a common aspect of social and technological networks that there are nodes and interactions in all networks. One should not forget the important task of differentiating between the various emergent qualities that technological networks and social networks have – emergent qualities that interact when these two kinds of networks are combined in the form of techno-social networks such as the Internet so that meta-emergent techno-social qualities appear.

The contradictions and fetishisms that one can partly find in Castells' work stem from a lack of engagement with social theory and show the importance of social theory as a theory of the Internet in contemporary society.

4.3. Communication Power, Social Media and Mass Self-communication

Mass Self-communication

Castells argues that mass self-communication is a novel quality of communication in contemporary society:

> It is mass communication because it can potentially reach a global audience, as in the posting of a video on YouTube, a blog with RSS links to a number of web sources, or a message to a massive e-mail list. At the same time, it is self-communication because the production of the message is self-generated, the definition of the potential receiver(s) is self-directed, and the retrieval of specific messages or content from the World Wide Web and electronic networks is self-selected. The three forms of communication (interpersonal, mass communication, and mass self-communication) coexist, interact, and complement each other rather than substituting for one another. What is historically novel, with considerable consequences for social organization and cultural change, is the articulation of all forms of communication into a composite, interactive, digital hypertext that includes, mixes, and recombines in their diversity the whole range of cultural expressions conveyed by human interaction. (Castells 2009, 55; see also 70)

Castells theorizes that mass self-communication is based on Umberto Eco's semiotic model of communication as the emergence of "the creative audience" (Castells 2009, 127–135) that engages in the "interactive production of meaning" (132) and is based on the emergence of the figure of the "sender/addressee" (130).

Autonomy

Castells argues that the contemporary Internet is shaped by a conflict between the global multimedia business networks that try to commodify the Internet and the "creative audience" that tries to establish a degree of citizen control of the Internet and to assert the right of communicative freedom without corporate control (Castells 2009, 80, 97, 136). Castells (2009) first introduces the notion of autonomy in mass self-communication on page 129 of *Communication Power*, but does not define it, which leaves the reader wondering what Castells wants to tell her/him by using this normatively and politically connoted term (see also Castells 2009, 302). The meaning of the concept of autonomy is not self-explanatory. Is it autonomy in the sense of Kant, understood as the autonomy of the will as the supreme principle of morality (Kant 2002, 58), the "quality of the will of being a law to itself" (Kant 2002, 63)? Or does autonomy mean the "true individualism" that Hayek (1948) had in mind, in which capitalism is conceived as spontaneous order that should be left to itself and should not be shaped by political rules (Hayek 1988)? Does it refer to freedom of speech, taste and assembly – "the liberty of thought and discussion" – in line with the harm principle, as postulated by John Stuart Mill (2002)? Or is autonomy the existence of functionally differentiated self-referential subsystems of society (Luhmann 1998)? Or does it, in a less individualistic sense, refer to the combination of individual autonomy, understood as subjectivity – that is "reflective and deliberative" and "frees the radical imagination" from "the enslavement of repetition" (Castoriadis 1991, 164) – and social autonomy, "the equal participation of all in power" (Castoriadis 1991, 136; see also Castoriadis 1998)? Does Castells' notion of autonomy confirm one of the two poles of the theoretically unreconciled relationship of private autonomy and public autonomy that Habermas (1996, 84) has critically examined, or does it refer to the dialectic of autonomy that Habermas has in mind when he speaks of a "coorignality of private and public autonomy" (Habermas 1996, 104) achieved in a "system of rights in which private and public autonomy are internally related" (Habermas 1996, 280) and "reciprocally presuppose each other" (Habermas 1996, 417)? Or does autonomy mean the "status of an organized people in an enclosed territorial unit" (Schmitt 1996, 19; for a critique of this approach see Habermas 1989a)? Or is autonomy a postmodern project of plural democracy with a multiplicity of subject positions (Laclau and Mouffe 1985)?

In short, there are all kinds of meanings of concepts such as autonomy, power, information, networks, etc. It is one of the tasks of social theory to clarify which meanings of concepts are feasible and suitable for the situation of contemporary society. The problems of Castells' lack of engagement with social theory become apparent in his unreflected use of terms.

Power and Counter-power on the Internet and Social Media

Castells says that mass self-communication (2009, 413) allows subjects to "watch the powerful", but those in power "have made it their priority to harness the potential of mass self-communication in the service of their specific interests" (414). Therefore, they engage in enclosing the communication commons (414). Castells speaks of a dialectical process in relation to mass self-communication. On the one hand, "web 2.0" business strategies result in "the commodification of freedom", the "enclosing of the commons of free communication and selling people access to global communication networks in exchange for surrendering their privacy and becoming advertising targets" (421). On the other hand, "once in cyberspace, people may have all kinds of ideas, including challenging corporate power, dismantling government authority, and changing the cultural foundations of our aging/aching civilization" (420). The typical web 2.0 business strategy is not, however, "selling people access", but that providers give users free access and sell them as a prosumer commodity to third parties in order to generate profit. This relationship is highly unequal. The actual power of corporations in web 2.0 "is much larger than the actual political counter-power that is exercised by the produsers. Castells acknowledges this in some instances, for example when he speaks of "unequal competition" (Castells 2009, 422), but he also contradicts this realism in some instances by a certain web 2.0 optimism, for example when he says that "the more corporations invest in expanding communication networks (benefiting from a hefty return), the more people build their own networks of mass self-communication, thus empowering themselves" (Castells 2009, 421).

There is an asymmetry between the power of corporations and other powerful groups and the actual counter-power of citizens. The dialectic of power is only a potential, but not an automatic actual or necessary dialectic. Political counter-power on the Internet faces a massive asymmetry that is due to the fact that the ruling powers control more resources, such as money, decision-making power, capacities for attention generation, etc. Power struggles are struggles of the less powerful against the powerful. There is no guarantee that they can emerge, that they can mobilize significant resources so that they do not remain precarious, or that they will be successful. There are examples of relatively successful counter-power struggles that have made use of the Internet, as Castells (2009) shows, but it is only a potential, not an automatism that citizens "overcome the powerlessness of their solitary despair by networking their desire. They fight the powers that be by identifying the networks that are" (Castells 2009, 431). The problem is that there are also forces of power in contemporary society, such as ideology and coercion, that might forestall such fights, that keep people occupied with struggling for survival so that they have no time, energy or thoughts for counter-power struggles. Communication counter-power should not be overestimated, but only assessed as potential.

Media Power as Cultural Power: John B. Thompson

John B. Thompson (1995) distinguishes four forms of power (see Table 4.1). The problem of Thompson's approach is that the media's power is reduced to the symbolic dimension and that the relationship of violence and power is unclear. Symbolic power is an important dimension of the media: the media not only have form, but also communicate content to the public, which allows attempts to influence the minds of the members of the public. But ideology is not the only aspect of the media. Rather, the media are a terrain where different forms of power and power struggles manifest themselves: the media have specific structures of private or public ownership that tend to be concentrated. There are attempts to politically control and influence the media and the media often have political roles in elections, social movement struggles, etc. Violence is a frequent topic in media content. The media are not just a realm of symbolic power, but also material and symbolic spaces where structures and contradictions of economic, political,

Table 4.1   John B. Thompson's four forms of power

Type of power	Definition	Resources	Institutions
Economic power	"Economic power stems from human productive activity, that is, activity concerned with the provision of the means of subsistence through the extraction of raw materials and their transformation into goods which can be consumed or exchanged in a market." (14)	Material and financial resources	Economic institutions
Political power	Political power "stems from the activity of coordinating individuals and regulating the patterns of their interaction" (14)	Authority	Political institutions (e.g. states)
Coercive power	"Coercive power involves the use, or threatened use, of physical force to subdue or conquer an opponent." (15)	Physical and armed force	Coercive institutions (military, police, carceral institutions, etc.)
Symbolic power	Symbolic power is the "capacity to intervene in the course of events, to influence the actions of others and indeed to create events, by means of the production and transmission of symbolic forms". (17)	Means of information and communication	Cultural institutions (church, schools, universities, media, etc.)

Based on Thompson 1995, 12–18.

coercive and symbolic power manifest themselves. Nick Couldry (2002, 4) defines media power as "the concentration in media institutions of the symbolic power of 'constructing reality'". Like Thompson's definition of power, the one given by Couldry also focuses on the symbolic and cultural dimensions of the media.

Media Power as Multidimensional Form of Economic, Political and Cultural Power

It is unclear why Thompson defines violence as a separate form of power. He reduces violence to direct physical violence, exerted, for example, if one kills or beats somebody. Johan Galtung (1990, 292) defines violence, in contrast, as "avoidable insults to basic human needs, and, more generally to life, lowering the real level of needs satisfaction below what is potentially possible". According to Galtung (1990), violence can be divided into three principal forms: direct violence (through physical intervention; an event), structural violence (through state or organizational mandate; a process), and cultural violence (dehumanizing or otherwise exclusionary representations; an invariance). This means that in exerting violence one can physically coerce somebody (physical violence), exclude him/her from access to vital resources (structural violence), or manipulate his/her mind or ruin his/her reputation (ideological violence). Violence exists not only if it is actually exerted, but also if it is only a threat: "Threats of violence are also violence" (Galtung 1990, 292). The three forms of violence are forms of how people or groups try to accumulate different forms of power.

Different forms of violence can be exerted in order to accumulate different forms of power. In modern society, economic, political and cultural power can be accumulated and tend to be asymmetrically distributed. Table 4.2 gives an overview of these three forms of power. Karl Marx (1867) stresses that the logic of accumulation (getting more and more of something) is vital for modern society. It has its origins in the capitalist economy. But it also shapes the logic of modern politics and culture that are focused on the accumulation of political and cultural power. Capitalism is therefore not just an economic system, but also a form of society. Physical, structural and ideological violence can be used in any of the three dimensions/fields of modern society for trying to accumulate power at the expense of others. Many structures of modern society are based on specific forms of violence that help accumulating power. For example, a corporation makes use of the structural violence of the market and private property in order to accumulate capital. Or the state uses the monopoly of physical violence and the institutional power of government institutions in order to make collective decisions.

The media and social media in contemporary society are shaped by structures of economic, political and cultural power:

- Social media have specific ownership structures. If social media's economic power is asymmetrically distributed, then a private class owns social media. If it is more symmetrically distributed, then a collective of users or all people own social media.

- Social media have specific decision-making structures. If social media's political power is asymmetrically distributed, then a specific group controls decision-making. If it is more symmetrically distributed, then all users or all people in society can influence decision-making.

Table 4.2 Three forms of power

Dimension of society	Definition of power	Structures of power in modern society
Economy	Control of use-values and resources that are produced, distributed and consumed.	Control of money and capital.
Politics	Influence on collective decisions that determine aspects of the lives of humans in certain communities and social systems.	Control of governments, bureaucratic state institutions, parliament, military, police, parties, lobby groups, civil society groups, etc.
Culture	Definition of moral values and meaning that shape what is considered as important, reputable and worthy in society.	Control of structures that define meaning and moral values in society (e.g. universities, religious groups, intellectual circles, opinion-making groups, etc.).

- Social media have specific mechanisms for the generation of reputation and popularity. If social media's cultural power is asymmetrically distributed, then the reputation and visibility of certain actors are in contrast to the attention and visibility given to others. Social media can also act as conveyors of ideologies that misrepresent reality. If highly visible actors communicate such ideologies, then it is likely that they will have some effect. If cultural power is more symmetrically distributed, then all users have a significant degree of visibility and attention.

James Curran (2002, chapter 5) has identified 11 dimensions of media power and seven dimensions of media counter-power. I have classified these dimensions according to the three dimensions of media power (see Table 4.3): economic media power, political media power and cultural media power. Curran stresses that media power is not just symbolic, but multidimensional. The distinction of three realms of society (economy, politics, culture) allows us to classify forms of media power (Table 4.3). Curran emphasizes the contradictory character of contemporary media: there are "eleven main factors that encourage the media to support dominant power interests" (Curran 2002, 148), but "the media are also subject to countervailing pressures which can pull potentially in the other direction" (Curran 2002, 151).

The Asymmetric Dialectic of Media Power

The systematic typology of media power that is based on Curran's approach shows that modern media can best be viewed dialectically: they are subject to elite control, but have potentials for acting as, and being influenced by, counter-powers that question elite control. This form of struggle is a potential, which means that it does not automatically arise. The power of dominant and alternative media tends to be distributed unequally (see Fuchs 2010a; Sandoval and Fuchs 2010): alternative media are often facing resource inequalities and have to exist based on precarious labour and resource precariousness.

Social media are spaces where media power and counter-power are played out. Dominant platforms, such as Facebook, Google/YouTube and Twitter, are privately owned and there are economic, political and ideological forms of media power at play; private ownership, concentration, advertising, the logic of consumption and entertainment, the high visibility of and attention given to elites and celebrities shape and filter communication on dominant social media platforms. At the same time, dominant structures are questioned by phenomena such as file-sharing, commons-based social media that are non-profit and non-commercial (e.g. Wikipedia, Diaspora*), social movements' use of social media for political purposes, the development of alternative social media, protests against the dominance of platforms like Google, protests and legal disputes over privacy violations, etc. Contemporary social media is a field of power struggles in which dominant actors command a large share of economic, political and ideological media power that can be challenged by alternative actors that have less resources, visibility and attention, but try to make best use of the unequal share

Table 4.3 Power and counter-power in the media

Dimension of media power	Forms of media power	Forms of media counter-power
Economic media power	High entry and operation costs; media concentration; private media ownership; influence of companies on the media via advertising	Public media, alternative grassroots media, public funding for alternative media
	Market pressure to produce homogeneous (often uncritical) content with wide appeal; content that appeals to wealthy consumers	Staff power (e.g. critical journalism, investigative reporting)
	The unequal distribution of economic resources (money) allows economic elites more influence on and control of the media	Consumer power (e.g. by support of alternative media in the form of donations)
Political media power	State censorship of the media	Media regulation that secures quality, fair reporting, diversity, freedom of expression, assembly and opinion
	Public relations of large (political and economic) organizations results in bureaucratic lobbying apparatus that aims to influence the media	Alternative news sources
	The unequal distribution of political resources (influence, decision power, political relations) allows economic elites more influence on and control of the media	State redistribution of resources from the more powerful to the less powerful
Cultural media power	Focus on content covering prestige institutions, celebrities and others who have high reputation; dominant ideologies influence dominant media to a certain degree; the unequal distribution of cultural resources (reputation, prestige) allows economic elites more influence on and control of the media	Creation of counter-organizations that develop counter-discourses and operate their own media

Based on Curran 2002, chapter 5.

of media power they are confronted with in order to fight against the dominant powers.

The Stratified Online Sphere

Castells (2009, 204) argues that in mass self-communication "traditional forms of access control are not applicable. Anyone can upload a video to the Internet, write a blog, start a chat forum, or create a gigantic e-mail list. Access in this case is the rule; blocking Internet access is the exception". Visibility and the attention economy form a central filter of the Internet that benefits powerful actors. Although everyone can produce and diffuse information easily in principle with the help of the Internet because it is a global, decentralized, many-to-many and one-to-many communication system, not all information is visible to the same degree or gets the same attention. The problem in the cyberspace flood of information is how users are drawn to specific information that flows in the huge informational online ocean.

Indymedia, a popular alternative online news platform, is only ranked number 12 278 in the list of the most accessed websites, whereas BBC Online is ranked number 54, CNN Online number 80, the New York Times Online number 120, Spiegel Online number 222, Bildzeitung Online number 250, or Fox News Online number 154 (data source: alexa.com, top 1 000 000 000 sites, accessed on February 28, 2013). This shows that there is a stratified online attention economy in which the trademarks of powerful media actors work as powerful symbols that help the online portals of these organizations to accumulate attention. This is not to deny the heavy use of "mass self-communication" platforms such as Blogger, Wordpress or Facebook, but political information generation and communication on such sites is much more fragmented, which is the reason why Jürgen Habermas speaks in relation to the Internet of a danger of the "fragmentation of large but politically focused mass audience into a huge number of isolated issue publics" (Habermas 2006, 423).

Web 2.0 and 3.0

Castells employs the terms "web 2.0 and 3.0" (see, for example, Castells 2009, 34, 56, 65, 97, 107, 113, 421, 429), which he defines as "the cluster of technologies, devices, and applications that support the proliferation of social spaces on the Internet" (Castells 2009, 65). We should also ask critical questions about "web 2.0":

- To what extent are the claims about the "new web" ideological and serve marketing purposes?
- What is novel about "web 2.0" and how can this novelty be empirically validated?
- What does it mean exactly to say that the web has become more social?
- Which notions of the social are employed when people speak of "web 2.0"?
- Which notion of sociality underlies "web 1.0" and how does this idea differ from the idea of sociality that underlies the concepts of web 2.0 and 3.0?
- What is the difference between web 1.0, 2.0 and 3.0?

In short, the talk about "web 2.0", "social media" and "social software" compels us to answer some basic questions: What is social about the Internet? What are the different forms of sociality that we find on the Internet? To answer these questions, we need to enter conceptual sociological discussions, and therefore social theory is important for understanding the contemporary Internet. Users do have the counter-power capacities to use web 2.0 against the intentions of the corporate operators in progressive ways and political struggles, but the corporate platform owners possess the power to switch users off the networks or to switch off entire networks. Furthermore, they also have an interest in and power to permanently control the online behaviour and personal data of users in order to accumulate capital with the help of targeted advertising. Economic surveillance is at the heart of capital accumulation in web 2.0. The power relationship between the corporate media and the creative users that Castells describes is an asymmetrical one that privileges the former. There are different media that can be used for trying to mobilize others to attend demonstrations, visit Occupy camps, etc.: face-to-face communication, phone communication (voice, SMS) and various commercial and non-commercial forms of online communication. There are positive correlations between the frequency of usage of many of these types of mobilization communication, which shows that activists tend to not limit their mobilization communication to one medium, but use multiple media.

4.4. Communication Power in the Arab Spring and the Occupy Movement

2011: The Year of the Rebirth of History and Dangerous Dreaming

The year 2011 will be remembered in history. It was a year of persistent global crisis and, in this respect, was not different from the preceding years 2008, 2009 and 2010. What made 2011 stand out is that it was a year of revolutions, major protests, riots and the emergence of various social movements. Alain Badiou (2012) argues, in this context, that 2011 was the year of the rebirth of history, a year in which people tried to change history by their protests. Slavoj Žižek (2012b) adds to Badiou's analysis that 2011 was the year of dreaming dangerously – the year in which people dared to try to make dreams of a different world a reality. History proved liberalism wrong. The new rebellious and revolutionary movements showed that "the world has long since dreamed of something of which it needs only to become conscious for it to possess it in reality" (Marx 1843b). 2011 was a year where dreams of a different world were put into political practice. Naturally, such developments are reflected in the intellectual realm by the publication of books that reflect on the causes, implications and consequences of the emergence of social movements. Manuel Castells' *Networks of Outrage and Hope: Social Movements in the Internet Age* (2012) is one of these books.

The Arab Spring and Occupy

Castells' (2012) *Networks of Outrage and Hope* analyzes the role of social media and communication power in the Tunisian and Egyptian revolutions as well as in protests in Iceland, the Spanish 15-M movement and the Occupy Wall Street movement (for a detailed discussion and criticism, see Fuchs 2012b). He argues that "the Arab uprisings were spontaneous processes of mobilization that emerged from calls from the Internet and wireless communication networks" (Castells 2012, 106). The Occupy movement "was born on the Internet, diffused by the Internet, and maintained its presence on the Internet" (168).

Castells puts a very strong emphasis on the mobilization capacities of the Internet. His argument implies that in the studied cases, Internet communication created street protests, which means that without the Internet there would have been no street protests. In the concluding chapter, Castells generalizes for all analyzed movements:

> The networked social movements of our time are largely based on the Internet, a necessary though not sufficient component of their collective action. The digital social networks based on the Internet and on wireless platforms are decisive tools for mobilizing, for organizing, for deliberating, for coordinating and for deciding. (Castells 2012, 229)

Twitter and Facebook Revolutions?

Formulations, such as the ones that the Internet resulted in the emergence of movements, that movements were born on the Internet, that protested were conveyed by the Internet, or that movements are based on the Internet, convey a logic that is based on overt technological determinism: technology is conceived as an actor that results in certain phenomena that have societal characteristics. Castells fails to see that it is not the Internet that creates sociality, but human actors who are embedded in antagonistic economic, political and ideological structures of society. The Internet is a techno-social system consisting of social networks that make use of a global network of computer networks. It is embedded in the antagonisms of contemporary society and therefore has no in-built effects or determinations. Collective social action that makes use of the Internet can have relatively few effects or dampen or intensify existing trends. The actual implications depend on contexts, power relations, resources, mobilization capacities, strategies and tactics as well as the complex and undetermined outcomes of struggles. Castells' model is simplistic: social media results in revolutions and rebellions. He shares the widespread ideological talk about "Twitter revolutions" and "Facebook rebellions" that, as already discussed, first became popular when the conservative blogger, Andrew Sullivan (2009), claimed that the "revolution will be twittered" in the context of the 2009 Iran protests.

Society's reality is more complex than Castells' behaviouristic model of protest (Internet as the stimulus, critical consciousness and political action as the response) suggests. The media – social media, the Internet and all other media – are contradictory because we live in a contradictory society. As a consequence, their effects are actually contradictory. They can dampen/forestall or amplify/advance protest or have not much effect at all. Also, different media (e.g. alternative media and commercial media) stand in a contradictory relation and power struggle with each other. The media are not the only factors that influence the conditions of protest – they stand in contradictory relations with politics and ideology/culture that also influence the conditions of protest.

Castells Falsified: Empirical Research on the Role of the Media in Social Movements

The Tahrir Data Project (http://tahrirdata.info) conducted a survey with Tahrir Square activists (N = 1056). Wilson and Dunn (2011) present data from the Tahrir Data Project, in which a survey (N = 1056) was conducted among Egyptian activists. The survey shows that face-to-face interaction (93%) was the most important form of activists' protest communication, followed by television (92%), phones (82%), print media (57%), SMS (46%), Facebook (42%), email (27%), radio (22%), Twitter (13%) and blogs (12%). Interpersonal communication, traditional media and telecommunications were more important information sources and communication tools in the revolution than social media and the Internet. Another part of the survey showed that Egyptian revolutionaries perceived phone communication, followed by face-to-face talk, as most important for their own protest, most informative and most motivating for participating in the protests. Facebook, email and Twitter were considered to be less important, less informative, less used and less motivating.

The Occupy General Survey that was conducted among Occupy Wall Street activists (see www.occupyresearch.net/2012/10/18/orgs-data-facet-browser/, accessed on July 2, 2013) showed that face-to-face communication and the Internet were activists' most important means of obtaining information about the Occupy movement. Facebook, word of mouth, websites and email played an especially important role. Both direct face-to-face interaction and mediated interaction have been crucial news sources for Occupy activists. This result was confirmed by the OccupyMedia! Survey (Fuchs 2013). Broadcasting and newspapers had a much less important role than the Internet. Facebook was a very popular source of information; however, older online media (email, websites) played a much more important role than YouTube, blogs, Twitter and Tumblr, which shows that one should not overestimate the role of what some have called "web 2.0" in protests. These empirical results falsify Castells' speculative argument that contemporary social movements emerged from and are largely based on the Internet, and live and act through digital media.

Jeffrey Juris, Paolo Gerbaudo and Miriyam Aouragh: For or against Castells?

Jeffrey Juris (2012), a former PhD student of Castells, conducted participant observation at Occupy Boston. He says that whereas the global justice movement primarily used mailing lists and was based on a logic of networking, the Occupy movement is based on a logic of aggregation, based on which social media result in "the viral flow of information and subsequent aggregations of large numbers of individuals in concrete physical spaces" (Juris 2012, 266). Individuals would "blast out vast amounts of information", make use of "ego-centered networks" so that "the use of Twitter and Facebook [. . .] tends to generate 'crowds of individuals'" (Juris 2012, 267). Like Castells, Juris assumes that social media "generate" protests. He claims that "social media such as Facebook, YouTube, and Twitter became the primary means of communication within #Occupy" (266), without empirically validating this claim.

In his book *Tweets and the Streets: Social Media and Contemporary Activism*, Paolo Gerbaudo (2012) challenges, on theoretical and empirical grounds, the assumption of Castells and others that the Internet brings about leaderless movements. He interviewed 80 activists in the USA, Egypt, Spain, the United Kingdom, Tunisia and Greece about their use of social media in protests and found that although contemporary social movements claim that they are leaderless networks, there are soft leaders who make use of social media for choreographing protests and "constructing a *choreography of assembly*" (Gerbaudo 2012, 139): "a handful of people control most of the communication flow" (Gerbaudo 2012, 135). The choreography of assembly means "the use of social media in directing people towards specific protest events, in providing participants with suggestions and instructions about how to act, and in the construction of an emotional narration to sustain their coming together in public space" (Gerbaudo 2012, 12). The movements' spontaneity would be organized "precisely because it is a highly mediated one" (Gerbaudo 2012, 164). The ethical problem would not be this movement choreography, but the denial that there are leaders because this would result in unaccountability.

Miriyam Aouragh (2012, 529) argues that the "overt fascination with social media gave the impression that the revolutions were mainly middle class and secular. Western experiences were taken as the model for Arab revolutions evaluated through the lens of modernity going hand in hand with the idea that social media plays an important role in developing a sense of modernity or, as this fascinating analysis claims".

Overcoming short-circuited analyses of the role of social media in revolutions would require a dialectical and historical Marxist analysis:

> explaining the value of the internet can never make sense without including a political and historic contextualisation. Rather than a sudden 'awakening', the region was already in turmoil, protests had been accumulating for almost a decade, starting with the outbreak of the Second Intifada and Ariel Sharon's massacre of Palestinians; the invasion of Iraq; anger over leaders seen as the local lackeys of the US and Israel. A widespread and deep anger over the regional politics overlapped with domestic issues and grew deeper as the economic impact of the neoliberal (IMF/WB) privatisation combined with the price increases caused by the global financial crisis. (Aouragh 2012, 529)

Miriyam Aouragh shares Paolo Gerbaudo's analysis, but connects it, in contrast to him, to a Marxist theory framework:

> I argued, echoing Rosa Luxemburg, that revolutionary change does not rely on spontaneous unorganized acts: it needs organizers, leaders, determination, and accountability. Discipline and structured organizing enables activists to generalize from complex and uneven realities and they are imperative for the survival of political movements. The activist networks do not confirm the view of leaderless swarms as often remarked when "new" Internet structures for political activism are concerned. It is mostly because it looked like it was a new, youth, non-ideological, online, horizontal movement that it gained attention and perhaps for many disillusioned with mainstream politics to give it the benefit of the doubt. (Aouragh 2012, 534)

4.5. Conclusion

Manuel Castells conceives of "social media" as a form of mass self-communication and as a social realm where communication power and counter-power are exerted. There are doubts about Castells' use of social theory, his notion of power, the use of computer science terms for analyzing society, the assessment and categorical description of the power distribution between global multimedia corporations and the creative audience, the feasibility of the notion of web 2.0, and the centrality of informationalism and communication power.

The global economic crisis resulted in a return of the importance of economic questions, which are also questions about class, in social theory, and has shown the huge power that the global financial and economic networks wield over our lives. The central political task might now be to develop counter-power against the commodification of everything. The task for social theory in the contemporary situation is to develop analyses of power and potential counter-power. Manuel Castells reminds us that the role of communication certainly should not be neglected in such endeavours. However, I have serious doubts that Castells' approach can advance the critical analysis of contemporary society or provide help for creating a better society.

We can summarize the main conclusions of this chapter:

- Castells mainly presents a history of the Internet and its context, and his work lacks a theory of society and a theory of modern society. His approach is neither a social theory, nor adequately theoretically grounded, but rather an arbitrary and unsystematic form of conceptualizing and collection of observations. Castells' concept of social media lacks an engagement with social theories that conceptualize power, autonomy, society, sociality and capitalism.

- Castells conveives of power and communication power as coercive, asymmetric, and violent features of all societies. He thereby naturalizes domination and overlooks the possibility of dominationless communication and a dominationless society.

- Manuel Castells uses computing language (terms like program, switches, protocols, kernel) for describing society. He conflates the logic of society with the logic of computing and cannot account for the special role of humans in society.

- In his discussion of social media in the Arab Spring, the Occupy movement and other 2011 uprisings, Castells shares the techno-euphoria and techno-determinism of thinkers like Clay Shirky (2008, 2011a, 2011b) and Andrew Sullivan (2009) by advancing the assumption that contemporary social movements emerged from and are largely based on the Internet and live and act through digital media.

A critical theory of social media and society is needed. Neither Jenkins nor Castells have provided such an approach. This book tries to contribute to the creation of some foundations of a critical theory of social media.

RECOMMENDED READINGS AND EXERCISES

Gaining an understanding of the concept of communication power can be achieved by engaging with the works of various thinkers, such as Manuel Castells, those who offer criticisms of Castells and the idea of the network society, such as Bob Jessop, Nicholas Garnham and Eran Fisher, thinkers who have theorized power and violence (e.g. Max Weber, Anthony Giddens, John P. Thompson, Johan Galtung, James Curran) and those who have studied social media in revolutions (e.g. Miriyam Aourgah, Paolo Gerbaudo).

Castells, Manuel. 2010b. *The rise of the network society*. The information age: economy, society and culture, Volume I (2nd edition with a new preface). Malden, MA: Wiley-Blackwell. Preface to the 2010 edition. Prologue: The Net and the self. Conclusion: The network society.

Jessop, Bob. 2003/2004. Informational capitalism and empire: The postmarxist celebration of US hegemony in a new world order. *Studies in Political Economy* 71/72: 39–58.

Garnham, Nicholas. 2000. "Information society" as theory or ideology. *Information, Communication & Society* 3 (2): 139–152.

Fisher, Eran. 2010. Contemporary technology discourse and the legitimation of capitalism. *European Journal of Social Theory* 13 (2): 229–252.

Fuchs, Christian. 2012. Capitalism or information society? The fundamental question of the present structure of society. *European Journal of Social Theory*, first published on November 20, 2012 as doi: 10.1177/1368431012461432.

Fuchs, Christian. 2009. Some reflections on Manuel Castells' book "Communication power". *tripleC: Open Access Journal for a Global Sustainable Information Society* 7 (1): 94–108.

Castells' *The Network Society* is the book that made his work appealing to a wide audience. It introduces the idea that we live in a network society. Critical theorists Bob Jessop and Nicholas Garnham are critical of this notion, which is expressed in their reviews of Castells' book. Eran Fisher contextualizes the network discourse and argues that it is a new ideology. Christian Fuchs stresses that it is important to talk about capitalism when discussing information technologies and that one needs a dialectical analysis for understanding their impact on society. He questions Castells' notion that the network society is a new society. Read the texts and in groups discuss the following questions:

- What is an ideology? Try to give a definition. You can search for and consult literature for this task.

- In respects are the information society and the network society ideologies? Which ideologies do the authors identify in the work of Castells? Construct an ordered and systematic typology of ideologies of the information and network society.

- Find examples of how the ideologies identified in the previous task can be found in public discourses about social media. Find examples by consulting media, debates, press releases, news clips, websites, etc.

- Do we live in an information society or not? Give reasons for your answer.

- How should contemporary society be characterized? What is your individual opinion and what is your group's opinion? What prefix should be used for characterizing contemporary society and why? Note: A prefixing term (as in "information society", "knowledge society", "modern society", "industrial society", "agricultural society", "reflexive society", "postmodern society", "digital society", "global society", "postindustrial society", "capitalist society", "labour society", "hyperreal society", "education society", "dynamic society", "functionally differentiated society", "flexible society", "adventure society", "divided society", "polycentric society", "risk society", "transcultural society", "multicultural society", "surveillance society", "transparent society", "responsible society", "virtual society", "ICT society", "Internet society", "cyber society", "world society", etc.) of society indicates that the prefix is the main characteristic of the society that is being described.

Castells, Manuel. 2009. *Communication power.* Oxford: Oxford University Press. Chapter 1: Power in the network society. Conclusion: Toward a communication theory of power.

In *Communication Power*, Castells provides an analysis of power in the context of social media.

- Search for reviews and criticisms of Castells' book with the help of Social Sciences Citation Index, Communication and Mass Media Complete, Scopus, Sociological Abstracts, Google Scholar, etc. Work in groups and construct a systematic and ordered list of points of criticism. Discuss these criticisms first in groups and then compare the results with the class.

Weber, Max. 1981. Selections from *Economy and Society*, volumes 1 and 2; and General economic history. In *Classes, power, and conflict: Classical and contemporary debates*, ed. Anthony Giddens and David Held, 60–86. Basingstoke: Macmillan.

Giddens, Anthony. 1984. *The constitution of society: Outline of the theory of structuration.* Cambridge: Polity Press. Chapter 1: Elements of the theory of structuration. Chapter 5: Change, evolution and power.

Giddens, Anthony. 1990. *The consequences of modernity.* Cambridge: Polity Press. Chapter II.

Max Weber and Anthony Giddens are two of the most important social theorists of the twentieth century. They have both provided theories of society that include important concepts of power.

- Compare Weber's and Giddens' concepts of power. What are commonalities and differences?

- Compare both Weber's and Giddens' concepts of power to Castells' concept of communication power.

- Find examples of communication power on social media based on a Weberian understanding of power.

- Find examples of communication power on social media based on a Giddensian understanding of power.

Movie: Manuel Castells: Lecture about "Communication power in the network society", http://webcast.oii.ox.ac.uk/?view=Webcast&ID=20081023_266&quality=high

Watch the video lecture. Ask yourself what you like about it and what points of criticism you have. Discuss the lecture in groups. Present the discussion results.

Work in groups: Try to find an example of communication power and counter-power on social media and look for a short video about this example that can be presented in the classroom. Prepare a presentation that focuses on the following questions:

- What is communication power? What is communication counter-power? How can the two terms be defined? Which definition should be employed – the one by Castells or another one, and why?

- Prepare an example of communication power and communication counter-power on social media. Use a short YouTube video that can be presented to your colleagues that is connected to the topic of communication power.

- Discuss aspects of communication power and communication counter-power in relation to your example video.

- Each group presents its example video and explains what aspects of communication power and communication counter-power can be found in the example and how these terms can best be understood.

Castells, Manuel. 2012. *Networks of outrage and hope: Social movements in the Internet age*. Cambridge: Polity Press. Chapters: Opening: Networking minds, creating meaning, contesting power;The Egyptian revolution; Occupy Wall Street: Harvesting the salt of the earth; Changing the world in the network society.

Fuchs, Christian. 2012. Some reflections on Manuel Castells' book "Networks of outrage and hope: Social movements in the Internet age". *tripleC: Communication, Capitalism & Critique: Open Access Journal for a Global Sustainable Information Society* 10 (2): 775–797.

Networks of Outrage and Hope is Castells' analysis of social media's role in the 2011 revolutions and uprisings. I have published the first English review of this book.

- Read the chapters listed above in Castells' book. Note especially how he uses the terms "power" and "communication power". Work in groups and compare these passages to the definitions of communication power in his previous book, *Communication Power* (2009). How exactly does Castells apply this concept? What kind of definition of power does he advance in the books? Are the definitions the same or do they vary?

- Read my criticism of Castells. Search for additional reviews and criticisms with the help of Social Sciences Citation Index, Communication and Mass Media Complete, Scopus, Sociological Abstracts, Google Scholar, etc. Work in groups and construct a systematic and ordered list of points of criticism. Discuss these criticisms first in groups and then compare the results with the class.

Thompson, John B. 1995. *The media and modernity: A social theory of the media.* Cambridge: Polity Press. Chapter 1: Communication and social context.

Galtung, Johan. 1990. Cultural violence. *Journal of Peace Research* 27 (3): 291–305.

John B. Thompson's *The Media and Modernity* is an influential book in media sociology. Chapter 1 includes a discussion of power. Johan Galtung is the founder of Peace and Conflict Studies and has written extensively on questions of violence. The works of these two thinkers are a helpful starting point for discussing the role of power and violence in the media. Read these two texts and discuss:

- How should the terms power and violence best be defined (try to give your own views and definitions)?

- Which forms of power are there (try to give your own views and definitions)?

- Which forms of violence exist (try to give your own views and definitions)?

- How can the relationship of power and violence best be conceptualized (try to give your own views and definitions)?

- Discuss how different forms of power and violence play a role in social media. Try to find examples and explain which forms of power and violence play a role and what role they have.

Curran, James. 2002. *Media and power.* London: Routledge. Chapter 5: Renewing the radical tradition.

Curran's book *Media and Power* discusses the multidimensional character of power in capitalism and how its economic, political and ideological dimensions relate to the media.

- Discuss James Curran's dimensions of media power and media counter-power and compare them to Table 4.3 in this chapter. Try to find examples for all forms of media power and media counter-power in the context of social media.

Aouragh, Miriyam. 2012. Social media, mediation and the Arab revolutions. *tripleC: Communication, Capitalism & Critique: Journal for a Global Sustainable Information Society* 10 (2): 518–536.

Gerbaudo, Paolo. 2012. *Tweets and the streets: Social media and contemporary activism.* London: Pluto Press. Introduction, Chapters 1 and 2.

Juris, Jeffrey S. 2012. Reflections on #occupy everywhere: Social media, public space, and emerging logics of aggregation. *American Ethnologist* 39 (2): 259–279.

Murthy, Dhiraj. 2013. *Twitter: Social communication in the Twitter age*. Cambridge: Polity Press. Chapter 6: Twitter and activism.

The four texts by Miriyam Aouragh, Paolo Gerbaudo, Jeffrey Juris and Dhiraj Murthy provide analyses of the role of social media in the 2011 revolutions and protests.

- Read the four texts. Compare all four positions to Castells' conceptualization of the role of social media in the Arab Spring and the 2011 protests.

- Compare the four authors' analyses to each other. What commonalities and differences are there? What role does critical thinking and theorizing play?

II
APPLICATIONS

The Power and Political Economy of Social Media

Key questions

- What are the ideologies and common myths that surround social media?
- What is meant by the political economy of social media and how does this work?
- What is digital labour and what role does it play within the political economy of social media?

Key concepts

Political economy of social media
Digital labour
Social media ideologies
Corporate colonization of social media
Prosumption

Audience commodity
Internet prosumer commodity
Targeted advertising
Prosumer surveillance
Panoptic sorting
Global division of digital labour

Overview

Political economy analyzes the structural features of capitalism, such as the causes of crises, whereas ideology critique analyzes the claims that are made about reality and how true they are. If one wants to understand power, then one needs to analyze both ideology and political economy. For a critical analysis of social media, this means that we have to take a look at both ideological aspects and political economy.

This chapter's task is to provide an introduction to the critical power structure analysis of social media. For this purpose, it will explain how surplus value production and exploitation work on corporate social media platforms, i.e. aspects of labour and capital accumulation are analyzed. I point out the limits of the participatory social media hypothesis (in section 5.1), introduce Marx's cycle of capital accumulation (5.2), which I apply to social media (5.3). I discuss the connection of unpaid user labour to other forms of labour (5.4) and, finally, draw some conclusions (5.5).

5.1. Social Media as Ideology: The Limits of the Participatory Social Media Hypothesis

Social Media: Participation as Ideology

Techno-deterministic approaches that assume that the rise of these technologies results in a more democratic society dominate studies of "web 2.0" and "social media". This becomes especially clear when representatives of this approach speak of "participatory social media". For example, Jenkins argues that increasingly "the Web has become a site of consumer participation" (Jenkins 2008, 137), Shirky (2008, 107) says that on web 2.0 there is a "linking of symmetrical participation and amateur production", Tapscott and Williams (2007, 15) argue that "the new web" has resulted in "a new economic democracy", Howe (2008, 14) speaks of social media crowdsourcing as a "manifestation of a larger trend toward greater democratization of commerce", Benkler (2006, 15) states that due to commons-based peer production "culture is becoming more democratic: self-reflective and participatory", Bruns (2008, 17) says that Internet produsage allows "participation in networked culture", Deuze (2007, 95) concludes that "new media technologies like the Internet have made visible [...] the participatory engagement of people with their media". To be fair, one has to say that Deuze (2008) has also written contributions in which he stresses the "corporate appropriation of participatory culture" (contribution title).

Approaches like the ones just mentioned miss a theoretically grounded understanding of participation. They use claims about implications for democracy, but miss that in democracy theory mainly the approach of participatory democracy theory (Held 2006) uses the term "participation". The earliest use of the term "participatory democracy" that I could trace in the literature is an article by Staughton Lynd (1965) that describes the grassroots organization of the student movement. Participatory democracy theory (for a more detailed discussion and its implications for the analysis of social media, see Fuchs 2011b, chapter 7) has two central features:

- the broad understanding of democracy as encompassing areas beyond voting, such as the economy, culture, and the household, and
- the questioning of the compatibility of participatory democracy and capitalism.

The Limits of YouTube

One should analyze the political economy of social media platforms when making judgements about their participatory character. If there are, for example, asymmetries in terms of visibility and attention, then it is questionable that corporate social media are truly participatory. It is therefore not enough to stress enabling and limiting potentials of the Internet, but one rather needs to analyze the actual distribution of advantages and disadvantages. It is also important to analyze the negative aspects of social media in order to temper the uncritical social media-optimism that is an ideological manifestation of the search for new capital accumulation models that wants to exploit user labour in order to raise the profit rate in the digital media industry. Critics have stressed in this context that web 2.0 optimism is uncritical and an ideology that serves corporate interests (Fuchs 2011b; Van Dijck and Nieborg 2009) or that web 2.0 users are more passive users than active creators (Van Dijck 2009).

Analysis of the ten most viewed videos on YouTube (see Table 5.1) shows that transnational media corporations, the organized exploiters of surplus value-generating labour, control YouTube's political attention economy. Entertainment and music are very popular on YouTube and Facebook (see also Table 5.2), whereas politics is a minority interest. An analysis of Facebook groups shows that the most popular groups are about IT and entertainment, whereas politics is of minor interest.

Table 5.1   The most viewed YouTube videos of all times

Rank	Title	Type	Owner	Views
1	Psy – Gangnam Style	Music	YG Entertainment	1 369 600 342
2	Justin Bieber – Baby	Music	Universal	835 366 175
3	Jennifer Lopez – On the Floor	Music	Universal	653 625 451
4	Eminem – Love the way you lie	Music	Universal	543 003 278
5	LMFAO – Party rock anthem	Music	Universal	523 909 234
6	Charlie bit my finger – again !	Entertainment	Private	513 822 064
7	Shakira – Waka Waka	Music	Sony	510 871 915
8	Lady Gaga – Bad Romance	Music	Universal	510 222 649
9	Michel Teló – Ai Se Eu Te Pego	Music	Universal	484 138 009
10	Carly Rae Jepsen – Call Me Maybe	Entertainment	Universal	415 625 906

Source: youtube.com, accessed on March 1, 2013.

Table 5.2   The most popular fan groups on Facebook

Rank	Facebook fan group	Type	Number of fans
1	Facebook for every phone	IT	208.3 million
2	Facebook	Internet	88.6 million
3	YouTube	Internet	71.0 million
4	Texas Hold'em Poker	Music	68.4 million
5	Rihanna	Music	67.2 million
6	Eminem	Music	66.9 million
7	The Simpsons	Entertainment	61.7 million
8	Shakira	Music	61.3 million
9	Coca-Cola	Brand	60.0 million
10	Harry Potter	Entertainment	59.9 million
51	Barack Obama	Politics	35.2 million
	Michael Moore	Alternative media producer	745 362
	Noam Chomsky	Political intellectual	551 117
	Karl Marx	Political philosopher, communist	176 447

Data source: http://statistics.allfacebook.com, accessed on March 1, 2013.

The Limits of Facebook

Powerful politicians, such as President Obama, dominate the attention given to the political Facebook groups, whereas alternative political figures, such as Michael Moore, Noam Chomsky and Karl Marx, have a much lower number of fans (Table 5.2).

The Limits of Google

The results yielded by a Google search for "political news" show that corporate news organizations dominate the top results (Table 5.3). Only one public service organization (BBC) and one non-profit organization (NPR) are under the top ten results. The top search keywords used on Google in 2010 show that the 12 most used keywords did not contain political topics. Instead, there was more interest in Whitney Houston, Gangnam Style, Hurricane Sandy, iPad 3, Diablo 3, Kate Middleton, Olympics 2012, Amanda Todd, Michael Clarke Duncan, Big Brother Brazil 12.[1]

The Limits of Twitter

Twitter is one of the most popular social media platforms. Blogger Andrew Sullivan wrote after the Iranian protests of 2009 that "the revolution will be

---

1 www.google.com/zeitgeist/, accessed on July 2, 2013.

Table 5.3 Top results of a Google search for "political news"

Rank	Website	Ownership status	Owner
1	cnn.com	Corporate	Time Warner
2	cbsnews.com	Corporate	CBS Corporation
3	Politico.com	Corporate	Allbritton Communications
4	abcnews.go.com/politics	Corporate	Walt Disney
5	bbc.co.uk	Public service	BBC
6	foxnews.com	Corporate	News Corporations
7	reuters.com	Corporate	Thompson Reuters
8	nbcnews.com	Corporate	Comcast
9	Yahoo.com/politics	Corporate	Yahoo
10	npr.org/sections/politics	Non-profit	Non-profit company

Data source: google.com, March 1, 2013.

Table 5.4 Twitter user profiles with the highest number of followers

Rank	Twitter user profile	Followers
1	Justin Bieber @justinbieber	35.2 million
2	Lady Gaga @ladygaga	34.6 million
3	Katy Perry @katyperry	33.0 million
4	Rihanna @rihanna	28.6 million
5	Barack Obama @barackobama	27.8 million
6	Taylor Swift @taylorswift13	24.5 million
7	Britney Spears @ britneyspears	24.3 million
8	YouTube @youtube	24.0 million
9	Shakira @shakira	19.9 million
10	Kim Karadashian @KimKaradashian	17.4 million
	Michael Moore @MMFlint	1 460 507
	Noam Chomsky @daily_chomsky	87 901
	Occupy Wall Street @OccupyWallSt	177 549
	Occupy London @OccupyLondon	38 056

Data source: www.socialbakers.com/twitter/, accessed on March 1, 2013.

twittered", which contributed to the myth of Twitter revolutions.[2] Can meaningful political debates be based on 140-character short messages? Short text invites simplistic arguments and is an expression of the commodification and speed-up of culture. Table 5.4 shows that nine out of the ten most followed Twitter users are entertainment-oriented. Barack Obama is the only exception in the top ten. But Table 5.4 also shows that politics has a stratified attention economy

---

2 www.theatlantic.com/daily-dish/archive/2009/06/the-revolution-will-be-twittered/200478/, accessed on August 20, 2011.

on Twitter: whereas Barack Obama has a very large number of followers, the number is much lower for representatives of alternative politics, such as Michael Moore, Noam Chomsky, Occupy Wall Street and Occupy London.

The Corporate Colonization of Social Media

Such data make clear that corporations and their logic dominate social media and the Internet and that the Internet is predominantly capitalist in character. Social media do not constitute a public sphere or participatory democratic space, but are rather colonized by corporations, especially by multimedia companies that dominate attention and visibility. Politics is a minority issue on social media. Georg Lukács argues that ideology "by-passes the essence of the evolution of society and fails to pinpoint it and express it adequately" (Lukács 1923/1972, 50). An ideology is a claim about a certain status of reality that does not correspond to actual reality. It deceives human subjects in order to forestall societal change. It is false consciousness (Lukács 1923/1972, 83).

Observers who argue that the contemporary web and social media are participatory, cause revolutions, facilitate democracy or advance the public sphere, facilitate an ideology that celebrates capitalism and does not see how capitalist interests predominantly shape the Internet. Not only management gurus and marketing agencies, but also scholars in academia advance social media ideology. They postulate a false social media reality that neglects the role of capitalism. The implication of the claims that are made is that social media result in a better world. However, as the method of ideology critique that empirically compares claims to reality has frequently shown, we have a much more stratified reality that is shaped by structures of domination.

The Internet and social media are today stratified, non-participatory spaces and an alternative, non-corporate Internet is needed (see Fuchs 2011b, chapters 7, 8 and 9). Large corporations colonize social media and dominate its attention economy. Even though Twitter and mobile phones supported the political rebellions, protests and revolutions in countries like Algeria, Bahrain, Egypt, Iran, Jordan, Libya, Morocco, Tunisia and Yemen in early 2011, and the publishing of videos about the effects of domination (as the video about the death of Neda Soltani in the Iranian protests in 2009 or the video about the death of Ian Tomlinson at the London anti-G20 protests in 2009) can support the communication of protest, one should not overestimate these potentials. There are no Twitter-, Facebook- or YouTube-revolutions. Only people who live under certain social conditions and organize collectively can make rebellions and revolutions. Technology is, in itself, not a revolution.

On corporate social media, the liberal freedom of association and assembly are suspended: big corporate and, to a lesser extent, political actors dominate and therefore centralize the formation of speech, association, assembly and opinion on social media. Liberal freedoms turn on capitalist social media into their opposite.

The concept of social media participation is an ideology. Given this empirical result, it seems both necessary and feasible to theorize "web 2.0" not as a participatory system, but by employing more negative, critical terms such as class, exploitation and surplus value. This requires us to ground the analysis of social media in the works of the founding figure of critical political economy – Karl Marx.

5.2. The Cycle of Capital Accumulation

In the three volumes of *Capital* (1867, 1885, 1894), Marx analyzes the accumulation process of capital. This process, as described by Marx, is visualized in Figure 5.1.

In the accumulation of capital, capitalists buy labour power and means of production (raw materials, technologies, etc.) in order to organize the production of new commodities that are sold with the expectation to make money profit that is partly reinvested. Marx distinguishes two spheres of capital accumulation: the circulation sphere and the sphere of production. In the circulation sphere, capital transforms its value form. First, money M is transformed into commodities (from the standpoint of the capitalist as buyer): the capitalist purchases the commodities labour power L and means of production Mp. The process M-C is based on the two purchases M-L and M-Mp. This means that due to private property structures workers do not own the means of production, the products they produce and the profit they generate. Capitalists own

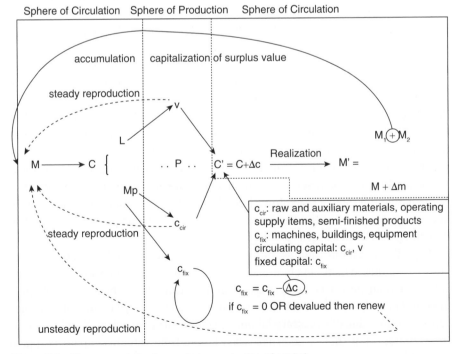

Figure 5.1 The accumulation/expanded reproduction of capital

these resources. In the sphere of production, a new good is produced: the value of labour power and the value of the means of production are added to the product. Value takes on the form of productive capital P. The value form of labour is variable capital v (which can be observed as wages), the value form of the means of production constant capital c (which can be observed as the total price of the means of production/producer goods).

In the sphere of production, capital stops its metamorphosis so that capital circulation comes to a halt. There is the production of new value V' of the commodity. V' contains the value of the necessary constant and variable capital and surplus value Δs of the surplus product. Unpaid labour generates surplus value and profit. Surplus value is the part of the working day that is unpaid. It is the part of the work day (measured in hours) that is used for producing profit. Profit does not belong to workers, but to capitalists. Capitalists do not pay for the production of surplus. Therefore the production of surplus value is a process of exploitation. The value V' of the new commodity after production is $V' = c + v + s$.

The commodity then leaves the sphere of production and again enters the circulation sphere, where capital conducts its next metamorphosis: it is transformed from the commodity form back into the money form by being sold on the market. Surplus value is realized in the form of money. The initial money capital M now takes on the form $M' = M + \Delta m$; it has been increased by an increment Δm. Accumulation of capital means that the produced surplus value/profit is (partly) reinvested/capitalized. The end point of one process M' becomes the starting point of a new accumulation process. One part of M', M_1, is reinvested. Accumulation means the aggregation of capital by investment and exploitation in the capital circuit M-C .. P .. C'-M', in which the end product M' becomes a new starting point M. The total process makes up the dynamic character of capital. Capital is money that is permanently increasing due to the exploitation of surplus value.

Commodities are sold at prices that are higher than the investment costs so that money profit is generated. Marx argues that one decisive quality of capital accumulation is that profit is an emergent property of production that is produced by labour, but owned by the capitalists. Without labour, no profit could be made. Workers are forced to enter class relations and to produce profit in order to survive, which enables capital to appropriate surplus. The notion of exploited surplus value is the main concept of Marx's theory, by which he intends to show that capitalism is a class society. "The theory of surplus value is in consequence immediately the theory of exploitation" (Negri 1991, 74). One can add: the theory of surplus value is the theory of class and, as a consequence, the political demand for a classless society.

Capital is not money per se, but is money that is increased through accumulation – "money which begets money" (Marx 1867, 256). Marx argues that the value of labour power is the average amount of time that is needed for the production of goods that are necessary for survival (necessary labour time). Wages represent the value of necessary labour time at the level of prices. Surplus labour time is labour time that exceeds necessary labour time, remains unpaid, is appropriated for free by capitalists, and transformed into money profit. Surplus value "is in substance the materialization of unpaid labour-time. The secret of the self-valorization of capital resolves itself into the fact that it has at its disposal a definite quantity of the unpaid labour of other people" (Marx 1867, 672). The production of surplus value is "the *differentia specifica* of capitalist production" (Marx 1867, 769) and the "driving force and the final result of the capitalist process of production" (Marx 1867, 976).

5.3. Capital Accumulation and Social Media

Many corporate social media platforms accumulate capital with the help of targeted advertising that is tailored to individual user data and behaviour. Capitalism is based on the imperative to accumulate ever more capital. To achieve this, capitalists have to either prolong the working day (absolute surplus value production) or increase the productivity of labour (relative surplus value production) (on relative surplus value, see Marx 1867, chapter 12).

Relative Surplus Value

Relative surplus value production means that productivity is increased so that more commodities and more surplus value can be produced in the same time period as before.

> For example, suppose a cobbler, with a given set of tools, makes one pair of boots in one working day of 12 hours. If he is to make two pairs in the same time, the productivity of his labour must be doubled; and this cannot be done except by an alteration in his tools or in his mode of working, or both. Hence the conditions of production of his labour, i.e. his mode of production, and the labour process itself, must be revolutionized. By an increase in the productivity of labour, we mean an alteration in the labour process of such a kind as to shorten the labour-time socially necessary for the production of a commodity, and to endow a given quantity of labour with the power of producing a greater quantity of use-value. [. . .] I call that surplus-value which is produced by lengthening of the working day, *absolute surplus-value*. In contrast to this, I call that surplus-value which arises from the curtailment of the necessary labour-time, and from the corresponding alteration in the respective lengths of the two components of the working day, *relative surplus-value*. (Marx 1867, 431f)

Sut Jhally (1987, 78) argues that "reorganizing the watching audience in terms of demographics" is a form of relative surplus value production. One can interpret targeted Internet advertising as a form of relative surplus value production: at one point in time, the advertisers show not only one advertisement to the audience, as in non-targeted advertising, but also different advertisements to different user groups depending on the monitoring, assessment and comparison of the users' interests and online behaviour. On traditional forms of television, all watchers see the same advertisements at the same time. In targeted online advertising, advertising companies can present different ads at the same time. The efficiency of advertising is increased: the advertisers can show more advertisements that are likely to fit the interests of consumers in the same time period as in non-targeted advertising. Partly the advertising company's wage labourers and partly the Internet users, whose user-generated data and transaction data are utilized, produce the profit generated from these advertisements. The more targeted advertisements there are, the more likely it is that users recognize ads and click on them.

The users' click-and-buy process is the surplus value realization process of the advertising company, in which surplus value is transformed into money profit. Targeted advertising allows Internet companies to present not just one advertisement at one point in time to users, but rather numerous advertisements so that there is the production of more total advertising time that presents commodities to users. Relative surplus value production means that more surplus value is generated in the same time period as earlier. Targeted online advertising is more productive than non-targeted online advertising because it allows presenting more ads in the same time period. These ads contain more surplus value than the non-targeted ads, i.e., more unpaid labour time of the advertising company's paid employees and of users, who generate user-generated content and transaction data.

Prosumption

Alvin Toffler (1980) introduced the notion of the prosumer in the early 1980s. It means the "progressive blurring of the line that separates producer from consumer" (Toffler 1980, 267). Toffler describes the age of prosumption as the arrival of a new form of economic and political democracy, self-determined work, labour autonomy, local production and autonomous self-production. But he overlooks that prosumption is used for outsourcing work to users and consumers, who work without payment. Thereby corporations reduce their investment costs and labour costs, jobs are destroyed, and consumers who work for free are extremely exploited. They produce surplus value that is appropriated and turned into profit by corporations without paying wages. Notwithstanding Toffler's uncritical optimism, his notion of the "prosumer" describes important changes of media structures and practices and can therefore also be adopted for critical studies.

Ritzer and Jurgenson (2010) argue that web 2.0 facilitates the emergence of "prosumer capitalism", that the capitalist economy "has always been dominated by presumption" (14), and that prosumption is an inherent feature of McDonaldization. The two authors' rather simplistic and one-dimensional analysis ignores that prosumption is only one of many tendencies of capitalism, not its only quality and not the dominant quality. Capitalism is multidimensional and has multiple interlinked dimensions. It is at the same time finance capitalism, imperialistic capitalism, informational capitalism, hyperindustrial capitalism (oil, gas), crisis capitalism, etc. Not all of these dimensions are equally important (Fuchs 2011b, chapter 5). Critical scholars have introduced concepts such as consumption work (Huws 2003) and Internet prosumer labour (Fuchs 2010c) for stressing how the boundaries between leisure and work, as well as production and consumption, have become liquid in contemporary capitalism.

Dallas Smythe, the Audience Commodity and Internet Prosumer Commodification

Dallas Smythe (1981/2006) suggests that in the case of media advertisement models, media companies sell the audience as a commodity to advertisers:

> Because audience power is produced, sold, purchased and consumed, it commands a price and is a commodity. [. . .] You audience members contribute your unpaid work time and in exchange you receive the program material and the explicit advertisements. (Smythe 1981/2006, 233, 238)

With the rise of user-generated content, free-access social networking platforms, and other free-access platforms that yield profit by online advertisement – a development subsumed under categories such as web 2.0, social software and social networking sites – the web seems to come close to accumulation strategies employed by capital on traditional mass media like TV or radio. Users who upload photos and images, write wall posting and comments, send mail to their contacts, accumulate friends or browse other profiles on Facebook, constitute an audience commodity that is sold to advertisers. The difference between the audience commodity on traditional mass media and on the Internet is that in the latter case the users are also content producers, there is user-generated content, the users engage in permanent creative activity, communication, community building and content-production. The fact that the users are more active on the Internet than in the reception of TV or radio content is due to the decentralized structure of the Internet, which allows many-to-many communication. Due to the permanent activity of the recipients and their status as prosumers, we can say that in the case of corporate social media the audience commodity is an Internet prosumer commodity (Fuchs 2010c).

The conflict between Cultural Studies and Critical Political Economy of the Media (see Ferguson and Golding 1997; Garnham 1995/1998; Grossberg 1995/1998) about the question of the activity and creativity of the user has been resolved in relation to web 2.0: on Facebook, Twitter, blogs, etc., users are fairly active and creative, which reflects Cultural Studies insights about the active character of recipients, but this active and creative user character is the very source of exploitation, which reflects Critical Political Economy's stress on class and exploitation.

Prosumer Surveillance

Economic surveillance on corporate social media is surveillance of prosumers, who dynamically and permanently create and share user-generated content, browse profiles and data, interact with others, join, create and build communities and co-create information. The corporate web platform operators and their third-party advertising clients continuously monitor and record personal data and online activities. They store, merge and analyze collected data. This allows them to create detailed user profiles and to know a lot about the users' personal interests and online behaviours. Social media that are based on targeted advertising sell prosumers as a commodity to advertising clients. There is an exchange of money for the access to user data that allows economic user surveillance. The exchange value of the social media prosumer commodity is the money value that the operators obtain from their clients. Its use value is the multitude of personal data and usage behaviour that is dominated by the commodity and exchange value form.

The corporations' surveillance of the prosumers' permanently produced use values, i.e., personal data and interactions, enables targeted advertising that aims at luring the prosumers into consumption and shopping. It also aims at manipulating prosumers' desires and needs in the interest of corporations and the commodities they offer. Whereas audience commodification in newspapers and traditional broadcasting was always based on statistical assessments of audience rates and characteristics (Bolin 2011), Internet surveillance gives social media corporations an exact picture of the interests and activities of users (Andrejevic 2007, 2012). The characteristics (interests and usage behaviour) and the size (the number of users in a specific interest group) of the Internet prosumer commodity can therefore be exactly determined and it can also be exactly determined who is part of a consumer group that should be targeted by specific ads and who is not.

Panoptic Sorting of Internet Prosumers

"The panoptic sort is a difference machine that sorts individuals into categories and classes on the basis of routine measurements. It is a discriminatory technology that allocates options and opportunities on the basis of those measures and the administrative models that they inform" (Gandy 1993, 15). It is a system of power and disciplinary surveillance that identifies, classifies and assesses (Gandy 1993, 15). The mechanism of targeted advertising on social media is the form of surveillance that Gandy has characterized as panoptic sorting: it *identifies* the interests of users by closely surveilling their personal data and usage behaviour, it *classifies* them into consumer groups, and *assesses* their interests in comparison to other consumers and to available advertisements that are then targeted at the users.

Social media prosumers are double objects of commodification: they are commodities themselves and through this commodification their consciousness becomes, while online, permanently exposed to commodity logic in the form of advertisements. Most online time is advertising time. On corporate social media, targeted advertising makes use of the users' personal data, interests, interactions, information behaviour, and also the interactions with other websites. So while you are using Facebook, Twitter, YouTube, etc., it is not just you interacting with others and browsing profiles; all of these activities are framed by advertisements presented to you. These advertisements come about by permanent surveillance of your online activities. Such advertisements do not necessarily represent consumers' real needs and desires because the ads are based on calculated assumptions, whereas needs are much more complex and spontaneous. The ads mainly reflect marketing decisions and economic power relations. They do not simply provide information about products as offers to buy, but information about products of powerful companies.

Capital Accumulation on Corporate Social Media

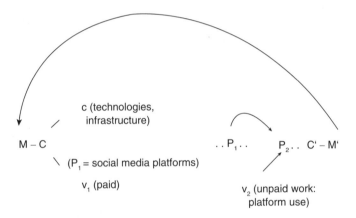

C' = **Internet prosumer commodity** (user-generated content, transaction data, virtual advertising space and time).
Most social media services are free to use, they are not commodities.
User data and the users are the social media commodity.

Figure 5.2 Capital accumulation on corporate social media platforms that are based on targeted advertising

Figure 5.2 shows the process of capital accumulation on corporate social media platforms that are funded by targeted advertising. Social media corporations invest money (M) for buying capital: technologies (server space, computers, organizational infrastructure, etc.) and labour power (paid employees). These are the constant capital (c) and the variable capital v_1 outlays. The outcome of the production process P_1 is not a commodity that is directly sold, but rather social media services (the specific platforms) that are made available without payment to users. As a consequence of this circumstance, management literature has focused on identifying how to make profit from free Internet services.

The waged employees, who create social media online environments that are accessed by users, produce part of the surplus value. The users employ the platform for generating content that they upload (user-generated data). The constant and variable capital invested by social media companies (c, v_1) that is objectified in the online environments is the prerequisite for their activities in the production process P_2. Their products are user-generated data, personal data, and transaction data about their browsing behaviour and communication behaviour on corporate social media. They invest a certain labour time v_2 in this process.

Corporate social media sell the users' data commodity to advertising clients at a price that is larger than the invested constant and variable capital. Partly the users and partly the corporations' employees create the surplus value contained in this commodity. The difference is that the users are unpaid and therefore infinitely exploited. Once the Internet prosumer commodity that contains the user-generated content, transaction data, and the right to access virtual advertising space and time is sold to advertising clients, the commodity is transformed into money capital and surplus value is transformed into money capital. A counter-argument to the insight that commercial social media companies exploit Internet prosumers is that the latter, in exchange for their work, receive access to a service. One can here, however, interpose that service access cannot be seen as a salary because users cannot "further convert this salary [...] [They] cannot buy food" (Bolin 2011, 37) with it.

The Profit Rate and Social Media

For Marx (1867), the profit rate is the relation of profit to investment costs:

$$p = s / (c + v) = \text{surplus value} / (\text{constant capital} (= \text{fixed costs}) + \text{variable capital} (= \text{wages})).$$

If Internet users become productive web 2.0 prosumers, then in terms of Marxian class theory this means that they become productive labourers who produce surplus value and are exploited by capital because, for Marx, productive labour generates surplus value (Fuchs 2010c). Therefore exploited surplus value producers are not merely those who are employed by web 2.0 corporations for programming, updating and maintaining the soft- and hardware, performing marketing activities, etc., but are also the users and prosumers who engage in the production of user-generated content.

New media corporations do not (or hardly) pay the users for the production of content. One accumulation strategy is to give them free access to services and platforms, let them produce content, and to accumulate a large number of prosumers that are sold as a commodity to third-party advertisers. No product is sold to the users, but the users are sold as a commodity to advertisers. The more users a platform has, the higher the advertising rates can be set. The productive labour time that capital exploits involves, on the one hand, the labour time of the paid employees and, on the other hand, all of the time that is spent online by the users. Digital media corporations pay salaries for the first type of knowledge labour. Users produce data that is used and sold by the platforms without payment. They work for free. There are neither variable nor constant investment costs. The formula for the profit rate needs to be transformed for this accumulation strategy:

$$p = s / (c + v_1 + v_2)$$

s: surplus value, c: constant capital, v_1: wages paid to fixed employees, v_2: wages paid to users

The typical situation is that $v_2 = > 0$ and that v_2 substitutes v_1 ($v_1 = > v_2 = 0$). If the production of content and the time spent online were carried out by paid employees, the variable costs (wages) would rise and profits would therefore decrease. This shows that prosumer activity in a capitalist society can be interpreted as the outsourcing of productive labour to users (in management literature the term "crowdsourcing" has been established; see Howe 2008) who work completely for free and help maximize the rate of exploitation:

$$e = s / v = \text{surplus value} / \text{variable capital}$$

The Rate of Exploitation and Social Media

The rate of exploitation (also called the rate of surplus value) measures the relationship of workers' unpaid work time and paid work time. The higher the rate of exploitation, the more work time is unpaid. Users of commercial social media platforms have no wages ($v = 0$). Therefore the rate of surplus value converges towards infinity. Internet prosumer labour is infinitely exploited by capital. This means that capitalist prosumption is an extreme form of exploitation, in which the prosumers work completely for free. Marx (1867) distinguishes between necessary labour time and surplus labour time. The first is the time a person needs to work in order to create the money equivalent for a wage that is required for buying goods that are needed for survival. The second is all additional labour time. Users are not paid on corporate social media (or for consuming other types of corporate media), hence they cannot generate money for buying food or other goods needed for survival. Therefore, all online time on corporate social media like Google, Facebook, YouTube or Twitter is surplus labour time.

The outsourcing of work to consumers is a general tendency of contemporary capitalism. Facebook has asked users to translate its site into other languages without payment. Javier Olivan, international manager at Facebook, commented that it would be cool to use the wisdom of the crowds.[3] Pepsi started a competition in which one could win US$10 000 for the best design of a Pepsi can. Ideabounty is a crowdsourcing platform that organizes crowdsourcing projects for corporations such as, for example, RedBull, BMW and Unilever. In such projects, most of the employed work is unpaid. Even if single individuals receive symbolic prize money, most of the work time employed by users and consumers is fully unpaid, which allows companies to outsource paid labour time to consumers or fans that work for free.

---

3 www.msnbc.msn.com/id/24205912, accessed on August 20, 2011.

Value and Social Media

Value is a complex concept (Fuchs 2014). Bolin (2011) identifies economic value, moral value, news value, public value, cultural value, aesthetic value, social value, educational value, political value and symbolic/sign value as specific interpretations of the term. Marx shared with Smith and Ricardo an objective concept of value. The value of a commodity is, for them, the "quantity of the 'value-forming substance', the labour, contained in the article", "the amount of labour socially necessary" for its production (Marx 1867, 129). Marx argues that goods in capitalism have a dual character. They have a use value-side (they are used for achieving certain aims) and a value-side. There are aspects of concrete and abstract labour. Concrete labour generates the commodity's use value (the good's qualitative character as a useful good that satisfies human needs), abstract labour the commodity's value (the good's quantitative side that allows its exchange with other commodities in the form of the relationship x amount of commodity A = y amount of commodity B). Subjective concepts of economic value, as held, for example, by classical French political economists such as Jean-Baptiste Say and Frederic Bastiat, or by representatives of the neoclassical Austrian school, assume that the worth of a good is determined by humans' cognitive evaluations and moral judgements, and interpret the notion of value idealistically. They say that the value of a good is the value given to them by the subjective judgements of humans.

One problem of the value concept is that its subjective and objective meanings are often mixed up. As the moral value of capitalism is economic value, one needs a precise concept of value (Fuchs 2014). To focus the meaning of the term "value" on economic value does not automatically mean to speak in favour of capitalism and commodification; it only reflects the important role the capitalist economy has in modern society and stresses commodity logic's tendency to attempt to colonize non-commodified realms. The goal is a world not dominated by economic value, but achieving this goal does not necessarily need a non-economic definition of the value concept. Marx made a difference between the concept of value and the concept of price. When we talk about the value of a good, we talk about the average number of hours needed for its production, whereas the price is expressed in quantities of money. "The expression of the value of a commodity in gold – x commodity A = Y money commodity – is its money-form or price" (Marx 1867, 189). Marx argued that the value and the price of a commodity do not coincide: "the production price of a commodity is not at all identical with its value [...] It has been shown that the production price of a commodity may stand above or below its value and coincides with it only in exceptional cases" (Marx 1894, 892). He also dealt with the question of how values are transformed into prices. Chapter 9 of *Capital Volume III* (Marx 1894, 254–272) is devoted to this question.

Information – A Peculiar Good

Information is a peculiar good:

- It is not used up in consumption.

- It can be infinitely shared and copied by one individual without losing the good itself. Several people can own it at the same time.

- It has no physical wear and tear. Its wear and tear is what Marx (1867, 528) called "moral depreciation": it is caused by competition and the drive of companies to establish new versions of informational commodities, such as the newest version of the iPod or iPad or a new song by an artist in order to accumulate ever more capital and by the creation of symbolic difference postulated by advertising and branding so that the older informational commodities appear to consumers to be "outdated".

- It can be easily and cheaply copied and quickly transmitted.

- It is a social good that reflects the history of social interactions and the history of knowledge.

- The value for producing the initial form of information is relatively high (it includes many hours of development costs), whereas, starting with the second copy, the value is relatively low (work time mainly is the time of copying and distributing the good).

- Information is, however, normally sold at a price that is higher than its value (measured in the amount of hours needed for its production). The difference between value and price is at the heart of profit making in the information industries.

A piece of artwork sold at a high price makes use of the value-price-differential and the ideological belief of the buyers in the superiority of the artist. Similarly, branding can constitute a value-price-differential. Branding is an ideological mechanism that wants to make consumers believe that a commodity has a symbolic value above its economic value. Consumers' ideological belief in the superiority of a certain commodity allows companies to achieve excess-profit, a profit higher than yielded for similar use values. Related phenomena are financial assets that are sold at prices that do not correspond to the profits the underlying commodities are yielding. Marx (1894) speaks in this respect of fictitious capital and David Harvey (2005b) talks of a temporal fix to overaccumulation that results in the deference of "the re-entry of capital values into circulation into the future" (Harvey 2005b, 109) so that the difference between profits and asset price can result in financial bubbles. Just like there can be a difference between value and price of a commodity, there can be a difference between profit and financial market worth of a financial asset.

Social Media Work

Bolin (2011) argues that in broadcasting, it is the statisticians, not the audiences, who work (see also: Maxwell 1991; Meehan 1984). The advertisers do not buy audiences, but the belief in a certain audience value generated by statisticians that relatively arbitrarily measure audience ratings. "Audiences do not work; it is rather the statisticians and market executives who do" (Bolin 2011, 84). From a Marxist perspective (that Smythe employed, see Fuchs 2014, chapter 4), audiences' work time is the time they consume commercial media. The exact quantity of labour value can never be determined. Therefore, Marx said that the "individual commodity counts [. . .] only as an average sample of its kind" (Marx 1867, 129f). Audiences create the value of the commercial media commodity, whereas audience statistics determine the price of the audience commodity by approximating average audience numbers based on a sample of a certain size.

There are two different basic understandings of the term "value". In a subjective sense, some people understand it is giving mental worth to something, considering it as important. In a more objective sense, value means monetary value or the number of hours that people spend working on something. On corporate social media, users create content, browse content, establish and maintain relations with others by communication, and update their profiles. All the time they spend on these platforms is work time. The Internet prosumer commodity that an advertiser buys on, for example, Facebook or Google is based on specific demographic data (age, location, education, gender, workplace, etc.) and interests (e.g. certain keywords typed into Google or certain interests identified on Facebook). Thereby, a specific group can be identified as target group. All time spent by members of this group on the specific social media platform constitutes the economic value (work time) of a specific Internet prosumer commodity. This work time contains time for social relationship management and cultural activities that generate reputation. Users spend time creating appreciation of others and appreciation of themselves by others in the form of social relations, affects, social bonds, friendships, personal relations, communities, etc. One therefore needs to reflect on how economic value production by the media is connected to what Bourdieu termed social, cultural and symbolic capital (Bolin 2011). Users employ social media because they strive for a certain degree to achieve what Bourdieu (1986a, 1986b) terms social capital (the accumulation of social relations), cultural capital (the accumulation of qualification, education, knowledge) and symbolic capital (the accumulation of reputation). The time that users spend on commercial social media platforms generating social, cultural and symbolic capital is in the process of prosumer commodification transformed into economic capital. Labour time on commercial social media is the conversion of Bourdieuian social, cultural and symbolic capital into Marxian value and economic capital. The subjective and economic understanding of the term "value" are connected by circumstance that human subjectivity is the foundation of capital accumulation on corporate social media.

The Social Media Prosumer Commodity's Price

How is the social media prosumer commodity's price determined and how is value transformed into money profit? Advertising clients are interested in the access to specific groups that can be targeted with individualized advertising that fit their interests. Access to this group and the data about their interests (who is a member of a specific consumer group that shares certain interests) is sold to advertisers. On Google and Facebook, advertisers set a maximum budget for one campaign and a maximum they are willing to pay for one click on their advertisement or for 1000 impressions (=presentations of an ad on a profile). The exact price for one click or for 1000 impressions is determined in an automated bidding process, in which all advertisers interested in a specific group (all ads targeted at this specific group) compete. In both models, every user is offered as a commodity and commodified, but only certain user groups are sold as a commodity. In the pay-per-click model, value is transformed into money (profit is realized) when a user clicks on an ad. In the pay-per-view model, value is transformed into money (profit is realized) when an ad is presented on a user's profile. Value and price of the social media prosumer commodity do not coincide; the price is mathematically determined by an algorithm and based on bids. The number of hours spent online by a specific group of users determines the value of the social media prosumer commodity. The price of this commodity is algorithmically determined.

All hours spent online by users of Facebook, Google and comparable corporate social media constitute work time, in which data commodities are generated, and potential time for profit realization. The maximum time of a single user that is productive (i.e. results in data commodities) is 100% of the time spent online. The maximum time that the same user contributes to profit realization by clicking on ads or viewing ads is the time that s/he spends on a specific platform. In practice, users only click on a small share of presented ads. So in the pay-per-click accumulation model, work time tends to be much larger than profit realization time. A lot of commodities that are offered for sale are created by online labour; only a certain share of it is sold and results in profits. This share is still large enough for companies like Google and Facebook to be able to generate significant profits. Online labour time is at the same time potential profit realization time. Capital tries to increase profit realization time in order to accumulate capital, i.e. to make an ever-larger share of productive labour time also profit realization time.

The Law of Value on Social Media

Marx formulated the law of value as saying that "the greater the labour-time necessary to produce an article, [. . .] the greater its value" (Marx 1867, 131). It also applies in the case of commercial social media: the more time a user spends on commercial social media, the more data about her/his interests and activities are available and the more advertisements are presented to him/her. Users spending a lot of time online create more data and more value (work time) that is potentially transformed into profit.

Time dimensions play a crucial role in determining the price of an ad: the number of times people click on an ad, the number of times an ad or target URL has already been viewed, the number of times a keyword has been entered, the time that a specific user group spends on the platform. Furthermore, the bidding maximums used as well as the number of ad clients competing for ad space influence the ad prices. In the pay-per-view method, Facebook and Google earn more with an ad that is targeted at a group that spends a lot of time on Facebook. The larger the target group, the higher Facebook's and Google's profits tend to be. In the pay-per-click method, Facebook and Google only earn money if users click on an ad. According to studies, the average click-through-rate is 0.1%.[4] This means that Facebook and Google tend to gain more profit if ads are presented to more users.

Generally, we can say that the higher the total attention time given to ads, the higher Google's and Facebook's profits tend to be. Attention time is determined by the size of a target group and the average time this group spends on the platforms. Online time on corporate social media is both labour time and attention time: all activities are monitored and result in data commodities, so users produce commodities online during their online time. In the pay-per-view mode, specific online time of specifically targeted groups is also attention time that realizes profit for Facebook or Google. In the pay-per-click mode, attention time that realizes profit is only the portion of the online time that users devote to clicking on ads that are presented to them. In both cases, online time is crucial for (a) the production of data commodities, and (b) the realization of profit derived from the sales of the data commodities. Both surveillance of online time (in the sphere of production) and attention time (in sphere of circulation) given to advertisements play an important role in corporate social media's capital accumulation model.

According to Google Trends, Michael Jackson was among the top trending search keywords on Google on June 27, 2012. Using the Google AdWords traffic estimator (on June 27, 2012) showed that by creating a campaign with a maximum CPC of €10 and a budget of €1000 per day, one can expect to attract 2867–3504 impressions and 112–137 clicks for total costs of €900–1100 per day if one targets Google users who search for "Michael Jackson". In comparison, I used the same settings for the keywords "Cat Power", an indie rock singer whose music I like and who is definitely much less popular than Michael Jackson. In a campaign that targets users who google "Cat Power", one can expect to attract 108–132 impressions and 3.9–4.7 clicks for total costs of €30.96–37.84 per day. The profit that Google makes with the data commodity associated with the keywords "Michael Jackson" is much larger than the one it makes with the keywords "Cat Power" because the first is more sought-after. And that a keyword is popular means that users spend more collective usage time per day entering the keyword and reading its result pages than for other keywords. The example shows that popular interests, for whose generation and result consumption users spend more labour time on the Internet than for not-so-popular keywords, tend to result in higher profits for Google than interests that are not so popular.

Possible Breakdown and Alternatives

That surplus value generating labour is an emergent property of capitalist production means that production and accumulation will break down if this labour is withdrawn. It is an essential part of the capitalist production process. That prosumers conduct surplus-generating labour can also be seen by imagining

---

4 Comscore. 2012. *The power of Like²: How social marketing works.* White Paper. www.comscore.com/ger/Press_Events/Presentations_Whitepapers/2012/The_Power_of_Like_2-How_Social_Marketing_Works, accessed on June 27, 2012.

what would happen if they stopped using Facebook: the number of users would drop, advertisers would stop investments because there are no objects for their advertising messages and therefore no potential customers for their products, the profits of the new media corporations would drop, and they would go bankrupt. If such activities were carried out on a large scale, a new economy crisis would arise. This thought experiment shows that users are essential for generating profit in the new media economy. Furthermore, they produce and co-produce parts of the products, and therefore parts of the use value, value, and surplus value that are objectified in these products.

Not all prosumer work on social media is commodified (just like not all audience work is commodified). Work that contributes content, attention or comments to non-commercial non-profit projects (such as Wikipedia or alternative online news media, such as Indymedia, Alternet, Democracy Now!, openDemocracy, WikiLeaks, or the use of social media by non-governmental organizations (NGOs)) is work in the sense that it helps to create use values (alternative news, critical discourse, etc.), but it is non-commodified work – it cannot be exploited, does not have exchange value and does not yield profit. Such projects are an expression of the struggle for a society and an Internet that is not ruled by the logic of commodities and exchange value. Although they are precarious, the existence of alternatives shows that social media and media in general are, in capitalism, shaped by (a) class structures, (b) ideological "incorporation and legitimation" and (c) "gaps and contradictions" that constitute "cracks and fissures" that allow "currents of criticism and movements of contestation" (Golding and Murdock 1978, 353). The question of the alternatives will be discussed in more detail in Chapters 9 and 10.

5.4. Free Labour and Slave Labour

The Social Factory

Unpaid Internet prosumer labour is a new form of labour that is connected to other forms of exploited labour (for foundations of a critical theory of digital labour see my book *Karl Marx and digital labour*, Fuchs 2014). The emergence of "playbour" does not replace Fordist and industrial forms of work that are based on the separation of labour time and reproductive spare time. It is a new quality of the organization of work that is connected to the rising importance of knowledge and creative work and the attempts of capital to overcome crises by reorganizing work.

In playbour, surveillance as a coercive means of work control is to a certain degree substituted or complemented by ideological forms of control, in which workers monitor and maximize their own performance or monitor themselves mutually. Surveillance thereby becomes transformed into control of the self. Playbour is an actual control strategy of humans that aims at enhancing productivity and capital accumulation. At the same time, it is an ideology that postulates (e.g. in management ideology, public debates, etc.) the democratization of work and thereby wants to create the illusionary impression that we have entered an age without alienation or exploitation.

The factory is the space for the production of economic value. Italian theorists such as Mario Tronti and Toni Negri have argued that, especially since the capitalist crisis in the 1970s, the production of value has diffused from the factory as a space for the organization of wage labour into the broader realm of society. The contemporary globalization of capitalism has dispersed the walls of the wage labour factory all over the globe. Due to the circumstance that capital cannot exist without non-wage labour and exploits the commons that are created by all, society has become a factory. Different forms of unpaid and low-paid work would be at the heart of what Autonomists call the social worker, who works in the social factory: "all of society lives as a function of the factory and the factory extends its exclusive domination over all of society" (Tronti, in Cleaver 1992, 137). Nick Dyer-Witheford (2010, 485) says that the rise of the social workers has resulted in the emergence of the "factory planet" – the factory as locus for the production of value and commodities is everywhere, commodification has become universal and total. The boundaries of the factory have enlarged from the wage labour place into society and thereby exploitation has become more global and more pervasive.

The factory is an inherent creation of capitalism. It is the space where the exploitation of labour and the creation of value take place. The factory is not static, but develops and changes its organizational forms along with the historical trajectory of capitalism. This means that there is not one type of factory in a historical period of capitalism, but there are different types of factories that are all connected to each other and are necessary organizational forms of capital accumulation. In contemporary capitalism, we find, for example, the blue-collar/white-collar factories, the Internet factory, the sweatshop factory, the domestic factory (household), etc.

The Social Factory Online

Social media and the mobile Internet make the audience commodity ubiquitous, and the factory is not limited to your living room and your wage workplace – the factory and workplace surveillance are also in all in-between spaces. The entire planet is today a capitalist factory. Internet user commodification is part of the tendency of the commodification of everything that has resulted in the generalization of the factory and of exploitation. Neoliberal capitalism has largely widened the boundaries of what is treated as a commodity.

Internet labour and its surveillance are based on the surveillance, blood and sweat of super-exploited labour in developing countries. Alain Lipietz (1995) has, in this context, spoken of the emergence of "bloody Taylorism" as a contemporary accumulation regime that is coupled with two other accumulation regimes (peripheral Fordism, post-Fordism). Bloody Taylorism is based on the "delocalization of certain limited Taylorist industrial activities towards social formations with very high rates of exploitation" (Lipietz 1995, 10). "To the traditional oppression of women, this strategy adds all the modern weapons of anti-labour repression (official unions, absence of civil rights, imprisonment and torture of opponents)"

(Lipietz 1995, 11). Taylorism has not been replaced, we do not live in an age of post-Taylorism; rather, we are experiencing an extension and intensification of Taylorism that is complemented by new ideological forms of workforce control. The emergence of "workplayplaces" is a tendency in contemporary capitalism that interacts with established forms of work, play and toil. The corporate Internet requires for its existence the exploitation of the labour that exists under bloody Taylorist conditions. On top of this foundation, which makes heavy use of traditional workplace surveillance, we find various workplayplaces on the Internet where users work without payment and deterritorialize the boundaries between play and work.

The iSlave behind the iPhone

Students & Scholars Against Corporate Misbehaviour (SACOM)[5] reported that Chinese Foxconn workers who produce iPhones, iPads, iPods, MacBooks and other ICTs are facing the withholding of wages, forced and unpaid overtime, exposure to chemicals, harsh management, low wages, bad work safety conditions, lack of basic facilities, etc. In 2010, 18 Foxconn employees attempted suicide, 14 of them succeeded.[6] SACOM describes Foxconn workers as "iSlave Behind the iPhone".[7] This example shows that the exploitation and surveillance of digital labour, i.e. labour that is needed for capital accumulation with the help of ICTs, is in no way limited to unpaid user labour, but includes various forms of labour – user labour, wage labour in Western companies for the creation of applications, and slave-like labour that creates hardware (and partly software) in developing countries under inhumane conditions (Fuchs 2014, Hong 2011, Qiu 2009, Sandoval 2013, 2014, Zhao 2008).

Surveillance of Foxconn workers is direct, coercive, disciplinary and Taylorist. "Foxconn's stringent military-like culture is one of surveillance, obedience and not challenging authority. Workers are told obey or leave".[8] "Supervisors yell at workers with foul language. Workers experience pressure and humiliation. Workers are warned that they may be replaced by robots if they are not efficient enough. Apart from scolding by frontline supervisors, other forms of punishment include being required to write confession letters and copying the CEO's quotations. A majority of workers have to stand for ten hours during work shifts. There is no recess as promised by Foxconn. Some workers suffer from leg cramps after work. Workers have extra workloads or have to skip the second meal break under the arrangement of 'continuous shifts'. [. . .] At the entrance of each building, there is a worker station to check the identities of the workers".[9]

---

5 Students & Scholars Against Corporate Misbehaviour (SACOM), iSlave Behind the iPhone: Foxconn Workers in Central China. http://sacom.hk/wp-content/uploads/2011/09/20110924-islave-behind-the-iphone.pdf, accessed on July 3, 2013.
6 http://en.wikipedia.org/wiki/Foxconn_suicides, accessed on April 16, 2013.
7 Ibid.
8 CNN Online, Apple Manufacturing Plant Workers Complain of Long Hours, Militant Culture. http://edition.cnn.com/2012/02/06/world/asia/china-apple-foxconn-worker/index.html, accessed on July 3, 2013.
9 SACOM, op cit.

The Joy of the Phone and Computer in the West is the Blood and Sweat of Africans and Asians

iPhones, iPads, iMacs, Nokia phones etc. are also "blood phones" and "blood pads", and "blood Macs" in another sense: many smartphones, laptops, digital cameras, mp3 players, etc. are made out of minerals (e.g. cassiterite, wolframite, coltan, gold, tungsten, tantalum, tin) that are extracted from mines in the Democratic Republic of Congo and other countries under slave-like conditions (Fuchs 2014, chapter 6). Delly Mawazo Sesete describes the production conditions:

> These minerals are part of *your* daily life. They keep your computer running so you can surf the internet. [. . .] While minerals from the Congo have enriched your life, they have often brought violence, rape and instability to my home country. That's because those armed groups fighting for control of these mineral resources use murder, extortion and mass rape as a deliberate strategy to intimidate and control local populations, which helps them secure control of mines, trading routes and other strategic areas. Living in the Congo, I saw many of these atrocities firsthand. I documented the child slaves who are forced to work in the mines in dangerous conditions. I witnessed the deadly chemicals dumped into the local environment. I saw the use of rape as a weapon. [. . .] That's why I'm asking Apple to make an iPhone made with conflict-free minerals from the Congo by this time next year.[10]

The Knowledge Labour Aristocracy

A software engineer at Google earns on average US$103 348 a year,[11] a software engineer at Facebook on average US$111 428.[12] They are highly paid and relatively wealthy, although, just like all workers, exploited. The mean average wage of software developers in the USA was $92 080 in May 2011, the mean average wage of telephone operators in call centres was $28 600.[13] Both types of activities fall under the broad category of knowledge work that is separated by internal class divisions.

The knowledge labour aristocracy derives wage benefits at the expense of other workers. On the one side there are precarious proletarianized knowledge workers, and on the other side a well-paid labour aristocracy that forms a "salaried bourgeoisie": the "members of the new bourgeoisie get wages, and even if they own part of their company, earn stocks as part of their remuneration ('bonuses' for their 'success'). This new bourgeoisie still appropriates surplus value, but in the (mystified) form of what has been called 'surplus wage': they are paid rather more than the proletarian 'minimum wage' (an often mythic point

10 Guardian Online, Apple: Time to Make a Conflict-Free iPhone. www.guardian.co.uk/commentisfree/cifamerica/2011/dec/30/apple-time-make-conflict-free-iphone, accessed on July 3, 2013.
11 www.glassdoor.com/Salary/Google-Salaries-E9079.htm, accessed on April 17, 2012.
12 www.glassdoor.com/Salary/Facebook-Salaries-E40772.htm, accessed on April 17, 2012.
13 Bureau of Labor Statistics, Occupational Employment Statistics. www.bls.gov/oes/, accessed on July 3, 2013.

of reference whose only real example in today's global economy is the wage of a sweatshop worker in China or Indonesia), and it is this distinction from common proletarians which determines their status" (Žižek 2012a).

The Internet as Global Division of Labour

The existence of the Internet in its current dominant capitalist form is based on various forms of labour: the relatively highly-paid wage work of software engineers and low-paid proletarianized workers in Internet companies, the unpaid labour of users, the highly exploited bloody Taylorist work, highly toxic e-waste labour that disassembles ICTs and slave work in developing countries producing hardware and extracting "conflict minerals" (Fuchs 2014). There is a class conflict between capital and labour that is constituted through exploitation.

The rate of exploitation is varied depending on the type and location of activity. In the case of the salaried knowledge worker bourgeoisie, capital pays relatively high wages in order to try to gain their hegemonic consensus, whereas low-paid knowledge workers, users, hardware and software producers and mineral extractors in developing countries are facing precarious work conditions and varying degrees and forms of slavery and exploitation that, as a whole, help advancing the profits of capital by minimizing the wage costs. Free-labouring Internet users and the workers in conflict mines have in common that they are unpaid. The difference is that the former gain pleasure through their exploitation, whereas the latter suffer pain and die through their exploitation which enables the pleasure of the former. The main benefit from this situation is monetary and goes to companies like Google, Apple and Facebook that are the contemporary slaveholders and slave masters.

Different forms of control are needed for exploiting digital labour. Self-control and playbour that feel like fun but create parts of the value constitute only one part of the labour process that has its foundation in a racist mode of production and exploitation of workers in developing countries. The exploitation of play workers in the West is based on the pain, sweat, blood and death of workers in developing countries. The corporate Internet needs for its existence both playbour and toil, fun and misery, biopolitical power and disciplinary power, self-control and surveillance. The example of the Foxconn factories and Congolese conflict minerals shows that the exploitation of Internet playbour needs as a precondition, and is coupled with, the bloody Taylorist exploitation of workers in the developing world.

5.5. Conclusion

The main results of this chapter can be summarized as follows:

- Contemporary social media are not participatory: large companies that centralize attention and visibility and marginalize politics, especially alternative politics, dominate them.
- Management gurus, marketing strategies and uncritical academics celebrate the democratic potentials of social media and neglect aspects of

capitalism. Their assumptions are ideologies that reinforce capitalist domination.

- Corporate social media use capital accumulation models that are based on the exploitation of the unpaid labour of Internet users and on the commodification of user-generated data and data about user behaviour that is sold as commodity to advertisers. Targeted advertising and economic surveillance are important aspects of this accumulation model. The category of the audience commodity becomes, in the realm of social media, transmogrified into the category of the Internet prosumer commodity.

- The exploitation of the Internet prosumer commodity is an expression for a stage of capitalism in which the boundaries between play and labour have become fuzzy and the exploitation of play labour has become a new principle. Exploitation tends to feel like fun and becomes part of free time.

- The existence of digital media is based on various forms of labour and different degrees of the exploited: the salaried bourgeoisie of highly-paid workers in Internet companies, low-paid precarious knowledge workers, unpaid Internet users, highly exploited workers in developing countries, and slave workers extracting minerals that are used as raw materials.

- Commercial social media are spheres of the exploitation of user play labour and at the same time objects of ideological mystifications that idealize social media in order to detract attention from their class character or advance the attraction of investors and the creation and expansion of spheres of capital accumulation. Commercial social media show that exploitation/capital accumulation and ideology are two important and entangled dimensions of the media in capitalism (Golding and Murdock 1978).

RECOMMENDED READINGS AND EXERCISES

The political economy of social media can best be approached by reading and discussing classical and newer texts that focus on aspects of labour and activity in the context of audiences and users. The recommended readings focus on the so-called Blindspot Debate, a classical foundational debate in Media and Communication Studies. It is a debate on the digital labour theory of value between Adam Arvidsson and I as well as four different positions on how to assess YouTube.

The Blindspot Debate

Smythe, Dallas W. 1977. Communications: Blindspot of Western Marxism. *Canadian Journal of Political and Social Theory* 1 (3): 1–27.

Smythe, Dallas W. 1981/2006. On the audience commodity and its work. In *Media and cultural studies*, ed. Meenakshi G. Durham and Douglas M. Kellner, 230–256. Malden, MA: Blackwell.

Murdock, Graham. 1978. Blindspots about Western Marxism: A reply to Dallas Smythe. In *The political economy of the media I*, ed. Peter Golding and Graham Murdock, 465–474. Cheltenham: Edward Elgar.

In 1977, Dallas Smythe published his seminal article "Communications: Blindspot of Western Marxism" (Smythe 1977), in which he argued that Western Marxism has not given enough attention to the complex role of communications in capitalism. The article's publication was followed by an important foundational debate of media sociology that came to be known as *the Blindspot Debate* (Murdock 1978; Livant 1979; Smythe answered with a rejoinder to Murdock: Smythe 1994, 292–299) and by another article of Smythe on the same topic, *On the Audience Commodity and its Work* (Smythe 1981, 22–51).

Ask yourself:

- What are Dallas Smythe's main arguments?

- What are Graham Murdock's main points of criticism?

- There are different types of media commodities. Think about different for-profit media and the way they make money. What is their commodity? Try to construct a complete and systematic typology of media commodities.

- How does the commodity in the case of corporate social media differ from other media commodities?

The Social Media Value Debate

Fuchs, Christian. 2010b. Labor in informational capitalism and on the Internet. *The Information Society* 26 (3): 179–196.

Arvidsson, Adam and Elanor Colleoni. 2012. Value in informational capitalism and on the Internet. *The Information Society* 28 (3): 135–150.

Fuchs, Christian. 2012. With or without Marx? With or without capitalism? A rejoinder to Adam Arvidsson and Eleanor Colleoni. *tripleC: Communication, Capitalism & Critique: Journal for a Global Sustainable Information Society* 10 (2): 633–645.

In 2010, I published an article about the relevance of Marx, his value and labour concepts for understanding social media. I presented excerpts from the article at the conference *The Internet as Playground and Factory* (New School, November 12–14, 2009, www.digitallabor.org). Conference organizer Trebor Scholz conveyed a pre-conference discussion on the mailing list of the Institute for Distributed Creativity (IDC). Adam Arvidsson, in this discussion, first formulated criticism of my insistence on the importance of Marx for understanding value creation on social media. Three years later he published this criticism in an article co-authored with Eleanor Colleoni. Arvidsson and Colleoni argue that the law of value no longer exists and cannot be applied online. I responded to their claims in another article.

Ask yourself:

- What is the law of value?

- Summarize Fuchs' arguments on why the law of value is applicable to social media.

- Summarize Arvidsson and Colleoni's arguments on why the law of value is not applicable to social media. Discuss the differences between the two approaches.

- The law of value has to do with labour time. Discuss what roles time plays on social media and what the differences are if one spends little or a lot of time on social media. Is time a fundamental determinant of the profits that social media companies make or not? Why? Why not? What is the role of reputation and emotions for the generation of profit on social media?

Andrejevic, Mark. 2009. Exploiting YouTube: Contradictions of user-generated labor. In *The YouTube reader*, ed. Pelle Snickars and Patrick Vonderau, 406–423. Stockholm: National Library of Sweden.

Miller, Toby. 2009. Cybertarians of the world unite: You have nothing to lose but your tubes! In *The YouTube reader*, ed. Pelle Snickars and Patrick Vonderau, 424–440. Stockholm: National Library of Sweden.

Gauntlett, David. 2011. *Making is connecting: The social meaning of creativity, from DIY and knitting to YouTube and Web 2.0.* Cambridge: Polity Press. Chapter 8: Web 2.0 not all rosy?

Jenkins, Henry, Sam Ford and Joshua Green. 2013. *Spreadable media: Creating value and meaning in a networked culture.* New York: New York University Press. Chapter 1: Where web 2.0 went wrong + pp. 125–128 (Audiences as commodity and labour).

These four contributions to discussions about social media present different interventions in the digital labour debate and partly refer to each other. They are written by four important scholars who study contemporary media and whose approaches to certain degrees overlap and diverge: Mark Andrejevic, David Gauntlett, Henry Jenkins and Toby Miller.

Work in groups and present your results:

- Summarize the basic arguments of each contribution.
- Compare the four contributions to each other. What are the commonalities and differences?
- What are the crucial points of difference between the authors? How do you individually think about these differences? Try to justify your opinion with theoretical arguments, statistics, concrete examples and political reasoning.

Google: Good or Evil
Search Engine?

Key questions

- How does Google's political economy work?
- How has Google been criticized?
- What ideologies exist about Google? How does Google see itself and how does it want to be seen by others? What is the reality behind Google-ideologies?

Key concepts

Digital labour
Surveillance
Ideology
Googology (Google ideology)
New spirit of capitalism
Biopolitical exploitation
Internet solutionism
Internet fetishism
Technological online rationality
Rational discrimination

Cumulative disadvantage
Moral panics
Privacy policy
Targeted advertising
Sensitive personal data
Terms of use
Play labour (playbour)
Antagonism between the productive
    forces and the relations of
    production

Overview

In the early days of the World Wide Web, there were many search engines that users employed for navigating the web. Some of them featured text-based searches. Others were ordered directories. Examples were Altavista, Excite, Infoseek, Lycos, Magellan, Yahoo. At the end of the second millennium, Google's search engine emerged. It uses an algorithm called PageRank that orders the results of a search based on how many links lead to each result page. It uses auto-mated software agents that crawl the WWW and count links to specific sites and analyze their results. Over the years, Google has become the dominant search engine in the world. Google's search is based on a single box as user interface, which makes a search intuitive and easy for most users.

This chapter analyzes Google's power, its advantages and disadvantages. A critical analysis of Google goes beyond moral condemnation or moral celebra-tion, but rather tries to understand the conditions and contradictions that shape the existence of Google and its users. This chapter therefore also wants to make a contribution to contextualizing normative questions about Google in the politi-cal economy of contemporary society. First, an introduction is given (in section 6.1). In section 6.2, I analyze Google's capital accumulation model. In section 6.3, I discuss the ideological implications of Google. Section 6.4 analyzes the working conditions at Google. Section 6.5 discusses the good and bad sides of Google, and I draw some conclusions in section 6.6.

6.1. Introduction

The Ubiquity of Google

Tim O'Reilly (2005a) argues that Google is "the standard bearer" for web 2.0 and social media because it is not sold in different versions as traditional software products, but is "delivered as a service" with "continuous improvement" and "context-sensitive" advertising. Google is one of the world's most accessed web platforms: 45.8% of worldwide Internet users accessed Google in a three-month period in 2012–2013 (data source: alexa.com, March 2, 2013).

Google has become ubiquitous in everyday life – it is shaping how we search, organize and perceive information in contexts like the workplace, private life, culture, politics, the household, shopping and consumption, entertainment, sports, etc. The phrase "to google" has even found its way into the vocabulary of some languages. *The Oxford English Dictionary* defines "to google" as "search for information about (someone or something) on the Internet, typically using the search engine Google" and remarks that the word's origin is "the proprietary name of a popular Internet search engine"[1].

Table 6.1   Google's ranking in the list of the largest public companies in the world

2005	2006	2007	2008	2009	2010	2011	2012
904	439	289	213	155	120	120	103

Data source: Forbes Global 2000, various years; the ranking is based on a composite index of profits, sales, assets and market value.

---

1 http://oxforddictionaries.com/view/entry/m_en_gb0342960#m_en_gb0342960, accessed on March 15, 2013.

6.2. Google's Political Economy

Google's Economic Power

Google, which was founded in 1998 by Larry Page and Sergey Brin, was transformed into a public company on August 19, 2004 (Vise 2005, 4). Google acquired the video-sharing platform YouTube for US$1.65 billion in 2006 and the online advertising service company DoubleClick for US$3.1 billion in 2008 (Stross 2008, 2).

In 2012, Google was, after IBM, the second largest computer service company in the world (Forbes Global 2000, 2012 list). In the list of the world's largest companies, Google has rapidly increased its ranking (Table 6.1). Profits in 2012 hit a record for Google: they reached US$10.79 billion (Google SEC Filings, Annual Report 2012), the largest amount since the company's creation in 1998. Since 2004, Google's annual profits have rapidly increased (see Figure 6.1).

Google and the Capitalist Crisis

In 2008, the year that a new world economic crisis hit capitalism, Google's market value dropped from US$147.66 billion (2007) to US$106.69 billion (data source: Forbes Global 2000, lists for the years 2007 and 2008). Google's profits remained constant in this period of world economic crisis (2007: $4.2 billion, 2008: $4.23 billion, Forbes Global 2000, lists for the years 2007 and 2008). In 2009, Google's market value increased to $169.38 billion (data source: Forbes Global 2000, year 2009). Google's profits reached a new all-time high of $6.52 billion in 2009 and skyrocketed to $8.5 billion in 2010, $9.75 billion in 2011 and $10.79 billion in

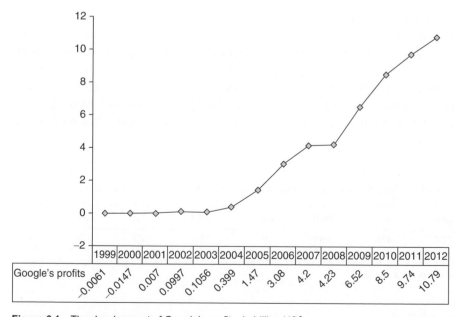

Figure 6.1   The development of Google's profits, in billion US$

Data source: SEC-filings, from 10-k, various years.

2012 (data source: Google SEC Filings, annual reports various years). So Google's profits were not harmed by the economic crisis that started in 2008. The company stabilized its profits in 2008 in comparison to 2007, achieved a 54% growth of its profits in 2009, 30.4% in 2010, 14.7% in 2011 and 10.7% in 2012.

An economic crisis results in the shrinking of the profits of many companies, which can have negative influences on advertising markets because companies with declining profits have less money to spend for marketing purposes. As a result, many advertising-financed media companies' profits declined in the financial years 2008 and 2009 (Fuchs 2011b, chapter 6). Google may have benefited from the crisis because at such times "advertisers are more concerned about the costs and direct results of their advertising campaigns" and Google offers good ways of "controlling and measuring [. . .] campaign's effectiveness" (Girard 2009, 215). In non-marketing research language, this means that Google provides a form of advertising that is based on the close surveillance of users. Google advertising clients know a lot about who clicks when on their ads. Surveillance makes Google advertising predictable. Capitalist companies seek to control unpredictability of investments, especially in times of crisis, and therefore welcome Google advertising because it is based on a form of economic user surveillance.

The Wealth and Power of Google's Owners

Ken Auletta (2010, 19) claims in his book *Googled* that Google is an egalitarian company and that Brin, Page and Schmidt have modest salaries. Can one speak of economic modesty if four persons control more than 70% of a corporation's voting power and more than 90% of its common stock (Table 6.3)? Page, Brin and Schmidt increased their personal wealth by a factor of five in the years 2004–2012

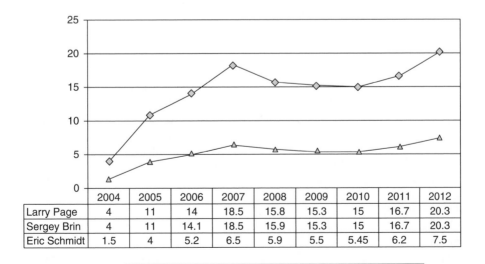

	2004	2005	2006	2007	2008	2009	2010	2011	2012
Larry Page	4	11	14	18.5	15.8	15.3	15	16.7	20.3
Sergey Brin	4	11	14.1	18.5	15.9	15.3	15	16.7	20.3
Eric Schmidt	1.5	4	5.2	6.5	5.9	5.5	5.45	6.2	7.5

—◇— Larry Page   —◇— Sergey Brin   —△— Eric Schmidt

Figure 6.2 Development of the wealth of Google's three richest directors, in billion US$

Data source: Forbes 400 List of the Richest Americans.

Table 6.2   Development of the ranking of Google's three richest directors in the list of the 300 richest Americans

	2004	2005	2006	2007	2008	2009	2010	2011	2012
Larry Page	43	16	13	5	14	11	11	15	13
Sergey Brin	43	16	12	5	13	11	11	15	13
Eric Schmidt	165	52	51	48	59	40	48	50	45

Data source: Forbes 400 List of the Richest Americans.

(Figure 6.2). They are among the richest Americans. Google is not more or less "evil" than any other capitalist company (Table 6.2). It is an ordinary capitalist company that accumulates profit and, as a result, the personal wealth of a few also grows because of the exploitation of many.

In 2012, four members of Google's board of directors (Larry Page, Sergey Brin, Eric Schmidt and L. John Doerr) owned 94.0% of Google's class B common stock and controlled 67.5% of the total voting power (see Table 6.3). In comparison, Google's 54 000 employees have almost no ownership or voting power share (the share of stock options and voting power can only be small if more than 90% and 70% respectively is owned/controlled by a power elite consisting of four persons) and Google's 1.1 billion users have no ownership or voting power share. Google's users and employees produce its surplus value and have made it into the powerful company that it is today. The people using Google or working for Google are permanently exploited and dispossessed of the profit that they create. The contemporary proletariat does not so much work at conveyor belts in industrial firms. To a certain degree it creates surplus value for Google (and other social media companies) by using and producing its services. The factory is today not only in spaces of waged employment, but also in the living room, the bedroom, the kitchen and public spaces – the factory is everywhere.

Table 6.3   Stock ownership shares and voting power shares at Google, 2012

Name	Role	Ownership share of Google's class B common stock	Share of total voting power
Larry Page	CEO, Director	39.6%	28.4%
Sergey Brin	Co-Founder, Director	39.0%	28.0%
Eric Schmidt	Executive Chairman	13.2%	9.5%
L. John Doerr	Director	2.2%	1.6%
53 861 employees (December 2012)	Surplus value production		
1.1 billion users (March 2013)	Surplus value production		
Total		94.0%	67.5%

Data sources: Google financial data: Google Proxy Statement 2012; employees: SEC FORM 10-K year 2012; worldwide Internet users: internetworldstats.com, accessed March 2, 2013; share of Google users in worldwide Internet users: alexa.com, top sites, accessed March 2, 2013.

How Google Accumulates Capital

These data show that Google is one of the most profitable media companies in the world. But how exactly does it achieve this profit? How does it accumulate capital? Answering this question requires a political economy analysis of Google's capital accumulation cycle.

Some existing analyses of Google stand in the political economy tradition.[2] In section 5.3 of this book, I introduced, based on Dallas Smythe's (1981/2006) concept of the audience commodity, the notion of Internet prosumer commodification for analyzing the political economy of social media. Google relates to Internet prosumer commodification in two ways. On the one hand, it indexes user-generated content that is uploaded to the web and thereby acts as a meta-exploiter of all user-generated content producers. Without user-generated content by unpaid users, Google could not perform keyword searches. Therefore Google exploits all users who create World Wide Web (WWW) content. On the other hand, users employ Google services and thereby conduct unpaid productive surplus-value generating labour.

Such labour includes, for example, searching for a keyword on Google's search portal, maintaining a social network on Google+, searching for a keyword on Google, sending an email via GMail, uploading or searching for a video on YouTube, searching for a book on Google Print, looking for a location on Google Maps or Google Earths, creating a document on GoogleDocs, maintaining or reading a blog on Blogger/Blogspot, uploading images to Picassa, translating a sentence with Google Translate, etc.

Google generates and stores data about the usage of these services in order to enable targeted advertising. It sells these data to advertising clients, who then provide advertisements that are targeted to the activities, searches, contents and interests of the users of Google services. Google engages in the economic surveillance of user data and user activities, thereby commodifing and infinitely exploiting users, and selling users and their data as Internet prosumer commodity to advertising clients in order to generate money profit. Google is the ultimate economic surveillance machine and the ultimate user-exploitation machine. It instrumentalizes all users and all of their data for creating profit.

Google does not pay for the circumstance that it uses web content as a resource, although results are provided to users when they search for keywords so that data about user interests are generated that are sold to advertising clients. Google benefits monetarily from the expansion of the web and user-generated content. The more websites and content there are on the WWW, the more content and pages Google can index in order to provide search results. The more and the better search results there are, the more likely users are to use Google and to be confronted with advertisements that match their searches, on which they might click.

The more users of Google's services there are, the more data about the services' users is stored and assessed. Google sells advertisements that match search

2 See, for example, Bermejo 2009; Jakobsson and Stiernstedt 2010; Kang and McAllister 2011; Lee 2011; Pasquinelli 2009; Petersen 2008; Vaidhyanathan 2011; Wasko and Erickson 2009.

keywords to ad clients that bid for advertising positions (Google AdWords). There are auctions for ad space connected to certain keywords and screen locations. Google sets the minimum bids. Ads that are clicked more frequently are displayed at a better position on the Google result pages (Girard 2009, 31). Users who conduct searches containing specific keywords are targeted by specific advertisements. Google AdSense enables website operators to include Google adverts on their websites and to achieve revenue for each click on an advertisement. Google shares parts of the ad revenue with the website operators that participate in the AdSense programme. Advertisements can be presented in a targeted way to specific groups of users. For doing so, Google collects a lot of information about users. It engages in user surveillance. It is important to study what kind of data about users Google collects, monitors and commodifies.

Google as a Surveillance Machine

Surveillance of user data is an important part of Google's operations. It is, however, subsumed under Google's political economy, i.e. Google engages in user surveillance for the end of capital accumulation. Google surveillance is therefore primarily a form of economic surveillance.

Google uses a powerful search algorithm. The details of the PageRank algorithm are secret. Basically small, automated programmes (web spiders) search the WWW, the algorithm analyzes all found pages, counts the number of links to each page, identifies keywords for each page, and ranks its importance. The results can be used for free via the easy user interface that Google provides. Google develops ever-newer services that are again offered for free. The PageRank algorithm is a form of surveillance that searches, assesses and indexes the WWW.

6.3. Googology: Google and Ideology

The Ideology of the 20% Rule

Googleplex, which is located in Mountain View, California, includes services for child care, personal trainers, hairdressers, bike repair, car wash, oil change as well as a laundry, restaurants, cafeterias, bars, sports halls, gyms, swimming halls, volleyball courts, etc. (Stross 2008, 13). Google adopted a work time regulation introduced by the 3M company: a certain share of the work time of the employees can be used for self-defined projects. Google uses the 20% rule: "We offer our engineers '20-percent time' so that they're free to work on what they're really passionate about. Google Suggest, AdSense for Content, and Orkut are among the many products of this perk".[3]

This statement is a contradiction in terms: on the one hand, Google says that its employees are "free to work on what they're passionate about"; on the other hand, the company seems to expect that the outcome of this work should be new

---

3 www.google.com/jobs/lifeatgoogle/englife/index.html, accessed on October 27, 2011.

services owned and operated and thereby monetized by Google. Would Google also grant its employees work time for engaging in building an anti-capitalist new media union or for writing and publishing an anti-Google manifesto? There seems to be "a lot of internal pressure to demonstrate progress with their personal projects, and employees that show little progress are seen as perhaps not being up to the Google standard" (Girard 2009, 67).

Gilles Deleuze (1995) has described the emergence of a society of control, in which individuals discipline themselves. He compared the individual in disciplinary society to a mole and the individual in the society of control to a serpent. The mole as a symbol of disciplinary society is faceless and dumb and monotonously digs his burrows; the snake is flexible and pluralistic. The Google worker is a serpent: s/he flexibly switches between different activities (leisure, work) so that the distinction between leisure and work, play and labour, collapses. Being employed by Google means having to engage in Google labour life and Google play life – Google employees are exploited playbourers. At Google, it becomes difficult to distinguish play and work.

Luc Boltanski and Éve Chiapello (2005) argue that the rise of participatory management means the emergence of a new spirit of capitalism that subsumes the values of the political revolt of 1968 and the subsequently emerging New Left, such as autonomy, spontaneity, mobility, creativity, networking, visions, openness, plurality, informality, authenticity, emancipation, and so on, under capital. The topics of the movement would now be put into the service of those forces that it wanted to destroy.

Google's management strategy is, on the one hand, based on the expectation that an integration of work time and free time in one space and the creation of happiness and fun inside the company make Google employees work longer and more efficiently. At Google, the boundaries between work time and playtime are fuzzy – the exploitation of Google workers is, as a tendency, the exploitation of play labour. Google play labour aims at what Marx (1867, chapter 16) termed (a) absolute surplus value production and (b) relative surplus value production: the production of more surplus value by (a) increasing the total labour time, (b) increasing the efficiency (output per unit of time) of production. On the other hand, Google's management strategy assumes that a relative freedom of action (the 20% policy) can generate new technologies that can be monetized and that this policy makes the workers happy so that they work more efficiently.

Biopolitical Exploitation

Google's Eric Schmidt dreams of storing "all of your information" so that "we would know enough about you to give you targeted information, the targeted news, the targeted advertising, to make instantaneous, and seamless, happen". He calls this "transparent personalization".[4] Google co-founder Sergey Brin

---

4 www.google.com/press/podium/ana.html, accessed on March 14, 2013.

suggested a Google Artificial Intelligence dimension, in which brains are "augmented by Google. For example you think about something and your cell phone could whisper the answer into your ear" (Sergey Brin, cited in Carr 2009, 213). As Brin says: "Perhaps in the future, we can attach a little version of Google that you just plug into your brain" (Sergey Brin, cited in Vise 2005, 292). Google wired with all human brains would be the ultimate form of constant biopolitical exploitation – all human thoughts could be directly transformed into commodities that are sold as data to advertising clients. A perfect dynamic profile of each individual could be created so that not only his/her general interests would be targeted by advertisements, but also commodity advertisements could be served in the second one thinks about a certain circumstance. Targeted advertisements could be directly and continuously transported to human brains.

Google's vision of Artificial Intelligence is constant real-time biopolitical exploitation. Hardt and Negri have argued, based on Foucault, that contemporary capitalism is based on a form of biopower. "Biopower thus refers to a situation in which what is directly at stake in power is the production and reproduction of life itself" (Hardt and Negri 2000, 24). Google, on the one hand, aims to commodify all knowledge on the Internet and to erect a panopticon that surveils all online user activities. It aims at the commodification of users' knowledge, which is an aspect of human subjectivity. On the other hand, Google dreams of the vision that its surveillance reaches directly into the brains of humans in order to monitor all human thoughts. In Google's vision, thinking should be exploited and commodified continuously in real time. Google's vision is one of total surveillance, exploitation and commodification of all human thoughts and activities.

Evgeny Morozov: Internet Solutionism

Google's directors have a vision of making the world completely knowable, controllable and predictable with the help of the Internet. They are proponents of an ideology that Evgeny Morozov (2013, 5) calls "technological solutionism": solutionism is recasting "all complex social situations either as neatly defined problems with definite, computable solutions or as transparent and self-evident processes that can be easily optimized – if only the right algorithms are in place". The consequence of solutionism would be the risk to create "unexpected consequences that could eventually cause more damage than the problems they seek to address". Morozov shows that solutionism is a typical ideology of Silicon Valley entrepreneurs and intellectuals who glorify the Internet as being the solution to societal problems, or what are seen as societal problems and may in fact not be problems at all. Thinkers that Morozov criticizes for being Internet centrists are, on the one hand, the likes of Eric Schmidt (Google) and Mark Zuckerberg (Facebook) and, on the other hand, intellectuals such as Yochai Benkler, Nicholas Carr, Jeff Jarvis, Kevin Kelly, Lawrence Lessig, Clay Shirky, Don Tapscott and Jonathan Zittrain. Internet-centrism and technological solutionism "impoverish and infantilize our public debate" (Morozov 2013, 43).

Ideologies Online: Internet Fetishism and Technological Online Rationality

Internet solutionism assumes that the Internet is the solution to society's problems and can perfect society and get rid of the existence of problems. Karl Marx
(1867) used the term "fetishism" for the logic of assuming that things are more
important than social relations between humans. Internet solutionism is a form
of Internet fetishism: it sees an artefact as a solution to human-made problems.
Max Horkheimer (1947) spoke in this context of instrumental reason and Herbert
Marcuse (1941/1998) of technological rationality: instrumental/technologi-
cal rationality assumes that society functions like machines, fully controllable
and programmable, like an algorithm. Internet fetishism assumes that society is
a machine and functions like the Internet and that the Internet is therefore the
solution for everything in society. Technological rationality wants to implement
"dictates of the apparatus" that use a "framework of standardized performances"
(Marcuse 1941/1998, 44). Google's standardized algorithms tell people what they
should like, defined as reality, where they should go, what they should consider
important, etc. A tool like Google Maps can indeed be helpful for finding your way
around, but it also allows Google (and, as a consequence, potentially also other
companies and the police) to track your movements and to subject movements in
space to the logic of advertising: targeted advertisements follow you wherever you
take your mobile phone and present reality, and what you should eat, drink, watch
and like according to the logic of advertisers: "Expediency in terms of technological
reason is, at the same time, expediency in terms of profitable efficiency" (Marcuse
1941/1998, 47). Marcuse (1941/1988) warned that organizing society according
to technological rationality can result in fascism and said that Nazi Germany was
ruled by "technical considerations of imperialistic efficiency and rationality".

Oscar Gandy: Rational Discrimination and Cumulative Disadvantage

Oscar Gandy (2009) shows that algorithmic prediction and control can easily
result in racist and other forms of discrimination. Discrimination (in law enforcement, marketing, the insurance business, etc.), based on statistics, occurs mainly
not because of individual actions, but "because an individual has been identified
as a member of a group" (Gandy 2009, 57). "Cumulative disadvantage refers to
the ways in which historical disadvantages cumulate over time, and across categories of experience" (Gandy 2009, 12). "People who have bad luck in one area,
are likely to suffer from bad luck in other areas as well" (Gandy 2009, 116). This
means that if by accident you have dark skin, are poor, live in a deprived neigh-
bourhood, have become unemployed or ill, you are more likely to be discriminated against and flagged as a risk group by data mining technologies.

The arbitrary disadvantages an individual has suffered cumulate and result in
further disadvantages that are enforced by predictive algorithms that calculate
that, based on certain previous behaviour, an individual is part of a risk group

and should therefore be discriminated against (by not being offered a service, being offered a lower quality service at a higher price (e.g. in the case of a loan or mortgage), by being considered as a criminal or terrorist, etc.). "Once they have been identified as criminals, or even as potential criminals, poor people, and black people in particular, are systematically barred from the opportunities they might otherwise use to improve their status in life" (Gandy 2009, 141). Data mining can easily intensify disadvantages and inequalities that structurally disadvantaged or racialized groups are facing. Being identified as belonging to a risk group and being therefore discriminated against can also result in a self-fulfilling prophecy and in the very behaviour that was predicted (crime, terrorism, etc.), even though it was not present in the first instance (Gandy 2009, 187).

Internet Fetishism and the Global Crisis

It is no accident that Internet centrism and technological solutionism have become so predominant in the early stage of the third millennium. After 9/11, policing has increasingly looked for security by algorithms in a world of high insecurity. It advances a fetishism of technology – the belief that crime and terrorism can be controlled by technology. Technology promises an easy fix to complex societal problems. 9/11 has resulted in "the misguided and socially disruptive attempts to identify terrorists and then predict their attacks" (Gandy 2009, 5). The world economic crisis that started in 2008 has added additional uncertainties and created a situation of high insecurity. 9/11 was indicative of a crisis of the hegemony of Western thought that was questioned by people and groups in Arab countries that put religious ideology against Western liberal and capitalist ideology. The "war against terror", the security discourse and the intensification of surveillance have resulted in a political crisis in which war and terrorism tend to reinforce each other mutually, which results in a vicious cycle that intensifies hatred and conflict. Financialization and neoliberalism made capitalism more unjust (which constitutes a social crisis) and also crisis-prone, which resulted in a new world economic crisis that started in 2008.

Capitalism faced a multidimensional crisis in and beyond the first decade of the twenty-first century. This crisis has further advanced ideologies of control and technological fixes that advance the ideology of the solvability of societal problems by technologies. Unemployment and lack of jobs? Social media will create them! Economic crisis? Invest in new Internet platforms and everything will be fine! Uprisings, revolutions and riots? All created by social media! It is no accident that ideological discourses like these proliferate in times of crisis: the Internet promises easy solutions to complex societal phenomena and contradictions intrinsic to capitalism, bureaucratic control and resulting inequalities.

Stuart Hall Revisited: The Internet as Ideological Culture of Control

Stuart Hall et al. (1978) describe how a moral panic about street robbery ("mugging") developed in the UK in the 1970s. They argue that this panic must be seen in the context of the crisis of the mid-1970s. This crisis would have been a global crisis of capitalism (recession), a crisis of political apparatuses (such as ruling-class and working-class parties), a crisis of the state, and a crisis of hegemony and political legitimacy (Hall et al. 1978, 317–319). In crises, people look for causes and answers. Ideology that wants to maintain the system does not engage with the systemic causes of crises, but rather displaces the causes ideologically. There is a "displacement effect": "the connection between the crisis and the way it is appropriated in the social experience of the majority – social anxiety – passes through a series of false 'resolutions'" (Hall et al. 1978, 322). Technological solutionism and Internet centrism are contemporary ideological false resolutions in situations of global crisis.

Technological solutionism and Internet/social media fetishism constitute a permanent form of what Hall et al. (1978) called signification spirals. In a signification spiral, a threat is identified and it is argued that "more troubling times" will come "if no action is taken", which results in the "call for 'firm steps'" (Hall et al. 1978, 223). If we do not act and use the latest Internet platform or app, the contemporary ideologues tell us, society cannot be saved and we will become the victims of criminals, terrorists, paedophiles, deviants, extremists and our own non-knowledge that can only be, as they want to tell us, technologically controlled. Today there are many Internet signification spirals, where the Internet is seen as cause of and/or solution to evils in the world.

In a moral panic, a "control culture" (such as police discourses about crime or terrorism) and a "signification culture" (like criminal hyperbole created by tabloid media) often act together (Hall et al. 1978, 76). The media, just like the police, then act as "an apparatus of the control process itself – an 'ideological state apparatus'" (Hall et al. 1978, 76). The Internet, as a relatively new medium of information, communication and collaboration (Fuchs 2008a), is inserted into contemporary moral panics in a different way from the mainstream media that simply tend to act as ideological control institutions. The Internet and social media act as an arena of ideological projections of fears and hopes that are associated with moral panics – some argue that they are dangerous spaces that are used by terrorists, rioters, vandals and criminals and therefore need to be policed with the help of Internet surveillance, whereas others argue that the Internet is a new space of political hope that is at the heart of demonstrations, rebellions, protests and revolutions that struggle for more democracy. What both discourses share is a strong belief in the power of technology, independently of society. They mistake societal phenomena (crime, terror, crises, political transformations) as being caused and controllable by technology. But societal phenomena merely express themselves in communicative and technological spaces; technologies do not cause them. Technological determinism inscribes power into technology; it reduces power to a technologically manageable phenomenon and thereby neglects the interaction of technology and society. The Internet is not like the mainstream mass media an ideological actor, but rather an object of ideological signification in moral panics and moral euphoria.

Google is not just a control machine that aims at controlling people's perception of reality and at transforming these perceptions into profits, it is also a symbol for the fetishism of control and technological determinism that have, as ideologies, accompanied the crisis-ridden first years of the third millennium.

The Ideology of Google's Privacy Policy

Google is a legally registered company with headquarters in Mountain View, California, United States. Its privacy policy is a typical expression of a self-regulatory privacy ideology, in which businesses can largely define themselves according to how they process personal user data. Privacy self-regulation by businesses is voluntary, therefore the number of organizations engaging in it tends to be very small (Bennett and Raab 2006, 171): "Self-regulation will always suffer from the perception that it is more symbolic than real because those who are responsible for implementation are those who have a vested interest in the processing of personal data". Google's terms of service and privacy policy are the legal foundations of economic user surveillance.

Google's general terms of services[5] that were valid from April 16, 2007 until the end of February 2012 applied to all of its services. It thereby enabled the economic surveillance of a diverse multitude of user data that is collected from various services and user activities for the purpose of targeted advertising: "Some of the Services are supported by advertising revenue and may display advertisements and promotions. These advertisements may be targeted to the content of information stored on the Services, queries made through the Services or other information".

Google+: Google and Social Networking Sites

On June 22, 2011, Google launched Google+ (G+), a social networking site (SNS). Facebook has dominated the SNS market, so G+ is a competing project. The competition is for users, which is at the same time a competition for advertising revenues. The main difference between G+ and Facebook is that G+ is based on the concept of friend circles: friends are organized in different groups and all information is shared with selected groups. G+ is governed by Google's general terms of service and privacy policy. There are additional regulations in the G+ Privacy Policy[6] that apply for the specifics of G+ as SNS.

It specified, for example: "We will record information about your activity – such as posts that you comment on and the other users with whom you interact – in order to provide you and other users with a better experience on Google services. We may also collect information about you from other users, such as when someone puts you in one of their circles or tags you in a photo". The surveillance of online activities and friendship networks certainly serves advertising purposes, although it is doubtful whether it provides users with "a better experience".

Google makes use of privacy policies and terms of service that enable the large-scale economic surveillance of users for the purpose of capital accumulation.

---

5 www.google.com/accounts/TOS, version from April 16, 2007.
6 www.google.com/intl/en_uk/+/policy/, version from June 28, 2011.

Advertising clients of Google that use Google AdWords are able to target ads, for example, by country, by the exact location of users and by the distance from a certain location, by the language users speak, by the type of device used (desktop/laptop computer, mobile device (specifiable)), the mobile phone operator used (specifiable), by gender or age group (data source: http://adwords.google.com, accessed on October 27, 2011).

The EU's Data Protection Regulation

On January 25, 2012, the EU released a proposal for a General Data Protection Regulation. It defines a right of individuals not to be subject to profiling, which is understood as "automated processing intended to evaluate certain personal aspects relating to this natural person or to analyse or predict in particular the natural person's performance at work, economic situation, location, health, personal preferences, reliability or behaviour" (article 20, 1). Targeted advertising is such a form of profiling. According to article 20, 2 (c), profiling is allowed if the data subject consents according to the conditions of article 7, which says that if the consent is given as part of a written declaration (e.g. as a website's terms of use or privacy policy), the "consent must be presented distinguishable in its appearance from this other matter" (article 7, 2).

Furthermore, the regulation proposes a right of citizens to be forgotten (article 17) – which also includes that third parties should be informed so that they can erase the same data (article 17, 2), the right to data portability (article 18) – which means that all personal data must be exportable from Facebook to other social networking sites, that by default only the minimum of data that is necessary for obtaining the purpose of processing is collected and stored (article 23), and fines of up to €1 000 000 and 2% of the annual worldwide turnover of a company are implemented (article 79). The EU regulation, to a certain extent, limits targeted advertising by the right to be forgotten and the special form in which consensus must be given. However, it does not make targeted advertising a pure opt-in option, which would be a more efficient way for protecting consumers' and users' privacy.

Google's 2012 Privacy Policy

As a result of the announcement of the EU Data Protection Regulation, overnight Google announced the change and unification of all its privacy policies and the change of its terms of use. Since 2012, the use of targeted advertising has no longer been defined in Google's terms of use, but rather in the privacy policy, as the version of Google's privacy policy that came into effect in 2012 shows: "We use the information we collect from all of our services to provide, maintain, protect and improve them, to develop new ones, and to protect Google and our users. We also use this information to offer you tailored content – like giving you more relevant search results and ads."[7]

---

7 Google Privacy Policy. www.google.com/intl/en/policies/privacy/, version from July 27, 2012.

Although Google presents its policies as a major privacy enhancement ("a simpler, more intuitive Google experience. [. . .] we're consolidating more than 60 into our main Privacy Policy. Regulators globally have been calling for shorter, simpler privacy policies – and having one policy covering many different products is now fairly standard across the web"[8]), the core of the regulations – the automatic use of targeted advertising – has not changed. The European Union does not require Google to base targeted ads on opt-in. Google offers two opt-out options for targeted ads: one can opt-out from the basing of targeted ads on (a) search keywords and (b) visited websites that have Google ads (Ads Preferences Manager, www.google.com/settings/ads/preferences/).

In Google's 2012 privacy policy, "user communications" are no longer mentioned separately as collected user information, but rather content is defined as part of log information: "Log information. When you use our services or view content provided by Google, we may automatically collect and store certain information in server logs. This may include: details of how you used our service, such as your search queries." Search keywords can be interpreted as the content of a Google search. The formulation that log information is how one uses a service is vague. It can be interpreted to also include all type of Google content, such as the text of a gMail message or a Google+ posting.

In the 2012 privacy policy, Google says: "We may combine personal information from one service with information, including personal information, from other Google services – for example to make it easier to share things with people you know. We will not combine DoubleClick cookie information with personally identifiable information unless we have your opt-in consent". This change is significant and reflects the circumstance of the EU data protection regulation's third-party regulation in the right to be forgotten (article 17, 2). The question of whether DoubleClick is used for Google's targeted ads is more or less based on the question how extensively and aggressively Google tries to make users to opt-in to DoubleClick. The effect is that Google will no longer be able to automatically use general Internet user data collected by DoubleClick. However, the unification of the privacy policies and the provision that information from all Google services and all Google ads on external sites can be combined allows Google to base targeted advertising on user profiles that contain a broad range of user data. The sources of user surveillance are now mainly Google services. As Google spreads its ad service all over the web, this surveillance is still networked and spread out. Google tries to compensate the limited use of DoubleClick data for targeted advertising with an integration of the data that it collects itself.

Sensitive Personal Data

Concerning the use of sensitive data, both the 2011 and the 2012 Google privacy policy specify: "We require opt-in consent for the sharing of any sensitive personal information." In addition, the 2012 privacy policy says: "When showing

---

8 http://googleblog.blogspot.com/2012/01/updating-our-privacy-policies-and-terms.html, accessed on March 13, 2013.

you tailored ads, we will not associate a cookie or anonymous identifier with sensitive categories, such as those based on race, religion, sexual orientation or health." Targeted ads use data from all Google services, including content data. The EU data protection regulation says that the processing of sensitive data (race, ethnicity, political opinions, religion, beliefs, trade-union membership, genetic data, health data, sex life, criminal convictions or related security measures) is forbidden, except if the data subject consents (article 9).

Google continued in 2012 to use content data (such as search queries) for targeting advertising that is based on algorithms that make an automatic classification of interests. By collecting a large number of search keywords by one individual, the likelihood that he or she can be personally identified increases. Search keywords are, furthermore, linked to IP addresses that make the computers of users identifiable. Algorithms can never perfectly analyze the semantics of data. Therefore, use of sensitive data for targeted advertising cannot be avoided as long as search queries and other content are automatically analyzed. Google's provision that it does not use sensitive data for targeted ads stands in contradiction with the fact that it says it uses "details of how you used our service, such as your search queries".

Complex Terms of Use

The overall changes introduced by Google's 2012 privacy policy and terms of use are modest, the main fundamental remains unchanged: Google uses targeted advertising as a default. DoubleClick is now less likely to be used for targeted advertising. Google has unified its privacy policies. Whereas Google presents this move as providing more transparency ("We believe this new, simpler policy will make it easier for people to understand our privacy practices as well as enable Google to improve the services we offer"[9]), it also enables Google to base its targeted ads on a wide range of user data that stem from across all its services. Google proclaims that it does not use sensitive data for targeted ads, which is contradicted by the definition of content data as log data that can be used for targeted ads.

Google's 2011 privacy terms (version from October 20, 2011) had 10 917 characters, whereas its 2012 privacy terms (version from July 27, 2012) have 14 218 characters, which is an increase of around 30%. The main privacy terms have thereby grown in complexity, although the number of privacy policies that apply to Google services was reduced from more than 70 to one.

6.4. Work at Google

Work at Google: Fun and Good Food?

What is it like to work at Google? In the description of its company culture, Google promises that it is fun and play to work for them. Furthermore, the food will be great and free and interesting people will come and visit the company:

---

9 http://googleblog.blogspot.com/2012/01/updating-our-privacy-policies-and-terms.html, accessed on March 14, 2013.

Googlers live and breathe a culture of openness. Our commitment to innovation depends on everyone being comfortable sharing ideas and opinions. [. . .] Googlers also have the opportunity to develop 20% Projects, where they take 20% of their work time to work on projects that they're personally passionate about. There are many examples of 20% projects that lead to meaningful impact on the company, such as Gmail. [. . .] Fun is a big part of Google culture. We consider each other not just colleagues, but friends and family, too. We play on Google sports teams together, have happy hours and throw each other birthday parties, baby showers and engagement celebrations – we like spending time together and we have fun and celebrate successes in many different ways. Our offices have all sorts of on-site entertainment, from pool tables to ping pong to bowling alleys to Mortal Kombat to Dance Dance Revolution dance-offs. [. . .] When the physical activity is over, Googlers need to recharge. We love to eat, and our amazing Culinary team creates a multitude of events and delicacies for our enjoyment. [. . .] Googlers enjoy visits from artists, authors, performers, politicians and celebrities who drop by throughout the year.[10]

The Reality of Work at Google: Working Long Hours

Is the reality of working at Google as the company promises? I tested these claims empirically.

Glassdoor is "a free jobs and career community that offers the world an inside look at jobs and companies" (www.glassdoor.com/about/index_input.htm). It has collected millions of reviews of how work, interviewing and salaries are conducted in specific companies. I analyzed job reviews for Google that contained a job title related to the keyword "software". This resulted in a total of 307 postings that were written between February 5, 2008 and December 15, 2012. In addition, I analyzed a thread on the social news site reddit (http://www.reddit.com/) that asked people to report anonymously on working conditions at Google (www.reddit.com/r/AskReddit/comments/clz1m/google_employees_on_reddit_fire_up_your_throw away/). I searched for and analyzed postings in which workers talked about working-time issues. The 307 postings on Glassdoor were written between February 5, 2008 and December 15, 2012. This resulted in a sample of 75 postings, 10 from the reddit thread and 65 from Glassdoor.

Glassdoor calculates salary averages for certain job positions. On January 17, 2013, the average salary for a Google software engineer in the USA was \$112 915 ($N = 2744$) and for a senior software engineer \$144 692 ($N = 187$). Given that the average salary of an application software developer was \$105 806 in California in 2012 (data source: State of California Employment Development Department[11]) it shows that Google seems to pay salaries that are above the average.

---

10 Google culture. www.google.com/intl/en/jobs/students/lifeatgoogle/culture/, accessed on March 15, 2013.
11 www.edd.ca.gov/

Most postings say nothing about working time, but rather focus on aspects such as free food. They therefore had to be excluded from the working time analysis.

In the conducted analysis, 18 postings mentioned positive aspects of working time at Google: 14 (78%) of them said that they value that there are flexible working times. A minority said that there is a good work–life balance (3, 17%) or that they work a regular eight hours a day (1, 5%). Fifty-eight postings mentioned negative aspects of working times at Google. The issue that all of these 58 postings exclusively focused on in relation to working time were long working hours and a resulting bad work–life balance. I have summarized typical comments in Table 6.4.

The picture that emerges from this analysis is that people tend to work long hours at Google, feel that the nice working environment that features free food, sports facilities, restaurants, cafés, events, tech-talks and other perks encourages employees to stay and work longer, that working long hours is not something that is formally dictated by the management, but that it is rather built into the company culture so that there is a lot of competitive peer-pressure to work long hours, and that one tends not to have enough time to make use of the 20% work for one's own projects or has to add these hours to more than 100% of working time. Google indirectly admits when describing its company culture that working days can be atypical: "Despite our size and expansion, Google still maintains a start-up culture. Google is not a conventional corporation, and our workdays are not the typical 9 to 5."[12]

Working Long Hours? Never Mind, just Sleep under your Desk, as Former Google Vice-President Marissa Mayer Does…

Where can long working hours lead to? To the fact that employees sleep under their desks in order to maximize performance. Former Google vice-president Marissa Mayer reports about her time at Google: "Part of Google was it was the right time and we had a great technology, but the other part was we worked really, really hard. […] It was 130 hour weeks. People say, 'there's only 168 hours in a week, how can you do it?' Well, if you're strategic about when you shower and sleeping under your desk, it can be done".[13] The ultimate consequence of such behaviour is that there is no life outside Google – life becomes Google and is, thereby, one-dimensional.

On the one hand, Google employees tend to have long working hours and a lot of overtime, whereas on the other hand, office hours are completely flexible and management does not see it as a negative feature if somebody does not work from 9 to 5. What is very striking about Google is a management strategy that uses soft and social forms of coercion: there is no formal contractual

12 Google culture. www.google.com/intl/en/jobs/students/lifeatgoogle/culture/, accessed on March 15, 2013.
13 http://it-jobs.fins.com/Articles/SBB0001424052702303404704577309493661513690/How-Google-s-Marissa-Mayer-Manages-Burnout, accessed on March 16, 2013.

Table 6.4 A selection of typical comments of Google employees about working hours

ID	Comment
5	I don't have much of a social life yet (workin' on it) so I tend to be at the office at retarded hours. [...] People don't look twice when I show up at noon. :3
6	The downside to google, you're asking? That's easy. Everything they do for you is in the interest of keeping you in the office as much as possible. They'll give you breakfast, lunch, dinner (all delicious, no crap). There's gyms, they'll do your laundry, they'll get you a massage, you can play sports, you can bring a pet. So for some people this is AWESOME. All I see is a bunch of people who are at the office 50–70 hours a week of their own volition, and don't separate their work from their everyday life.
7	It's not uncommon for people to be there late, work late @home, and work a few hours over the weekend.
8	By the end my typical day was 14 hours long and I was starting to underperform on my primary responsibilities. [...] The fast pace and competitive environment simply make it an easy trap for Googlers to fall into.
9	Google is specifically catering to people who work very long hours. The breakfast is at 8:30, and the dinner is at 6:30 (and it's considered tacky to eat dinner and leave right away).
14	The food was great, and while I stayed in the office for long hours every day, my work schedule didn't feel oppressive to me, simply because it was such a nice work environment.
17	In my group, people usually work from 9:00am to 7:00pm everyday.
24	Everybody is very very career focused, they mostly dont have any other aspiration in life. So they spent a lot of hour in office. And it creates tremendous peer pressure. [...] If you want a stable work pressure, with stable work life balance, and other interest than the job, this is not your place for sure.
26	All the benefits are designed to get you to work more.
27	Cons – Too much time spent at work (50–60hrs/week).
29	Cons – over-time work. seems everyone works late on weekends.
32	Cons – too much time spent on work, sometimes too much time thinking of work even when you're out.
33	The opportunities for 20% time are real, but you may not have enough time and energy to make use of them.
35	Also, the availability of free food, gym, etc. on campus and the plenty of fun distractions on its corp network make it easy to spend more time there.
37	Cons – Company policy, not that fun when you working, pressure, dead line, pushing, sometime you have to give up some life for the work.
38	Pros – The free food is good. Cons – The working hours are long. The pay is not worth all the time spent at work. Management is not great.
43	Cons – too much work and very weird hours! Advice to Senior Management – have a good work life balance.
45	"Death march" schedules and random priority changes becoming more common
47	Bad balance between work and personal life.
49	Cons – Growth within the company is difficult unless you're prepared to sacrifice personal life and sleep.

(Continued)

Table 6.4 (Continued)

ID	Comment
50	There may not be a lot of external pressure from management to pull long hours, but folks tend to do it anyway because they want to accomplish something great. It's an easy place to feel you're below average, even when you've been tops everywhere else.
51	bad work/life balance
54	Cons – Very long hours. At least where I was, people would seriously work 12–14 hours a day (out of which 90% would be "effective hours", churning away tons of code). [...] Google is not that magic place to work for anymore: pay better, think of the work-life balance (I mean, actually think of it, not just pretend you are).
56	Cons – Long work hours – 10+ hours/day is typical for many engineers.
58	Cons – Many people work very long hours, so it feels that you must do likewise in order to be considered a good employee.
61	Because the peer group is so good, expectations run high, as a result many people have to put in long hours.
62	Work–life balance doesn't really exist, as working 10+ hours a day seemed to be expected with people working 8–9 hours at work and then 2+ hours at home at night. [...] Advice to Senior Management – Don't stress working so much and be more open in general.
63	Cons – Can have long hours because you don't want to disappoint high-achieving coworkers.
65	Cons – There is a culture of working long hours there, and 20% time is pretty much a myth now. If anything, it's 120% time.
67	There's a culture of working long hours.
70	Culture encourages one to give up the rest of his/her life for their job.
73	Cons – Long hours! Not the place for people who want to have a life outside of work, but then they aren't the type who wind up getting hired anyway.
74	Cons – Because of the large amounts of benefits (such as free foods) there seems to be an unsaid rule that employees are expected to work longer hours. Many people work more than 8 hours a day and then will be on email or work for a couple hours at home, at night as well (or on the weekends). It may be hard to perform extremely well with a good work/life balance. Advice to Senior Management – Give engineers more freedom to use 20% time to work on cool projects without the stress of having to do 120% work.

requirement to work overtime, but the company culture is based on project-based work, social pressure between colleagues, competition, positive identification with the job, a fun and play culture, performance-based promotion, incentives to stay for long periods at the workplace (sports, restaurants, cafés, massages, social events, lectures, etc.) and a blurring of the boundaries between work and play. As a result, employees tend to work long hours, the work–life balance is damaged and Google tends to become synonymous with life itself: lifetime becomes work time and time spent creating value for Google. Google is a prototypical company for the realization of what Luc Boltanski and Ève Chiapello (2005) call the new spirit of capitalism[14] – the anti-authoritarian values of the political revolt of 1968 and the subsequently emerging New Left, such as autonomy, play, freedom, spontaneity, mobility, creativity, networking, visions,

14 For an application of this concept to the critique of Internet ideologies, see Fisher 2010a, 2010b.

openness, plurality, informality, authenticity, emancipation, are subsumed under the logic of capital.

In the early times of capitalism that Marx describes in *Capital, Volume 1* (1867), the lengthening of the working day was achieved by control, surveillance, disciplinary measures and legitimation by state laws. The price was an increase of class struggles that pressed for a reduction in working hours. Google's main way of increasing surplus value production is also absolute surplus value production, i.e. the lengthening of the working day, but it takes a different approach: the coercion is ideological and social, is built into the company's culture of fun, playbour (play labour), employee services and peer pressure. The result is that the total average working time and unpaid working hours per employee tend to increase. Marx described this case as a specific method of absolute and relative surplus value production, in which the productivity and intensity of labour remain constant, whereas the length of the working day is variable: if the working day is lengthened and the price of labour (wages) remain the same, "the surplus-value increases both absolutely and relatively. Although there is no absolute change in the value of labour-power, it suffers a relative fall. [. . .] Here, [. . .] the change of relative magnitude in the value of labour-power is the result of the change of absolute magnitude in surplus-value" (Marx 1867, 663). What Marx explains in this passage is that the wages tend to relatively decrease, the more hours employees work unpaid overtime because they then create additional surplus value and profit. This can be illustrated for the case of Google: 12 of the analyzed postings indicated average working hours per week, which allows calculation of an average weekly working time of 62 hours.[15]

This evidence is certainly only anecdotal, but given the large number of comments that stated that working long hours is common at Google, this result seems to be indicative. The Fair US Labor Standards Act (Section 13 (a) 17) provides an exemption from overpay for computer systems analysts, software engineers or similar workers if they earn at least US$27.63 an hour. This means that if it is assumed that software engineers at Google, on average, work 22 hours overtime per week, that their salary average of US$112,915 stands for a 155% time employment, which means that 55% of the working time is unpaid extra work time. During these 22 hours a week, the employee creates surplus value and profit for Google. If we assume 47 weeks of work per year, then the unpaid overtime lengthens work on average by 1034 hours a year.

6.5. Google: God and Satan in One Company

Many popular science accounts of Google are celebratory, whereas a lot of social science analyses point out the dangers of the company. One should go beyond one-sided assessments of Google and think dialectically: Google is at the same time the

---

15 For example, if an employee wrote that s/he works 55–70 hours per week, then this circumstance was coded as an average of 62.5 hours.

best and the worst that has ever happened on the Internet. Google is evil like the figure of Satan and good like the figure of God. It is the dialectical Good Evil. Google is part of the best Internet practices because its services can enhance and support the everyday life of humans. It can help them to find and organize information, to access public information, to communicate and co-operate with others. Google has the potential to greatly advance the cognition, communication and co-operation of humans in society. It is a manifestation of the productive and socializing forces of the Internet. The problem is not the technologies provided by Google, but the capitalist relations of production that organize these technologies. The problem is that, in providing its services, Google necessarily has to exploit users and engage in the surveillance and commodification of user-oriented data.

Marx and the Antagonism between Productive Forces and Relations of Production

Marx spoke of an antagonism of the productive forces and the relations of production: "the material productive forces of society come into conflict with the existing relations of production. [. . .] From forms of development of the productive forces these relations turn into their fetters. Then begins an era of social revolution" (Marx 1859, 263).

> In the development of productive forces there comes a stage when productive forces and means of intercourse are brought into being, which, under the existing relationships, only cause mischief, and are no longer productive but destructive forces (machinery and money); and connected with this a class is called forth, which has to bear all the burdens of society without enjoying its advantages, which, ousted from society, is forced into the most decided antagonism to all other classes; a class which forms the majority of all members of society. (Marx and Engels 1846, 60)

The class relations framing Google, in which all Google users and web users are exploited by Google and in which the privacy of all of these individuals is necessarily violated by Google's business activities, are destructive forces – they destroy consumer privacy and people's interest in being protected from exploitation.

Google In and Beyond Capitalism

Google's cognitive, communicative and co-operative potentials point beyond capitalism. The social and co-operative dimension of corporate social media anticipates and points towards "elements of the new society with which old collapsing bourgeois society itself is pregnant" (Marx 1871, 277); new relations, which mature "within the framework of the old society" (Marx 1859, 263); "new forces and new passions" that "spring up in the bosom of society, forces and passions which feel themselves to be fettered by that society" (Marx and Engels 1848, 928); "antithetical forms", which are "concealed in society" and "mines to explode it" (Marx 1857/1858, 159).

Google is a sorcerer of capitalism. It calls up a spell that questions capitalism itself: "Modern bourgeois society with its relations of production, of exchange, and of property, a society that has conjured up such gigantic means of production and of exchange, is like the sorcerer who is no longer able to control the powers of the nether world whom he has called up by his spells" (Marx and Engels 1848, 214).

At the level of the technological productive forces, we see that Google advances socialization, the co-operative and common character of the online-productive forces: Google tools are available for free, Google Documents allows the collaborative creation of documents; G+, GMail, Blogger and Buzz enable social networking and communication, YouTube supports sharing videos, Google Scholar and Google Books help to establish better access to worldwide academic knowledge, etc. These are all applications that can give great benefits to humans. But at the level of the relations of production, Google is a profit-oriented, advertising-financed money-making machine that turns users and their data into a commodity. And large-scale surveillance and the immanent undermining of liberal democracy's intrinsic privacy value are the result. Liberal democratic values thereby constitute their own limit and immanent critique. So on the level of the productive forces, Google and other web 2.0 platforms anticipate a commons-based public Internet from which all benefit, whereas at the same time Google enables a form of freedom (free service access) that works by online surveillance and user commodification that threaten consumer privacy. Google is a prototypical example of the antagonisms between networked productive forces and capitalist relations of production in the capitalist information economy (Fuchs 2008a).

"The conditions of bourgeois society are too narrow to comprise the wealth created by them" (Marx and Engels 1848, 215). Google's class character limits its immanent potentials that can enhance human life. These potentials cannot be realized within capitalism. The critical discussion that maintains that Google advances the surveillance society points towards Google's immanent limit as a capitalist company.

Google is an antagonistic way of organizing human knowledge. Marx pointed out that knowledge and other productive forces constitute barriers to capital: "The barrier to *capital* is that this entire development proceeds in a contradictory way, and that the working-out of the productive forces, of general wealth etc., knowledge etc., appears in such a way that [. . .] this antithetical form is itself fleeting, and produces the real conditions of its own suspension" (Marx 1857/1858, 541f).

Google has created the real conditions of its own suspension. It is a mistake to argue that Google should be dissolved, or to say that alternatives to Google are needed or that its services are a danger to humanity. Rather, Google would lose its antagonistic character if it were expropriated and transformed into a public, non-profit, non-commercial organization that serves the common good. Google permanently expropriates and exploits Internet users by commodifying their content and user data. The best solution is the expropriation of the Google expropriator – the transformation of Google into a public search engine.

Google stands at the same time for the universal and the particular interests on the Internet. It represents the idea of the advancement of an Internet that benefits humanity and the reality of the absolute exploitation of humanity for business purposes. Google is the universal exploiter and has created technologies that can advance a universal humanity if, in an act of universal appropriation, humans act as a universal subject and free themselves and these technologies from exploitative class relations.

6.6. Conclusion

We can summarize the main results of this chapter as follows:

- Google's accumulation model is based on the exploitation and commodification of users through the economic surveillance of users' interests and activities (demographic, technological, economic, political, cultural, ecological data), communications, networks and collaborations. This data is sold for the purpose of accumulating money capital by way of targeted advertising.
- Google's internal company ideology is based on the advancement of play labour. Google does not show sensitivity for privacy issues, which contradicts its philosophy of wanting to do no evil.
- Google says that work in its offices is fun and play. Empirical analysis indicates that work at Google is highly paid and based on working long hours, which can result in a lack of work-life-balance and feelings of stress.
- Many analyses of Google are undialectical. They miss that Google's activities are embedded into the capitalist antagonism between networked productive forces and class relations. Google advances the socialization of the networked productive forces and at the same time uses these as destructive forces for exploiting users.

One should think about Google in terms of commodity logic and ideology, but at the same time one should see how, from this very logic, potential alternatives emerge. Karl Marx stressed that the globalization of production and circulation necessitates institutions that allow individuals to inform themselves about complex conditions. He said that "institutions emerge whereby each individual can acquire information about the activity of all others and attempt to adjust his own accordingly" and that these "interconnections" are enabled by "mails, telegraphs etc." (Marx 1857/1858, 161). Is this passage not the perfect description of the concept of the search engine? We can therefore say that Larry Page and Sergey Brin did not invent Google, but that rather Karl Marx was the true inventor of the search engine and of Google. But if Marx's thinking is crucial for the concept of the search engine, shouldn't we then think about the concept of a public search engine?

What could a public search engine look like? Google services could be run by non-profit organizations, for example universities (Maurer, Balke, Kappe,

Kulathuramaiyer, Weber and Zaka 2007, 74), and be supported by public funding. A service like Google Books could then serve humanity by making the knowledge of all books freely available to all humans without drawing private profit from it. A public search engine does not require advertising funding if it is a non-profit endeavour. In this way, the exploitation and surveillance of users and the privacy violation issues that are at the heart of Google could be avoided. Establishing a public Google could lead to the dissolution of the private business of Google. This may only be possible by establishing a commons-based Internet in a commons-based society. Doing so will require the first steps in the class struggle for a just humanity and a just Internet to be taken. These include, for example, the suggestion to require Google by law to make advertising an opt-in option and to surveil the surveillor by creating and supporting Google watchdog organizations that document the problems and antagonisms of Google. Google's 20% policy is, on the one hand, pure capitalist ideology that wants to advance profit maximization. On the other hand, it makes sense that unions pressure Google to make the 20% of work time really autonomous from Google's control. If this could be established in a large company like Google, then a general demand for a reduction of labour time without wage decreases would be easier to attain. Such a demand is a demand for the increase of the autonomy of labour from capital.

Another Google is possible, but this requires class struggle for and against Google in order to set free the humanistic (cognitive, communicative, co-operative) potentials of Google by overcoming its class relations.

RECOMMENDED READINGS AND EXERCISES

For understanding Google it makes sense to engage with classical (Stuart Hall, Herbert Marcuse) and newer (Evgeny Morozov) versions of ideology critique. More exercises follow on Google's terms of service, privacy policy and financial data.

Hall, Stuart, Chas Critcher, Tony Jefferson, John Clarke and Brian Roberts. 1978. *Policing the crisis: Mugging, the state and law and order*. London: Macmillan. Chapter 9: The law-and-order society: towards the "exceptional state" (273–323).

Marcuse, Herbert. 1941/1998. Some social implications of modern technology. In *Technology, war and fascism*, ed. Douglas Kellner, 39–65. London: Routledge.

Morozov, Evgeny. 2013. *To save everything, click here: Technology, solutionism and the urge to fix problems that don't exist*. London: Allen Lane. Chapter 1: Solutionism and its discontents. Chapter 2: The nonsense of "the Internet" – and how to stop it.

Stuart Hall is one of the most important representatives of Cultural Studies. Herbert Marcuse was, besides Horkheimer and Adorno, the major representative of Frankfurt School Critical Theory. Evgeny Morozov is a writer who is critical of Internet fetishism and techno-centrism.

Ask yourself:

- What do Stuart Hall et al. describe as characteristic elements of ideologies and moral panics during the crisis of the 1970s?

- Make a list of the characteristics of technological rationality that Herbert Marcuse identifies.

- Try to define what Evgeny Morozov understands by Internet solutionism and Internet centrism. Try to find some examples in the daily press. Try to also find examples that relate to Google.

- Discuss if, and how, the notions of technological solutionism and Internet centrism are connected to Stuart Hall et al.'s analysis of ideologies in times of crisis and Herbert Marcuse's notion of technological rationality.

Read Google's latest Terms of Service and ask yourself:

- What rights does Google have in relation to the content that you create on its services?

- If you feel treated in an illegal manner by Google, how can you hold it legally reliable? Which court is responsible?

- Try to find more information on how national regulations (e.g. the ones in your home country) work for a global system like the Internet?

Read Google's latest Privacy Policy and ask yourself the following questions:

- Make a systematic and ordered list of data that Google collects about users.

- Discuss which data Google uses for targeted advertising. Find out how exactly this form of advertising works. Which data does Google use about you for targeted advertising?

- Are there mechanisms for limiting targeted advertising on Google? Do you think they are sufficient? Why? Why not?

- How do you politically assess targeted advertising?

- Are there alternative organization models for social media that do not use targeted advertising? Which ones? How do you think social media should best be organized?

Read Google's latest Proxy Statement and its Annual Financial Report. You can find both on its website under SEC Filings. Ask yourself:

- How does Google present itself in these documents?

- Try to make sense of and interpret the financial data presented in the reports. What does Google's ownership structure and its financial operations look like?

- According to these reports, what role does advertising play in Google's operations?

Work in groups and then present the results to the class:

- Search for videos, documents, press releases, blog posts etc., in which Google presents itself. What kind of image does Google construct of itself? What are the major themes in the discourse? What is the role of corporate responsibility in Google's public relations?

- Search for documents, interviews, news articles, reports by critical scholars, critical journalists, civil society representatives, privacy and data protection advocates, consumer protection advocates and organizations as well as watchdog organizations that criticize the topics that Google presented in a positive light in the material you found earlier. Summarize the basic points of criticism. Compare them to how Google presents itself. Discuss which assessments you find more convincing and provide reasons for your assessments.

Work in groups and present the results to the class:

- Select a specific Internet or social media company. Try to find out how the company presents the working conditions of its employees in public discourse. Register at glassdoor.com (you have to write a review of an employer to get full access to other reviews). Collect reviews about a specific job category at your selected company. Conduct a content analysis to assess what the working conditions are like at this company.

Facebook: A Surveillance Threat to Privacy?

Key questions

- How does Facebook's political economy work?
- How has Facebook been criticized?
- What ideologies exist on and about Facebook? How does Facebook present itself to the world? What is the reality behind Facebook-ideologies?
- Are there alternatives to Facebook?

Key concepts

Digital labour	Opt-out
Privacy	Targeted advertising
Social media & privacy	Instant personalization
Facebook ideologies	Commodification
Privacy fetishism	Private property
Privacy policy	Alternative social media

Overview

Facebook is the most popular social networking site (SNS). SNSs are web-based platforms that integrate different media, information and communication technologies that allow at least the generation of profiles that display information describing the users, the display of connections (connection list), the establishment of

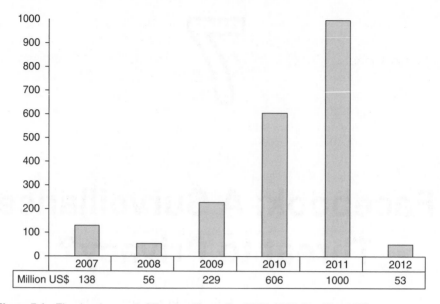

Figure 7.1   The development of Facebook's profits, 2007–2012, in million US$

Data source: SEC Filings, Form-S1 Registration Statement: Facebook, Inc., Form 10-K: Annual Report 2012.

connections between users displayed on their connection lists, and communication between users (Fuchs 2009b).

Mark Zuckerberg, Eduardo Saverin, Dustin Moskovitz and Chris Hughes, who were then Harvard students, founded Facebook in 2004. This chapter's task is to discuss the power of Facebook, the role of surveillance and implications for privacy. First, I discuss Facebook's economic development (section 7.1). Section 7.2 introduces the notion of privacy. Then, I criticize the dominant kind of analysis of Facebook privacy by characterizing it as a form of privacy fetishism (section 7.3). In section 7.4, I analyze Facebook's political economy. Finally, I draw some conclusions and outline strategies for alternative online privacy politics in section 7.5 and the alternative social networking site Diaspora* is introduced.

7.1. Facebook's Financial Power

Facebook's Profits

Facebook became a public company on February 1, 2012. As part of this process, financial data required for the registration as public company was published.[1] Facebook says that it generates "a substantial majority" of its "revenue from advertising": 98.3% in 2009, 94.6% in 2010, 85% in 2011 and

---

1 SEC Filings, Form-S1 Registration Statement: Facebook, Inc. www.sec.gov/Archives/edgar/data/1326801/000119312512034517/d287954ds1.htm, accessed on March 26, 2012. Annual Report 2012, Form 10-K, http://investor.fb.com/secfiling.cfm?filingID=1326801-13-3&CIK=1326801, accessed on March 3, 2013.

84% in 2012.[2] It says that the "loss of advertisers, or reduction in spending by advertisers with Facebook, could seriously harm our business".[3] Facebook's self-assessment of this risk shows that it is coupled to the broader politi-cal economy of capitalism: an advertising-based capital accumulation model depends on a constant influx of advertisement investments and the belief of companies that specific forms of advertisement on specific media can increase their profits. A general economic crisis that results in decreasing profits can result in a decrease of advertisement investments.

Figure 7.1 shows the development of Facebook's profits in the years 2007–2012. Since 2007, the company's annual profits have increased by a factor of 7.2 from US$138 million in 2007 to US$1 billion in 2011. There was a slump in 2008 ($56 million, −60% in comparison to 2007), which was due to the big economic crisis that took effect in 2008 all over the world. Since 2009, Facebook's profits have almost exploded. At the same time, there was a large increase of users: the number of monthly active users was 197 million in March 2009, 431 million in March 2010, 680 million in March 2011, 845 million in December 2011 and 1.06 billion in December 2012.[4] On May 17, 2012, Facebook became a public company. Its shares were offered at an initial price of $38 per piece.

2012: Facebook's Decreasing Profits and Increasing Revenues

In 2012, Facebook's profits decreased dramatically from $1 billion to $53 mil-lion, which is a factor of 19 or a decrease of profits by 95%. Facebook increased its revenues in 2012 from $3.7 billion in the previous year to $5.1 billion. Facebook's investment costs for fixed goods, compensation, research and development, marketing, general costs and advertising more than doubled to $4.6 billion. According to Facebook's annual report 2012, the cause of the decrease of profits was investment in employees, data centres and employee compensation in stocks. Facebook had 3200 employees in December 2011 (Form-S1 Registration Statement: Facebook, Inc.) and 4619 in December 2012 (Form 10-K: Annual Report 2012). The 2012 Annual Report says:

> Prior to January 1, 2011 we granted Pre-2011 RSUs [restricted stock units] to our employees and members of our board of directors that vested upon the satisfaction of both a service-based condition, generally over four years, and a liquidity condition. The liquidity condition was satisfied in connection with our IPO [initial public offering] in May 2012. Because the liquidity condition was not satis-fied until our IPO, in prior periods we had not recorded any expense

2 Ibid., 12, 50.
3 Ibid., 12.
4 Ibid., 44.

relating to the granting of the Pre-2011 RSUs. In the second quarter
of 2012, we recognized $986 million of stock-based compensation
expense associated with Pre-2011 RSUs that vested in connection
with our IPO.

This means that Facebook to a certain degree compensated its directors and
employees with stock options that had to be redeemed in order that the company could become a public corporation that sells stocks on the stock market.
So although Facebook's revenues increased, its investments and salary costs
increased to such an extent that its overall profits massively decreased in 2012.

7.2. The Notion of Privacy

Different Definitions of Privacy

Tavani (2008) distinguishes between the restricted access theory, the control
theory, and the restricted access/limited control theory of privacy. The restricted
access theory of informational privacy sees privacy achieved if one is able to limit
and restrict others from access to personal information (Tavani 2008, 142ff).
The classical form of this definition is Warren and Brandeis' notion of privacy:
"Now the right to life has come to mean the right to enjoy life – the right to be let
alone" (Warren and Brandeis 1890, 193). They discussed this right especially in
relation to newspapers and spoke of the "evil of invasion of privacy by the newspapers". Although some scholars argue that Warren and Brandeis' (1890) paper
is the source of the restricted access theory (for example, Bloustein 1964/1984;
Rule 2007, 22; Schoeman 1984b; Solove 2008, 15f), already John Stuart Mill had
formulated the same concept 42 years before Warren and Brandeis in his 1848
book *Principles of Political Economy* (Mill 1965, 938). This circumstance shows
the inherent connection of the modern privacy concept and liberal ideology. The
control theory of privacy sees privacy as control and self-determination over
information about oneself (Tavani 2008, 142ff).

Westin (1967, 7) provided the most influential control definition of privacy:
"Privacy is the claim of individuals, groups or institutions to determine for themselves when, how, and to what extent information about them is communicated
to others" (Westin 1967, 7). In a control theory of privacy, there is privacy even
if one chooses to disclose all personal information about oneself. In an absolute
restricted access theory of privacy, there is only privacy if one lives in solitary
confinement without contact with others.

The restricted access/limited control theory (RALC) of privacy tries to combine both concepts. It distinguishes "between the concept of privacy, which it
defines in terms of restricted access, and the management of privacy, which is
achieved via a system of limited controls for individuals" (Tavani 2008, 144; see
also Moor 2000).

All three kinds of definitions of informational privacy have in common that
they deal with the moral questions of how information about people should be

processed, who shall have access to this data, and how this access shall be regulated. All have in common the normative value that some form of data protection is needed.

Criticisms of Privacy

Etzioni (1999) stresses that it is a typical American liberal belief that strengthening privacy can cause no harm. He stresses that privacy can undermine common goods (public safety, public health). Countries like Switzerland, Liechtenstein, Monaco and Austria have a tradition of relative anonymity of bank accounts and transactions. One sees money and private property as aspects of privacy, about which the public should have no information. In Switzerland, the Federal Banking Act (§47) defines the bank secret. The Swiss Bankers' Association sees bank anonymity as a form of "financial privacy"[5] that needs to be protected and speaks of "privacy in relation to financial income and assets".[6] Most countries treat information about income and the profits of companies (except for public companies) as a secret, a form of financial privacy. The privacy-as-secrecy conception is typically part of the limited access concept of privacy (Solove 2008, 22).

Control theories and limited access/control theories of privacy, in contrast, do not stress absolute secrecy of personal information as desirable, but rather stress the importance of self-determination in keeping or sharing personal information and the different contexts in which keeping information to oneself or sharing it is considered important. In this vein, Helen Nissenbaum argues that the "right to privacy is neither a right to secrecy nor a right to control but a right to appropriate flow of personal information" (Nissenbaum 2010, 127). In all of these versions of privacy theories, secrecy of information plays a certain role, although the exact role and desirability of secrecy is differently assessed.

The problem of secret bank accounts/transactions and the intransparency of richness and company profits is not only that financial privacy can support tax evasion, black money and money laundering, but also that it hides wealth gaps. Financial privacy reflects the classical liberal account of privacy. So, for example, John Stuart Mill formulated a right of the propertied class to economic privacy as "the owner's privacy against invasion" (Mill 1965, 232). Economic privacy (the right to keep information about income, profits or bank transactions secret) protects the rich, companies and the wealthy. The anonymity of wealth, high incomes and profits makes income and wealth gaps between the rich and the poor invisible and thereby ideologically helps legitimizing and upholding these gaps. It can therefore be considered an ideological mechanism that helps to reproduce and deepen inequality.

Privacy: A Bourgeois Value?

It would nonetheless be a mistake to dismiss privacy rights as bourgeois values. Liberal privacy discourse is highly individualistic. It always focuses on the

---

5 www.swissbanking.org/en/home/qa-090313.htm, accessed on August 24, 2011.
6 www.swissbanking.org/en/home/dossier-bankkundengeheimnis/dossier-bankkundengeheimnis-themen-geheimnis.htm, accessed on August 24, 2011.

individual and his/her freedoms. It separates the public and private sphere. Privacy in capitalism can best be characterized as an antagonistic value that is, on the one side, upheld as a universal value for protecting private property, but is at the same time permanently undermined by corporate surveillance into the lives of people for profit purposes and by political surveillance for administrative purposes, defence and law enforcement. Capitalism protects privacy for the rich and companies, but at the same time legitimates privacy violations of consumers and citizens. It thereby undermines its own positing of privacy as a universal value.

Privacy and Surveillance

In modern society, privacy is inherently linked to surveillance. Based on Foucault's (1977, 1994) notions of surveillance as disciplinary power, one can define surveillance as a specific kind of information gathering, storage, processing, assessment, and use that involves potential or actual harm, coercion, violence, asymmetric power relations, control, manipulation, domination, disciplinary power (Fuchs 2011a, 2011c). Surveillance is instrumental and a means for trying to derive and accumulate benefits for certain groups or individuals at the expense of other groups or individuals. Surveillance is based on the logic of competition. It tries to bring about or prevent certain behaviours of groups or individuals by gathering, storing, processing, diffusing, assessing and using data about humans so that potential or actual physical, ideological or structural violence can be directed against humans in order to influence their behaviour. This influence is brought about by coercive means and brings benefits to certain groups at the expense of others. In modern societies, privacy is an ideal rooted in the Enlightenment.

Capitalism is grounded in the idea that the private sphere should be separated from the public sphere, should not be accessible by the public, and that therefore autonomy and anonymity of the individual are needed in the private sphere. The rise of the idea of privacy in modern society is connected to the rise of the central ideal of the freedom of private ownership. Private ownership is the idea that humans have the right to as much wealth as they want, as long as it is inherited or acquired through individual achievements. There is an antagonism between private ownership and social equity in modern society. Many contemporary societies treat how much and what exactly a person owns as an aspect of privacy. Keeping ownership structures secret is a precautionary measure against the public questioning of or the political and individual attack against private ownership.

Capitalism requires anonymity and privacy in order to function. But full privacy is also not possible in modern society because strangers enter social relations that require trust or enable exchange. Building trust requires knowing certain data about other persons, especially in capitalist market relations. It is therefore checked with the help of surveillance procedures if a stranger can be trusted. This means that companies try to find out as much as possible about job applicants, workers, consumers and competitors and that various forms of monitoring and espionage are common means for doing so. Corporations have the aim of accumulating ever more capital. That is why they have an interest in knowing as much as possible about their workers (in order to control them) and the interests, tastes and behaviours of their customers. This results in the surveillance of workers/employees and consumers.

The ideals of modernity (such as the freedom of ownership) also produce phenomena such as income and wealth inequality, poverty, unemployment, precarious living and working conditions. The establishment of trust, socio-economic differences and corporate interests are three qualities of modernity that necessitate surveillance. Therefore modernity, on the one hand, advances the ideal of a right to privacy, but on the other hand, it must continuously advance surveillance that threatens to undermine privacy rights. An antagonism between privacy ideals and surveillance is therefore constitutive of capitalism.

An Alternative Notion of Privacy

When discussing privacy on Facebook, we should therefore go beyond a bourgeois notion of privacy and try to advance a socialist notion of privacy that attempts to strengthen the protection of consumers and citizens from corporate surveillance. Economic privacy is posited as undesirable in those cases where it protects the rich and capital from public accountability, but as desirable where it tries to protect citizens from corporate surveillance. Public surveillance of the income of the rich, and of companies and public mechanisms that make their wealth transparent, are desirable for making wealth and income gaps in capitalism visible, whereas privacy protection from corporate surveillance is also important. In a socialist privacy concept, the existing privacy values have to be reversed. Whereas today we mainly find surveillance of the poor and of citizens who are not owners of private property and surveillance for the protection of private property, a socialist privacy concept focuses on surveillance of capital and the rich in order to increase transparency and privacy protection of consumers and workers.

A socialist privacy concept conceives privacy as the collective right of dominated and exploited groups that need to be protected from corporate domination that aims at gathering information about workers and consumers for accumulating capital, disciplining workers and consumers, and for increasing the productivity of capitalist production and advertising. The liberal conception and reality of privacy as an individual right within capitalism protects the rich and the accumulation of ever more wealth from public knowledge. A socialist privacy concept as the collective right of workers and consumers can protect humans from the misuse of their data by companies. The question therefore is, privacy for whom? Privacy for dominant groups in regard to the ability to keep wealth and power secret from the public can be problematic, whereas privacy at the bottom of the power pyramid for consumers and normal citizens can be a protection from dominant interests.

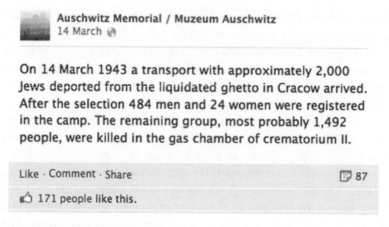

On 14 March 1943 a transport with approximately 2,000 Jews deported from the liquidated ghetto in Cracow arrived. After the selection 484 men and 24 women were registered in the camp. The remaining group, most probably 1,492 people, were killed in the gas chamber of crematorium II.

Like · Comment · Share   87

171 people like this.

Figure 7.2   An example of 'likes' on Facebook

Privacy rights should therefore be differentiated according to the position people and groups occupy in the power structure.

7.3. Facebook and Ideology

Like as Facebook Ideology: "I Like Auschwitz"

Facebook advances an ideology of liking in the form of its "Like button". It is only possible to like pages and postings, but not to dislike them. Facebook wants to spread an affirmative atmosphere, in which people only agree and do not disagree or express discontent and disagreement. One can imagine that it could be harmful for Facebook's profits if users would massively dislike certain companies that are important advertising clients of the platform. This may explain why, after Zuckerberg said in 2010 that Facebook is "definitely thinking about" introducing a dislike button,[7] nothing happened.

Figure 7.2 shows an example of the problem of Facebook's like-ideology. Many people liked a posting on the Facebook page of the Auschwitz Memorial page that says that 70 years ago 1500 Jews were killed in the gas chambers in Auschwitz.[8] One can assume that most of the users who pressed "like" are not neo-Nazis, but rather wanted to express their dismay about what had happened. Facebook's "happy-go-like" ideology does not allow expressing negative emotions. It turns Auschwitz mourners into Auschwitz likers. Likes sell, whereas dislikes contain the risk that companies obtain negative assessments. So it is more profitable for Facebook, by design, to make people like companies and also to make them "like" Auschwitz.

---

7 CNN, Should Facebook add a dislike button? July 22, 2010. http://articles.cnn.com/2010-07-22/tech/facebook. dislike.cashmore_1_facebook-users-facebook-ceo-mark-zuckerberg-dislike-button?_s=PM:TECH
8 The "I like Auschwitz" Facebook example was introduced to academic discourse by Bunz (2013, 138).

The Liberal Fetishism of Privacy

Liberal privacy theories typically talk about the positive qualities that privacy entails for humans or speak of it as an anthropological constant in all societies, without discussing the particular role of privacy in capitalist society. Solove (2008, 98) summarizes the positive values that have been associated with privacy in the existing literature: autonomy, counter-culture, creativity, democracy, eccentricity, dignity, freedom, freedom of thought, friendship, human relationships, imagination, independence, individuality, intimacy, psychological well-being, reputation, self-development. The following values can be added to this list (see the contributions in Schoeman 1984a): emotional release, individual integrity, love, personality, pluralism, self-determination, respect, tolerance, self-evaluation, trust.

Analyses that associate privacy with universal positive values tend not to engage with actual and possible negative effects of privacy or the relationship of modern privacy to private property, capital accumulation and social inequality. They give unhistorical accounts of privacy by arguing that privacy is a universal human principle that brings about positive qualities for individuals and society. They abstract from issues relating to the political economy of capitalism, such as exploitation and income/wealth inequality. But if there are negative aspects of modern privacy, such as the shielding of income gaps and of corporate crimes, then such accounts are problematic because they neglect negative aspects and present modern values as characteristic for all societies.

Karl Marx characterized the appearance of the "definite social relation between men themselves" as "the fantastic form of a relation between things" (Marx 1867, 167) as fetishistic thinking. Fetishism mistakes phenomena that are created by humans and have social and historical character as being natural and existing always and forever in all societies. Phenomena such as the commodity are declared to be "everlasting truths" (Marx 1867, 175, fn34). Theories of privacy that do not consider privacy as historical, that do not take into account the relation of privacy and capitalism or only stress its positive role, can, based on Marx, be characterized as privacy fetishism. In contrast to privacy fetishism, Barrington Moore (1984) argues, based on anthropological and historical analyses of privacy, that it is not an anthropological need "like the need for air, sleep, or nourishment" (Moore 1984, 71), but "a socially created need" that varies historically (Moore 1984, 73). The desire for privacy, according to Moore, develops only in societies that have a public sphere that is characterized by complex social relationships, which are seen as "disagreeable or threatening obligation" (Moore 1984, 72). Moore argues that this situation is the result of stratified societies, in which there are winners and losers. The alternative would be the "direct participation in decisions affecting daily lives" (Moore 1984, 79).

Privacy Fetishism in Research about Facebook

A specific form of privacy fetishism can also be found in research about Facebook and social networking sites in general. The typical standard study of privacy on Facebook and other social networking sites focuses on the analysis of information disclosures by users (in many cases younger users).[9] Bourgeois scholars argue that users' privacy is under threat because they disclose too much information about themselves and thereby become targets of criminals and harassment. Such approaches see privacy as an individual phenomenon that can be protected if users behave in the correct way and do not disclose too much information. Such approaches ignore all issues relating to the political economy of Facebook, such as advertising, capital accumulation, the appropriation of user data for economic ends, and user exploitation. One can therefore characterize such analyses as Facebook privacy fetishism.

Marx has stressed that a critical theory of society does "not preach *morality* at all" (Marx and Engels 1846, 264) because human behaviour is an expression of the conditions individuals live in. Critical theorists "do not put to people the moral demand: love one another, do not be egoists, etc.; on the contrary, they are very well aware that egoism, just as much selflessness, *is* in definite circumstances a necessary form of the self-assertion of individuals" (Marx and Engels 1846, 264). The implication of uncritical analyses of social networking sites is moral condemnation and the simplistic conclusion that it is morally bad to make personal data public. Paraphrasing Marx, critical theorists, in contrast, do not put moral demands on users not to upload personal data to public Internet platforms, because they are very well aware that this behaviour is, under capitalist circumstances, a necessary form of the self-assertion of individuals.

One can also characterize Facebook privacy fetishism as victimization discourse. Such research concludes that social networking sites pose threats that make users potential victims of individual criminals, such as in the case of cyberstalking, sexual harassment, threats by mentally ill persons, data theft, data fraud, etc. Frequently, these studies also advance the opinion that the problem is a lack of individual responsibility and knowledge, and that as a consequence users put themselves at risk by putting too much private information online and not making use of privacy mechanisms, for example by making their profile visible for all other users. One problem of the victimization discourse is that it implies young people are irresponsible, passive and ill informed, that older people are more responsible, that the young should take the values of older people as morally superior and as guidelines, and especially that there are technological fixes to societal problems. It advances the view that increasing privacy levels will technologically solve societal problems and ignores that this might create new problems because decreased visibility may result in less fun for the users, less contacts, and therefore less satisfaction, as well as in the deepening of information inequality. Another problem is that such approaches implicitly or explicitly conclude that communication technologies as such have negative effects. These are pessimistic assessments of technology that imply that it carries are inherent risks.

---

9 For example, Acquisti and Gross 2006; Barnes 2006; Dwyer 2007; Dwyer, Hiltz and Passerini 2007; Fogel and Nehmad 2009; Gross, Acquisti and Heinz 2005; Hodge 2006; Lewis, Kaufman and Christakis 2008; Livingstone 2008; Stutzman 2006; Tufekci 2008.

The causality underlying these arguments is one-dimensional: it assumes that technology causes only one negative effect on society. But both technology and society are complex, dynamic systems (Fuchs 2008a). Such systems are to a certain extent unpredictable and their complexity makes it unlikely that they will have only one effect (Fuchs 2008a). It is much more likely that there will be multiple, at least two, contradictory effects (Fuchs 2008a). The techno-pessimistic victimization discourse is also individualistic and ideological. It focuses on the analysis of individual usage behaviour without seeing or analyzing how this use is conditioned by the societal context of information technologies, such as surveillance, the global war against terror, corporate interests, neoliberalism and capitalist development.

In contrast to Facebook privacy fetishism, Critical Internet Studies' task is to analyze Facebook privacy in the context of the political economy of capitalism.

7.4. Privacy and the Political Economy of Facebook

Privacy and Private Property

Karl Marx positions privacy in relation to private property. The liberal concept of the private individual and privacy would see man as "an isolated monad, withdrawn into himself. [. . .] The practical application of the right of liberty is the right of private property" (Marx 1843c, 235). Modern society's constitution would be the "constitution of private property" (Marx 1843a, 166).

For Hannah Arendt, modern privacy is an expression of a sphere of deprivation, where humans are deprived of social relations and "the possibility of achieving something more permanent than life itself" (Arendt 1958, 58). "The privation of privacy lies in the absence of others" (Arendt 1958, 58). Arendt says that the relation between private and public is "manifest in its most elementary level in the question of private property" (Arendt 1958, 61).

Habermas (1989c) stresses that the modern concept of privacy is connected to the capitalist separation of the private and public realms. Habermas sees privacy as an illusionary ideology – "pseudo-privacy" (Habermas 1989c, 157) – that in reality functions as a community of consumers (Habermas 1989c, 156) and enables leisure and consumption as a means for the reproduction of labour power so that it remains vital, productive and exploitable (Habermas 1989c, 159).

The theories of Marx, Arendt and Habermas have quite different political implications, but all three authors stress the importance of addressing the notions of privacy, the private sphere and the public by analyzing their inherent connection to the political economy of capitalism. A critical analysis should not simply discuss privacy on Facebook as the revelation of personal data, but also inquire into the political economy and ownership structures of personal data on Facebook. Most contemporary analyses of privacy on web 2.0 and social networking sites neglect this dimension that Marx, Arendt and Habermas stressed. These three authors remind us that it is important to focus on the political economy of privacy when analyzing Facebook.

Facebook is a capitalist company. Therefore its economic goal is to achieve financial profit. It does so with the help of targeted personalized advertising, which means that it tailors advertisements to the consumption interests of the users. Social networking sites are especially suited for targeted advertising because they store and communicate a vast amount of personal likes and dislikes of users that allow surveillance of these data for economic purposes and to identify and calculate which products the users are likely to buy. This explains why targeted advertising is the main source of income and the business model of most profit-oriented social networking sites.

Facebook uses mass surveillance because it stores, compares, assesses and sells the personal data and usage behaviour of several hundred million users. But this mass surveillance is personalized and individualized at the same time, because the detailed analysis of the interests and browsing behaviour of each user and the comparison to the online behaviour and interests of other users allow Facebook to sort the users into consumer interest groups and to provide each individual user with advertisements that, based on algorithmic selection and comparison mechanisms, are believed to reflect the users' consumption interests. Facebook surveillance is mass self-surveillance (Fuchs 2011a). Mass self-surveillance (Fuchs 2011a) is the shadow side of mass self-communication (Castells 2009) under capitalist conditions. The users' permanent input and activity is needed for this form of Internet surveillance to work. The specific characteristics of web 2.0, especially the upload of user-generated content and permanent communicative flows, enable this form of surveillance.

In order to understand the political economy of Facebook, I analyze its legal-political framework (p. 164) and its accumulation model (p. 169).

Facebook's Privacy Policy
Critical Discourse Analysis

The use of targeted advertising and economic surveillance is legally guaranteed by Facebook's privacy policy. In this section of the chapter, I will conduct a qualitative critical discourse analysis of those parts of the Facebook privacy policy that are focused on advertising. It is an important principle of critical discourse analysis to contextualize texts (Van Dijk 1997, 29). Therefore the advertising-focused passages of the Facebook privacy context are put into the context of the political economy of capitalism. Another principle is to ask what meaning and functions the sentences and words have (Van Dijk 1997, 31). Therefore I discuss which meaning and role the advertising-related passages have in light of the political economy context. Critical discourse analyses challenge taken-for-granted assumptions by putting them into the context of power structures in society. "The goals of critical discourse analysis are also therefore 'denaturalizing'" (Fairclough 1995, 36). The task is to denaturalize assumptions about privacy and advertising in the Facebook privacy policy by putting them into the context of structures of power and capitalist exploitation. "One crucial presupposition of adequate critical discourse analysis is understanding the nature of social power and dominance. Once we have such an insight, we may begin to formulate ideas about how discourse contributes to their reproduction" (Van Dijk 1993, 254). By analyzing the role of advertising in the Facebook privacy policy, one can understand how self-regulatory legal mechanisms reproduce economic power and dominance.

Self-regulation

Facebook can largely regulate itself in what it wants to do with user data because it is a company that is legally registered in Palo Alto, California, USA. Facebook's privacy policy is a typical expression of a self-regulatory privacy regime, in which businesses largely define themselves by how they process personal user data. The general perception in privacy and surveillance studies is that there is very little privacy protection in the United States and that the United States lags behind Europe in protecting privacy (Tavani 2010, 166; Wacks 2010, 124; Zureik and Harling Stalker 2010, 15). Also, US data protection laws only cover government databanks and, due to business considerations, leave commercial surveillance untouched in order to maximize profitability (Ess 2009, 56; Lyon 1994, 15; Rule 2007, 97; Zureik 2010, 351).

Facebook's terms of use and its privacy policy are characteristic of the liberal US data protection policies that are strongly based on business self-regulation. They also stand for the problems associated with a business-friendly self-regulatory privacy regime: if privacy regulation is voluntary, the number of organizations engaging in it tends to be very small (Bennett and Raab 2006, 171): "Self-regulation will always suffer from the perception that it is more symbolic than real because those who are responsible for implementation are those who have a vested interest in the processing of personal data." "In the United States, we call government interference domination, and we call marketplace governance freedom. We should recognize that the marketplace does not automatically ensure diversity, but that (as in the example of the United States) the marketplace can also act as a serious constraint to freedom" (Jhally 2006, 60).

Joseph Turow (2006, 83f) argues that privacy policies of commercial Internet websites are often complex, written in turgid legalese, but formulated in a polite way. They would first assure the user that they care about his/her privacy and then spread over a long text advance elements that mean that personal data is given to (mostly unnamed) "affiliates". The purpose would be to cover up the capturing and selling of marketing data. Turow's analysis can be applied to Facebook.

Privacy Policy

Facebook wants to assure users that it deals responsibly with their data and that users are in full control of privacy controls. Therefore as an introduction to the privacy issue, it wrote: "Facebook is about sharing. Our privacy controls give you the power to decide what and how much you share."[10] Facebook's December 2012 privacy policy is 56 494 characters long (approximately 16 single-spaced A4 print pages)[11] and has increased in length in comparison to the previous versions that had 52 366 characters (version from June 8, 2012), 40 086 characters (version from September 17, 2011) and 35 709 characters (version from December 22, 2010). The policy's complexity and length makes it unlikely that users read it in detail. Facebook, on the one hand, says that it "take[s] safety issues very seriously",[12] but on the other hand, uses targeted advertising in which it sells user data to advertisers:

> When an advertiser creates an ad, they are given the opportunity to choose their audience by location, demographics, likes, keywords, and any other information we receive or can tell about you and other users. For example, an advertiser can choose to target 18 to 35 year-old women who live in the United States and like basketball. An advertiser could also choose to target certain topics or keywords, like "music" or even people who like a particular song or artist. If you indicate that you are interested in topics, such as by liking a Page, including topics such as products, brands, religion, health status, or political views, you may see ads related to those topics as well.

In its privacy policy Facebook avoids speaking of selling user-generated data, demographic data and user behaviour. It instead uses the phrase "sharing information" with third parties, which is a euphemism for the commodification of user data. The words sharing/share appear 85 times in Facebook's December 2012 privacy policy, the terms sell/selling/sale not a single time.

Unambiguous Consent?

There are no privacy settings on Facebook that allow users to disable advertisers' access to their data (there are only minor privacy settings relating to "social advertising" in Facebook friend communities). Facebook does not ask users if they find targeted advertising necessary and agree to it.

Facebook says that it does "not share any of your information with advertisers (unless, of course, you give us permission)", but targeted advertising is always activated, there is no opt-in and no opt-out option. Users must agree to the privacy terms in order to be able to use Facebook and thereby they agree to the use of their self-descriptions, uploaded data and transaction data to be sold to advertising clients. Given the fact that Facebook is the second most used web platform in the world, it is unlikely that many users refuse to use Facebook because doing so will make them miss the social opportunities to stay in touch with their friends and colleagues, to

---

10 www.facebook.com/privacy/explanation.php, accessed on January 19, 2011.
11 Facebook Data Use Policy, version from December 11, 2012, www.facebook.com/about/privacy/, accessed on December 14, 2012.
12 Facebook Data Use Policy, version from September 23, 2011.

make important new contacts, and may result in being treated as outsiders in their communities. Facebook coerces users into agreeing to the use of their personal data and collected user behaviour data for economic purposes.

If you do not agree to the privacy terms that make targeted advertising possible, you are unable to use the platform. Users are not really asked if their data can be sold to advertisers, therefore one cannot speak of user consent. Facebook utilizes the notion of "user consent" in its privacy policy in order to mask the commodification of user data as consensual. It bases its assumption on a control theory of privacy and assumes that users want to sacrifice consumer privacy in order to be able to use Facebook. When Facebook advances the idea in its privacy policy that advertising-financed social networking is needed in order to "generally make Facebook better" and to "make Facebook easier or faster to use",[13] then also a form of fetishism is at play. The idea that social networking sites can be run on a non-profit and non-commercial basis, as is attempted by the alternative social networking project Diaspora*, for example, is forestalled by presenting advertising on social networking sites as purely positive mechanisms that help improve the site. The potential problems that are posed by advertising for users are never mentioned.

Opt-out?

Advertisers not only receive data from Facebook for targeting advertising, they also use small programs, so-called cookies, to collect data about user behaviour. Facebook provides an opt-out option from this cookie setting that is not visible in the normal privacy settings, but deeply hidden in the 2012 privacy policy with a link to a webpage, where users can deactivate 97 advertising networks' usage of cookies (as of December 14, 2012). The fact that this link is hard to find makes it unlikely that users opt-out. This reflects many commercial websites' attitude towards privacy protection mechanisms as being bad for business. It also shows that Facebook values profit much higher than user privacy, which explains the attempt to make the usability for opting-out of cookie use for targeted advertising as complex as possible.

Facebook reduces the privacy issue to the topic whether users' information is visible to other users or not and under which circumstances this is the case. In the privacy settings, users can only select which information to show or not to show to other users, whereas they cannot select which data not to show to advertisers. Advertising is not part of the privacy menu and is therefore not considered as a privacy issue by Facebook. The few available advertising settings (opt-out of social advertising, use of pictures and name of users for advertising) are a submenu of the "account settings". Targeted advertising is automatically activated and cannot be deactivated in the account and privacy settings, which shows that Facebook is an advertising and economic surveillance machine that wants to store, assess and sell as much user data as possible in order to maximize its profits.

---

13 Facebook Data Use Policy, version from December 11, 2012.

Targeted Advertising

Facebook's privacy policy also enables the collection of data about users' behaviour on other websites and commodifies this data for advertising purposes (December 2012 version): "Sometimes we get data from our affiliates or our advertising partners, customers and other third parties that helps us (or them) deliver ads, understand online activity, and generally make Facebook better. For example, an advertiser may tell us information about you (like how you responded to an ad on Facebook or on another site) in order to measure the effectiveness of – and improve the quality of – ads." "Sometimes we allow advertisers to target a category of user, like a 'moviegoer' or a 'sci-fi fan.' We do this by bundling characteristics that we believe are related to the category. For example, if a person 'likes' the 'Star Trek' Page and mentions 'Star Wars' when they check into a movie theater, we may conclude that this person is likely to be a sci-fi fan. Advertisers of sci-fi movies, for example, could ask us to 'target' 'sci-fi fans' and we would target that group, which may include you. Or if you 'like' Pages that are car-related and mention a particular car brand in a post, we might put you in the 'potential car buyer' category and let a car brand target that group, which would include you."

Instant Personalization

Another quality of Facebook's 2012 privacy policy is the "instant personalization" feature. Facebook shares certain user data with other platforms, with which it has entered business partnerships. The first time a user goes to the partner website, the platform should inform him/her that it uses Facebook information about the user. In Facebook's privacy settings, one can turn off instant personalization for all of Facebook's partner sites. This is, however, an opt-out solution, which shows that Facebook wants to share the information it collects about users with partner sites so that they can also use the data for targeted advertising. This circumstance is typical for the networked character of Internet commerce and shows how strongly advertising culture shapes social media and the World Wide Web (WWW).

If a user at some point in time decides to deactivate instant personalization, but has used a Facebook partner site that employs instant personalization before, the data that the partner site uses is not automatically deleted: "If you turn off an instant personalization site or app after you have been using it or visited it a few times (or after you have given it specific permission to access your data), it will not automatically delete your data received through Facebook. Like all other apps, the site is required by our policies to delete information about you if you ask it to." This means that the user has to explicitly write to Facebook's partner sites to delete personal data. Furthermore, it is not transparent for a single user which data exactly Facebook partners store about him or her. Facebook's instant personalization feature increases the non-transparency of data storage.

7.4.2. Exploitation on Facebook

Based on Dallas Smythe's (1977, 1981/2006) notion of the audience commodity, the concept of the Internet prosumer commodity was introduced in section 5.3 of this book. Internet prosumer commodification in combination with economic surveillance that enables targeted advertising is at the heart of many commercial social media's capital accumulation strategy.

Commodification and Digital Labour on Facebook

Surveillance on Facebook is surveillance of prosumers, who dynamically and permanently create and share user-generated content, browse profiles and data, interact with others, join, create, and build communities, and co-create information. The corporate web platform operators and their third-party advertising clients continuously monitor and record personal data and online activities; they store, merge and analyze collected data. This allows them to create detailed user profiles and to know about the personal interests and online behaviours of the users. Facebook sells its prosumers as a commodity to advertising clients. Money is exchanged for the access to user data that allows economic surveillance of the users. The exchange value of the Facebook prosumer commodity is the money value that the operators obtain from their clients. Its use value is the multitude of personal data and usage behaviour that is dominated by the commodity and exchange value form. Corporations' surveillance of the prosumers' permanently produced use values, i.e. personal data and interactions, allows targeted advertising that aims at luring the prosumers into consumption and at manipulating their desires and needs in the interest of corporations and the commodities they offer.

First, corporate platform operators commodify Facebook prosumers. The latter are sold as commodities to advertising clients. Second, this process results in the users' intensified exposure to commodity logic. They are double objects of commodification, they are commodities themselves and through this commodification their consciousness becomes, while online, permanently exposed to commodity logic in the form of advertisements. Most online time is advertising time. On Facebook, targeted advertising makes use of users' personal data, interests, interactions, information behaviour, and also interactions with other websites. So while you are using Facebook, it is not just you interacting with others and browsing profiles – all of these activities are framed by advertisements presented to you. These advertisements come about by permanent surveillance of your online activities. Such advertisements do not necessarily represent consumers' real needs and desires because the ads are based on calculated assumptions, whereas needs are much more complex and spontaneous. The ads mainly reflect marketing decisions and economic power relations: the ads do not simply provide suggestions to buy certain commodities, they provide suggestions by companies that have enough money for buying advertising for specific commodities, whereas other companies or non-profit organizations cannot purchase ads, which shows how selective and driven by financial power advertising actually is. As Douglas Rushkoff (2013) says:

Facebook has never been merely a social platform. Rather, it exploits
our social interactions the way a Tupperware party does. [...] The true
end users of Facebook are the marketers who want to reach and influence us. They are Facebook's paying customers; we are the product.
And we are its workers. The countless hours that we – and the young,
particularly – spend on our profiles constitute the unpaid labor on
which Facebook justifies its stock valuation.

Surveillance and Privacy Violations on Facebook

Daniel Solove (2008, chapter 5) has worked out a model of different privacy violations that is based on a model of information processing. There is a data subject and a data holder. Privacy violation can occur in relation to the data subject
(invasion) or in relation to the data holder (information collection, processing or
dissemination). Based on these four groups of harmful violations, Solove distinguishes 16 forms of privacy violations. Many of these forms can be found when
analyzing the economic operations of Facebook:

- Facebook watches and records usage behaviour and personal data uploaded
  and entered by users (surveillance).
- It aggregates information about users that is obtained from its own site and
  other sites (aggregation).
- Based on aggregation, it identifies the consumer interests of users
  (identification).
- It is unclear with whom exactly the data is shared for economic purposes
  (exclusion from knowledge about data use; here one can also speak of the
  intransparency of data use).
- The data are exploited for profit generation and therefore for economic purposes (data appropriation, understood as "the use of the data subject's identity to serve another's aims and interests" (appropriation; Solove 2008, 105).

The surveillance, aggregation, identification, intransparency and appropriation
of personal data and usage data are essential activities of Facebook that serve
economic purposes. They are all part of Facebook's business model that is based
on targeted personalized advertising. Solove defines secondary use as a privacy
violation, where data is used for a purpose without the data subject's consent.
Commercial social networking sites are primarily used because they allow users
to communicate with their friends, colleagues and others and to establish new
relationships (Fuchs 2009c, 2010d, 2010e). Their privacy policies tend to be
complex and long. Although users formally agree to the commercial usage of
their data, they do not automatically morally agree and express concerns about
data appropriation for economic purposes (Fuchs 2009c, 2010e). Here, therefore, one can also speak of a secondary data use in a specific normative sense.

The Private on Facebook: Private Ownership

Hannah Arendt (1958) and Jürgen Habermas (1989c) stress that capitalism has traditionally been based on a separation of the private and the public sphere. Facebook is a typical manifestation of a stage of capitalism in which the relation of public and private, and labour and play, collapses, and in which this collapse is exploited by capital. "The distinction between the private and the public realms [. . .] equals the distinction between things that should be shown and things that should not be hidden" (Arendt 1958, 72). Facebook monitors, commodifies and uses all private data and user behaviour, whereas the users do not know what exactly happens with their data and to whom these data are sold for the task of targeting advertising. The intransparency of the company's use of personal data that is based on the private appropriation of user data is the main form of privacy on Facebook. Facebook privacy is privacy for the company, not user privacy.

Facebook usage's private dimension is that individual users generate content (user-generated content). When this data is uploaded to Facebook or other social media, parts of it (to a larger or smaller degree depending on the privacy settings the users choose) become available to a lot of people, whereby the data obtains a more public character. The public availability of data can have both advantages (new social relations, friendships, staying in touch with friends, family, relatives over distance, etc.) and disadvantages (job-related discrimination, stalking, etc.) for users (Fuchs 2009c, 2010d, 2010e). The private–public relation has another dimension on Facebook: the privately generated user data and the individual user behaviour become commodified on Facebook. This data is sold to advertising companies so that targeted advertising is presented to users and Facebook accumulates profit that is privately owned by the company. Facebook commodifies private data that is used for public communication in order to accumulate capital that is privately owned. The users are excluded from the ownership of the resulting money capital, i.e., they are exploited by Facebook and are not paid for their creation of surplus value (Fuchs 2010c). Facebook is a huge advertising, capital accumulation, and user-exploitation machine. Data surveillance is the means for Facebook's economic ends.

7.5. Conclusion

Facebook: Ideology and Political Economy

Facebook founder and CEO, Mark Zuckerberg, says that Facebook is about the "concept that the world will be better if you share more" (*Wired Magazine*, August 2010). Zuckerberg has repeatedly said that he does not care about profit, but wants to help people with Facebook's tools and to create an open society. Kevin Colleran, Facebook advertising sales executive, argued in a *Wired* story that "Mark is not motivated by money" (*Wired Magazine*, August 2010). In a *Times* story,[14] Zuckerberg said: "The goal of the company is to help people to share more in order

---

14 *The Times*, October 20, 2008, http://business.timesonline.co.uk/tol/business/industry_sectors/technology/article4974197.ece, accessed on August 24, 2011.

to make the world more open and to help promote understanding between people. The long-term belief is that if we can succeed in this mission then we will also be able to build a pretty good business and everyone can be financially rewarded. [. . .] The Times: Does money motivate you? Zuckerberg: No."

Zuckerberg's view of Facebook is contradicted by the analysis presented in this chapter, which has shown that Facebook's privacy strategy masks the exploitation of users. If Zuckerberg really does not care about profit, why is Facebook not a non-commercial platform and why does it use targeted advertising? The problems of targeted advertising are that it aims at controlling and manipulating human needs; that users are normally not asked if they agree to the use of advertising on the Internet, but have to agree to advertising if they want to use commercial platforms (lack of democracy); that advertising can increase market concentration; that it is intransparent for most users what kind of information about them is used for advertising purposes; and that users are not paid for, and are infinitely exploited in the value creation they engage in, when using commercial social media platforms and uploading data. Surveillance on Facebook is not only an interpersonal process, where users view data about other individuals that might benefit or harm the latter, it is primarily economic surveillance, i.e., the collection, storage, assessment and commodification of personal data, usage behaviour and user-generated data for economic purposes. Facebook, and other web 2.0 platforms, are large advertising-based capital accumulation machines that achieve their economic aims by economic surveillance.

Facebook's privacy policy is the living proof that the platform is primarily about profit-generation by advertising. "[T]he world will be better if you share more"? The real question is for whom will the world be better? "Sharing" on Facebook in economic terms means primarily that Facebook "shares" information with advertising clients. "Sharing" is the euphemism for selling and commodifying data. Facebook commodifies and trades user data and user behaviour data. Facebook does not make the world a better place; it makes the world a more commercialized place, a big shopping mall without an exit. It makes the world a better place only for companies interested in advertising, not for users.

We can summarize the main results of this chapter as follows:

- The modern concept of privacy is a highly individualistic ideology that legitimates private property relations and social inequality. It is a universal Enlightenment ideal that finds its own limit and its critique in capitalism's immanent tendencies for the surveillance of employees and consumers in the economy and the surveillance of citizens by the state that enable the accumulation of money capital and power.

- The mainstream of social networking site privacy research focuses on the topic of information revelation and ignores the political economy of privacy that is related to the exploitation of prosumer labour and targeted advertising. An uncritical, individualistic notion of privacy underlies these studies.

- Facebook's privacy policy is the legal mechanism that enables prosumer exploitation. It is complex, an expression of the self-regulatory US privacy regime, and sugar-coats the surveillance of users' personal data. Furthermore, Facebook has minimal advertising control settings, has implemented a complex usability for the few available advertising opt-out options, and conceives reducing privacy to an individual and interpersonal issue.

- Facebook's capital accumulation model commodifies the digital labour of users: (demographic and interest-oriented) profile information, user-generated content, social contacts, browsing behaviour on Facebook and other websites are monitored, stored, assessed and sold as commodity to advertising clients, who provide targeted ads to specific user groups. Facebook usage time is labour time that produces a digital data commodity that is sold to advertisers.

Aspects of ideology and commodification shape privacy on Facebook. An individualistic and uncritical concept of privacy underlies the mainstream of Facebook research. It neglects the contradictions and the political economy of capitalism. Facebook advances ideology in its privacy policy by guaranteeing users that it protects their privacy, but in the same privacy policy it enables the commodification of user data for the purpose of targeted advertising. This strategy is ideological in the sense of a constituted difference between claim and reality: Facebook claims to protect its users' privacy, but violates their privacy for economic ends. This ideological strategy serves the purpose of capital accumulation that is based on Internet prosumer commodification.

Ideology and commodification are two central aspects of Critical Political Economy (see Marx 1867: in chapters 1.1.–1.3, Marx stresses the role of the commodity in capitalism; in chapter 1.4 he outlines, with the help of the concept of fetishism, how ideology is connected to commodification). At the same time, Critical Political Economy is interested in helping to create alternatives. In the concluding chapter of this book, some elements of a socialist privacy protection strategy will be identified. We can anticipate this discussion here and say that alternatives are needed – alternatives to Facebook, alternatives to the corporate Internet, alternatives to capitalism.

Diaspora*: An Alternative to Facebook?

One strategy of socialist Internet politics is to establish and support non-commercial, non-profit Internet platforms. It is not impossible to create successful non-profit Internet platforms, as the example of Wikipedia – which is advertising-free, provides free access and is financed by donations – shows. The most well-known alternative social networking site project is Diaspora*, which tries to develop an open source alternative to Facebook. Other examples are Budypress, Crabgrass, Cryptocat, Elgg, Friendica, kaioo, Lorea, N-1, Occupii (see Cabello, Franco and Haché 2013; Sevignani 2012, 2013). Diaspora* is a project created by four New York University students – Dan Grippi, Maxwell Salzberg, Raphael Sofaer and Ilya Zhitomirskiy. Diaspora* defines itself as a "privacy-aware, personally controlled, do-it-all, open source social network".[15] It is not funded by advertising, but by

---

15 www.joindiaspora.com, accessed on November 11, 2010.

donations. The three design principles of Diaspora* are choice, self-ownership of data and simplicity.[16]

The Diaspora* team is critical of the control of personal data by corporations. It describes Facebook as "spying for free".[17] The basic idea of Diaspora* is to circumvent the corporate mediation of sharing and communication by using decentralized nodes that store data that is shared with friends.[18] Each user has his/her own data node that s/he fully controls. As Ilya Zhitomirskiy states: "On Diaspora, users are no longer dependent on corporate networks, who want to tell you that sharing and privacy are mutually exclusive."[19]

So Diaspora* aims to enable users to share data with others and at the same time to protect them from corporate domination and from having to sacrifice their data to corporate purposes in order to communicate and share. Diaspora* can therefore be considered as a socialist Internet project that practically tries to realize a socialist privacy concept. The Diaspora* team is inspired by the ideas of Eben Moglen, author of the *dotCommunist Manifesto* (2003). He says that an important political goal and possibility today is the "liberation of information from the control of ownership" with the help of networks that are "based on association among peers without hierarchical control, which replaces the coercive system" of capitalist ownership of knowledge and data (Moglen 2003). "In overthrowing the system of private property in ideas, we bring into existence a truly just society, in which the free development of each is the condition for the free development of all" (Moglen 2003).

Many Facebook users have diffuse feelings of discontent with Facebook's privacy practices that have manifested themselves into groups against the introduction of Facebook Beacon, news feed, mini-feed, etc., the emergence of the web 2.0 suicide machine (http://suicidemachine.org/), or the organization of a Quit Facebook Day (www.quitfacebookday.com/). These activities are mainly based on liberal and Luddite ideologies, but if they were connected to ongoing class struggles against neoliberalism (like the ones that have taken place throughout the world in the aftermath of the new global capitalist crisis) and the commodification of the commons, they could grow in importance.

On Facebook, the "audience" is an exploited worker-consumer – a slave-prosumer. How can socialist privacy protection strategies be structured? The overall goal is to drive back the commodification of user data and the exploitation of prosumers by advancing the decommodification of the Internet and society.

---

16 www.joindiaspora.com, accessed on March 21, 2011.
17 *New York Times*, www.nytimes.com/2010/05/12/nyregion/12about.html, March 10, 2013, accessed on August 25, 2011.
18 http://vimeo.com/11242736, accessed on March 10, 2013.
19 http://vimeo.com/11099292, accessed on March 10, 2013.

RECOMMENDED READINGS AND EXERCISES

For understanding Facebook, it makes sense to engage with its statement of rights and responsibilities, data use policy, financial statements as well as criticisms of the platform.

Read Facebook's latest Statement of Rights and Responsibilities and discuss the following questions in groups. Ask yourself:

- What rights does Google have in relation to the content that you create on its services?

- If you feel you have been treated in an illegal manner by Google, how can you hold it legally reliable? Which court is responsible?

- Try to find more information on how national regulations (e.g. the ones in your home country) work for a global system like the Internet?

Read Facebook's latest Data Use Policy and ask yourself the following questions:

- Make a systematic and ordered list of data that Facebook collects about users.

- Discuss which data Facebook uses for targeted advertising. Find out how this form of advertising works. Which data does Facebook use about you for targeted advertising?

- Are there mechanisms for limiting targeted advertising on Facebook? Do you think they are sufficient? Why? Why not?

- How do you politically assess targeted advertising?

- Are there alternative organization models for social media that do not use targeted advertising? Which ones? How do you think social media should best be organized?

Read Facebook's latest Proxy Statement and its Annual Financial Report. You will find both on its website under SEC Filings. Ask yourself:

- How does Facebook present itself in these documents?

- Try to make sense of and interpret the financial data presented in the reports. What do Google's ownership structure and its financial operations look like?

- According to these reports, what role does advertising play in Google's operations?

Work in groups and present the results of the following exercises to the class.

Facebook has faced a lot of criticism. These exercises focuses on engagement with this criticism.

- Search for videos, documents, press releases, blog posts etc., in which Facebook presents itself. What kind of image does Facebook construct of itself? What are the major themes in its discourse?

- Search for documents, interviews, news articles, reports by critical scholars, critical journalists, civil society representatives, privacy and data protection advocates, consumer protection advocates and organizations as well as watchdog organizations that criticize the topics that Google presented in a positive light in the material you found earlier. Summarize the basic points of criticism. Compare them to how Facebook presents itself. Discuss which assessments you find more convincing and provide reasons for your assessments.

- The initiative Europe vs. Facebook filed a complaint about Facebook to the Irish Data Protection Commissioner. First, read the basic complaint documents and the Irish Data Protection Commissioner's audit. Conduct a search about how Facebook, Europe vs. Facebook and other data protection commissioners (e.g. Thilo Weichert in Germany and others) have reacted to the audit report. Document the discussion and its basic arguments. Position yourself on the involved political issues. Present your results.

Fuchs, Christian. 2011. How to define surveillance? *MATRIZes* 5 (1): 109–133.

Gandy, Oscar H. 1996. Coming to terms with the panoptic sort. In *Computers, surveillance & privacy*, ed. David Lyon and Elia Zureik, 132–155. Minneapolis, MN: University of Minnesota Press.

Mathiesen, Thomas. 1997. The viewer society: Michel Foucault's "Panopticon" revisited. *Theoretical Criminology* 1 (2): 215–334.

Fuchs, Christian. 2012. Political economy and surveillance theory. *Critical Sociology*, first published on April 2, 2012 as doi: 10.1177/0896920511435710

Allmer, Thomas. 2011. Critical surveillance studies in the information age. *tripleC: Communication, Capitalism & Critique: Open Access Journal for a Global Sustainable Information Society* 9 (2): 566–592.

These readings deal with the notion of surveillance in the context of computing. Read the texts and ask yourself:

- How should surveillance best be defined?

- What is the relevance of Michel Foucault's works for studying surveillance?

- What is the panoptic sort? What is the synopticon?

- Do the panoptic sort and the synopticon matter for understanding social media? Try to find examples that you can analyze with the help of these concepts.

- What are aspects of the political economy of surveillance on social media? Try to give some examples.

Arendt, Hannah. 1958. *The human condition* (2nd edition). Chicago, IL: University of Chicago Press. Chapter 8: The private realm: property. Chapter 9: The social and the private.

Habermas, Jürgen. 1989c. *The structural transformation of the public sphere*. Cambridge, MA: MIT Press. Chapter 17: The polarization of the social sphere and the intimate sphere.

Fuchs, Christian. 2011. Towards an alternative concept of privacy. *Journal of Information, Communication and Ethics in Society* 9 (4): 220–237.

Allmer, Thomas. 2011. A critical contribution to theoretical foundations of privacy studies. *Journal of Information, Communication and Ethics in Society* 9 (2): 83–101.

Fuchs, Christian. 2012. The political economy of privacy on Facebook. *Television & New Media* 13 (2): 139–159.

Ask yourself:

- What are Arendt and Habermas' basic criticisms of privacy? In which respect do these criticisms matter for understanding Facebook and other social media critically?

- In light of the criticisms of privacy, do you think there is anything that is politically valuable about this concept? If so, why and what? If not, why not?

- Discuss what the advantages and disadvantages of the privacy concept are and how they relate to Facebook and other social media.

Fuchs, Christian, Kees Boersma, Anders Albrechtslund, Marisol Sandoval, eds. 2012. *The Internet and surveillance: The challenges of web 2.0 and social media*. New York: Routledge. Chapter by Christian Fuchs: Critique of the political economy of web 2.0 surveillance. Chapter by Mark Andrejevic: Exploitation in the data mine. Chapter by Daniel Trottier and David Lyon: Key features of social media surveillance.

Ask yourself:

- Make a systematic and ordered typology of characteristics of social media surveillance. Give a name to each dimension and take care that the dimensions are not overlapping. Constructing such a typology presupposes that you understand and can define the terms "social media" and "surveillance".

- Have a look at your characteristics of social media surveillance. Give two examples that relate to specific platforms for each dimension.

Atton, Chris. 2002. *Alternative media*. London: SAGE. Chapter 1: Approaching alternative media: Theory and methodology. Chapter 2: The economics of production.

Sandoval, Marisol. 2009. A critical contribution to the foundations of alternative media studies. *Kurgu – Online International Journal of Communiation Studies* 1: 1–18.

Fuchs, Christian. 2010. Alternative media as critical media. *European Journal of Social Theory* 13 (2): 173–192.

Sandoval, Marisol and Christian Fuchs. 2010. Towards a critical theory of alternative media. *Telematics and Informatics* 27 (2): 141–150.

Sevignani, Sebastian. 2012. The problem of privacy in capitalism and the alternative social networking site Diaspora*. *tripleC: Communication, Capitalism & Critique: Open Access Journal for a Global Sustainable Information Society* 10 (2): 600–617.

Social networking sites like Diaspora*, Occupii and N-1 are alternative social networking sites. Make a list of 10 alternative social networking sites. This presupposes that you have an understanding of what an alternative medium is. Ask yourself:

- What is an alternative medium? Discuss different meanings of the term and devise a working definition.

- In which respect can the social networking sites that you selected be considered as being alternatives to Facebook? What does the term "alternatives" here mean? In what respect are the platforms different from Facebook?

- Compare the terms of use and privacy policy of these platforms to the ones of Facebook. What are the differences and commonalities?

Rushkoff, Douglas. 2013. Why I'm quitting Facebook. *CNN*, February 25, 2013. http://edition.cnn.com/2013/02/25/opinion/rushkoff-why-im-quitting-facebook, accessed on July 4, 2013.

Scholz, Trebor. 2010. Facebook as playground and factory. In *Facebook and philosophy*, ed. Dylan E. Wittkower, 241–252. Chicago, IL: Open Court.

Kiss, Jemina. 2010. "Facebook should be paying us". *The Guardian*, August 9, 2010. www.guardian.co.uk/media/2010/aug/09/facebook-users-union-demands-payment

Ask yourself:

- What are the basic points of criticism of Facebook formulated by Douglas Rushkoff, Trebor Scholz and Richard Buchanan?

- Which strategies of resistance are mentioned? What commonalities and differences are there? What other strategies are there? What do you think about such strategies?

- One strategy is to demand a wage from Facebook for platform usage. This demand is based on the assumption that Facebook usage is labour that creates value. Another strategy is to build, use and support alternative non-commercial platforms such as Diaspora*. What are the differences of these strategies? What do you think about them? What are their ultimate goals?

Twitter and Democracy:
A New Public Sphere?

Key questions

- What is a public sphere?
- Does Twitter contribute towards the creation of a public sphere?
- How has Twitter been criticized?
- What are the political economic limits of Twitter?
- Is Twitter emancipatory? What are the limits of political communication on Twitter?
- Can the 2011 rebellions (Arab spring, Occupy etc) be called Twitter revolutions and Twitter protests?

Key concepts

Public sphere
Jürgen Habermas's concept of the public sphere
Political communication
Public sphere as immanent critique
Private sphere
Communicative capitalism

Slacktivism and clicktivism
Visibility on Twitter
Pseudo public sphere
Manufactured public sphere
Technological determinism
Social revolution
Social media revolutions

Overview

A blog is a website that features periodically published postings that are organized in reverse chronological order so that the newest postings are shown first. A microblog is a further development of the blog concept: one shares short messages with the public and each user has a contact list of persons who are following these messages. Microblogging is like sending SMS online to a large number of people. A microblog is "an Internet-based service in which: (1) users

have a public profile where they broadcast short public messages/updates [...]
(2) messages become publicly aggregated together across users; and (3) users
can decide whose messages they wish to receive, but not necessarily who can
receive their messages" (Murthy 2013, 10). The two most popular microblogs in
the world are Twitter and Weibo. The Chinese company SINA owns Weibo, which
was created in 2009. Twitter was created in 2006. It is owned by Twitter Inc., a
company founded by Jack Dorsey that is based in San Francisco.

Lotan, Graeff, Ananny, Gaffney, Pearce and boyd (2011) analyzed 168 663
tweets from the Tunisian revolution and 230 270 from the Egyptian one. They
found that journalists and activists were the main sources of retweets and that
bloggers and activists were the most active retweeters. However, it is hard to see
why the presented evidence should support the authors' claim that "the revolutions were, indeed, tweeted" (1401). The analysis says nothing about what role
these tweets had in mobilizing activists on the streets and how relevant Twitter
was for street activists. In contrast to surveys and interviews with Egyptian activists, the analysis of tweets cannot provide conclusive evidence about the role of
social media in the revolution. In March 2011, only 0.00158% of the Egyptian
population used Twitter (Murthy 2013, 107). It is therefore likely that "much of
Twitter's prominence in relation to the 'Arab Spring' arose from individuals in
the West tweeting and retweeting" (Murthy 2013, 112), which may have helped
to "raise global awareness" (113), but cannot be considered to have caused a
revolution. Lotan et al.'s assumption that the Tunisian and Egyptian revolutions
were tweeted is characterized by the "self-absorption and parochialism" of much
Western media research (Curran and Park 2000, 3) that assesses what is happening in non-Western countries from a Western perspective and through the lenses
of Western technology. Daya Thussu (2009, 24) has, in this context, called for the
"decolonization of thoughts and theory".

Twitter revolution claims imply that Twitter constitutes a new public sphere
of political communication that has emancipatory political potentials. This chapter questions these assumptions. It asks the question: Is Twitter a political public sphere? Lindgren and Lundström (2011, 1015) argue that Twitter and the
Internet have "a particularly strong potential" to create a space for what Ulrich
Beck terms subpolitics: politics that are not "governmental, parliamentary, and
party politics", but take place in "all the other fields of society" (Beck 1997, 52).
This chapter asks the question how large this potential is and what its limits are.
Its analysis belongs to the field of political Twitter research, in which the topic of
the public sphere has thus far been rather neglected.

Concepts of the public sphere are strongly connected to Jürgen Habermas's
theory (see Calhoun 1992a; Roberts and Crossley 2004a). Dealing with the posed
research question requires, therefore, a close engagement with Habermas's concept of the public sphere and a discussion of its relation to the Internet (section 8.1). Section 8.2 discusses how some scholars conceive the impact of social
media on the public sphere. I will discuss the approaches of Clay Shirky, Zizi
Papacharissi, Jodi Dean, Malcolm Gladwell and Evgeny Morozov and argue that
the public sphere has two main aspects: political communication and political
economy. Based on the theory framework, I present in section 8.3 an empirical

analysis of the role of Twitter and social media in the public sphere's political communication, and in section 8.4 how Twitter and social media's political economy impact the public sphere. Section 8.5 connects these results to Habermas's theory and section 8.6 draws some conclusions.

8.1. Habermas's Concept of the Public Sphere

What is the Public Sphere?

Habermas has defined the notion of the public: "We call events and occasions 'public' when they are open to all, in contrast to close or exclusive affairs" (Habermas 1989c, 1). Habermas (1989c, 6) argues that the concept of the public is related to the notion of the common that is associated with ideas like *Gemeinschaft* (German), community, the common use of resources like a marketplace or a fountain, and communal organization (in German: *genossenschaftliche*, Organisation) (Habermas 1989c, 6).

Habermas characterizes some important dimensions of the public sphere (Habermas 1989b, 136, 1989c, 27):

- Formation of public opinion.
- All citizens have access.
- Conference in unrestricted fashion (freedom of assembly, freedom of association, freedom to expression and publication of opinions) about matters of general interest.
- Debate over the general rules governing relations.

Habermas's original concept of the public sphere is grounded in Marxian political theory (see Habermas 1989c, 122–129). In his discussion of Marx's relevance for the concept of the public sphere, Habermas stresses:

- Private property and skills are required for participating in the public sphere, but wageworkers have been excluded from these resources.
- The bourgeois class serves and advances particular interests (its own profit interests), not the general interests of society.
- Marx imagined alternatives to the bourgeois state that serves class interests when he described the Paris Commune (March–May 1871) as a specific kind of public sphere.

The Working-class Critique of the Public Sphere Concept

There have been two common critiques of Habermas's theory of the public sphere. The *working-class critique* stresses that Habermas focuses on the bourgeois movement and neglects other popular movements that existed in the seventeenth, eighteenth and nineteenth centuries, such as the working-class movement. Oskar Negt's and Alexander Kluge's (1972) notion of a pro-letarian (counter) public sphere can be read as both a socialist critique and a radicalization of Habermas's approach (see Calhoun 1992b, 5; Jameson 1988).

Such criticism should, however, see that Habermas acknowledged in the preface of *Structural Transformation* the existence of a "plebeian public sphere", like in the Chartist movement or the anarchist working class (Habermas 1989c, xviii), and that he pointed out that the "economically dependent masses" would only be able to contribute "to the spontaneous formation [. . .] of opinion [. . .] to the extent to which they had attained the equivalent of the social independence of private property owners" (Habermas 1992, 434).

The Feminist Critique of the Public Sphere Concept

The feminist critique points out that the public sphere has been a sphere of educated, rich men, juxtaposed to the private sphere that has been seen as the domain of women. Women, gays and lesbians, and ethnicities would have been excluded from the public sphere. It would therefore today be more promising that struggles against oppression take place in multiple subaltern counter publics than in one unified sphere. The criticism also stresses that an egalitarian society should be based on a plurality of public arenas in order to be democratic and multicultural (Eley 1992; Fraser 1992; Roberts and Crossley 2004b). Habermas agrees that his early account in *The Structural Transformation of the Public Sphere* (Habermas 1989c), published in 1962, has neglected proletarian, feminist and other public spheres (Habermas 1992, 425–430).

The danger of pluralistic publics without unity is, however, that they will in social struggle focus on mere reformist identity politics without challenging the whole, which negatively affects the lives of all subordinated groups, and that in an egalitarian society common communication media are needed for guaranteeing cohesion and solidarity and a strong democracy. Postmodernists and post-Marxists are so occupied with stressing difference that they do not realize that difference can become repressive if it turns into a plurality with-out unity. One needs unity in diversity in order to struggle for participatory democracy and for maintaining this condition once it is reached. It is prefer-able and more effective to have a few widely accessible and widely consumed broad critical media than many small-scale special interest media that sup-port the fragmentation of struggles. Nicholas Garnham argues in this context for the need of a single public sphere and says that the postmodernists risk "cultural relativism" if they do not see that democracy is in need of "some common normative dimensions" and "more generalized media" (Garnham 1992, 369).

The Public Sphere: Political Communication and Political Economy

In discussions about the Internet and the public sphere, many authors have stressed the potential or limit of the Internet to advance political communication (for example, Benkler 2006; Dahlberg 2001, 2004; Dahlgren 2005, 2009; Papacharissi 2002, 2009), whereas a smaller number have also stressed that aspects of the political economy of the media and the Internet relate directly to the concept of the public sphere (for example, Garnham 1992; Sparks 2001).

It is important to see that Habermas stresses both aspects of (a) political communication and (b) political economy as being constitutive for the public sphere. So he stresses (a) that the proper task of the public sphere is that "society [is] engaged in critical public debate" (Habermas 1989c, 52). But Habermas also points out (b) that the public sphere is a question of the command of resources (property, intellectual skills) by its members: "But even under ideally favorable conditions of communication, one could have expected from economically dependent masses a contribution to the spontaneous formation of opinion and will only to the extent to which they had attained the equivalent of the social independence of private property owners" (Habermas 1992, 434).

Habermas stresses that Marx's work is especially relevant for the second dimension of the public sphere. Marx's "critique demolished all fictions to which the idea of the public sphere of civil society appealed. In the first place, the social preconditions for the equality of opportunity were obviously lacking, namely: that any person with skill and 'luck' could attain the status of property owner and thus the qualifications of a private person granted access to the public sphere, property and education. The public sphere with which Marx saw himself confronted contradicted its own principle of universal accessibility" (Habermas 1989c, 124).

Habermas: No Idealization of the Public Sphere, but rather Public Sphere as Concept of Immanent Critique

Habermas does not idealize the bourgeois public sphere, but rather applies an elegant dialectical logic to show that the bourgeois ideals and values find their own limits in the existence of stratification and class. Habermas showed, based on Marx (critique of the political economy: class character of the public sphere) and Horkheimer (ideology critique: manipulated public sphere), how the very principles of the public sphere are stylized principles that in reality within capitalist society are not realized due to the exclusory character of the public sphere and the manipulation of the public sphere by particularistic class interests.

Habermas's theory of the public sphere is an ideology-critical study in the tradition of Adorno's (1951/2003) method of immanent critique that confronts the ideals of the public sphere with its capitalist reality and thereby uncovers its ideological character. The implication is that a true public sphere can only exist in a participatory society.

Liberal ideology postulates individual freedoms (of speech, opinion, association, assembly) as universal rights, but the particularistic and stratified class character of capitalism undermines these universal rights and creates inequality and therefore unequal access to the public sphere. There are specifically two immanent limitations of the bourgeois public sphere that Habermas discusses:

- The limitation of freedom of speech and public opinion: individuals do not have the same formal education and material resources for participating in public sphere (Habermas 1989c, 227).
- The limitation of freedom of association and assembly: big political and economic organizations "enjoy an oligopoly of the publicistically effective and politically relevant formation of assemblies and associations" (Habermas 1989c, 228).

The bourgeois public sphere creates its own limits and thereby its own immanent critique.

For discussing whether the Internet or certain Internet platforms constitute a public sphere, one should take both the level of political communication and the level of political economy into account. This allows asking specific questions that can help to determine whether we can speak of the existence of a public sphere.

1) Analysis of the political economic dimension of mediated communication:

   1(a) Ownership:

      Is there a democratic ownership of the media organization and resources?

   1(b) Censorship:

      Is there political and/or economic censorship?

   1(c) Exclusion:

      Is there an overrepresentation of viewpoints of corporate elites or of uncritical and pro-capitalist viewpoints? To which degree are critical viewpoints present?

   1(d) Political content production:

      Who can produce content? How visible, relevant and influential is the produced content?

2) Analysis of political communication:

   2(a) Universal access:

      How relevant/frequently used are political communication sites or political communication forums/features/contents within more general platforms? Who has access and who uses the sites for political communication (income, education level, age, gender, ethnicity, origin, etc.)? How relevant is political communication in relation to other forms of communication (for example, as pure entertainment)? Who has access and who uses the sites for political communication (income, education level, age, gender, ethnicity, origin, etc.)?

2(b) Independence:

How independent are the sites and discussions from economic and state interests?

2(c) Quality of political discussion:

How valid (right, true, truthful, understandable), inclusive, attentive, sincere, reflexive and inclusive is political online discussion?

8.2. Twitter, Social Media and the Public Sphere

The rise of blogs (e.g. Wordpress, Blogspot, Tumblr), social networking sites (e.g. Facebook, LinkedIn, Diaspora*, VK), microblogs (e.g. Twitter, Weibo), wikis (e.g. Wikipedia) and content sharing sites (e.g. YouTube, Flickr, Instagram) has resulted in public discussions on the implications of these media for the political realm. There are, on the one hand, more optimistic and, on the other hand, more sceptical views. This section introduces five approaches that have in common that they focus on discussing the role of social media in politics.

Clay Shirky: Social Media as Radically New Enhancers of Freedom

Clary Shirky argued in 2008 that the political use of "social media" ultimately enhances freedom: "Social tools create what economists would call a positive supply-side shock to the amount of freedom in the world. [. . .] To speak online is to publish, and to publish online is to connect with others. With the arrival of globally accessible publishing, freedom of speech is now freedom of the press, and freedom of the press is freedom of assembly" (Shirky 2008, 172).

Whereas one assumption in this discourse is that new media have predominantly positive effects, another one is that they bring about radical change: "Our social tools are dramatically improving our ability to share, co-operate, and act together. As everyone from working biologists to angry air passengers adopts those tools, it is leading to an epochal change" (Shirky 2008, 304).

Zizi Papacharissi: The Idealization of Individualization – The Private Sphere

Papacharissi (2010, 21) has advanced an approach that is comparable to the one by Shirky, in which she argues that political activities that were in former times "activities pursued in the public realm" are today practised in the private realm "with greater autonomy, flexibility, and potential for expression". Social media like Twitter would make the private sphere "a sphere of connection and not isolation, as it serves primarily to connect the personal to the political, and the self to the polity and society" (Papacharissi 2010, 164).

New forms of politics would include tweeting, "participating in a MoveOn.org online protest, expressing political opinion on blogs, viewing or posting content on YouTube, or posting a comment in an online discussion group" (Papacharissi 2010, 131). Such online activities would constitute "an expression of dissent with a public agenda. [. . .] these potentially powerful acts of dissent emanate from a private sphere of interaction, meaning that the citizen engages and is enabled politically through a private media environment located within the individual's personal and private space" (Papacharissi 2010, 131).

Papacharissi assumes that social media like Twitter have resulted in a collapse of the boundaries between the private sphere and the political public sphere so that the private sphere becomes the realm of the political. She overlooks that co-presence and physicality matter also in a networked world. A huge mass of people gathering in physical places is a visible threat to those in power and it can have material effects (like blocking streets, occupying squares and buildings, etc.).

It is no surprise that the main protests during the new global capitalist crisis have been associated with physical spaces: Tahrir Square in Cairo, Egypt; Syntagma Square in Athens, Greece; Puerta del Sol in Madrid, Spain; Plaça Catalunya in Barcelona, Spain; Zuccotti Park (Liberty Plaza Park) in New York, USA. Physical spaces allow an agglomeration of individuals that gives them a visibility that those in power likely perceive as a threat. They also provide opportunities for building and maintaining interpersonal relations that involve eye contact, communication of an emotional aura, and bonding activities (like drinking a beer or coffee together) that are important for the cohesion of a political movement and can hardly be communicated over the Internet.

Papacharissi reduces collective action to individual action and the public sphere to the private sphere. She ignores the materiality of protest action. Her approach is individualistic, reductionist and philosophically idealistic. I thereby do not say that social media never matter. I rather want to stress that social media cannot replace collective action that involves spatio-temporal presence. Social media can, given a good organization, high interest and a lot of resources, serve as protest co-ordination and organization tools. However, the reality of protests shows that they cannot replace collective protest action and experience.

Online activism can cause material and symbolic harm and be a threat to the powerful, as the hacking activities of the Anonynous group (e.g. blocking of the sites of Amazon, MasterCard, PostFinanc, PayPal and Visa as revenge for the companies' blocking of payments to WikiLeaks, blocking of government websites in Tunisia, Egypt, Libya and Syria in solidarity with the Arab Spring, the hacking of sites by Koch Industries that supported anti-union groups as part of the 2011 Wisconsin protests) show, but a lot of "online politics" is harmless (writing a blog, posting a tweet or YouTube video, signing an online petition, joining a Facebook group, etc.) and can simply be ignored by the powerful.

danah boyd (2010, 39) defines a networked public as "(1) the space constructed through networked technologies and (2) the imagined collective that emerges as a result of the intersection of people, technology, and practice". Expressions in networked publics would be persistent (recorded, archived), replicable, scalable and searchable. Audiences in these publics would often be invisible, social contexts collapsed and the boundary between public and private would often blur. For boyd, Facebook and Twitter are prototypes of networked publics. Whereas Papacharissi idealizes private individuals' political use of social media as new forms of the public sphere, boyd generalizes the notion of the public from a political context to the whole realm of social media so that the notion of the public (sphere) loses any critical dimension. The notion of the networked public is not only an apolitical concept; it is at the same time one that idealizes corporate social media: the notions of being public and being networked create a purely positive image of human activity without conceptualizing potential problems. As a consequence, the concept of social media as "networked publics" predominantly creates positive associations; it lacks any critical dimension that addresses power asymmetries, the exploitation of digital labour, asymmetric visibility, commercial culture and targeted advertising, corporate and state surveillance and other problems that manifest themselves on dominant social media platforms.

Jodi Dean: Social Media Politics as Ideology

Jodi Dean (2005) argues, therefore, that the Internet has in the context of communicative capitalism become a technological fetish that advances post-politics. What Papacharissi (2010) calls the emergence of a political private sphere is, for Dean, the foreclosure of politics proper. "File sharing is political. A website is political. Blogging is political. But this very immediacy rests on something else, on a prior exclusion. And, what is excluded is the possibility of politicization proper" (Dean 2005, 65).

> Busy people can think they are active – the technology will act for them, alleviating their guilt while assuring them that nothing will change too much. [. . .] By sending an e-mail, signing a petition, responding to an article on a blog, people can feel political. And that feeling feeds communicative capitalism insofar as it leaves behind the time-consuming, incremental and risky efforts of politics. [. . .] It is a refusal to take a stand, to venture into the dangerous terrain of politicization. (Dean 2005, 70)

Malcolm Gladwell: Social Media – No Natural Enemies of the Status Quo

In response to the techno-euphoria about social media, Malcolm Gladwell (2010) argued that activists in revolutions and rebellions risk their lives and risk becoming victims of violence conducted by the police or the people their protest is directed at. Taking the courage to face these dangers would require strong social ties and friendships with others in the movement. Activism would involve high risks. "The kind of activism associated with social media isn't like this at all. The platforms of social media are built around weak ties" (Gladwell 2010, 45).

Facebook and Twitter activism would only succeed in situations that do not require people "to make a real sacrifice" (Gladwell 2010, 47), such as registering in a bone-marrow database or getting back a stolen phone. "The evangelists of social media", such as Clay Shirky, "seem to believe that a Facebook friend is the same as a real friend and that signing up for a donor registry in Silicon Valley today is activism in the same sense as sitting at a segregated lunch counter in Greensboro in 1960" (Gladwell 2010, 46). Social media would "make it easier for activists to express themselves, and harder for that expression to have any impact" (Gladwell 2010, 49). Social media "are not a natural enemy of the status quo" and "are well suited to making the existing social order more efficient" (Gladwell 2010, 49).

Evgeny Morozov: Social Media and Slacktivism/Clicktivism

Evgeny Morozov (2009) speaks in line with Gladwell's argument of slacktivism as:

> feel-good online activism that has zero political or social impact. It gives those who participate in "slacktivist" campaigns an illusion of having a meaningful impact on the world without demanding anything more than joining a Facebook group. [. . .] "Slacktivism" is the ideal type of activism for a lazy generation: why bother with sit-ins and the risk of arrest, police brutality, or torture if one can be as loud campaigning in the virtual space?

Morozov (2010) argues that the notion of "Twitter revolution" is based on a belief in cyber-utopianism – "a naive belief in the emancipatory nature of online communication that rests on a stubborn refusal to acknowledge its downside" (Morozov 2010, xiii) that, combined with Internet-centrism, forms a techno-deterministic ideology

Shirky's Response to Gladwell and Morozov

In an article that can be read as a kind of response to criticism, Clay Shirky (2011b, 29), mentioning both Gladwell and Morozov, acknowledges that the use of social media "does not have a single preordained outcome". Social media would be "coordinating tools for nearly all of the world's political movements, just as most of the world's authoritarian governments (and, alarmingly, an increasing number of democratic ones) are trying to limit access to it" (Shirky 2011b, 30). Shirky admits that there are attempts to control, censor and monitor social media, but argues at the same time that these attempts are unlikely to be successful in the long run and that social media are "long-term tools that can strengthen civil society and the public sphere" (Shirky 2011b, 32).

Social media would facilitate shared awareness and result in "the dictator's dilemma"/"the conservative dilemma" (Shirky 2011b, 36):

> The dilemma is created by new media that increase public access to speech or assembly; with the spread of such media, whether photo-copiers or Web browsers, a state accustomed to having a monopoly on public speech finds itself called to account for anomalies between its view of events and the public's. The two responses to the conserv-ative dilemma are censorship and propaganda. But neither of these is as effective a source of control as the enforced silence of the citizens. The state will censor critics or produce propaganda as it needs to, but both of those actions have higher costs than simply not having any critics to silence or reply to in the first place. But if a government were to shut down Internet access or ban cell phones, it would risk radicalizing otherwise pro-regime citizens or harming the economy. (Shirky 2011b, 36f)

Shirky sees two sides of social media, but argues that the positive side over-determines the negative one and that in the last instance social media have posi-tive effects on democracy. So although acknowledging contradictions in order to make his argument more complex, Shirky postulates the techno-deterministic equation: social media = more democracy = more freedom. Shirky (2011b, 38) argues that the slacktivism argument is irrelevant because "the fact that barely committed actors cannot click their way to a better world does not mean that committed actors cannot use social media effectively".

In a response to Shirky, Gladwell wrote that Shirky "has to convince read-ers that in the absence of social media, those uprisings would not have been possible" (Gladwell and Shirky 2011, 153). Shirky answered that "social media allow insurgents to adopt new strategies" that are crucial, "allow com-mitted groups to play by new rules" and that "as with the printing press", social media "will result in a net improvement for democracy" (Gladwell and Shirky 2011, 154). So, asked for clarification, Shirky confirmed the view that, although acknowledging complexity, the formula remains in the last instance "the Internet = increase of democracy".

Clay Shirky and Zizi Papacharissi, on the one hand, and Jodi Dean, Malcolm Gladwell and Evgeny Morozov, on the other hand, have opposing views on the question of whether Twitter and other social media, under the given societal context, advance or harm the political public. For readers of this book, it will be obvious that I am sceptical of the first position and have sympathies with the second one. But one can only give a definitive answer to this question by empirical inquiries that cover aspects of both political communication and political economy.

8.3. Political Communication on Twitter

The Stratification of Twitter and Microblog Usage

The typical Twitter user was, in 2013, between 18 and 34 years old, held a university degree and had no children.[1] The relative majority of users came from the USA (20.9%, ibid.). In contrast, 92.4% of Weibo's users are located in China.[2] In the United States, the typical Twitter user was, in 2013, part of a younger age group of up to 34 years (62%), white (67%) and earned more than US$100 000 per year (58%).[3]

Stratification patterns that are created by age, ethnicity and class shape the use of Twitter and microblogs in general. The hypothesis of the end of information inequality (what is in a misleading way often called the "digital divide") due to the rapid adoption of the Internet (for example, as claimed by Compaine 2001) is a myth. Stratification no longer so much concerns physical access to the Internet, but rather the use of this technology and the skills required for this use. As long as there is a stratified society, information inequality will exist.

This pattern is not only specific to Twitter use in Western countries; as already mentioned, 93.4% of all Weibo users live in China. The typical user is 25–34 years old, has attended university and has no children.[4] Just like in the West, the urban middle-class also dominates microblogging in China, whereas workers, farmers, old people and others are rather excluded. Inequality in China and the West is a feature that shows that a similar neoliberal logic shapes both systems (Zhao 2008).

The Asymmetrical Power of Visibility on Twitter

In 2009, only 7% of the top Twitter trend topics were political topics and 38% were entertainment-oriented topics. In 2010, only 3% were about politics, 28% about entertainment and 40% about hashtags (#). An analysis of the most-used hashtags in 2010 shows that politics was marginal and that music and dating were the most used hashtag topics.[5] Table 8.1 documents the top Twitter trends in 2009, 2010, 2011 and 2012. The statistics show that Twitter topics are dominated by entertainment. Politics is not a particularly important topic in contrast to entertainment. Table 5.4 in Chapter 5 of this book shows a ranking of Twitter users ordered by number of followers. Celebrities from the entertainment business, particularly pop stars, dominate attention measured by number of Twitter followers. Politics is much less represented and mainly in the form of influential political actors, such as Barack Obama, CNN and *The New York Times*, that dominate the political field in terms of influence, resources and reputation. Alternative political figures, such as political documentary producer Michael Moore, have far

---

1 www.alexa.com/siteinfo/twitter.com, accessed on March 4, 2013.
2 www.alexa.com/siteinfo/weibo.com, accessed on March 4, 2013.
3 www.quantcast.com/twitter.com, accessed on March 4, 2013.
4 www.alexa.com/siteinfo/weibo.com, accessed on March 3, 2013.
5 http://mashable.com/2010/12/22/top-twitter-trends-2010-charts/, accessed on August 20, 2011.

Table 8.1 Top trends on Twitter (C = crisis, E = entertainment, I = instrument, T = technology, P = politics, EV = event)

#	2012 top Twitter trends	Type	2011 top Twitter trends	Type	2010 top Twitter trends	Type	2010 top hashtags	Type	2009 top Twitter hashtags	Type
1	Olympics	EV	Justin Bieber	E	Gulf Oil Spill	C	#rememberwhen	E	#musicmonday	E
2	Election 2012	P	Soccer/Sport	E	FIFA World Cup	E	#slapyourself	E	#iranelection	P
3	Justin Bieber	E	Lady Gaga	E	Inception	E	#confessiontime	E	#sxsw	E
4	Hurricane Sandy	C	NBA	C	Haiti Earthquake	C	#thingsimiss	E	#swineflu	C
5	MTV Music Awards	E	Jonas Brothers	E	Vuvuzela	I	#ohjustlikeme	E	#nevertrust	E
6	Euro 2012	EV	Christmas	EV	Apple iPad	T	#wheniwaslittle	E	#mm	E
7	Super Bowl	EV	Super Junior	EV	Google Android	T	#haveuever	E	#rememberwhen	E
8	Whitney Houston	E	Britney Spears	E	Justin Bieber	E	#icantlivewithoutit	E	#3drunkwords	E
9	Kony	E	Japan Earthquake	C	Harry Potter & the Deathly Hallows	E	#thankful	E	#unacceptable	E
10	One Direction	E	One Direction	E	Pulpo Paul	E	#2010disappointments	E	#iwish	E

Data sources: 2012: http://blog.hootsuite.com/twitter-trends-2012/; 2011: http://mashable.com/2011/12/06/top-twitter-trends-2011/; 2010: http://mashable.com/2010/12/13/top-twitter-trends-2010/, http://yearinreview.twitter.com/trends/; 2009: http://3.bp.blogspot.com/_14cEenKeR04/Sygl8Gp0F9I/AAAAAAAADY/hELPQB1mQKo/s1600-h/2009trends_large.png.

fewer followers, which is an expression of the asymmetrical political attention economy of capitalism that discriminates critical voices by lack of resources and attention: Those who have a lot of reputation, fame, money or power tend to have many more followers than everyday people. Their tweets also tend to be much more often re-tweeted than common people's tweets.

Dhiraj Murthy (2013, 31) argues that "the influence of ordinary people on Twitter" may be minimal, but that "the medium can potentially be democratizing in that it can be thought of as a megaphone that makes public the voices/conversations of any individual or entity". The important question is, however, how society needs to be changed so that asymmetrical visibility disappears. Capitalist structures of accumulation operate not just in the economy, but also in culture, where they result in the accumulation of reputation, visibility and attention of a few. Murthy continues to argue that tweets circulate in the form of re-tweets and that as a result a single individual's voice "can potentially be amplified exponentially" if other users pick up their tweets and re-tweet them (Murthy 2013, 21). This potential does not, however, mean that Twitter is a democratic medium because the power of amplification is also stratified: highly visible users determine what gets amplified and what does not. Twitter's reality is one of asymmetric visibility; its democratic potentials are limited by the reality of stratified attention and the visibility characteristic for a capitalist culture.

The Degree of Interactivity of Political Communication on Twitter

For analyzing the degree of information, communication and interactivity of political Twitter use, I have selected two cases: WikiLeaks and the Egyptian revolution. WikiLeaks was in the news media all over the world in December 2010 after it had released the diplomatic cables on November 28 and a European-wide arrest warrant was issued against Julian Assange on December 6. I collected 985 667 tweets that have the hashtag #wikileaks from the archive http://twapperkeeper.com (time period: November 28, 2010, 00:00:00–January 1st, 2011, 00:00:00).

The revolution in Egypt began on January 25, 2011, with mass protests in Cairo and other cities. On February 11, President Mubarak resigned. I collected 73 395 tweets with the hashtag #25jan (time period: January 25th, 2011, 00:00:00–February 12th, 2011, 00:00:00) from Twapper Keeper. Twitter users employed this hashtag for communication about the Egyptian revolution.

For addressing other users, it is common that one uses the "@" symbol followed by the username in tweets. There are two types of addressing: the re-posting of a Twitter message ("re-tweet") and the commenting on another posting. Twitter does not allow making downloadable archives of its posts. Twapper Keeper outputs a maximum of 25 000 results on screen. I manually generated these lists and copied them into Excel files that were then further analyzed. I analyzed the Twitter streams by identifying all tweets that address somebody ("@"). Then I decided for

Table 8.2 Levels of information and communication for tweets relating to WikiLeaks and the Egyptian revolution

Hashtag	Number of tweets	Time period	Comment	Re-tweets	Information
#wikileaks	985 667	11-28-2010, 00:00:00 – 01-01- 2011 00:00:00	23.1%	51.3%	25.6%
#25jan	73 395	time period: 01-25-2011, 00:00:00 – 02-12- 2011, 00:00:00	12.9%	54.4%	32.7%

each of these tweets whether it was a re-tweet or not by looking for the identifier "RT @", which signifies a re-tweet in the output generated by Twapper Keeper. This procedure allowed me to identify which average share of postings is purely informational, a re-tweeting of another post or a comment on another tweet. The results are displayed in Table 8.2.

The results show that more than 50% of the postings are re-tweets in both cases and there is a low level of commenting (23.1% and 12.9% repectively). As re-tweeting is also a form of information, the total level of information provision was 76.9% in the WikiLeaks case and 87.1% in the Egyptian case.

Communication can be one-way or two-way (McQuail 2010, 552). In the first case, one person talks to the other, who does not talk back or does not have the means to do so. In two-way communication (interaction; McQuail 2010, 560), there is mutual meaningful symbolic interaction. In order to get a first idea of the quality of communication of postings, I analyzed all postings in the #wikileaks stream that were posted in the time period November 28, 2010, 00:00:00–01:00:00 that mentioned other users. There were a total of 110 postings, of which there were 44 re-tweets (40%), one mutual interaction consisting of two postings (1.8%), and 64 informational postings (58.2%). This sample is an indication that mutual symbolic interaction is rare in political Twitter communication and that Twitter communication mostly consists of one-way comments. Single messages like the following ones were typical interactions:

> @userA @userB A large number of your countrymen would disagree with you. Most humans disagree with you. http://bit.ly/i7pJy0 #wikileaks Sun Nov 28 00:27:26

> @userC @userD <----------#Racist #idiot #wikileaks Sun Nov 28 00:00:43

> @userE @userF <------------SPAM Don't retweet #wikileaks #SPAM Sun Nov 28 00:58:52

Re-tweets typically contained links or information that users assessed as important. For example:

> @userG RT @userH: #Wikileaks next release contains 251,287 diplo-
> matic cables: report [ibtimes] http://j.m ... Sun Nov 28 00:45:17

> @userI RT @userF: UK Sunday papers have got it all wrong about
> #wikileaks #embassy cables. Not worth reading. Wait for the #guard-
> ian! Sun Nov 28 00:56:00

The only mutual interaction in the analyzed stream section of #wikileaks was a
short dialogue:

> @userJ @userK #Assange is a traitor to whom? He is not a citizen of
> the US. He is a whistle blower #wikileaks Sun Nov 28 00:07:10

> @userK @userJ You misunderstood my tweet.... #Assange #wikileaks
> Sun Nov 28 00:19:28

The 2011 Protests and Revolutions:
Twitter and Facebook Revolutions?

The question of whether the 2011 revolutions and protests were Twitter or
Facebook revolutions also has to do with Internet access rates. Since 2008
the Internet access rate in the countries where such protests took place varies between 3.1% (Mauritania) and 97.8% (Iceland), and the Facebook usage
rate varies between 2.6% of the population (Yemen) and 69.1% (Iceland) (see
Table 8.3). Given such different conditions of Internet usage, the question
arises as to whether one can really so easily generalize, as some observers do,
that the Internet and social media created and amplified revolutions and rebellions. Data on media use in the Egyptian revolution show that the revolutionaries considered phone communication and face-to-face talk were much more
important for spreading information than "social media" (Wilson and Dunn
2011). In December 2011, 26.4% of the Egyptian population had access to the
Internet and in June 2012, 13.6% of the Egyptian population were Facebook
users (data source: internetworldstats.com, accessed on October 28, 2012).
The Facebook page كلنا خالد سعيد ("We are all Khaled Said"), which has been
moderated by Whael Ghonim (see Ghonim 2012), is said to have played a role
in spreading the protests after Khaled Said was beaten to death by Egyptian
police forces on June 6, 2010. It had 2.5 million likes (Arab version; English
version: 278 000) on December 8, 2012. However, it is unclear how many of
the likes come from Egyptian users who participated in the Tahrir Square
occupation and protests.

eMarketing Egypt conducted a survey about the Internet and the revolution in
Egypt.[6] Of the respondents, 71% said that Facebook was the prime medium "used
to tie up with events and news". The problem is, however, that the survey only
focused on Egyptian Internet users, who make up a minority of the population

---

6 For more details, see www.emarketing-egypt.com/1st-study-about-the-Internet-and-the-Egyptian-Revolution:-
Survey-Results/2/0/18, accessed on December 12, 2012.

Table 8.3 Internet penetration rate and Facebook usage rate (relative to the entire population) in selected countries that witnessed revolutions or rebellions in 2011

Country	Internet access rate (%)	Facebook usage rate (% of population)
Algeria	13.4%	9.5%
Bahrain	77%	30.0%
Egypt	26.4%	13.6%
Greece	46.9%	33.1%
Iceland	97.8%	69.1%
Jordan	38.1%	38.1%
Kuwait	74.2%	31.2%
Lebanon	52.0%	38.0%
Libya	5.9%	10.0%
Mauritania	3.1%	2.7%
Morocco	49.0%	14.2%
Oman	68.8%	16.9%
Portugal	50.7%	38.8%
Saudi Arabia	49.0%	20.9%
Spain	65.6%	33.5%
Sudan	9.3%	n/a
Syria	22.5%	n/a
Tunisia	36.3%	28.9%
United Arab Emirates	70.9%	38.6%
United Kingdom	84.1%	48.6%
United States	78.1%	46.4%
Western Sahara	n/a	n/a
Yemen	14.9%	2.6%

Data source: www.internetworldstats.com, accessed on October 30, 2012; n/a = not available.

(26.4%, see Table 8.3), and not on the Egyptian population as a whole. The results are therefore necessarily techno-centric.

The Role of Social Media in the Egyptian Revolution

The Tahrir Data Project (http://tahrirdata.info) conducted a survey with Tahrir Square activists (N = 1056). Wilson and Dunn (2011) present some results from the survey that focused on activists' media use. Interestingly, Castells (2012) ignores Wilson and Dunn's results, in his techno-deterministic analysis of social media in the Arab spring, although they were published in the *International Journal of Communication* that he co-founded. The survey shows that face-to-face interaction (93%) was the most important form of activists' protest communication, followed by television (92%), phones (82%), print media (57%), SMS (46%), Facebook (42%), email (27%), radio (22%), Twitter (13%) and blogs (12%). Interpersonal communication, traditional media and telecommunications were more important information sources and communication tools in the revolution than social media and the Internet. Another part of the survey showed that Egyptian revolutionaries perceived phone communication followed by face-to-face talk as most important for their own protest, most informative and most motivating for participating in the protests. Facebook, eMail and Twitter were considered to be less important, less informative, less used and less motivating. The study illustrates that "digital media was not as central to protester communication and organization on the ground as the heralds of Twitter revolutions would have us hyperbolize" (Wilson and Dunn 2011, 1252). James Curran (2012, 53) argues that the Arab Spring has "deep-seated economic, political and religious causes". Digital media "contributed to the build-up of dissent, facilitated the actual organisation of protests, and disseminated news of the protests across the region and to the wider world. If the rise of digital communications technology did not cause the uprisings, it strengthened them" (Curran 2012, 54).

The Role of Social Media in the Occupy Wall Street Movement

Table 8.4 shows results from the Occupy General Survey that was conducted among Occupy Wall Street activists (see www.occupyresearch.net/2012/10/18/orgs-data-facet-browser/): face-to-face communication and the Internet were activists' most important means for obtaining information about the movement. In particular, Facebook, word of mouth, websites and email played an important role (for a detailed empirical analysis of social media in the Occupy movement, see my book *OccupyMedia! The Occupy movement and social media in crisis capitalism*, Fuchs 2013). Twitter was a relevant medium used by 41.9% of the respondents for informing themselves politically, but it was less important than many other online and offline media. These results show that both direct face-to-face interaction and mediated interaction have been crucial news sources for Occupy activists. Broadcasting and newspapers had a much less important role than the Internet. Facebook was a very popular source of information, although older online media (email, websites) played a much more important role than YouTube, blogs, Twitter and Tumblr, which shows that one should not overestimate the role of what some have called "web 2.0" in protests. This data is certainly limited because it does not take into account the use of non-commercial platforms (such as or N-1, Occupii) and non-commercial social movement media (such as the Occupied Wall Street Journal, the Occupied Times, Occupy News Network, etc.). There may also be a difference between activists' media use as information source and as mobilization tool and co-ordination tool during demonstrations, which is not reflected in the survey. This shows that further empirical research on the media use of Occupy is needed. However, the results allow us

Table 8.4 Share of respondents in the Occupy Wall Street movement who answered that they used a specific medium for informing themselves about the movement at least once a week or more frequently

Media dimension of the survey question "These are some sources that you might or might not use for news and information about the Occupy movement. Please indicate whether you used these sources for news and information about the Occupy movement"	Share of respondents who used the specific medium at least once or more often in the past week for informing themselves about the Occupy movement	N
Email	79.1%	1132
Occupy websites	83.4%	1127
Facebook	89.7%	1126
Word of mouth	85.2%	1125
Discussions face-to-face or at Occupy camps	51.9%	1117
YouTube	72.2%	1113
Livestreams	61.4%	1109
Local newspapers	52.4%	1099
National or international newspapers	58.5%	1099
Local radio	52.4%	1099
Blogs	62.8%	1090
Twitter	41.9%	1078
Local television	33.1%	1073
National or international television	45.1%	1064
Chat rooms/IRC	21.2%	1057
Tumblr	20.5%	1052

Data source: Occupy General Survey, www.occupyresearch.net/orgs, accessed on December 7, 2012.

to conclude that the Occupy movement makes use of multiple communication channels and that the alleged newness of "social media" should not blind us to the importance of interpersonal face-to-face communication and older online media when analyzing the information structures of social movements.

Available data indicates that in the Egyptian revolution, interpersonal communication, broadcasting and the phone were more important communication tools than the Internet. Data from the Occupy General Survey indicates that interpersonal communication and online communication were important information and news sources for activists. These data are certainly limited and could/should be extended by studies that ask further and more detailed questions. However, they are sufficient for falsifying Castells' hypothesis that contemporary social movements emerged from and are largely based on the Internet and live and act through digital media. These empirical results deconstruct the myth that the Arab Spring was a Twitter revolution, a Facebook revolution, a social media revolution or revolution 2.0. Social media and the Internet played a role as one among several media (especially interpersonal communication), but empirical evidence does not sustain the assumption that social media were necessary conditions of the revolution. The Arab revolutions and other protests (such as the ones by Occupy) were not tweeted, blogged or liked. Social media played a role in protest communication, but it was one role among different media types.

8.4. Twitter's Political Economy

Twitter's Terms of Service and Targeted Advertising

Twitter started as a profit-oriented corporation without a business model. At first it did not use advertising. In September 2009, it revised its terms of use, so that advertising and targeted advertising became possible. But advertising was not used. In April 2010, Twitter announced that advertising would be introduced in the near future.[7] Twitter's terms of use significantly grew in length and complexity, and set out the company's ownership rights with respect to user-generated content. In 2011, Twitter's business model that is based on targeted advertising came into full effect.

Capital Accumulation on Twitter

Twitter's capital accumulation model uses three mechanisms: *promoted tweets, promoted trends, promoted accounts*. Promoted tweets are advertising tweets that appear at the top of search result lists for searches conducted by specifically targeted user groups. "Use Promoted Trends to drive conversations and interest around your brand or product by capturing a user's attention on Twitter".[8] "The Promoted Account is featured in search results and within the Who To Follow section. Who To Follow is Twitter's account recommendation engine and identifies similar accounts and followers to help users discover new businesses, content, and people on Twitter."[9]

When one searches on Twitter for content or a hashtag, current tweets, people results/accounts and worldwide Twitter trends are displayed. Twitter's advertising strategy manipulates the selection of Twitter search results, displayed accounts and trends. Not those tweets, accounts and trends that attain most attention are displayed, but preference is given to tweets, accounts and trends defined by Twitter's advertising clients. Twitter advances a class-structured attention economy that privileges economically powerful actors over everyday users. If you are a large company with a huge advertising budget, then it is easy for you to buy attention on Twitter. If you are an everyday user without an advertising budget and without much time, you will, in contrast, have a much harder time promoting your tweets and your accounts as trend on Twitter.

Users who tweet constitute an audience commodity (Smythe 1977, 1981/2006) that is sold to advertisers (see Chapter 5 in this book). The difference between the

---

7 See http://news.bbc.co.uk/2/hi/8617031.stm, accessed on April 13, 2010.
8 http://business.twitter.com/advertise/promoted-trends, accessed on March 4, 2013.
9 http://business.twitter.com/advertise/promoted-accounts, accessed on March 4, 2013.

audience commodity on traditional mass media and on Twitter is that in the latter case the users are also content producers; there is user-generated content and the users engage in permanent creative activity, communication, community building and content-production (Fuchs 2010c). The fact that the users are more active on Twitter than in the reception of TV or radio content is due to the decentralized structure of the Internet, which allows many-to-many communication. Due to the permanent activity of the recipients and their status as prosumers, we can say that in the case of the Internet the audience commodity is a prosumer commodity. The category of the Internet prosumer commodity does not signify a democratization of the media towards a participatory or democratic system, but the total commodification of human creativity. Twitter users work for free, without payment; they generate surplus value by creating tweets and log data that are sold as commodity to advertisers that then target their ads to specific user groups. In order that capital accumulation can work on Twitter, the economic surveillance of user data is needed (Fuchs 2011a). Twitter surveillance is subsumed under the capitalist political economy.

8.5. @JürgenHabermas #Twitter #PublicSphere

The Public Sphere and Political Communication on Twitter

Habermas argues that political communication and political economy are two important aspects of the public sphere. According to Habermas (1989b, 1989c), the public sphere is a sphere of political debate. It is therefore important to test how communicative political Twitter use is. What is the role of political communication on Twitter? Twitter is dominated by the young, educated middle class and excludes other groups, such as workers, farmers and elderly people. Those with higher incomes and better education, who are more politically interested and informed, dominate political communication. The result is "a rather homogenous climate of opinion" (Habermas 1989c, 213).

Politics is a minority topic on Twitter, which is dominated by entertainment. Twitter is predominantly an information medium, not a communication tool. It is predominantly about entertainment, not about politics. Celebrities from the entertainment industry have the most-followed profiles on Twitter. Concerning political profiles, mainly established high-profile political actors with a lot of resources have a large number of followers, whereas critical political actors have much less visibility and fewer followers. An analysis of a large number of tweets from two political events (discussions about WikiLeaks in 2010, the Egyptian revolution in 2011) has shown that political tweets tend to be primarily information-based postings, especially re-tweets, and not conversations. The interactive postings are mainly one-way comments and not two-way interactions.

There is a limitation of freedom of speech and public opinion on Twitter: individuals do not have the same formal education or material resources for participating in the public sphere (Habermas 1989c, 227). The proper task of a public sphere, a "society engaged in critical public debate" (Habermas 1989c, 52) about politics, is not achieved on Twitter in the current societal context. One important question arises in this context: Can meaningful political debates be based on 140-character short messages? Short text may invite simplistic arguments and be an expression of the commodification and speeded-up nature of culture.

The Public Sphere and the Visibility of the Powerful on Twitter

In 2013 Twitter had around 180 million unpaid users and a rather small number of waged employees that together create surplus value. Twitter's political economy is stratified in two ways:

a) Twitter users and waged employees are exploited, which generates a dispossessed and non-owning class that is opposed to the Twitter-owning class. Given these circumstances, it is no surprise that Twitter's 2010 revenue of US$45 million[10] grew to $139.5 million in 2011[11] and $ 288.3 in 2012.[12]

b) Twitter is a profit-oriented commercial company that stratifies visibility of tweets, profiles and trends in favour of advertising clients and at the expense of everyday users in order to accumulate capital.

The analysis of Twitter's political economy shows that Twitter's stratified economy is detrimental to the character of a public sphere. On Twitter, the powerful (especially entertainers and celebrities) "enjoy an oligopoly of the publicistically effective and politically relevant formation of assemblies and associations" (Habermas 1989c, 228). There is a limitation of freedom of association and assembly.

The Pseudo- and Manufactured Public Sphere

These results allow no other conclusion than the one that Twitter is not a public sphere. Twitter shows the continued importance of Habermas's argument that the bourgeois public sphere has created, as Marx has already observed, its own limits and thereby its own immanent critique. "The public sphere with which Marx saw himself confronted contradicted its own principle of universal accessibility" (Habermas 1989c, 124). Habermasian public sphere analysis with the help of the epistemological method of immanent critique compares an actual public sphere (political economy and political communication) to

---

10 http://online.wsj.com/article/SB10001424052748703716904576134543029279426.html?KEYWORDS= twitter, accessed on July 3, 2013.

11 http://www.emarketer.com/newsroom/index.php/strong-2011-twitter-ad-revenues-grow-86-259-million-2012/, accessed on July 3, 2013.

12 http://www.emarketer.com/newsroom/index.php/strong-2011-twitter-ad-revenues-grow-86-259-million-2012/, accessed on July 3, 2013.

the ideal and values of the public sphere that bourgeois society promises (freedom of speech, freedom of public opinion, freedom of association, freedom of assembly). The immanent analysis conducted in this chapter found that Twitter's reality contradicts the promises of bourgeois society. Twitter is a "pseudo-public sphere" (Habermas 1989c, 162) and a "manufactured public sphere" (Habermas 1989c, 217).

8.6. Conclusion

Critical voices have warned about the claims that Twitter constitutes a new public sphere. Evgeny Morozov (2010) argues that the notion of "Twitter revolution" is based on a belief in cyber-utopianism – "a naive belief in the emancipatory nature of online communication that rests on a stubborn refusal to acknowledge its downside" (Morozov 2010, xiii). Christian Christensen (2011) argues that the logic of technological determinism that ignores societal contexts, such as "the political-economic, historical or sociological implications of social media use in relation to development or political change" (Christensen 2011, 248), frequently shapes policy and academic discourses about Twitter.

Politicians and mainstream media have made a claim related to the myth of Twitter revolutions in the context of the UK riots in August 2011, namely that Twitter results in violence and riots. They invented the notions of "Twitter mobs" and "Blackberry mobs". "Rioting thugs use Twitter to boost their numbers in thieving store raids. [. . .] THUGS used social network Twitter to orchestrate the Tottenham violence and incite others to join in as they sent messages urging: 'Roll up and loot'. [. . .] Gang members used Blackberry smart-phones designed as a communications tool for high-flying executives to organise the mayhem" (*The Sun*, August 8, 2011; *The Telegraph*, August 8, 2011).

Whereas the notion of Twitter revolution is a belief in cyber-utopianism and in the power of Twitter to strengthen the political public sphere, the notion of Twitter mob is an expression of techno-pessimism, the assumption that the Internet in all contexts has necessarily bad consequences for society and that it is the Internet or specific platforms that are the cause of negative phenomena. Both are expressions of technological determinism.

Technological Determinism

One of the reasons why critical theory is important for analyzing media, technology and information is that it allows us to question and provide alternatives to technological determinism and to explain the causal relationship of media and technology, on the one hand, and society, on the other hand, in a complex way that avoids one-dimensionality and one-sidedness. Technological determinism is a kind of explanation of the causal relationship of media/technology and society that assumes that a certain medium or technology has exactly one specific effect on society and social systems (see Figure 8.1). In the case that this effect is assessed positively, we can speak of techno-optimism. In the

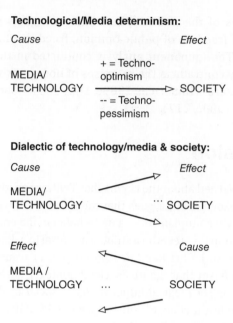

Figure 8.1 Two logics of the relationship between media technology and society

case that the effect is assessed negatively, we can speak of techno-pessimism. Techno-optimism and techno-pessimism are the normative dimensions of technological determinism.

The problem of techno-optimistic and techno-pessimistic arguments is that they are only interested in single aspects of technology and create the impression that there are only one-sided effects (see Figure 8.1). They lack a sense of contradictions and the dialectics of technology and society and can therefore be described as technological deterministic forms of argumentation. Technological determinism is a fetishism of technology (Robins and Webster 1999), "the idea that technology develops as the sole result of an internal dynamic, and then, unmediated by any other influence molds society to fit its pattern" (Winner 1980/1999, 29).

Technological determinism overestimates the role of technology in society; it ignores the fact that technology is embedded into society and that it is the people living under and rebelling against power relations, not the technology, who conduct unrest and revolutions. The rise of new technologies often creates an "eruption of feeling that briefly overwhelms reason" (Mosco 2004, 22). Technological determinism ignores the political economy of events. Social media determinism is an expression of the digital sublime, the development that "cyberspace has become the latest icon of the technological and electronic sublime, praised for its epochal and transcendent characteristics and demonized for the depth of the evil it can conjure" (Mosco 2004, 24).

An alternative that avoids technological and social determinisms is to conceptualize the relationship of technology and society as dialectical (see Figure 8.1):

society conditions the invention, design and engineering of technology and technology shapes society in complex ways. Technology is conditioned, not determined by society, and vice versa. This means that societal conditions, interests and conflicts influence which technologies will emerge, but technology's effects are not predetermined because modern technologies are complex wholes of interacting parts that are to certain extents unpredictable. Technology shapes society in complex ways, which means that frequently there are multiple effects that can stand in contradiction with each other. Because society and technology are complex systems, which means that they have many elements and many interactions between these elements, it is unlikely that the interaction of the two complex systems of technology and society will have one-dimensional effects. Technology is a medium (enabling and constraining) and outcome of society.

A Dialectical Concept of Technology and Society

A critical theory of media and technology is based on dialectical reasoning (see Figure 8.1). This allows us to see the causal relationship of media/technology and society as multidimensional and complex: a specific media/technology has multiple, at least two, potential effects on society and social systems that can co-exist or stand in contradiction to each other. Which potentials are realized is based on how society, interests, power structures and struggles shape the design and usage of technology in multiple ways that are also potentially contradictory. Andrew Feenberg says in this context that Critical Theory "argues that technology is not a thing in the ordinary sense of the term, but an 'ambivalent' process of development suspended between different possibilities" (Feenberg 2002, 15).

The revolution in Egypt was not a Twitter revolution, but related to the context of a highly stratified society. Real wages have been decreasing over 20 years, strikes were forbidden, there has been repression against the political left and unions, the gap between the rich and the poor has been large, poverty has constantly increased, wages in industry have been low, the global economic crisis has resulted in mass lay-offs and a food crisis, Mubarak – together with the army – controlled Egyptian politics and bureaucracy since 1981, the illiteracy rate has been high, and there has been a contradiction between Islamic traditions and the values of modernization (Björklund 2011).

Pierre Bourdieu (1986b) distinguished between economic capital (money), political capital (power) and cultural capital (status, skills, educational attainments). Egypt was, under Mubarak, a society with a highly stratified class structure: there was a class that controlled the political-economic-military complex and accumulated economic, political and cultural capital at the expense of the masses of Egyptian people. The Egyptian revolution was a revolution against capitalism's multidimensional injustices, in which social media were used as a tool of information and organization, but were not the cause of the revolution.

The UK riots were not a Twitter mob, but related to the societal structure of the UK. The latter has a high level of income inequality; its Gini level was 32.4 in

2009 (0 means absolute equality, 100 absolute inequality), a level that is only topped by a few countries in Europe and that is comparable to the level of Greece (33.1) (data source: Eurostat). Of the UK population, 17.3% had a risk of living in poverty in 2009 (data source: Eurostat). In early 2011, the youth unemployment rate in the UK rose to 20.3%, the highest level since these statistics started being recorded in 1992.[13] The UK is not only one of the most advanced developed countries today, it is at the same time a developing country with a lot of structurally deprived areas. Is it a surprise that riots erupted, especially in East London, the West Midlands and Greater Manchester? The UK Department of Communities and Local Government reported in its analysis, *The English Indices of Deprivation 2010*:[14] "Liverpool, Middlesbrough, Manchester, Knowsley, the City of Kingston-upon Hull, Hackney and Tower Hamlets are the local authorities with the highest proportion of LSOAs amongst the most deprived in England. [...] The north east quarter of London, particularly Newham, Hackney and Tower Hamlets, continue to exhibit very high levels of deprivation" (1, 3). Decades of UK capitalist development, shaped by deindustrialization and neoliberalism, have had effects on the creation, intensification and extension of precariousness and deprivation. Capitalism, crisis and class are the main contexts of unrests, uproar and social media today.

Social media are not the causes of revolutions and violence; they are rather a mirror of the power structures and structures of exploitation and oppression that we find in contemporary society.

A Model of (Social) Media and Revolution

Especially the dialectical philosophies of Herbert Marcuse and Ernst Bloch allow conceiving the relationship of human subjects (agents) and societal objects (structures) as dialectical so that existing structures enable and constrain human action and open up a field of possible developments for society and social systems, based on which humans reproduce existing structures or create new structures (Fuchs 2011b, chapter 2). The possibilities and the likelihood of fundamental social change are therefore based on existing power structures. The subject–object dialectic of Marcuse and Bloch is a viable alternative to structuralist–functionalist forms of dialectic that underestimate the importance of humans in the dialectic of society and reduce societal development to automatic processes without human subjects. Dialectical philosophy allows conceptualizing the relationship of media and society, the relationship of a different type and organization of media to each other, and the relationship of movements and the media as contradictory and grounded in the contradictions of contemporary antagonistic societies (Fuchs 2011b).

A theoretical model that I suggest for conceiving the relationship of media and revolution conceptualizes the relationship between rebellions and (social) media as dialectical: in the form of contradictions. Figure 8.2 shows a dialectical model of revolts and the media.

---

13 www.guardian.co.uk/business/2011/jan/19/youth-unemployment-heads-towards-1-million.
14 www.communities.gov.uk/documents/statistics/pdf/1871538.pdf.

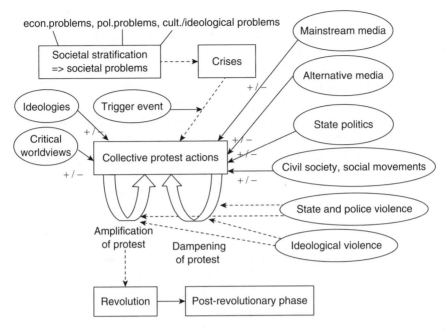

Figure 8.2 A model of protests and revolutions and the role of crises, the media, ideology and politics

Protests have an objective foundation that is grounded in the contradictions of society, i.e. forms of domination that cause problems that are economic, political and cultural in nature. Societal problems can result in (economic, political, cultural/ideological) crises[15] if they are temporally persistent and cannot be easily overcome. Crises do not automatically result in protests, but are an objective and necessary, although not sufficient, condition of protest. If crisis dimensions converge and interact, then we can speak of a societal crisis. Protests require a mass of people's perception that there are societal problems, that these problems are unbearable and a scandal and a sign that something needs to be changed. Often actual protests and movements are triggered and continuously intensified by certain events (such as the arrest of Rosa Parks in the US civil rights movement, the public suicide of Mohamed Bouazizi in the 2011 Tunisian revolution, the police's killing of Khaled Mohamed Said in Egypt, the pepper-spraying of activists by New York Police Department officer Anthony Bologna and the mass arrest of Occupy activists on Brooklyn Bridge in the Occupy Wall Street movement, etc.).

It is precisely here that Castells' (2012) focus on the emotions of outrage and hope plays a role – in the potential transition from crises to protests. Subjective

---

15 There are of course also ecological crises that can threaten the existence of humankind. For social theory, the question is how nature relates to society. Humans have to enter into a metabolism with nature in order to survive. They have to appropriate parts of nature and change it with their activities in order to produce use-values that serve the needs of society. This means that the process where the interaction of nature and society is directly established takes place in the economy. We therefore do not discern ecological crises separately, but see them as one specific subtype of economic crises.

perceptions and emotions are, however, not the only factor because they are conditioned and influenced by politics, the media and culture/ideology. The way state politics, mainstream media and ideology, on the one hand, and oppositional politics/social movements, alternative media and alternative worldviews, on the other hand, connect to human subjects influences the conditions of protests. Each of these factors can have either amplifying or dampening effects on protests. So, for example, racist media coverage can advance racist stereotypes and/or the insight that the media and contemporary society are racist in-themselves. It can also advance both views, namely in respect to different individuals or groups that then enter into an antagonism with each other.

The media – social media, the Internet and all other media – are contradictory because we live in a contradictory society. As a consequence, their effects are actually contradictory, they can dampen/forestall or amplify/advance protest or have not much effect at all. Also, different media (e.g. alternative media and commercial media) stand in a contradictory relation and power struggle with each other. The media are not the only factors that influence the conditions of protest – they stand in contradictory relations with politics and ideology/culture that also influence the conditions of protest. So whether protest emerges or not is shaped by multiple factors that are so complex that it cannot be calculated or forecast whether protest will emerge as result of a certain crisis or not. Once protests have emerged, media, politics and culture continue to have permanent contradictory influences on them and it is undetermined whether these factors have rather neutral, amplifying or dampening effects on protest. Protests in antagonistic societies often call forth policing and police action. In this case, the state reacts to social movements with its organized form of violence. State violence against protests and ideological violence against movements (in the form of attacks of delegitimization conducted by the media, politicians and others) can again have amplifying, dampening or insignificant effects on protests.

If there is a protest amplification spiral, protest may grow to larger and larger dimensions, which can eventually, but not necessarily, result in a revolution – a breakdown and fundamental reconstitution/renewal of the economy, politics and worldviews caused by a social movement's overthrow of society that puts the revolutionary forces into power and control of the major economic, political and moral structures (see Goodwin 2001, 9). Every revolution results in a post-revolutionary phase, in which the reconstruction and renewal of society begins and the legacy of conflict and the old society can pose challenges and new contradictions.

Social media in a contradictory society (made up of class conflicts and other conflicts between dominant and dominated groups) are likely to have a contradictory character: they do not necessarily and automatically support/amplify or dampen/limit rebellions, but rather pose contradictory potentials that stand in contradictions with influences by the state, ideology and capitalism.

Summary

We can summarize the main results of this chapter as follows:

- Habermas's concept of the public sphere stresses that a public sphere is (a) a space of political communication and (b) that access to resources that allow citizens to participate in the public sphere is crucial.

- Habermas's notion of the public sphere is a critical concept that helps to analyze whether modern society lives up to its own expectations. It allows testing if the freedom of speech and public opinion are realized or rather limited by the distribution of educational and material resources. Furthermore, it enables the same test for the values of freedom of association and assembly by analyzing whether there are powerful actors that dominate visibility and influence.

- Twitter is not a public sphere. It should neither be the subject of hope for the renewal of democracy and publication, nor the cause of concerns about violence and riots. What should first and foremost concern us is inequality in society and how to alleviate inequality. Habermas's notion of the public sphere has not primarily been about the media, but about the creation of a concept that allows the criticism of structures that lack public concerns about common goods and limit the availability of the commons for all people.

- Social media do not cause revolutions or protests. They are embedded into contradictions and the power structures of contemporary society. This also means that in society, in which these media are prevalent, they are not completely unimportant in situations of uproar and revolution. Social media have contradictory characteristics in contradictory societies: they do not necessarily and automatically support/amplify or dampen/limit rebellions, but rather pose contradictory potentials that stand in contradiction with influences by the state, ideology, capitalism and other media.

Contemporary societies are today experiencing highly damaged common goods and services as the result of decades of neoliberalism. The result has been a global crisis of capitalism that allows us to also think about the possibility of strengthening the commons. Strengthening the commons requires common struggle, which also involves, among other things, common communication. The struggle for a commons-based society that overcomes neoliberalism should also be the struggle for communication commons. The stratified structures of Twitter are an expression of the limits of the public sphere. Another society is possible. Is another Twitter possible?

RECOMMENDED READINGS AND EXERCISES

For critically understanding Twitter, it is useful to engage with works by Jürgen Habermas and debates about Twitter's role in politics.

Habermas, Jürgen. 1989. *The structural transformation of the public sphere.* Cambridge, MA: MIT Press.

Jeffrey, Stuart. 2010. A rare interview with Jürgen Habermas. *Financial Times Online,* April 30, 2010.

There are many myths about Habermas's famous book *The Structural Transformation of the Public Sphere*. I therefore recommend that you read the entire book in order to understand its content and the notion of the public sphere. Ask yourself:

- What is the public sphere according to Habermas? How has it developed historically?

- What are characteristics and limits of the bourgeois public sphere?

- How is the notion of the public sphere connected to Karl Marx's thinking?

- What does Habermas mean by refeudalization of the public sphere?

- Think of social media in contemporary politics and society: which aspects of political communication, limits of the public sphere and refeudalization are there? Try to find examples.

- How do you interpret the fact that a fake Habermas posted about the public sphere on Twitter under Habermas's name and caused some irritation? What are the implications for the public sphere?

Morozov, Evgeny. 2009. The brave new world of slacktivism. http://neteffect.foreignpolicy. com/posts/2009/05/19/the_brave_new_world_of_slacktivism, accessed on July 3, 2013.

Gladwell, Malcolm. 2010. Small change. Why the revolution will not be tweeted. *The New Yorker*, October: 42–49.

Morozov, Evgeny. 2010. *The net delusion: How not to liberate the world.* London: Allen Lane. Chapter 7: Why Kierkegaard hates slacktivism.

Shirky, Clay. 2011. The political power of social media. *Foreign Affairs* 90 (1): 28–41.

Gladwell, Malcolm and Clay Shirky. 2011. From innovation to revolution: Do social media make protests possible? *Foreign Affairs* 90 (2): 153–154.

These readings focus on a debate between Clay Shirky, Malcolm Gladwell and Evgeny Morozov concerning the question of whether digital media help to liberate the world and strengthen democracy or not.

- Summarize and compare the basic arguments of Shirky, Gladwell and Morozov about social media's role in politics.
- Try to find logical, theoretical and empirical evidence to describe what the relationship between social media, politics and protests looks like.

Identify Twitter hashtags for a current political event and a current entertainment event. Observe, collect and store all postings for these two hashtags for one day. Conduct a content and discourse analysis that focuses on the topics of discussion and their frequency, the interactivity of the tweets (the degree of re-tweeting/information/communication), the overall number of tweets, the number of participants, the number of postings per participant and the share of tweets for each participant in the total number of tweets, the use of emoticons, abbreviations and affects. If there are disagreements, how are they expressed? Are these disagreements further discussed? Observe also how the number of followers of the most active participants changes during the day. How many new followers does s/he gain?

- Interpret the results of your small study in the light of Habermas's public sphere theory.

WikiLeaks: Can We Make Power Transparent?

Key questions

- What does WikiLeaks tell us about power and counter-power?
- What is transparency and how does it relate to WikiLeaks?
- What kind of medium is WikiLeaks?
- Does WikiLeaks provide an alternative medium?
- Can WikiLeaks be called a form of journalism?

Key concepts

Transparency	Liberalism
Disciplinary power	Socialism
Watchdog	Alternative media
Watch platform	Journalism

Overview

WikiLeaks (www.wikileaks.org) is a non-commercial and non-profit Internet whistleblowing platform that has been online since 2006. Julian Assange founded it. It is funded by online donations. Whistleblowers can upload documents that are intended to make the misbehaviour and crimes of governments and corporations transparent, i.e. visible to the public. One can upload such documents anonymously by making use of an online submission form.

In April 2010, WikiLeaks published a video (entitled "Collateral Murder") that shows a situation where the US air force kills civilians and journalists in Iraq. The topic that made the news about WikiLeaks in late July 2010 was that the platform published more than 90 000 top-secret documents (reports of soldiers about operations, protocols of surveillance operations, etc.) from American military sources about military operations in Afghanistan. According to news sources (*Der Spiegel*, 30/2010, pp. 70–86), the files:

- show that special command forces like the US Task Force 373 have killed enemies that were defined on death lists,
- document failed operations (including the killing of civilians),
- document that the Americans and their allies have faced serious problems in the military conflict with the Taliban and Al Qaeda,
- document that unmanned fighter drones used in Afghanistan are error prone and have had many accidents.

WikiLeaks released almost 400 000 US Army documents about the Iraq war ("Iraq War Logs") in October 2010 and one month later more than 250 000 files documenting correspondence between the US State Department and diplomats ("Diplomatic Cables").

These are just some of the most well-known leaks. In December 2010, WikiLeaks was permanently in the world news because Julian Assange was sought with a European Arrest Warrant issued in Sweden for the suspected sexual assault of two women. This event followed the release of the US Diplomatic Cables, which spurred speculation. After Assange turned himself in to British authorities on December 7, 2010, there were reports that the US Justice Department planned to accuse Assange of espionage ("U.S. Prosecutors Study WikiLeaks Prosecution", *New York Times*, December 7, 2010). The circumstance that an Internet-based political project has had the power to become the subject of world politics shows the relative importance of political online communication today and that studying WikiLeaks is an important task for Media and Communication Studies and Internet Studies.

The circumstance that WikiLeaks has become a subject of world politics has led some academics, such as Yochai Benkler (2011, 2013) and Manuel Castells (2010a) who are two of the primary techno-optimistic Internet scholars, to stress in a techno-euphoric manner the political power of the Internet and social media (for a more critical analysis, see Žižek 2011). Contrary to this deterministic optimism, this chapter suggests that it is necessary to realistically assess the potentials of WikiLeaks and the problems it faces based on a political economy.

In section 9.1, I analyze WikiLeaks with the help of the categories of power, surveillance and transparency. In section 9.2, I assess the political worldview underlying WikiLeaks. I apply the notions of journalism and

alternative media to WikiLeaks in section 9.3, and finally, I draw some conclusions in section 9.4.

9.1. WikiLeaks and Power

Uncritical Definitions of Surveillance

In general, one can distinguish between general and more specific definitions
of surveillance (Fuchs 2011c[1]). General definitions see surveillance as having both normatively positive and negative aspects, whereas the more specific
definitions see surveillance as a normatively negative form of coercive power
and domination.

General concepts of surveillance make one or more of the following assumptions:

- There are positive aspects of surveillance (Haggerty 2006, 36).
- Surveillance has two faces: it is enabling and constraining (Lyon 1994, ix;
  Marx 2007, 535; Zureik 2003, 42).
- Surveillance is a fundamental aspect of all societies (Norris and Armstrong
  1999, 5; Rule 2007, 14).
- Surveillance is necessary for organization (Dandeker 1990; Giddens 1984,
  1985, 1987).
- Any kind of systematic information gathering is surveillance (Ball and Webster
  2003, 1; Bogard 2006, 98f; Dandeker 2006, 225; Haggerty and Ericson 2006,
  3; Hier and Greenberg 2007, 381; Rule 2007, 14; Wall 2007, 230).

There are a number of problems that general surveillance concepts face:

- A general notion of surveillance puts negative and positive aspects of surveillance on one categorical level and therefore may trivialize repressive
  information gathering and usage.
- General surveillance studies support the ideological celebration and normalization of surveillance.
- A general surveillance concept does not allow for distinguishing between
  information gathering and surveillance. Therefore, one cannot draw a distinction between a surveillance society and an information society and
  cannot distinguish between surveillance studies and information society
  studies.
- One should not assume a dialectic at the categorical level of surveillance,
  but at a meta-level that allows one to distinguish between surveillance and
  solidarity as positive and negative sides respectively of systematic information gathering.

---

1 Thomas Allmer (2012, chapters 2 and 4) makes a comparable distinction between non-panoptic and panoptic
theories of surveillance and Internet surveillance.

- Etymologically, the term "surveillance" implies a relationship of asymmetrical power, domination, hierarchy and violence.

WikiLeaks and the Value-neutral Definition of Surveillance

General surveillance concepts can also be characterized as being "neutral" or "neutralizing" concepts because, by identifying the potential positive meanings of the term "surveillance", they neutralize the critical potential of the term when engaging in a fundamental critique of power and domination. They create a conceptual confusion and conflationism that is a disservice for a critical theory of society. WikiLeaks makes information about organizations that abuse power available to the public by enabling the anonymous submission of secret documents that are analyzed, summarized and presented on the WikiLeaks website. If WikiLeaks were understood as being a form of surveillance in the general neutral understanding of the term, then it could not be distinguished from other Internet projects, like Wikipedia, because both Wikipedia and WikiLeaks are systematic forms of gathering and assessing information, which is the core of neutral surveillance definitions. The difference, however, is that WikiLeaks is engaging in political struggles, is an explicitly politically motivated project, and wants to make information public that has to do with the abuse of power.

Critical Definitions of Surveillance

A notion of surveillance different from the general, neutral concept of surveillance is needed for theorizing WikiLeaks because it is a project that makes available knowledge that stems from political conflicts and struggles. We therefore have to turn to negative, critical notions of surveillance for better understanding WikiLeaks.

A negative concept of surveillance characterizes an aspect of the negativity of power structures, contemporary society and heteronomous societies (Allmer 2012, Fuchs 2011c). It uses the notion of surveillance for denunciating and indicting domination and dominative societies. By doing so, it wants to point towards emancipation and a dominationless society, which is conceived as being also a society without surveillance. In a negative theory, surveillance is a concept that is inherently linked to information gathering for the purposes of domination, violence and coercion, and thereby at the same time accuses such states of society and makes political demands for a participatory, co-operative, dominationless society that is not only one in which co-operative modes of production and ownership replace classes and the exploitation of surplus value, but also one in which care and solidarity substitute surveillance. Therefore, a negative theory is not just opposed to something, it is at the same time positive because it analyzes the conditions for the establishment of a better society. Such a concept of surveillance is inspired by critical theory's analysis and accusation of domination and exploitation and its identification of the need for struggles against dominative and exploitative orders of society (see Chapter 1). A neutral concept of surveillance is a disservice for a critical theory of surveillance: it makes critique more difficult and may support the ideological celebration and normalization of surveillance.

Foucault on Disciplinary Power

Michel Foucault's theory is the most well-known negative theory of surveillance. Foucault (1977) sees surveillance as a form of disciplinary power. Surveillance prepares "a knowledge of man" (Foucault 1977, 171), a knowledge about "whether an individual" is "behaving as he should, in accordance with the rule or not" (Foucault 1994, 59). WikiLeaks wants to make public knowledge about powerful institutions in order to monitor whether they are behaving as they should, in accordance with certain normative rules:

> The power of principled leaking to call governments, corporations and institutions to account is amply demonstrated through recent history. The public scrutiny of otherwise unaccountable and secretive institutions forces them to consider the ethical implications of their actions. Which official will chance a secret, corrupt transaction when the public is likely to find out? What repressive plan will be carried out when it is revealed to the citizenry, not just of its own country, but the world? When the risks of embarrassment and discovery increase, the tables are turned against conspiracy, corruption, exploitation and oppression. (WikiLeaks 2010, 13, 2011, 30)

For Foucault, surveillance is also a purposefully systematically organized act of observation for controlling human subjects. Surveillance is "permanent, exhaustive, omnipresent" (Foucault 1977, 214). It is based on "a principle of compulsory visibility" (187), is a "system of permanent registration" (196), in which "all events are recorded" (197). Foucault argues that in order to secure domination, disciplines make use of certain methods such as the hierarchical observation, the normalizing judgement and the examination (170ff). The instrument of hierarchical observation establishes the connection disciplines–surveillance because the "exercise of discipline presupposes a mechanism that coerces by means of observation" (170).

WikiLeaks and Critical Theory

WikiLeaks as an organization is in contrast to the cases of a detective agency, a secret service, corporate workplace surveillance or consumer surveillance not involved in systematically gathering data about powerful institutions that show how they abuse power. Others, who have access to certain data, supply them to WikiLeaks. Sometimes systematic data gathering that is permanent, exhaustive, omnipresent and deliberately recorded without the knowledge of the monitored institutions results in submissions to WikiLeaks. But in many cases, powerful institutions know about the existence of the leaked documents submitted to WikiLeaks. The data are not gathered by external operations, but stem from its inside operations. Powerful institutions want to keep certain information unknown to the public in order to protect their own power.

The analysis shows that the documents submitted to WikiLeaks share two aspects with the notion of negative surveillance:

a) One parallel is the aspect of the negative surveillance concept as disciplinary power that wants to show whether powerful organizations are abusing power or not. The task that WikiLeaks has set itself is to discipline powerful organizations: leaking "is a motivating force for governments and corporations to act justly" (WikiLeaks 2010, paragraph 20, 2011, 36). "When the risks of embarrassment and discovery increase, the tables are turned against conspiracy, corruption, exploitation and oppression" (WikiLeaks 2011, 30).

b) The documents submitted to WikiLeaks are normally not the result of systematic, purposeful, permanent surveillance operations carried out by WikiLeaks, but rather only partly stem from systematic, purposeful and permanent acts of surveillance. Documents are also sourced from individuals who have access to data that document the abuse of power and that stem from the actions and information generated by powerful organizations themselves. These individuals submit material to WikiLeaks, which then analyzes, systematizes and presents this material to the public.

A main difference between WikiLeaks and corporate and government surveillance is that the latter remains hidden, secret and in many cases without the knowledge of the surveilled subjects. In contrast, WikiLeaks wants to make data about powerful organizations available to the public. WikiLeaks does not employ the term "surveillance" for describing itself, but rather employs the notion of transparency:

> Today, with authoritarian governments in power in much of the world, increasing authoritarian tendencies in democratic governments, and increasing amounts of power vested in unaccountable corporations, the need for openness and transparency is greater than ever. WikiLeaks interest is the revelation of the truth. Unlike the covert activities of state intelligence agencies, as a media publisher WikiLeaks relies upon the power of overt fact to enable and empower citizens to bring feared and corrupt governments and corporations to justice. (WikiLeaks 2011, paragraph 31; see also WikiLeaks 2010, paragraph 13)

WikiLeaks "is a global group of people with long standing dedication to the idea of improved transparency in institutions, especially government. We think better transparency is at the heart of less corruption and better democracies. By definition, spy agencies want to hoard information. We want to get it out to the public" (WikiLeaks 2010, paragraph 55).

WikiLeaks, Watchdogs and Transparency

Corporate watch platforms (such as CorpWatch Reporting, Transnationale Ethical Rating, The Corporate Watch Project) and WikiLeaks are attempts by those resisting against asymmetric economic and political power relations to struggle against powerful classes by documenting data that should make power transparent. There is a difference between surveillance used for erecting visibility over oppressed groups, which is the attempt to control and further oppress them, and the attempt to make the powerful transparent, which is a self-defence mechanism and a form of struggle of the oppressed or on behalf of the oppressed in order to try to defend themselves against oppression. "'Surveillance' suggests the operation of authority, while 'transparency' suggest the operation of democracy, of the powerful being held accountable" (Johnson and Wayland 2010, 25). Johnson and Wayland (2010) point out that one should use the notion of transparency in relation to economic and political power.

WikiLeaks is a project that tries to make power transparent by leaking secret documents about political and economic power. It does not so much itself engage in collecting information about the powerful, but relies on anonymous online submissions by insiders, who witness the wrongdoings of institutions and want to provide more transparency of what is happening. WikiLeaks has, to a certain degree, a focus on both political and economic transparency:

> Publishing improves transparency, and this transparency creates a better society for all people. Better scrutiny leads to reduced corruption and stronger democracies in all society's institutions, including government, corporations and other organisations. A healthy, vibrant and inquisitive journalistic media plays a vital role in achieving these goals. We are part of that media. (WikiLeaks 2011, paragraph 8)

WikiLeaks: Watching the Watchers Online

WikiLeaks has some parallels with corporate watch platforms. They have in common that they are both Internet projects that try to make powerful structures transparent as part of the struggle against powerful institutions. The Internet provides means for documenting such behaviour. It can help to watch the watchers and to raise public awareness.

The use of media (like the Internet in the case of online watch organizations and WikiLeaks) as a means to resist and struggle against domination by making the latter transparent is not new and not specific to the Internet. There are parallels to the use of earlier media, such as the video camera, in the attempt to establish watchdog media. The Los Angeles Police Department (LAPD) stopped the Afro-American Rodney King in his car on March 3, 1991, after a freeway chase. King resisted his arrest, which resulted in a brutal beating by the police, causing fractures of his leg and facial bone. An LA court tried the four police officers – Briseno, Koon, Powell and Wind – for police brutality and acquitted them in April 1992. George Holiday filmed the beating of King with a low-technology home video camera. When the news of the acquittal of the officers and the video made their way to the mass media, outrage spread and many observers came to hold the view that both the LAPD and the justice system engaged in racism against Afro-Americans. The event triggered riots in Los Angeles in April 1992.

Today, we live in an age where the Internet shapes the lives of many of us. The Internet has become a new key medium of information, communication and co-production. Therefore, paraphrasing Fiske (1996, 224f), we can say that the Internet extends the panoptic eye of power, but it also enables those who are normally the object of surveillance to turn their eyes, ears and voice on the powerful and reverse the power of surveillance. In such cases, we can speak of Internet counter-surveillance or "subveillance". WikiLeaks and corporate watchdog organizations make data about powerful organizations public. They are attempts to make the secrecy of power public and transparent. Whereas surveillance is mainly kept secret and unknown to those who are monitored, watching is a self-defence reaction, on behalf of the dominated, to the accumulation of power and the surveillance and oppression of citizens, workers, consumers and prosumers.

The concept of watching the powerful shares with Foucault's theory of surveillance the idea that subjects are made visible with the help of knowledge. However, watchdog organizations do not necessarily – or only partly – systematically and permanently collect data in a secret way, but rather make existing data available to the public. They generate new knowledge about the powerful (e.g. ethical ratings) and publish unknown facts. The main difference between surveillance conducted by the powerful and watchdog organizations is that the latter's main task is the publication of data about the powerful. The parallel between the powerful surveilling dominated groups and watchdog organizations making power transparent is mainly the potential effect: disciplinary power.

Powerful groups try to advance the accumulation of power (money, decision power, hegemony) by controlling the behaviour and thoughts of subordinated groups and individuals with the help of surveillance procedures. They discipline their behaviour, but keep the collected data secret. Watchdog organizations collect and publish or leak information about powerful organizations in order to contribute to the limitation or abolishment of asymmetric power. Watchdog organizations' potential disciplinary power is a form of counter-power that is a reaction to the disciplinary power exerted by powerful institutions (companies, governments, etc.) – watching is an information-based self-defence mechanism and counter-power struggle against domination.

Theories of Power

Power can be theorized in different ways. Thinkers like Max Weber define power as the "chance of a man or a number of men to realize their own will in a social action even against the resistance of others who are participating in the action" (Weber 1978, 926). Power here is necessarily a form of violence and coercion. This definition's problem is that it does not allow a clear line of separation between power and domination. Weber defines the latter as "probability that a command with a given specific content will be obeyed by a given group of persons" (Weber 1978, 54), which is quite similar to his definition of power. It is therefore theoretically more feasible to conceive power as a more general phenomenon than domination.

Differently from Weber, Anthony Giddens defines power as "'transformative capacity', the capability to intervene in a given set of events so as in some way to alter them" (Giddens 1985, 7), as the "capability to effectively decide about courses of events, even where others might contest such decisions" (Giddens 1985, 9). Giddens sees power as related to (allocative and authoritative) resources, to material facilities and means of control. Power characterizes all social relationships, "is routinely involved in the instantiation of social practices" and is "operating in and through human action" (Giddens 1981, 49f). Where Giddens differs from Weber is that Giddens has a general concept of power that is not necessarily associated with violence and coercion. For Giddens, power can be distributed in different ways (more symmetrically or more asymmetrically), whereas for Weber power is always imposed on others and is always asymmetrical.

Based on this alternative tradition of theorizing power, we can define "power" as the disposition over the means required to influence processes and decisions in one's own interest and "domination" as the disposition over the means of coercion required to influence others or processes and decisions. This means that power (the control of resources like money, political influence, definition capacities) can be distributed in more symmetric and asymmetric ways. Dictatorship is a centralization of economic and/or political and/or ideological power, whereas participatory democracy is a more symmetric or equal distribution of economic, political and cultural power.

WikiLeaks and the Power of Visibility

Watchdog organizations like WikiLeaks exist because we live in societies that are shaped by asymmetrical economic, political and cultural power structures. They are reactions to these situations. They try to build counter-power to the exertion of asymmetrical power that excludes, dominates, oppresses or exploits humans and struggle for a more symmetric distribution of power by trying to make information about powerful institutions available to the public.

The power elite – large corporations, governments and military institutions – distinguishes itself from ordinary citizens and most civil society organizations by two features:

1. These actors have a lot of economic and/or political power, which allows them to strongly shape our world.
2. They also have the resources to keep parts of their activities invisible (Mills 2000).

Therefore, for example, corporate crime frequently remains undetected. Power is based on a dialectic of visibility and invisibility: powerful actors want to make their enemies and opponents visible, while they want to remain invisible themselves. They engage in surveillance in order to make others visible and in order to keep their own operations and gathered information invisible. Asymmetric power is always related to making information about enemies and opponents visible, while at the same time making and keeping the collected information non-transparent, inaccessible and secret.

WikiLeaks and corporate watchdog organizations cut into the power dialectic of visibility of the surveilled and invisibility of the powerful by helping to make invisible power structures visible. This is itself a process of power-making and power-generation because these are processes that try to force visibility on the powerful. WikiLeaks and other watchdog organizations engage in watching the powerful. During the Vietnam War, television made visible the horrors of the killing fields that would have otherwise remained invisible. In a similar fashion, WikiLeaks has made visible hidden and secret realities of warfare today.

The Structural Discrimination of Watchdog Organizations

There are certainly limits to what watchdog organizations can do. They are generally civil society projects because it is unlikely that big corporations or governments support initiatives that tend to criticize corporations and governments with big amounts of money. Therefore such projects are frequently based on precarious, self-exploitative labour, and are confronted with a lack of resources such as money, activists, time, infrastructure, influence, etc. If political or economic institutions offer support, then there is a danger that they try to influence the activities of such projects, which can severely damage or limit the autonomy and critical facility of such projects. They seem to be trapped in an antagonism between resource precariousness and loss of autonomy that is caused by the fact that the control of resources is vital for having political influence in contemporary society and that resources in this very society are unequally distributed so that corporations and established political actors have much more power and influence than other actors. Given this situation, it would be a mistake not to try to organize citizens' initiatives, but one should bear in mind that due to the stratified character of capitalism it is more likely that such initiatives will fail and remain unimportant than that they will be successful in achieving their goals. Only the challenging of different resources towards watchdog organizations can contribute to weakening these limits.

In December 2010, Visa, PayPal, Western Union, the Bank of America and MasterCard disabled the means by which individuals could donate money to WikiLeaks using these services. The Swiss bank PostFinance closed Julian Assange's personal bank account. Private capitalist companies reacted to the US government's criticism of WikiLeaks, which shows that companies are highly instrumental and influenced by governments' demands. In October 2011, WikiLeaks had to suspend its operation due to a lack of funds and published a call for donations. Julian Assange said that this financial blockade had wiped out 95% of the donations and that "WikiLeaks' work takes a lot of resources. We cannot permit these banks to control our lives."[2]

---

2 www.youtube.com/watch?v=kbOibFK2ZpU&feature=player_embedded#t=130s, accessed on October 28, 2011.

WikiLeaks' financial problems show how difficult it is for alternative critical media to operate in a capitalist word. In order to exist, media need labour and resources. If they are, like WikiLeaks, not organized as businesses, they face existential pressures by the political economy of capitalism. Alternative media are facing resource inequalities in capitalism: corporate media are more powerful due to their control of capital. They therefore require financial and individual help (donations, voluntary work) in order to exist. Neglecting the profit imperative makes alternative media politically independent and potentially more critical, but at the same time more prone to censorship exerted by market forces and the lack of resources that result in precariousness. The circumstance that WikiLeaks has problems of keeping up its operations shows two areas where capitalist society is not free:

a) The rule of the media landscape by capitalist logic marginalizes alternative media and limits freedom of speech. There is no freedom of speech and of the press in a capitalist media world because alternative voices are systematically discriminated against.

b) Governments and corporations have to a certain extent similar interests, which can result in joint repressive action against critical alternatives.

Capitalism necessarily restricts liberal freedom. It is its own immanent limit. WikiLeaks' censorship by economic means shows that it is necessary to overcome capitalism in order to democratize the media and society.

The question arises about what the political goals and interests of this watchdog organization look like. Watchdog organizations are not critical *per se*; rather, underlying worldviews and political practices shape their character. Therefore, in the next section I analyze the worldviews that are related to WikiLeaks.

9.2. Wikileaks, Liberalism and Socialism

What is Liberalism?

Reviewing classical and contemporary concepts of liberalism, Gaus and Courtland (2011), in an encyclopaedic article about liberalism, argue that a common characteristic is that "liberals accord liberty primacy as a political value". Liberalism differs in this respect from radical democracy/participatory democracy: "Radical democrats assert the overriding value of equality" (Gaus and Courtland 2011). In liberalism, "freedom is normatively basic, and so the onus of justification is on those who would limit freedom, especially through coercive means" (Gaus and Courtland 2011). The *Fundamental Liberal Principle* is that "political authority and law must be justified, as they limit the liberty of citizens. Consequently, a central question of liberal political theory is whether political authority can be justified, and if so, how" (Gaus and Courtland 2011).

Freedom of speech, religious toleration extended to wide toleration of competing conceptions of the good life, antiestablishmentarianism (aimed at both religion and substantive views of human perfection), and a sphere of privacy are fundamental liberal commitments. Liberal public concerns focus on honoring these commitments but also on protecting fundamental civil interests, such as bodily integrity. Civil interests also include the maintenance of some sort of justified system of property rights. (Gaus 1996, 175)

What is Socialism?

Socialists, in contrast to liberals, think that "the rewards of production [. . .] are due to society as a whole, and to its members equally, rather than to particular individuals" (Barker 1991, 485). In the realm of property and labour, "means of production are commonly possessed" in a socialist society (Barker 1991, 485). Important values in socialist thought include: equality, communal and co-operative production, workers' control of production/self-managed companies (Barker 1991), and socio-political solidarity (Buzby 2010). Socialism maintains that the source of human value is human creativity and co-operation liberated from class power: "Socialist humanism declares: liberate men from slavery to things, to the pursuit of profit or servitude to 'economic necessity'. Liberate man, as a creative being – and he will create, not only new values, but things in super-abundance" (Thompson 1957).

The notion of socialism is not limited to the economic realm, although socialists see the economy as an important foundation of society. Held (2006, 215) says that a key feature of participatory democracy is the "direct participation of citizens in the regulation of the key institutions of society, including the workplace and local community". Participatory democracy, the political dimension of socialism, involves the "democratisation of authority structures" (Pateman 1970, 35) in all decision-making systems, such as government, the workplace, the family, education, housing, etc. "If individuals are to exercise the maximum amount of control over their own lives and environment then authority structures in these areas must be so organised that they can participate in decision making" (Pateman 1970, 43). Participatory democracy theory uses a wide notion of the political that extends beyond the sphere of government into the economy and culture. "Spheres such as industry should be seen as political systems in their own right" (Pateman 1970, 43). Socialism is, on the one hand, based on the idea that there should be an economy "within which the means of production are socially owned" and, on the other hand, on the idea that "the allocation and use of resources for different social purposes is accomplished through the exercise of what can be termed 'social power'", which is "power rooted in the capacity to mobilize people for co-operative, voluntary collective actions of various sorts" (Wright 2010, 121). Socialism has an economic and a political dimension. Table 9.1 summarizes some main differences between liberalism and socialism.

WikiLeaks and Political Worldviews

How does WikiLeaks relate to political worldviews? To answer this question, it is best to analyze WikiLeaks' self-description with the help of critical discourse

Table 9.1 Differences between liberalism and socialism

	Liberalism	Socialism
Basic value	Freedom	Equality
View of society	Individualism	Sociality, solidarity
Economy	Private property	Collective ownership
Source of wealth	Capital	Co-operation of creative human beings freed from exploitation
State and politics	Private affairs are not controlled by the state	Grassroots democracy
Culture	Plurality of interests and worldviews	Universal rights and interests
Political struggle against:	Regulating state	Capital interests, exploitation, capitalist state, ideology

analysis. I apply one specific principle of critical discourse analyis: focus analysis (Van Dijk 2011, 398). Focus analysis assesses how and to what extent focus (special stress) is given to certain topics and how these topics are predicated.

Until December 3, 2010, WikiLeaks was accessible on the website wikileaks. org. On the same day, the domain service provider EveryDNS cancelled WikiLeaks' URL. With the help of the Pirate Party Switzerland, WikiLeaks moved its official site to wikileaks.ch. The old and the new site have different mission statements (wikileaks.org: WikiLeaks 2010, wikileaks.ch: WikiLeaks 2011). Later, wikileaks. org reappeared and in 2013 held the same content as wikileaks.ch. These mission statements express the self-understanding and self-definition of WikiLeaks and are therefore suited for critical discourse analysis. The content of these self-definitions is related to liberal and socialist political worldviews both in a quantitative and a qualitative way.

I numbered each paragraph in the two WikiLeaks' self-definitions. For each paragraph I classified which topics were discussed, which resulted in a category system consisting of seven topics. Table 9.2 shows the total number of occurrences of each topic in the two documents and the corresponding paragraph numbers.

The analysis shows that the most important element in both self-definitions of WikiLeaks is that it wants, by document leaking, to make government power transparent, watch governments and advance the establishment of open governments. Making corporate power visible is a secondary topic: there are only 11 paragraphs that discuss this topic in both WikiLeaks' self-understandings, as opposed to 22 and 16 paragraphs respectively that discuss government transparency. In the first self-definition, the word "government" is mentioned 41 times, in the second 36 times (WikiLeaks 2010, 2011). In the first, the term "company/companies" is mentioned once, in the second three times, and the term "corporate/corporation(s)" 17 times in the first and 21 times in the second (WikiLeaks 2010, 2011). WikiLeaks (2011, paragraph 22) provides a list of its most important leaks: 29 (63%) leaks concern governments, 13 (28%) companies and banks, and four (9%) religion. This circumstance confirms that WikiLeaks gives more weight to politics than to political economy and ideology.

Table 9.2 Results of a quantitative analysis of topics occurring in WikiLeaks' two self-understandings

Category	Total number (paragraphs in WikiLeaks' self-definition 1)	Total number (paragraphs in WikiLeaks' self-definition 2)
Whistleblowing, leaking documents	10 (1, 11, 12, 30, 36, 37, 42, 45, 46, 47)	6 (5, 6, 13, 22, 28, 32)
Making government transparent, watching governments, open government	22 (2, 3, 4, 5, 6, 7, 8, 9, 13, 14, 15, 16, 17, 18, 19, 20, 21, 28, 29, 55, 56, 60)	16 (8, 9, 10, 11, 23, 24, 25, 26, 27, 29, 30, 31, 33, 37, 44, 45)
Explanation of technology	8 (10, 33, 38, 39, 40, 41, 43, 44)	2 (2, 17)
Making corporate power transparent	11 (13, 15, 16, 17, 20, 22, 23, 24, 25, 26, 27)	11 (8, 11, 30, 31, 33, 38, 39, 40, 41, 42, 43)
Free speech	10 (19, 20, 31, 32, 34, 35, 43, 49, 50, 51)	10 (3, 7, 18, 19, 20, 21, 32, 34, 35, 36)
Journalism	3 (48, 52, 53)	7 (1, 4, 8, 12, 13, 14, 16)
WikiLeaks organization	6 (54, 55, 56, 57, 58, 59)	3 (2, 9, 15)

Data source: WikiLeaks 2010, 2011.

WikiLeaks' self-definition has a liberal bias because it sees big governments as the main problem, which reflects the liberal tendency to never trust governments. It also has a strong focus on the liberal core value of freedom (WikiLeaks is defined as a freedom of speech and freedom of information project) and the value of information plurality.

"Good Governance"

WikiLeaks mentions as one of its goals the promotion of "good governance": "Open government answers injustice rather than causing it. Open government exposes and undoes corruption. Open governance is the most effective method of promoting good governance" (WikiLeaks 2010, 13). The International Monetary Fund (IMF) employed the concept of "good governance" to describe the conditions indebted and poor countries have to fulfil in order to get an IMF loan. These conditions include, on the one hand, the commitment of the debtor countries to fight corruption and, on the other hand, the commitment of "improving the management of public resources through reforms covering public sector institutions" and "supporting the development and maintenance of a transparent and stable economic and regulatory environment conducive to efficient private sector activities" (IMF 1997). This means that the concept of good governance is an expression of neoliberal international politics that aim at deregulating, liberalizing and privatizing the public sector, cutting state budgets for education, welfare, social security and health care in poor countries, and opening investment opportunities for Western companies that transfer wealth and profit created in poor countries back to the West.

David Harvey (2007) gives examples of how IMF austerity programmes have resulted in the increase of poverty and inequality. He argues that the management

and manipulation of crises by the IMF and other institutions results in the "deliberative redistribution of wealth from poor countries to the rich" (Harvey 2007, 162)
and is an expression of neoliberal accumulation by dispossession. Good governance is a measure for orienting the state on "conditions for economic expansion"
(Jessop 2002, 267). Given the fact that WikiLeaks to a certain degree is concerned
about the negative effects of corporate power (WikiLeaks 2010, 22–27, 2011,
29–43), it is surprising and self-contradictory that it employs the neoliberally connoted notion of "good governance" in its self-definition.

Watching Corporate Power

WikiLeaks does not ignore the importance of criticizing and watching corporate
power in its mission statements, but subordinates it to government watching.
Corporate power is frequently relegated to one form of corruption among others:
"WikiLeaks may be at the heart of another global revolution – in better accountability by governments and other institutions" (WikiLeaks 2010, 60). Leaking
affects "authoritarian governments, oppressive institutions and corrupt corporations" (WikiLeaks 2010, 17, 2011, 33). One cannot only observe here that governments are always mentioned first, but there is also a strange separation that
implies that corporations are not necessarily oppressive institutions, but only in
those cases where they are corrupt. The banking blockade that WikiLeaks has
experienced is itself a good example that shows the interconnection of capitalist
power and state power: the capitalist economy is always political economy.

The problem of WikiLeaks' self-understanding is that it idealizes freedom of
speech and information and liberal values, and separates corporate domination
from state domination. The very liberal values that WikiLeaks embraces (freedom
of speech, freedom from government intervention, freedom of information) have
in modern society never been realized because markets and capitalism privilege
corporations that tend to dominate public expression and opinion by privately
controlling large parts of the means of expression, information and speech. Liberal
values are their own immanent critique because they have never been realized in
capitalism and are contradicted by liberalism's emphasis on private property rights.
Jürgen Habermas has stressed in this context that the liberal public sphere limits its
own value of freedom of speech and public opinion because citizens in capitalism
do not have the same formal education and material resources for participating in
the public sphere (Habermas 1989c, 227), and that it limits its own value of freedom of association and assembly because big political and economic organizations
"enjoy an oligopoly of the publicistically effective and politically relevant formation
of assemblies and associations" (Habermas 1989c, 228).

The non-transparency of power that WikiLeaks criticizes is not external to
liberal values, but is an integral part of liberal-capitalist regimes. Corporate
power and the support of corporate power by the capitalist state is kept
secret in order to maintain and expand capitalist rule, and is legitimized by
liberal values such as privacy and private property. Corporate domination
and state domination are not separated in modern societies, but connected.

Contemporary states support corporate rules by protecting private property, enforcing neoliberal policies and fighting wars that install a global new imperialist rule (Fuchs 2011b, chapter 5; Harvey 2005b). WikiLeaks has a liberal bias; it argues for liberal values and thereby ignores that liberalism is a core cause of the phenomena that WikiLeaks questions. The question that will therefore be covered in the next section is whether WikiLeaks has the potential to act as a socialist alternative medium.

9.3. WikiLeaks, Journalism and Alternative Media

What is a Journalist?

McQuail (2010, 561) defines a journalist as a person who creates "informational reports of recent or current events of interest to the public". In an earlier version of the same book, McQuail (2000, 340) defined journalism as "paid writing (and the audiovisual equivalent) for public media with reference to actual and ongoing events of public relevance", which led Harcup (2009, 3) to ask: "Can journalism never be unpaid?" McQuail's shift towards a more general definition of the journalist may reflect the rise of phenomena like political blogging, participatory journalism (Deuze 2010), grassroots journalism (Gillmor 2006), citizen journalism (Allan 2010; Bruns 2008), alternative online journalism (Atton 2009, 2010) and radical online journalism that "questions taken-for-granted forms of doing journalism" (Atton 2004, 60) and provides news that is created by those affected by power.

The question "Who is a journalist?" remains contested, with, on the one hand, traditional scholars arguing that journalists are professionals that "are hired to make profits by selling their products. This has always been the case throughout the development of the profession" (Donsbach 2010, 39). On the other hand, there are observers who say that "participatory journalism is any kind of news work at the hands of professionals and amateurs, of journalists and citizens, and of users and producers benchmarked by what Benkler calls commons-based peer production" (Deuze 2010, 271). Notwithstanding this discussion, there seems to be a general consensus that at the most basic level the definition of journalism has to include a focus on "finding things out, then telling people about them via newspapers, radio, television or the Internet" (Kinsey 2005, 124). If an important aspect of journalism is the systematic creation, publishing and provision of news stories, then the question arises as to whether WikiLeaks is a journalistic project.

The Iceland-based company the Sunshine Press operates WikiLeaks. Its content is stored on web servers. WikiLeaks provides content to the public and creates summaries as news stories. It can therefore be considered to satisfy the broad consensus definition of journalism as the systematic creation, publication and provision of news stories. WikiLeaks is a form of journalism that can best be characterized as watchdog journalism. Watchdog journalists are interventionist because they advocate the interests of disadvantaged groups, are critical of power, and tend to define their activities and goals in terms of the public interest instead of market interests (Hanitzsch 2007). Deuze (2005) argues that journalism is an ideology that is characterized by five elements that, without a doubt, can also be found in the self-understanding of WikiLeaks: public service, objectivity, autonomy from power, immediacy/actuality, ethics. Deuze (2003) sees alternative online media as a form of online journalism that questions mainstream news-making media.

WikiLeaks and Mainstream Media

Mainstream media like *The Guardian*, *The New York Times* and *Der Spiegel* have the economic, reputational and political power to reach the public, whereas an alternative medium, like WikiLeaks, is less likely to be recognized, read or mastered by the everyday citizen. It is a reflection of the political economy of the media in capitalism that, on the one hand, *The New York Times* was, in 2013, ranked #120 in the list of the world's most accessed websites, *Der Spiegel Online* was #227, *The Guardian* #196 and that, on the other hand, WikiLeaks.org is much less accessed and known, and was ranked in 2013 as #20 080 (data source: alexa.com, top 1 000 000 sites, accessed on March 4, 2013). Mainstream media are prone to pressures by advertisers, companies, lobbyists and governments that can result in filtered, censored news that is uncritical and excludes critical voices. It is therefore no surprise that *The New York Times* reported that there was US government pressure not to release news about the "Afghanistan Diaries" (The war logs articles, *The New York Times*, July 25, 2010). It is desirable that alternative media like WikiLeaks do not have to rely on corporate channels in order to reach the public, but have the power and visibility to reach a mass public directly. The unequal media and communication power structures that are a characteristic of the capitalist media system make this difficult and thereby create the risk that leaked documents published by WikiLeaks will be censored, distorted or ignored. Changing this situation requires that we give more economic power, political power and attention to alternative media. It requires steps towards the end of the capitalistic media landscape.

Economic, Political and Cultural Censorship of WikiLeaks

The economy, politics and culture are three basic realms of all societies (Fuchs 2008a). The economy is about the production of use-values that satisfy human needs, politics about taking collective decisions that govern society and culture about the establishment of social meanings of society. In capitalism, all three realms are stratified: elites control property, collective decision-making and dominant ideas, and interpretation. The example of WikiLeaks shows that censorship is not just a political process, where state apparatuses imprison media and political activists, criminalize media organizations or stop the publication and availability of certain media. It is also an economic and ideological process.

First, there was *political censorship*: states tried to silence WikiLeaks. The US government imprisoned Bradley Manning, a soldier who allegedly leaked the Collateral Murder, and put him on trial for the alleged disclosure of data classified by the US military. The US government also demanded, by court rules, access to the social media profiles and content of everyone involved in WikiLeaks, such as the Icelandic parliamentarian Birgitta Jónsdóttir:

> The American government demanded access to my personal Twitter messages, my IP numbers, and various other personal data in a desperate attempt to criminalize everyone who volunteered for WikiLeaks in 2009/2010. Not only was Twitter forced to hand over my personal data, but so were three other companies which the courts are refusing to reveal to me. (Jónsdóttir 2013, xiii)

US Vice President Joe Biden said that Assange is "closer to being a hi-tech terrorist than the Pentagon papers" in the 1970s and that he "has done things that have damaged and put in jeopardy the lives and occupations of people in other parts of the world".[3] Given such statements and the good political relations between Sweden and the USA, Julian Assange's fear that he could be extradited to the USA, put on trial for espionage or treason and even face the death penalty is realistic.

Second, there were also attempts to *ideologically censor* WikiLeaks, i.e. to create negative public opinion about the project. One media ideological strategy that is part of the tabloidization of the commercialization of the media is to focus on personal affairs and scandals of public figures. The coverage of Julian Assange in the mainstream media has strongly focused on discussing his personality and two alleged cases of rape in Sweden. Thereby the media and politicians tried to construct a negative public image of Assange and to discredit WikiLeaks as a political project. A very good example is Bill Keller's article "Dealing with Assange and the WikiLeaks secrets" that was published in *The New York Times* on January 26, 2011.[4] Keller was then the newspaper's editor. He describes Assange in this article as "an eccentric former computer hacker of Australian birth and no fixed residence" and continues with formulations such as:

- "'He's tall – probably 6-foot-2 or 6–3 – and lanky, with pale skin, gray eyes and a shock of white hair that seizes your attention', Schmitt wrote to me later. 'He was alert but disheveled, like a bag lady walking in off the street, wearing a dingy, light-colored sport coat and cargo pants, dirty white shirt, beat-up sneakers and filthy white socks that collapsed around his ankles. He smelled as if he hadn't bathed in days.'"
- "The reporters came to think of Assange as smart and well educated, extremely adept technologically but arrogant, thin-skinned, conspiratorial and oddly credulous."

---

3 http://www.guardian.co.uk/media/2010/dec/19/assange-high-tech-terrorist-biden, accessed on March 29, 2013.
4 http://www.nytimes.com/2011/01/30/magazine/30Wikileaks-t.html?pagewanted=all&_r=0, accessed on March 29, 2013.

- "But while I do not regard Assange as a partner, and I would hesitate to describe what WikiLeaks does as journalism, it is chilling to contemplate the possible government prosecution of WikiLeaks for making secrets public, let alone the passage of new laws to punish the dissemination of classified information, as some have advocated."

- "Assange was transformed by his outlaw celebrity. The derelict with the backpack and the sagging socks now wore his hair dyed and styled, and he favored fashionably skinny suits and ties. He became a kind of cult figure for the European young and leftish and was evidently a magnet for women. Two Swedish women filed police complaints claiming that Assange insisted on having sex without a condom; Sweden's strict laws on nonconsensual sex categorize such behavior as rape, and a prosecutor issued a warrant to question Assange, who initially described it as a plot concocted to silence or discredit WikiLeaks. I came to think of Julian Assange as a character from a Stieg Larsson thriller – a man who could figure either as hero or villain in one of the megaselling Swedish novels that mix hacker counterculture, high-level conspiracy and sex as both recreation and violation."

Tabloidization focuses on the personal, crime, show business, tragedy, drama, sensationalism, disaster, pictures, brevity and entertainment. "Tabloidization is the progressive displacement of citizen-enhancing material with material which has *no other purpose* than to shock, provoke, entertain or retain viewers; and the progressive erosion of professional journalistic values in favour of televisual techniques involving sensationalism, distortion, misrepresentation and dramatization of the trivial" (Barnett 2011, 169). Tabloidization displaces politics. By tabloidization, the public sphere is "transmogrified into a sphere of culture consumption" and becomes a "pseudo-public sphere" (Habermas 1989c, 162). Habermas (1989c, 171f) noted that part of this process is that the media present public developments as private affairs so that they are "distorted to the point of unrecognizability" (172), that stars attain publicity and that there is a publicizing of private biographies. The focus on Julian Assange's personality in many mainstream media tried to politically discredit WikiLeaks by using tabloidization as an ideological strategy.

Bendetta Brevini and Graham Murdock (2013) argue that WikiLeaks faces multiple forms of economic censorship:

- The cancellation of the provision of server space and domain names (Amazon, EveryDNS).
- The cancellation of the provision of software services (WikiLeaks app on Apple iPhones and iPads).
- The disabling of bank accounts and donations via bank transfers and credit cards (PayPal, PostFinance, MasterCard, Visa, Bank of America).
- The labour required for organizing and maintaining WikiLeaks was constrained by the diminishing donations.

- The analytical labour needed for analyzing leaked documents had to be outsourced to mainstream media organizations.

WikiLeaks has faced economic, political and ideological censorship. As alternative medium, there is a limited availability of resources and labour for operating WikiLeaks and for analyzing documents. As a consequence, WikiLeaks, due to a lack of resources, had to collaborate with corporate media giants such as *The New York Times*, *The Guardian* and *Der Spiegel* that are subject to corporate, political and ideological filters that can censor the published content. As Julian Assange himself states: "If you want to have an impact and you're an organization which is very small, you have to co-opt or leverage the rest of the mainstream press" (Assange and Žižek 2013, 257). Economically, donation possibilities were restricted and technological infrastructure provision was cancelled. Ideologically, many mainstream media started a tabloid-like campaign against Assange in order to discredit WikiLeaks. "Counterinstitutions based on ideals of public service" (Brevini and Murdock 2013, 52) that are funded by donations or taxes are attempts to offset the structural and direct discrimination and censorship of alternative media. However, they are still faced with the resource power of corporate media, the political power of the state and the ideological power of opinion leaders. In order to overcome this inequality, it is necessary to overcome the inequalities of economic, political and cultural power that are immanent in the current economic, political and ideological orders.

WikiLeaks: An Alternative Medium?

Is WikiLeaks an alternative medium? Alternative media can, on the one hand, be defined as self-organized journalistic production projects and, on the other hand, as journalistic projects that voice non-mainstream views (Fuchs 2010a; Sandoval 2009; Sandoval and Fuchs 2010;). Five main differences between mainstream media and alternative media can be identified (see Table 9.3). According to Fuchs and Sandoval (Fuchs 2010a; Sandoval 2009; Sandoval and Fuchs 2010;), the most relevant dimension for speaking of an alternative medium is critical content. They therefore speak of alternative media as critical media.

Critical media, according to this perspective, provide oppositional content that presents alternatives to dominant, repressive, heteronomous perspectives that reflect the rule of capital, patriarchy, racism, sexism, nationalism, etc. Such content expresses oppositional standpoints that question all forms of heteronomy and domination. So there is counter-information and counter-hegemony that includes the voices of the excluded, oppressed, dominated, enslaved, estranged, exploited, dominated. One goal is to give voices to the voiceless, media power to the powerless as well as to transcend filtering and censorship of information by corporate information monopolies, state monopolies, or cultural monopolies in public information and communication. For judging whether WikiLeaks is

Table 9.3   Potential dimensions of traditional and alternative media (Fuchs 2010a)

Dimension	Capitalist mass media	Alternative media
Journalistic production	Elite journalism	Citizens' journalism
Media product structures	Ideological form and content	Critical form and content
Organizational media structures	Hierarchical media organizations	Grassroots media organizations
Distribution structures	Marketing and public relations	Alternative distribution
Reception practices	Manipulative reception	Critical reception

a critical medium, it must be analyzed as to the extent to which it questions contemporary forms of domination and exploitation, i.e. the extent to which it reflects what in section 9.2 has been characterized as a socialist worldview.

This chapter has argued that WikiLeaks' goals have a liberal bias, which does not automatically mean that its practices are completely alien from socialism. WikiLeaks' self-understandings have a section that is devoted to corporate power and corporate corruption (WikiLeaks 2010, 22–27, 2011, 38–43): WikiLeaks argues that large corporations have tremendous economic and political power. It makes eleven points about what is problematic about corporate power (WikiLeaks 2010, 24, 2011, 40). These points can be summarized as focusing on the following topics: corporations have centralized decision power, they provide no civil rights for employees (no freedom of speech and association, human rights are limited, no privacy, permanent surveillance), and their economy is centrally planned. These are good points that are certainly elements of a socialist worldview, but one important criticism of corporations is missing: that they are centrally owned by a class of private owners who exploit the labour power of workers and employees in order to accumulate profit that is their private property. Questions concerning class and exploitation are left out. One gets the impression that WikiLeaks sees companies as just another form of oppressive government and reduces corporations to government mechanisms. The difference is, however, that companies not only oppress; in contrast to governments, they also have the general feature of exploiting labour power.

Another problem is the assumption that it is possible to civilize corporations: "WikiLeaks endeavors to civilize corporations by exposing uncivil plans and behavior. Just like a country, a corrupt or unethical corporation is a menace to all inside and outside it" (WikiLeaks 2010, 27). "Corporations will behave more ethically if the world is watching closely" (WikiLeaks 2011, 43). One can hear daily stories about corporate irresponsibility – stories such as the one that BP (British Petroleum) caused one of the worst ecological disasters are in all news formats, or that iPods and iPads are produced in China under such inhumane conditions that workers commit suicide because they cannot stand the working conditions, etc. The problem is that such a multitude of stories, and here

WikiLeaks is no exception and directly admits this in its self-description, makes us believe that corporate irresponsibility and corporate crimes against humanity are the exception from the rule and can therefore be fixed within capitalism by "civilizing corporations".

But what if corporations are uncivilized as such, if their behaviour is always exploitative and irresponsible? Then capitalism and corporations cannot be civilized and made ethical, and exposing uncivil plans and behaviour should be aimed at transforming and civilizing the whole. What is a corporation? A machine-like organization that accumulates capital by exploiting workers who create surplus value that is transformed into profit. Exploitation is always uncivilized and degrades humans to an inhumane status. Therefore corporations cannot be civilized and can never act ethically. In order to civilize society, corporatism and all other forms of domination need to be abolished. In its new mission statement, WikiLeaks (2011) abolished the passage about civilizing corporations, which could be an indication that is has changed its political assessment of capitalism.

WikiLeaks can be seen as an alternative media project: it tries to provide information that uncovers the misuse of power by powerful actors. It is an Internet-based medium that enables critiques of power structures. It is, however, thus far only to a limited extent a critical project because it seems to aim at reforming and not abolishing structures of exploitation and domination, underestimates the exploitative character of corporate power, and therefore falls short of aiming at the categorical imperative of criticism to help overthrow all relations that alienate them from their human essence by exploiting and oppressing them. WikiLeaks has, however, a potential to be not only an alternative medium that watches power abuse, but a critical medium that helps and aims at overcoming structures of domination. This requires that WikiLeaks overcomes its liberal bias by changing its self-understanding and engages more in the practice of corporate watching that is currently subordinated to government watching.

9.4. Conclusion

WikiLeaks has made visible the scale of brutality, violence and horror of the wars in Afghanistan and Iraq. These and subsequent leaks about the US government and other powerful institutions have resulted in the circumstance that ruling groups perceive WikiLeaks as a threat and define it as the enemy. It is therefore no surprise that following "Cablegate" in December 2010, EveryDNS cancelled WikiLeaks' domain and Amazon, PayPal, the Swiss bank PostFinance, MasterCard, Visa, Apple and the Bank of America stopped the provision of payment and other services to WikiLeaks. WikiLeaks' counter-power against dominant powers was answered by the latter powers' turning against WikiLeaks itself. Sarah Palin said that Assange "is an anti-American operative with blood on his hands. His past posting of classified documents revealed the identity of more than 100 Afghan sources to the Taliban. Why was he not pursued with the same urgency we pursue Al Qaeda and Taliban leaders?"[5]

The publication of the Iraq and Afghanistan documents on WikiLeaks is certainly a political move intended to help put an end to the US invasion of Iraq and Afghanistan. Julian Assange talks openly about his anti-war motivations: "The most dangerous men are those who are in charge of war. And they need to be stopped."[6] The wars in Afghanistan and Iraq not only help to secure the United State's global political hegemony, they also secure the access to economic resources and markets and are therefore expressions of the new imperialism. These wars are examples of how the violence of the political economy of capitalism works. WikiLeaks, however, does not realize in its self-understanding that these wars and contemporary power structures in general are not matters of bad governance, but the imperialistic intersection of state, corporate and military interests. WikiLeaks threatens the imperialist military–state–corporate complex and should therefore better realize and acknowledge its own critical potentials. The positive potential of WikiLeaks is that it transcends its own values and realizes its potential for becoming a critical, socialist watchdog medium. Socialist watchdog projects are not an end-in-itself, but rather self-defence mechanisms in social struggles that aim at the establishment of participatory democracy. It is not an alternative to WikiLeaks that is needed, but a redefinition of WikiLeaks. WikiLeaks is its own alternative.

We can summarize the main results of this chapter as follows:

- WikiLeaks is an alternative medium and watchdog journalism project. It makes use of Internet document leaking to try to make power structures transparent.

- The worldviews and practices underlying WikiLeaks give more weight to politics than to political economy and ideology critique, have a liberal bias characterized by a focus on "good governance", and a lack of understanding of class and exploitation in contemporary capitalism.

- As a liberally biased project, WikiLeaks poses a threat to the military-state-corporate complex. Its own liberal self-understanding, in practice, goes beyond liberalism itself, dialectically inverts itself, and anticipates a qualitatively different project. WikiLeaks has the potential to become a critical, socialist watchdog medium, but to do so needs to acknowledge socialist theory and practices and the radical critique of capitalism, and has to overcome its liberal bias.

---

5 www.alternet.org/news/149032/noam_chomsky:_wikileaks_cables_reveal_%22profound_hatred_for_democracy_on_the_part_of_our_political_leadership%22/?page=5, accessed on March 20, 2013.
6 www.spiegel.de/international/world/0,1518,708518,00.html, accessed on March 20, 2013.

RECOMMENDED READINGS AND EXERCISES

For understanding WikiLeaks, it is useful to read texts that discuss what journalism and alternative media are and to conduct exemplary analyses of documents leaked on the platform.

Donsbach, Wolfgang. 2010. Introduction: Recrafting news and journalism. In *The Routledge companion to news and journalism*, ed. Stuart Allan, xxiii–xliv. Abingdon: Routledge.

Atton, Chris. 2010. Alternative journalism. In *The Routledge companion to news and journalism*, ed. Stuart Allan, 169–178. Abingdon: Routledge.

Atton, Chris and James F. Hamilton. 2008. *Alternative journalism*. London: SAGE. Chapter 7: Theorizing alternative journalism. Chapter 2: Political-economic pressures that shape alternative journalism.

Deuze, Mark. 2010. Journalism and convergence culture. In *The Routledge companion to news and journalism*, ed. Stuart Allan, 267–276. Abingdon: Routledge.

Ask yourself:

- What are commonalities and differences in how the three authors of these chapters conceptualize journalism?

- How do you define journalism?

- According to each of the three texts, is WikiLeaks a form of journalism or not? Why? Why not?

- Is WikiLeaks, according to your definition, a form of journalism? If so, how does it differ from other forms of journalism? If not, why not?

Sandoval, Marisol and Christian Fuchs. 2010. Towards a critical theory of alternative media. *Telematics and Informatics* 27 (2): 141–150.

- Discuss the limits, problems and structural discriminations that alternative media are facing. Construct a systematic typology of these limits.

- How does each of these limits affect WikiLeaks? Try to give concrete examples.

- How can such limits be overcome? What needs to change in order to overcome them?

Fuchs, Christian. 2012. Implications of Deep Packet Inspection (DPI) Internet surveillance for society. The Privacy & Security-Research Paper Series, ed. Emilio Mordini and Christian Fuchs. ISSN 2270-7467. Research Paper Number 1. EU FP7 project

"PACT – Public Perception of Security and Privacy: Assessing Knowledge, Collecting Evidence, Translating Research into Action". 125 pages. http://fuchs.uti.at/wp-content/uploads/DPI.pdf

- Read the research report, study and discuss how WikiLeaks was used as a data source.

- Create an overview of the leaks that WikiLeaks has published. Select one topic. Download a significant number of leaked documents. Analyze what these documents are all about with the help of a content and/or discourse analysis. Document and present your results.

10

Wikipedia: A New Democratic Form of Collaborative Work and Production?

Key questions

- How does Wikipedia work and how does it differ from corporate social media such as Facebook?
- Positivistic or utopian? Exploitative or emancipatory? What are the political implications of Wikipedia's organization model?
- What is a commons-based Internet and why should we think about this model?

Key concepts

Collaborative work
Communal production
Commons

Participatory democracy
Well-rounded individuality
Communication commons

Overview

This chapter's task is to analyze the political economy of Wikipedia and its implications for economic democracy. Wikipedia is the sixth most visited web platform in the world (data source: alexa.com, accessed on March 4, 2013). It was founded in 2001. It deviates strongly from other dominant web platforms, such as Google, Facebook, YouTube, Yahoo, Baidu, Twitter, QQ, MSN and LinkedIn, because it is operated by a non-profit organization (the Wikimedia Foundation) and is advertising-free.

Wikipedia describes itself in the following way:

> Wikipedia [...] is a multilingual, web-based, free-content encyclope-
> dia project based on an openly editable model. [...] Wikipedia is writ-
> ten collaboratively by largely anonymous Internet volunteers who
> write without pay. Anyone with Internet access can write and make
> changes to Wikipedia articles (except in certain cases where editing
> is restricted to prevent disruption or vandalism). [...] Since its crea-
> tion in 2001, Wikipedia has grown rapidly into one of the largest ref-
> erence websites, attracting 470 million unique visitors monthly as of
> February 2012. There are more than 77,000 active contributors work-
> ing on more than 22,000,000 articles in more than 285 languages. As
> of today, there are 4,178,041 articles in English. [...] Wikipedia is a
> live collaboration differing from paper-based reference sources in
> important ways. Unlike printed encyclopedias, Wikipedia is continu-
> ally created and updated, with articles on historic events appearing
> within minutes, rather than months or years. Older articles tend to
> grow more comprehensive and balanced; newer articles may contain
> misinformation, unencyclopedic content, or vandalism. Awareness of
> this aids obtaining valid information and avoiding recently added mis-
> information.[1]

Wikipedia is based on general principles, the *Five Pillars of Wikipedia*:[2]

- "Wikipedia is an online encyclopedia. [...]
- Wikipedia is written from a neutral point of view. [...]
- Wikipedia is free content that anyone can edit, use, modify, and distribute. [...]
- Editors should interact with each other in a respectful and civil manner. [...]
- Wikipedia does not have firm rules. Rules in Wikipedia are not carved in stone, and their wording and interpretation are likely to change over time."

This chapter advances the argument that Wikipedia's mode of production bears a strong resemblance to what Marx and Engels described as communism. First, I discuss the renewal of the idea of communism undertaken by thinkers such as Slavoj Žižek and Alain Badiou and give an overview of Marx's principles of com-munism (section 10.1). Then I discuss the relationship between communism and communication (section 10.2) and present an analysis of Wikipedia's political economy (section 10.3).

The literature published on Wikipedia (for an overview, see: http://en.wikipedia.org/wiki/Wikipedia:Wikipedia_in_academic_studies) lacks atten-tion to societal implications, economic property, economic production and participatory democracy. It is very positivistic and has no critical focus. An exception is Erik Olin Wright (2010), who discusses Wikipedia based on a critical

---

1 http://en.wikipedia.org/wiki/Wikipedia:About, accessed on March 4, 2013.
2 http://en.wikipedia.org/wiki/Wikipedia:Five_pillars, accessed on March 4, 2013.

framework and points out its implications for "real utopias". He discusses four emancipatory aspects of Wikipedia:

1) non-market relations (voluntary, unpaid contributions, free access),
2) egalitarian participation,
3) direct deliberative interactions,
4) democratic governance and adjunction (Wright 2010, 194–203).

The problem is that Wright ignores aspects of ownership of Wikipedia's content (its Creative Commons licence) and the contradictory nature of free labour as both a source of unlimited exploitation for corporate ends and communist potentials. While he asserts the emancipatory characteristics of Wikipedia's mode of governance, he does not seem to see the potential of Wikipedia in terms of political economy and its mode of production. Wikipedia is important in the sense that it presents a new way of collaborative decision-making and a new way of producing, owning, consuming and distributing goods.

10.1. The Communist Idea

The Return of Marx

One interesting thing about Marx is that he keeps coming back at moments when people least expect it, in the form of various Marxisms that keep haunting capitalism like ghosts, as Jacques Derrida (1994) has stressed. It is paradoxical that almost 20 years after the end of the Soviet Union, capitalism seems to have falsified itself because its neoliberal mode of development has intensified global problems, caused severe poverty and a rise of unequal income distribution, and as a result has brought a return of the economic in the form of a worldwide economic crisis and with it a re-actualization of the Marxian critique of capitalism. Although a persistent refrain is "Marx is dead, long live capitalism", Marx has come back again today.

The Marxian focus on machinery, means of communication and the general intellect anticipated the importance of technology, knowledge and the media in contemporary capitalism (see, for example, Dyer-Witheford 1999; Fuchs 2008a, 2011b). The new global economic crisis that started in 2008 has shown that Marxist crisis theory is still important today (Foster and Magdoff 2009). Capitalism seems to be inherently crisis-ridden.

The renewed discussion about the relevance of Marx's critique of the political economy (see Eagleton 2011; Žižek 2008) as an analytical tool for understanding the crisis of capitalism has been accompanied by a discussion about the need for establishing a democratic form of communism as an alternative to capitalism (Badiou 2008; Dean 2012; Hardt and Negri 2009; Harvey 2010a, 2010b, 2012; Žižek and Douzinas 2010; for a detailed discussion see Fuchs 2011b, chapter 9).

Three Dimensions of Communism

The negation of class is the classless society – communism. Marx and Engels did not mean by the term communism as a totalitarian society that monitors all human beings, operates forced labour camps, represses human individuality, installs conditions of general shortage, limits the freedom of movement, etc. Rather, they saw communism as a society that strengthens common co-operative production, common ownership of the means of production, and enriches the individual sphere of activities and thereby individuality. We will discuss each of these three aspects that constitute communism (Fuchs 2011b, chapter 9). In production, human subjects engage in co-operative social relations (subjective dimension) and by making use of the means of production (technologies, resources) create a new good or service (objective dimension). The overall process has effects on individuals and on society. The production process has a subjective, an objective and an effects dimension. All three dimensions are transformed by the transition from a capitalist to a communist society.

The Subjective Dimension

(1) The subjective dimension of production: communism as the co-operative form of production.

For Marx and Engels, communism is a community of co-operating producers that operate in a highly productive economy, use the means of production together to produce use values that satisfy the needs of all, and take decisions in the production process together.

   Marx speaks of communism as "general co-operation of all members of society" (MEW 4, 377), "communal production" (Marx 1857/1858, 172) and the "positing of the activity of individuals as immediately general or social activity" (Marx 1857/1858, 832).

The Objective Dimension

(2) The objective dimension of production: communism as the common ownership of the means of production.

Communism does not mean, for Marx and Engels, that there are no longer any private goods for consumption. The main difference from capitalist society is rather that there is no longer only a small group, but all producers own the means of production (the technologies of production, the firms, the decision power in firms, etc.). Communism is a democratic form of organizing industry and the economy. It extends economic property from a small group to all producers. Communist firms are self-managed and do not have a power division between owners and workers – all workers are at the same time owners.

   Marx and Engels extended the notion of the commons to all means of production. Marx spoke of "an association of free men, working with the means of production held in common, and expending their many different forms of labour-power in full self-awareness as one single social labour force" (Marx 1867, 171). In this association, machines are the "property of the associated workers" (Marx 1857/1858, 833) so that "a new foundation" of production emerges. This new system implements "the common utilization of all instruments of production and the distribution of all products according to common agreement – in a word, what is called the communal ownership of goods" (MEW 4, 370f).

Marx and Engels described communism using terms such as "social property" (Marx 1867, 930), "conditions of production" as "general, communal, social conditions" (Marx 1894, 373), "common appropriation and control of the means of production" (Marx 1857/1858, 159), "common ownership of the means of production" (Marx and Engels 1968, 305), "industry controlled by society as a whole" (MEW 4, 376), "a system in which all these branches of production are operated by society as a whole" (MEW 4, 370), or by speaking of individuals who "appropriate the existing totality of productive forces" (MEW 3, 67).

For Marx, individuals in capitalism are not yet fully developed social beings because they do not co-operatively own the means of production and operate the production process. He therefore spoke of the emergence of "social individuals" in communism (Marx 1857/1858, 832). Communism is "the complete return of man to himself as a social (i.e. human) being" (Marx 1844, 102). For Marx, communism is a not a dictatorship, but a form of humanism, it is the "advent of practical humanism" (Marx 1844, 164).

Marx argued that it is not the capitalists who produce money capital and commodities, but the activities of many producers and "the united action of all members of society" that contribute diverse activities enable production. Therefore, it is not only a small class of capitalists who should profit from production, but all should benefit.

Communism does not put an end to private consumption, but an end to the exploitation of the labour of individuals: "Communism deprives no man of the power to appropriate the products of society; all that it does is to deprive him of the power to subjugate the labour of others by means of such appropriation" (Marx and Engels 1968, 48).

A communist economy is not based on money and the exchange of goods: "money would immediately be done away with" (Marx 1885, 390); "producers do not exchange their products" (Marx and Engels 1968, 305). Rather the economy is so productive that consumers receive all goods for free. In communism, the "productive forces have also increased with the all-round development of the individual, and all the springs of common wealth flow more abundantly", which allows the economy to be based on the principle: "from each according to his abilities, to each according to his needs" (Marx and Engels 1968, 306).

Communism = Participatory Democracy

Marx's notion of a communist economy is what Crawford Macpherson (1973) and Carole Pateman (1970) described as participatory democracy in the economic realm. Participatory democracy involves the intensification of democracy and its extensions into realms beyond politics. This also involves the insight that the capitalist economy is an undemocratic dictatorship of capital that should be democ-ratized. Democracy is, in capitalism, limited to the realm of voting and parliament. Participatory democracy theory asks the questions why democratic ideals are given up once one enters the realm of the workplace and how one can speak of a demo-cratic society if the economy is excluded from the realm of democracy. It wants to go beyond a narrow understanding of the concept of democracy and broaden its mean-ing and practice. Macpherson and Pateman argue that participatory democracy requires that the means and the output of labour are no longer private property, but become common property. Pateman (1970) terms the grassroots organization of firms and the economy in a participatory democracy "self-management".

The Subject-Object Dimension

(3) The effect dimension of production: communism as the emergence of well-rounded individuals.

When a subject interacts with an object, some change is the result. A new quality of the overall system or an entirely new system emerges. Hegel (1991) terms this outcome the subject-object. The subject-object is the unity of the subjective and the objective (Hegel 1991, §212). In a democratic communist economy, collabora-tive work based on an associated means of production is connected to a high level of productivity. The result is the emergence of a new form of work organization.

For Marx and Engels, communism also means that productivity has developed to such a high degree that in combination with common ownership of the means of production and the abolition of the division of labour, the time for self-directed activities can be enlarged so that humans can engage in many-sided activities and can thereby realize and develop creative potentials that benefit society as a whole. A new form of work organization emerges. For Marx, a true form of indi-viduality develops through the co-operative character of production.

With the technological increase of the productivity of labour in communism, "the part of the social working day necessarily taken up with material production is shorter and, as a consequence, the time at society's disposal for the free intel-lectual and social activity of the individual is greater" (Marx 1867, 667). There is a "general reduction of the necessary labour of society to a minimum, which then corresponds to the artistic, scientific etc. development of the individuals in the time set free" (Marx 1857/1858, 706). Based on the development of the produc-tive forces, "the realm of freedom really begins only where labour determined by necessity and external expediency ends" (Marx 1894, 958f). Freedom is here the freedom to determine one's own activities.

Reducing necessary labour time by high technological productivity is, for Marx, a precondition of communism. "Real economy" consists "of the saving of labour time" (Marx 1857/1858, 711). "The multiplicity of its [society's] develop-ment, its enjoyment and its activity depends on economization of time. Economy of time, to this all economy, ultimately reduces itself" (Marx 1857/1858, 173).

Wealth would then result from the free activities of humans: "When the limited bourgeois form is stripped away, what is wealth other than the universality of individual needs, capacities, pleasures, productive forces etc., created through universal exchange" (Marx 1857/1858, 488). "Labour in the direct form has [then] ceased to be the great well-spring of wealth" (Marx 1857/1858, 705). "The measure of wealth is then not any longer, in any way, labour time, but rather disposable time" (Marx 1857/58, 708). "Disposable time will grow for all" (Marx 1857/1858, 708). "For real wealth is the developed productive power of all individuals" (Marx 1857/1858, 708).

Marx sees high technological productivity and the increase of disposable time as the foundation for rich human individuality. He spoke of the emergence of the well-rounded individual. The "highest development of the forces of production" is "the richest development of the individuals" (Marx 1857/1858, 541). "The saving of labour time [is] equal to an increase of free time, i.e. time for the full development of the individual" (Marx 1857/1858, 711). "The appropriation of these forces is itself nothing more than the development of the individual capacities corresponding to the material instruments of production. The appropriation of a totality of instruments of production is, for this very reason, the development of a totality of capacities in the individuals themselves" (MEW 3, 67f).

The most well-known passage that describes the emergence of "complete individuals" (MEW 3, 68), "well-rounded human beings" (MEW 4, 376), and of "a society in which the full and free development of every individual forms the ruling principle" (Marx 1867, 639) can be found in the *German Ideology*:

> In communist society, where nobody has one exclusive sphere of activity but each can become accomplished in any branch he wishes, society regulates the general production and thus makes it possible for me to do one thing today and another tomorrow, to hunt in the morning, fish in the afternoon, rear cattle in the evening, criticise after dinner, just as I have a mind, without ever becoming hunter, fisherman, herdsman or critic. (MEW 3, 33)

Guattari and Negri (1990) stress that real communism is based on a dialectic of community and rich individuality.

For discussing the notion of communism, I have deliberately used many quotations by Marx and Engels in order to show that they see communism not as a repressive and totalitarian society, but as a form of humanism that is based on co-operation, participatory economic democracy, and well-rounded human individuality. Communism is not the Soviet Union, Stalin, Mao and the Gulag, but participatory democracy. Stalin, Mao and the Soviet Union called themselves communist, but had nothing in common with participatory democracy and therefore were alien to the Marxian idea of communism. Communism was, for Marx, the "struggle for democracy" (MEW 4, 481). By democracy, Marx means a specific kind of democracy – participatory democracy.

10.2. Communication and Communism

The Communication Commons

Raymond Williams (1983, 70–72) points out that the term "commons" stems from the Latin word *communis*, which means that something is shared by many or all. The notion has to do with the generality of humankind and that something is shared. Williams (1983, 73) argues that there are affinities and overlaps between the words "communism" and "commons". The notion of the commons is also connected to the word "communication" because to communicate means to make something "common to many" (Williams 1983, 72).

Communication is an essential feature of human society. There can be no society without communication; humans create and maintain social relationships by communication and thereby continuously reproduce their social existence. Media, such as the Internet, are a means of communication. They are tools that enable the production of communication and human sociality. Means of communication, like the Internet, are therefore essential necessary features of human society, just like nature, education, love, care, knowledge, technology, affects, entertainment, language, transportation, housing, food, cities, cultural goods and traditions, etc. Communication and the means of communication are part of the commons of society – all humans continuously create, reproduce and use them in order to exist. Denying humans the means to communicate is like denying them fresh air to breathe; it undermines the conditions of their survival. Therefore the commons of society should be available for free (without payment or other access requirements) for all and no class should own them privately.

The freedom of the commons includes the creation of a commons-based Internet, the communist Internet. The communist Internet is an association of free produsers that is critical, self-managed, surveillance-free, beneficial for all, freely accessible for all, fostering wealth for all, co-operative, classless and universal. On the communist Internet, there is no profit and no advertising and there are no corporations. In a communist Internet age, programmers, administrators and users control Internet platforms by participatory self-management. Network access is provided free to all there are no corporate Internet service providers. Internet literacy programs are widely available in schools and adult education in order to enable humans to develop capacities that allow them to use the Internet in meaningful ways that benefit themselves and society as a whole. All humans have free access to web platforms, computer software and hardware. Computing is non-profit, non-commercial, non-commodified and advertising-free. There is no corporate mediation of Internet communication; humans engage more directly with each other over the Internet without the mediation by corporations that own platforms and exploit communicative labour.

The Commons-based Internet

On the commons-based Internet:

1) humans co-create and share knowledge,

2) humans are equal participants in the decision-making processes that concern the platforms and technologies they use,

3) the free access to and sharing of knowledge, the remixing of knowledge, and the co-creation of new knowledge help to create well-rounded individuals.

A commons-based Internet is only possible in a commons-based society. If you, for example, make all copyrighted knowledge available for free on the Internet within a capitalist society, this will either result in precarious working conditions for cultural producers or an accumulation strategy based on targeted advertising and massive surveillance. A true communist Internet therefore requires together with a redesign of the Internet (e.g. the abolishment of targeted ads and other similar commercial design principles) the end of wage labour, the common ownership of all means of production, the free availability of all goods instead of exchange and money, the end of the division of labour, the abolition of classes, etc.

10.3. The Political Economy of Wikipedia

David Harvey argues that "communists are all those who work incessantly to produce a different future to that which capitalism portends. [. . .] If, as the alternative globalization movement of the late 1990s declared, 'another world is possible', then why not also say 'another communism is possible'" (Harvey 2010b, 259). My claim is that, based on Harvey, we can say that one of these communist practices is the production and usage of Wikipedia, which means that Wikipedians are prototypical contemporary communists. Communism is not a distant society; it exists to a certain degree in each society. Communism is a dream that the world has always possessed. In this context, Marx says that "the world already possesses the dream of a thing, of which it has only to possess the consciousness to possess it truly" (MEGA, Section 3, Vol. 1, 56). My claim is that there are communist elements in contemporary society of which Wikipedia is one such form, and that these communist cells need to be developed, extended and intensified in order to create a communist Internet and a communist society. I will show in this section why Wikipedia should be considered as being a communist project and anticipates a communist mode of production. The mode of production at work in Wikipedia goes beyond the production of the collaborative encyclopaedia and is also present in the production of, for instance, free software. This mode of production, which bears so many resemblances to the model of communism, works with the making of information. This is why it can be called *info-communism*.

According to Marx (1859, 263; Marx and Engels 1846, chapter I.A), a mode of production is a combination of:

- The productive forces: (a) labour power, the capacity to systematically transform nature and create use-values in work processes; (b) the means of production, materials, land, or objectified crystallization of previous labour power, i.e. tools, infrastructures and other technologies.

- The relations of production: ways in which humans relate to one another to determine how work is organized, how property is distributed, who controls the productive forces, etc.

The Subjective Dimension of Wikipedia Production: Co-operative Labour

Info-communism relies heavily on intellectual work. In Wikipedia, the labour force is constituted by thousands of intellectual workers. Wikipedians are today mainly Western youth and "elite workers": the highly educated, students, white-collar workers, programmers, who have sufficient income, skills and time to work on Wikipedia in their leisure time (Glott, Schmidt and Ghosh 2010; Jullien 2011). This circumstance reflects the general stratification patterns of capitalism and shows that a truly info-communist mode of production requires a communist society in which free time, skills and material wealth become universal.

The work on Wikipedia is co-operative. No one can reclaim the authorship of an article, as it is often the result of dozens of people writing and debating together about what should be written. Most of the articles have between seven and 21 co-authors (Auray, Poudat and Pons 2007, 194). Wikipedians have developed an *ad hoc* decision-making process based on debate and consensus, which enables them to collaboratively edit Wikipedia articles. This method is supported and enabled by the *wiki* web software, which generates webpages that can be edited by anyone and that supports discussion between the users. A temporary consensus is achieved if an article or passage in it stays unchanged for some time. If there is disagreement over a passage, then users have to discuss and try to find a solution and a joint formulation. Each Wikipedia article has an edit page and a discussion page. Also its history is documented.

The Objective Dimensions of Wikipedia Production
The Common Ownership of the Means of Production

Wikipedia uses the free software MediaWiki for its website. The Wikimedia Foundation, which is a public, non-profit charity under US regulations, operates Wikipedia. Its self-defined purpose is to "empower and engage people around the world to collect and develop educational content under a free license or in the public domain, and to disseminate it effectively and globally".[3] Wikipedia's expenses are mainly funded by individual donations of users. There is no advertising on Wikipedia and Wikipedia does not have a business model. Wikipedia's terms of use (http://wikimediafoundation.org/wiki/Terms_of_use) and privacy policy (http://wikimediafoundation.org/wiki/Privacy_policy) therefore do not mention advertising – there is no need for commercial income.

---

3 Bylaws of the Wikimedia Foundation, Article II. http://goo.gl/2Wdy2, accessed on May 27, 2011.

In info-communism, the means of production belong to the workers. Programs and servers can be considered as common property managed by the Wikimedia Foundation. MediaWiki is based on a copyleft licence that makes it a free software commons:

- The code is free to use and to analyze.
- The users can copy and share the software with others.
- The code can be modified, and modified copies can be distributed.
- It is illegal to use and/or modify part of a code under copyleft without the resulting work being implemented under the copyleft licence, which prevents a future proprietary enclosure of the commons.

Wikimedia's servers are becoming *de facto* public goods for the community of workers running the project because the users control the production of and access to Wikipedia content. Wikipedia does not serve capital accumulation purposes. The Wikipedia community elects the top managers of the Wikimedia Foundation and thereby has some control over the Foundation.

Relations of Production: Participatory Democracy in the Economic Realm

In the info-communist mode of production, the works manage production themselves. The workers make all decisions together and control the production process, which is an expression of economic participatory democracy. In Wikipedia, Wikipedians decide about the rules structuring co-operation in common. One applies the same debate/consensus decision-making process as in the editing process to bring about Wikipedia's rules (http://en.wikipedia.org/wiki/Wikipedia:CONPOL#CONPOL gives an overview of Wikipedia's policies). A policy proposal usually emerges from a discussion in the village pump – the general Wikipedia forum.[4] One then discusses policy proposals. Other than in liberal representative democracy, it is not the vote, but consensus that constitutes the mode of decision-making. Wikipedia's decision modus therefore parallels grassroots democracy.

The Use-value of Wikipedia: Free Content

The use of the means of production by workforces within definite relations of production results in the creation of use-values that serve human needs. In capitalism, these use-values are exchange values and commodities; in communism, they are commonly owned and all people can access them without payment.

The motto of Wikipedia is: "Imagine a world in which every single person on the planet is given free access to the sum of all human knowledge."[5] This shows

---

4 http://en.Wikipedia.org/wiki/Wikipedia:Village_pump, accessed on March 6, 2013.
5 Wikimedia Foundation, Annual report 2009–2010. http://upload.wikimedia.org/wikipedia/commons/9/9f/AR_web_all-spreads_24mar11_72_FINAL.pdf, accessed on March 6, 2013.

that Wikipedia's intrinsic reason for production is different from capitalism's. Capitalism is based on profit interests, whereas Wikipedia is based on voluntary work and users' desire and pleasure to work on the provision of encyclopaedic knowledge as a common good that is available without payment to all. Wikipedia's products are collaboratively authored articles, which are available without payment to the world. Their character is dynamic and open; they are not a one-time product, but a product in flux that invites users to participate in developing the content and therefore can potentially change according to the number of participants who become involved in its development.

According to Wikipedia's terms of use, articles are licensed under the Creative Commons Attribution-ShareAlike License and the GNU Free Documentation License. These licences grant the users the same rights we described earlier for free software that uses a copyleft licence: the right to freely use the Wikipedia content, to share it with others, and to modify it as long as the resulting work is under the same licence. As a result of a decision by Wikipedia founder Jimmy Wales (Enyedy and Tkacs 2011, 114), only the GNU Free Documentation License (GFDL) is applied to Wikipedia content. In June 2009, Wikipedia adopted, in addition, the Creative Commons Attribution-ShareAlike (CC-BY-SA) License,[6] which allows the commercial use of content as long as others are allowed to use and distribute the content under the same conditions. A vote taken in April 2009 resulted in the decision to introduce this licence. Voting and not consensus was, in this case, used as the decision-mechanism to broaden the participation. Of a total of 15 071 voters, 87.9% were in favour of the adoption of the new licence.

It is therefore now allowed that somebody can print and sell a book that contains Wikipedia articles as long as others are allowed to copy, share and remix/edit the content. So a commercial publishing house could publish a book or paper encyclopaedia that is sold for making a profit and that contains Wikipedia articles. Wherever such a commodification of Wikipedia knowledge happens, the work of Wikipedians is infinitely exploited (see Chapter 5 of this book and Fuchs 2010c) because the users create surplus value that is fully unpaid, which results in the circumstance that the rate of surplus value rs = s/v (surplus value/variable capital, profit/wages) converges towards infinity. This means that commodified Wikipedia work is, like slave labour, extremely exploited and unremunerated. But it is voluntary slavery because none other than the slave Wikipedians have opted for a policy that allows commodification of their labour. This circumstance shows that Wikipedia is to a certain degree entangled into the capitalist relations of production. In order to go beyond them, Wikipedians would, among other things, have to change Wikipedia's licence from a Creative Commons Attribution-ShareAlike Unported License to a Creative Commons Attribution-NonCommercial 3.0 Unported License, which would prohibit the commercial exploitation of Wikipedia.

---

6 http://meta.wikimedia.org/wiki/Licensing_update/Result, accessed on August 23, 2011.

The Effect Dimension of Wikipedia Production: The Pleasure of Co-operative Intellectual Work

Why do Wikipedians work voluntarily and without payment for the project? Studies have shown that their main incentive is that they derive pleasure from intellectual and co-operative work and believe in the importance of making encyclopaedic knowledge available to the world as common good (Bauwens 2003; Foglia 2008; Hars and Ou 2002). The work process is self-determined. Wikipedians work on whatever article they choose according to their time resources and own preferences. Wikipedia work is, in contrast to capitalist wage labour, not coercive, it is not conducted for surviving by earning a wage that allows the buying of food and other nutrition. The Wikipedia workforce is non-commodified, it has no exchange value, it is not exchanged against money, but has a voluntary character. The time Wikipedians work on Wikipedia is self-determined work time, an expression and anticipation of the communist mode of production, in which all work is self-determined and an expression of well-rounded individuality.

At the same time, Wikipedia work is stratified today; those who have the time and skills required for Wikipedia production are part of a well-educated elite. Not all have the intellectual skills and the wealth of time needed to contribute actively to Wikipedia because global capitalism is a class society that creates classes of wealthy and poor people: the wealthy are rich in material resources, skills, time, relations, networks, etc., and the poor are deprived of these. These class structures are fluid, overlapping and many-folded (the material rich are not automatically the culturally rich or most educated, although they can use money to try to convert money capital into cultural capital, etc.). Wikipedia is embedded into global capitalism. A global elite that can afford its own elite status operates and contributes to the platform. A truly democratic and communist Wikipedia can only be achieved if we overcome class society and establish a classless society in which all humans have wealth in terms of resources, time, skills, networks, relations, capacities, etc. – a society of well-rounded individuals.

10.4. Conclusion

The main results of this chapter are as follows:

- Communism is not about the establishment of a repressive state-centred society, but the struggle for establishing a participatory democracy. There is a need for a renewed debate about democratic communism and a renewal of the critique of the political economy.
- Wikipedia has communist potentials that are antagonistically entangled into capitalist class relations.

- Wikipedia is based on co-operative work, grassroots decision-making, and content that is made available without payment. Furthermore, a non-profit organization that is non-commercial (no use of advertisement) operates Wikipedia. Wikipedia work is voluntary, self-determined and non-commodified.
- These communist potentials are, however, antagonistic because of the use of the Creative Commons Attribution-ShareAlike license that allows the selling of Wikipedia content as commodity. In those cases where an article is sold, all underlying voluntary work is unpaid labour and the involved Wikipedians are infinitely exploited.

A new mode of production develops within an old one. "The economic structure of capitalist society has grown out of the economic structure of feudal society" (Marx 1867, 875). But there is no guarantee that the roots of a new society can be realized because realization is a task of political practice. The social and co-operative dimension of Wikipedia points towards "elements of the new society with which old collapsing bourgeois society itself is pregnant" (Marx 1871, 277); new relations, which mature "within the framework of the old society" (Marx 1859, 263); "new forces and new passions" that "spring up in the bosom of society, forces and passions which feel themselves to be fettered by that society" (Marx and Engels 1848, 928); "antithetical forms", which are "concealed in society" and "mines to explode it" (Marx 1857/1858, 159). In order to compete with and supersede capitalism, the info-communist mode of production needs to grow in terms of the number of members engaging in it, the number of projects being part of it, and the resources controlled. Such a growth is only possible if info-communist seeds grow, expand in size, can command ever more resources and overcome its own antagonistic character.

There are therefore two possible futures for info-communism: in the first scenario, communist class struggle nourishes info-communism against capitalist hegemony so that info-communism drives back the capitalist mode of production; in the second scenario, some of the characteristics of info-communism, such as the principle of free access and free content provision and online mass collaboration, are absorbed by capitalism, which thereby destroys the communist character of info-communism.

Capitalism is a violent and imperialistic system that has always colonized non-capitalist spaces and has always used the violence of the law and warfare to destroy alternatives. Informational communism is a potential and Wikipedia is the brightest communist star on the Internet's class struggle firmament. It is possible that capitalism subsumes the transcendent elements of info-communism just like it has done before with many anti-capitalist worldviews and practices (Boltanski and Chiapello 2005, chapter 3). The primary political task for concerned citizens should therefore be to resist the commodification of everything and to strive for democratizing the economy and the Internet.

RECOMMENDED READINGS AND EXERCISES

For understanding Wikipedia, it is useful to engage with the idea of the commons, different assessments of the platform and to gather experiences of it that are systematically analyzed.

Hardt, Michael. 2010. The common in communism. In *The idea of communism*, ed. Slavoj Žižek and Costas Douzinas, 131–144. London: Verso.

Žižek, Slavoj. 2010. How to begin from the beginning. In *The idea of communism*, ed. Slavoj Žižek and Costas Douzinas, 209–226. London: Verso.

Williams, Raymond. 1983. *Keywords*. New York: Oxford University Press. Entries: Common, Communication, Communism (pp. 70–75).

Fuchs, Christian. 2011. *Foundations of critical media and information studies*. New York: Routledge. Chapter 9: Conclusion (pp. 323–349).

These readings introduce the ideas of the commons and the communication commons. They are good foundations for thinking about the relevance of the commons in respect to the Internet. Ask yourself:

- What are the commons? What kinds of commons are there? Try to construct an ordered and systematic typology. Identify a theoretical category that you can use for distinguishing the categories in your typology. Take care that the types do not overlap and that the typology is complete (i.e. involves all forms of commons that exist).

- What are communication commons?

- In which respects is Wikipedia a communications commons?

Wright, Erik Olin. 2010. *Envisioning real utopias*. London: Verso. Chapter 1: Why real utopias? Chapter 8: Real utopias II: Social empowerment and the economy. Conclusion: Making utopias real.

Carr, Nicholas. 2010. Questioning Wikipedia. In *Critical point of view: A Wikipedia reader*, ed. Geert Lovink and Nathaniel Tkacz, 309–324. Amsterdam: Institute of Network Cultures.

O'Neil, Mathieu. 2010. Wikipedia and authority. In *Critical point of view: A Wikipedia reader*, ed. Geert Lovink and Nathaniel Tkacz, 309–324. Amsterdam: Institute of Network Cultures.

O'Neil, Mathieu. 2011. The sociology of critique in Wikipedia. *Critical Studies in Peer Production* RS 1.2: 1–11.

van Dijck, José. 2013. *The culture of connectivity: A critical history of social media*. Oxford: Oxford University Press. Chapter 7: Wikipedia and the neutrality principle.

The authors of these readings have different opinions of Wikipedia. Work in groups on the questions below and present your results to the class.

- Discuss how Wikipedia differs from Google Docs, Facebook, Twitter and YouTube.

- Make a list of commonalities and differences in the assessments of Wikipedia that these three authors give. Which criteria for assessing Wikipedia does each text employ?

- There are points of disagreement on the overall assessment of Wikipedia in the works of the four authors. Formulate your own opinion individually and a group opinion on these questions. Do you think that Wikipedia is the germ form of an alternative Internet? If so, in which respect? If not, why not?

Conduct a group project: Select a topic that is currently hotly debated in society and whose Wikipedia entry at the moment is frequently updated. As a group, set yourselves the goal of contributing to the improvement of this article. Together as a group, conduct academic research on this topic. Try to make new additions to the article. Enter the world of Wikipedia and discuss with others on the article's talk page how to improve certain paragraphs. Continue this work for one week. In the next week, write down your experiences: What was positive? What was not so positive? What did it feel like to be actively contributing Wikipedians? How do you assess Wikipedia as a project? What did you learn as a group by working together on a knowledge project? Make a group presentation and discuss your results with the results of other groups.

III

FUTURES

11

Conclusion: Social Media and its Alternatives – Towards a Truly Social Media

Key questions

- What common social media ideologies exist?
- How does the exploitation of digital labour undermine the social aspect of social media?
- What alternatives are there to corporate social media? What could truly public, social and common media look like?

Key concepts

Corporate social media
Neoliberalism
Crisis
Alternative social media

Commons
Social media commons
Commons-based social media

11.1. Social Media Reality: Ideologies and Exploitation

Ideology

The London police's shooting of Mark Duggan on August 4 2011 in Tottenham triggered riots in London areas such as Tottenham, Wood Green, Enfield Town, Ponders End, Brixton, Walthamstow, Chingford Mount, Hackney, Croydon and Ealing, and in other areas of UK cities such as Toxteth (Liverpool), Handsworth (Birmingham), St. Ann's (Nottingham), West Bromwich, Wolverhampton, Salford and Central Manchester. Parts of the mass media started blaming social media for being the cause of the violence. *The Sun* reported on August 8: "Rioting thugs use Twitter to boost their numbers in thieving store raids. [. . .] THUGS used social network Twitter to orchestrate the Tottenham violence and incite others to join in as they sent messages urging: 'Roll up and loot'". *The Telegraph* wrote on the same day:

> How technology fuelled Britain's first 21st century riot. The Tottenham riots were orchestrated by teenage gang members, who used the latest mobile phone technology to incite and film the loot-ing and violence. Gang members used Blackberry smart-phones designed as a communications tool for high-flying executives to organise the mayhem.

The Daily Mail wrote on August 7 that there were "fears that violence was fanned by Twitter as picture of burning police car was re-tweeted more than 100 times".

And also, as usual in moral panics, the call for policing technology could be heard. *The Daily Express* (August 10) wrote:

> Thugs and looters are thought to have sent messages via the BlackBerry Messenger (BBM) service to other troublemakers, alerting them to riot scenes and inciting further violence. Technology writer Mike Butcher said it was unbelievable the service had not already been shut down. He said: "Mobile phones have become weaponised. It's like text messaging with steroids – you can send messages to hundreds of peo-ple that cannot be traced back to you." Tottenham MP David Lammy appealed for BlackBerry to suspend the service.

The police published pictures of rioters recorded by CCTV and asked the public to identify the people. The mass media published these pictures. *The Sun* called for "naming and shaming a rioter" and for "shopping a moron". The mass media also reported on citizens who had self-organized over social media in order to gather in affected neighbourhoods to clean up the streets. A few months before we had been told we had "Twitter revolutions" and "Facebook revolutions" in Egypt and Tunisia, and now we heard about "Twitter mobs", "Facebook mobs" and "Blackberry mobs" in the UK.

There were calls for more police, greater surveillance and crowd control. Popular culture (rap music) and social media were blamed as having caused the riots. It is too late to cast blame once riots erupt. One should not blame social media or popular culture, but the violent conditions of society for the UK riots. The mass media and politics' focus on surveillance, law and order politics, and the condemnation of social media will not solve the problems. A serious discussion about class, inequality and racism is needed, which also requires a change of policy regimes. The UK riots were not a Blackberry mob and not a Twitter mob; they were the effects of the structural violence of neoliberalism. Capitalism, crisis and class are the main contexts of unrest, uproar and social media today. The mass media presented a simplistic picture about the role of the Internet in society. And yet these discussions and the riots themselves showed that it has become so obvious today that we do not simply live in a society, but that we live in capitalist societies and that capitalism needs to be considered as the context of the Internet.

Technological determinism overestimates the role of technology in society; it ignores the fact that technology is embedded in society, and that it is not technology, but humans living under and rebelling against power relations who create revolutions and unrest. The rise of new technologies often creates an "eruption of feeling that briefly overwhelms reason" (Mosco 2004, 22). Technological determinism ignores the political economy of events. Social media determinism is an expression of the digital sublime, the development that "cyberspace has become the latest icon of the technological and electronic sublime, praised for its epochal and transcendent characteristics and demonized for the depth of the evil it can conjure" (Mosco 2004, 24).

Critical Theory and Critical Political Economy of the Media analyze how exploitation, domination, commodification and ideology interact in shaping media communication in society, what potentials for alternatives there are, and how struggles can use and advance these potentials.

Talking about social media requires that we engage with the concept of the "social" and social theory. It requires us to specify which notions of the social we are using. Applying a multidimensional understanding shows that we are experiencing at the same time continuity and discontinuity of the sociality of the media. The media's development is dialectical.

Exploitation

I have stressed throughout this book the double logic of commodification and ideology that shapes corporate social media. Capital accumulation on corporate social media is based on Internet prosumer commodification, the unpaid labour of Internet users, targeted advertising and economic surveillance. Google is the dominant player in Internet prosumer commodification. It has developed a sophisticated targeted advertising system that collects a multitude of data about user interests and activities (demographic, technological, economic, political, cultural, ecological information), communications, networks and collaborations. Facebook is the dominant social networking site. It has developed a prosumer commodification system that is especially based on commodifying networks, contacts, user profiles and user-generated content that are created by unpaid user labour. Twitter is a microblog platform that has become the object of political mythologizing.

The analysis has shown that politics is a minority issue on Twitter, that the urban middle class dominates the platform, and that Twitter is not a political public sphere. Non-profit non-commercial Internet projects like Wikipedia question the logic of common production, common control and common ownership. Alternative online media (such as WikiLeaks, Indymedia, AlterNet, Democracy Now!, OpenDemocracy, etc.) try to make alternative, critical information available and to foster critical debates (see Fuchs 2010a; Sandoval and Fuchs 2010).

Social Media: Anticipative and Limited Sociality

Management gurus, marketing strategists and uncritical academics have used the notions of "web 2.0", "social media" and "social software" as ideology that overemphasizes novelty and democratic potentials. One of the goals of this ideology has been to create new business models and attract financial capital investments. In contemporary capitalism, the boundaries between play and labour have become fuzzy. Google's management philosophy is characterized by stressing play labour (playbour), which is the expression of a new spirit/ideology of capitalism. Many analyses of Google are one-dimensional and therefore ideological in the sense that they only see positive or negative aspects. Google is a dialectical system reflecting the contradictions of contemporary capitalism. It advances the socialization of the networked productive forces and has thereby created new potentials for cognition, communication and co-operation, but within capitalist class relations limits, and exploits these potentials for commodity purposes. The mainstream of social networking sites research is based on an individualistic and bourgeois privacy ideology that sees information sharing as necessarily bad and ignores the problems created by targeted advertising and user exploitation. Corporate social media use privacy policies and terms of use that legally legitimate Internet prosumer commodification. They are expressions of a privacy regime that is based on the ideology of corporate self-regulation of privacy. In these terms and policies, social media corporations tend to assure the users that they responsibly deal with user data, but at the same time define and enable consumer privacy violations so that these terms and policies become ideological documents. There are many claims about political social media use: that Twitter and other platforms re-vitalize the political public, cause political revolutions, are the source of violence, etc. Neither techno-optimism nor techno-pessimism is the appropriate method for analyzing social media. Rather, one needs to decentre the analysis from technology and focus on the interaction of the power structures of the political economy of capitalism with social media.

Social media in their current forms advance the socialization of human activities. But these activities are on corporate social media trapped in private relations of ownership so that social media advance social production and private ownership of data in the form of commodification of data, human creativity and social relations. Corporate social media are incompletely social: they are controlled and owned in a particularistic manner by an elite, although their social form of production points towards an existence beyond capitalism. Social media anticipate a full sociality of human existence, but in their corporate form this potential is limited by capitalist structures of ownership and capital accumulation. Social media today have an anticipative and simultaneously limited sociality: they anticipate a full socialization of human existence that is limited by the capitalist reality of social media. Alternatives are needed.

11.2. Social Media Alternatives

The Internet and the Logic of the Commons

Exploitation and ideology can and should be questioned and challenged. Capitalism is not the end of history. The capitalist Internet is not the end of history. An alternative society is possible. An alternative Internet is possible. Both changes of the design of the Internet and society's fundamental structures are needed. But alternatives require struggles. We have seen that alternative platforms like Diaspora*, Wikipedia and WikiLeaks have a contradictory character. They are shaped by the logics of commodification and bourgeois ideology, but at the same time have potentials that point beyond capitalism and the capitalist Internet. They anticipate a commons-based Internet that is not based on capital accumulation, advertising, profit, ideology and a stratified attention economy, but rather enables knowledge, communication and collaboration for their own sake as social activities between humans. A commons-based Internet is possible – an Internet on which people share, communicate, decide, discuss, play, create, criticize, network, collaborate, find, maintain and build friendships, fall in love, entertain themselves and each other, educate themselves as common activity without corporate mediation.

The logic of the commons is the logic of a common humanity that has realized that all humans should be equal participants and beneficiaries in society (see Dyer-Witheford 1999, 2007, 2009; Fuchs 2011b; Hardt and Negri 2009; Žižek 2010). Technology and the media are not the main, but a part of society. Therefore all humans should be able to truly participate and benefit from media and technology, which is not the case today. Capitalism is a class society. The capitalist Internet is a class-structured Internet: corporations and other central actors dominate attention, symbolic, social and material benefits. A just society is a classless society. A just Internet is a classless Internet.

Capitalism, Neoliberalism, Crisis

All forms of capitalism are contradictory and create crises. The world economic crisis that started in 2008 was the result of decades of neoliberal capitalism. Neoliberalism is based on "the subordination of the totality of socio-economic fields to the accumulation process so that economic functions come to occupy the dominant place within the state" (Jessop 2008, 132). Neoliberal ideology's focus is almost exclusively on capital accumulation:

> Neoliberalism is in the first instance a theory of political economic practices that proposes that human well-being can be best advanced by liberating individual entrepreneurial freedoms and skills within an institutional framework characterized by strong private rights, free markets and free trade. [. . .] It holds that the social good will be maximized by maximizing the reach and frequency of market transactions,

and it seeks to bring all human action into the domain of the market. This requires technologies of information creation and capacities
to accumulate, store, transfer, analyze, and use massive databases to
guide decisions in the global marketplace. (Harvey 2007, 2–3)

Negative social consequences are subordinated to economic logic: "The fundamental mission of the neoliberal state is to create 'a good business climate' and therefore
to optimize conditions for capital accumulation no matter what the consequences
are for employment or social well-being" (Harvey 2005a, 19).

   All forms of capitalism are contradictory and create crises. Neoliberalism
has intensified inequality. Table 11.1 shows an almost continuous increase of
income inequality in selected Organization for Economical and Co-operative
Development (OECD) countries (measured by the Gini coefficient) since the
mid-1970s. The development was most drastic in the USA and the UK, but
also Scandinavian countries, which were long praised for their welfare states
that express universalistic socialist values, have experienced neoliberal influences and rising inequality. And this situation exploded in the crisis and its
aftermath.

Struggles

The main political reaction to the crisis has been the rise of hyper-neoliberalism. Hyper-neoliberalism is an intensification of neoliberalism that uses
employees' tax money for consolidating the financial system and, as a result,
extends and intensifies budget cuts to social security, education, health care
and the pension system, and has resulted in a shift towards the right and
extreme-right in elections in many countries. Large protests in countries such
as Greece, Portugal and Spain, student protests in many countries, rebellions
and revolutions in Arab and North African countries (for example Tunisia and

Table 11.1   Inequality in selected OECD countries (Gini coefficient, after taxes and transfers)

Country	Mid-1970s	Mid-1980s	Around 1990	Mid-1990s	Around 2000	Mid-2000s	Late 2000s
Canada	0.304	0.293	0.287	0.289	0.318	0.317	0.324
Finland	0.235	0.209		0.218	0.247	0.254	0.259
Germany		0.251	0.256	0.266	0.264	0.285	0.295
Italy		0.309	0.297	0.348	0.343	0.352	0.337
Japan		0.304		0.323	0.337	0.321	0.329
Norway		0.222	0.243	0.261	0.261	0.276	0.25
Sweden	0.212	0.198	0.209	0.211	0.243	0.234	0.259
UK	0.268	0.309	0.354	0.336	0.352	0.331	0.342
USA	0.316	0.337	0.348	0.361	0.357	0.38	0.378

Data source: OECD Social and Welfare Statistics.

Egypt), the emergence of the Occupy movement and riots have constituted another important, although weaker, consequence of the crisis. However different these consequences may be, they express discontent with capitalism and remind us that we need a classless society in order to overcome inequality. There seem to be only two options today: (a) continuance and intensification of the 200-year-old barbarity of capitalism or (b) socialism.

Struggles for a commons-based Internet need to be connected to struggles for socialism. In Chapter 8, I introduced the concept of socialist privacy protection. One can achieve privacy protection of consumers, prosumers and workers only in an economy that is not ruled by profit interests, but controlled and managed by prosumers, consumers and producers. If there were no profit motive on Internet platforms, then there would be no need to commodify the data and usage behaviour of Internet users. Achieving such a situation is, however, not primarily a technological task, but one that requires changes in society. Socialist privacy policies are part of a struggle for a just society. Oscar Gandy (2011, 183) argues that just as societies have, in respect to pollution, realized that "markets will not work on their own to insure the maintenance of healthy and sustainable environments" and "agree that the regulation of pollution and other threats to the environment should be treated as explicit and important public policy goals", they should realize the need for consumer protection in cyberspace as part of a policy that protects the information environment.

Five strategies for achieving this goal are: (1) the use of data protection legislation (see p. 259), (2) the advancement of opt-in online advertising (p. 260), (3) civil society surveillance of Internet companies (p. 261), (4) the establishment and support of alternative platforms (p. 264), and (5) the establishment of an alternative societal context of Internet use (section 11.3).

Data Protection Laws

One strategy is to use existing data protection laws to force Internet corporations not to put profit interests above user interests, and to struggle for strict data protection laws that protect consumer interests.

Struggles against the corporate and commercial character of the Internet can also make use of existing data protection laws. On August 18, 2011, members of the initiative "Europe vs. Facebook", which was founded by Austrian law students, filed a complaint against Facebook to the Irish Data Protection Commissioner. Facebook Europe is legally registered in Ireland. The initiative's members made 16 complaints and asked the Commissioner to check whether Facebook violates European data protection laws in these 16 privacy areas.

One complaint is that Facebook engages in excessive processing of data. One of the complainers demanded that Facebook send him the data it stores about him. Although he had deleted his account, he received a print-out of 1200 pages of personal data stored about him by Facebook. This topic is addressed in the complaint under point 15: "After using facebook.com for 3 years, Facebook Ireland gathered more than 1.200 pages of personal information about me (in fact Facebook Ireland might hold a much bigger amount of data, see Complaint 10), even though

I have deleted just about everything I could (e.g. all my posts, all messages, and many friends)."[1]

The Irish Data Protection Act (DPA) says that data "(iii) shall be adequate, relevant and not excessive in relation to the purpose or purposes for which they were collected or are further processed, and (iv) shall not be kept for longer than is necessary for that purpose or those purposes" (DPA §2 (1) (c) (iii) (iv)). The EU Data Protection Directive regulates that "Member States shall provide that personal data must be: [. . .] (c) adequate, relevant and not excessive in relation to the purposes for which they are collected and/or further processed" (Directive 95/46/EC of the European Parliament, §6 (1) (c)).

The initiative also made the complaint that Facebook does not use opt-in options and thereby may breach the regulation that users have to give consent to the processing of their personal data. This regulation is specifically important for other topics and for targeted advertising, which is organized without an opt-in on Facebook.

> 2A. (1) Personal data shall not be processed by a data controller unless section 2 of this Act (as amended by the *Act of 2003*) is complied with by the data controller and at least one of the following conditions is met: (*a*) the data subject has given his or her consent to the processing or . . . (Irish Data Protection Act, §2A (1) (a))

> Member States shall provide that personal data may be processed only if: (a) the data subject has unambiguously given his consent. (Directive 95/46/EC of the European Parliament, §7 (a))

Opt-in Advertising Policies

Oscar Gandy (1993) argues that an alternative to opt-out solutions to targeted advertising are opt-in solutions that are based on the informed consent of consumers. Opt-in to advertising and automatically activated Do-Not-Track cookies in all web browsers as standard setting are progressive design principles that can help changing the problematic reality of the internet. Consumer organizations and data protectionists typically favour opt-in privacy policies, whereas companies and marketing associations tend to prefer opt-out and self-regulation advertising policies in order to maximize profit (Bellman et al. 2004; Federal Trade Commission 2000; Gandy 1993; Quinn 2006; Ryker et al. 2002; Starke-Meyerring and Gurak 2007). Socialist privacy legislation could require all commercial Internet platforms to use advertising only as an opt-in option, which would strengthen the users' possibility for self-determination.

Within capitalism, forcing corporations by state laws to implement opt-in mechanisms is certainly desirable, but at the same time it is likely that corporations will not consent to such policies because opt-in is likely to reduce the actual amount of surveilled and commodified user data significantly, which results in a drop in

---

1 www.europe-v-facebook.org/Complaint_15_Excessive.pdf, accessed on May 20, 2013.

advertising profits. Organizing targeted advertising as opt-in instead of as opt-out or no option does not establish economic user privacy, but is a step towards strengthening the economic privacy of users.

Corporate Watch Platforms as a Form of Struggle against Corporatism

In order to circumvent the large-scale surveillance of consumers, producers and consumer-producers, movements and protests against economic surveillance are necessary. Kojin Karatani (2005) argues that consumption is the only space in capitalism where workers become subjects that can exert pressure by consumption boycotts on capital. I do not think that this is correct because strikes also show the subject position of workers that enables them to boycott production, to cause financial harm to capital, and to exert pressure in order to voice political demands. However, Karatani in my opinion correctly argues that the role of the consumer has been underestimated in Marxist theory and practice. The fact that in the contemporary media landscape media consumers become media producers who work and create surplus value shows the importance of the role of consumers in contemporary capitalism and of "the transcritical moment where workers and consumers intersect" (Karatani 2005, 21). For political strategies this brings up the actuality of an associationist movement that is "a transnational association of consumers/workers" (Karatani 2005, 295) and engages in "the class struggle against capitalism" of "workers qua consumers or consumers qua workers" (Karatani 2005, 294).

Critical citizens, critical citizens' initiatives, consumer groups, social movement groups, critical scholars, unions, data protection specialists/groups, consumer protection specialists/groups, critical politicians and critical political parties should observe closely the surveillance and exploitation operations of Internet corporations and document these mechanisms, and the instances where corporations and politicians take measures that threaten privacy or increase the surveillance of citizens. Such documentation is most effective if it is easily accessible to the public. The Internet provides the means for documenting such behaviour. It can help to watch the watchers and to raise public awareness. In recent years, corporate watch organizations that run online watch platforms have emerged. Examples for corporate watch organizations are:

- CorpWatch Reporting (www.corpwatch.org)
- Transnationale Ethical Rating (www.transnationale.org)
- The Corporate Watch Project (www.corporatewatch.org)
- Multinational Monitor (www.multinationalmonitor.org)
- Responsible Shopper (www.greenamerica.org/programs/responsible-shopper/)
- crocodyl: Collaborative Research on Corporations (www.crocodyl.org)

- Endgame Database of Corporate Fines (www.endgame.org/corpfines.html)
- Corporate Crime Reporter (www.corporatecrimereporter.com)
- Corporate Europe Observatory (www.corporateeurope.org)
- Corporate Critic Database (www.corporatecritic.org)
- Students and Scholars against Corporate Misbehaviour (http://sacom.hk)
- China Labor Watch (www.chinalaborwatch.org)
- Center for Media and Democracy's PR Watch (www.prwatch.org)

For example, Transnationale Ethical Rating aims at informing consumers and research about corporations. Its ratings include quantitative and qualitative data about violations of labour rights, violations of human rights, layoff of employees, profits, sales, earnings of CEOs, boards, president and managers, financial offshoring operations, financial delinquency, environmental pollution, corporate corruption and dubious communication practices. Dubious communication practices include an "arguable partnership, deceptive advertising, disinformation, commercial invasion, spying, mishandling of private data, biopiracy and appropriation of public knowledge".[2] Corporate watchdog organizations' task is to document corporate irresponsibility. Corporate watch platforms can not only monitor ICT corporations and the corporate media (as well as corporations in general), but can also situate corporate behaviour in the larger political-economic context of corporate social irresponsibility (the counterpart of the corporate social responsibility (CSR) ideology).

Figure 11.1 shows as an example Transnationale Ethical Rating's entry for Google. The "infocom" violations include "spying": "By downloading Google's browser, Chrome, users agree to give up copyright to their own files."[3] Online corporate watchdog organizations document and gather data about the corporate irresponsibility of corporations.

On the one hand, it is important that watchdog organizations document and gather data about the corporate irresponsibility of Internet corporations. On the other hand, it looks like these data are not very complete and not many Internet corporations are thus far included. So one could, for example, also document Google's targeted advertising practices and many other irresponsible practices (see Chapter 7). These practices are highly opaque to users and they leave it unclear for the single user what data exactly about her/him is stored and commodified. In any case, more efforts are required in order to advance the documentation of corporate social irresponsibility of Internet corporations and to contextualize privacy violations within the process of watching the watchers.

Corporate watch platforms are attempts by those resisting asymmetric economic power relations to struggle against the powerful class of corporations by documenting data that should make economic power transparent. Online

---

2 www.transnationale.org/aide.php, accessed on March 21, 2011.
3 www.transnationale.org/companies/google.php, accessed on March 21, 2011.

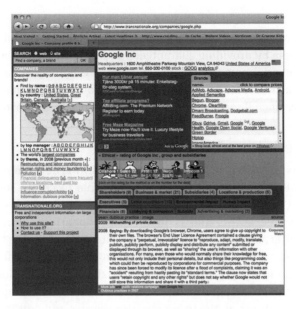

Figure 11.1   An example page about Google from transnationale.org

corporate watchdog organizations document and gather data about the corporate irresponsibility of corporations. Making data about corporate irresponsibility available to the public does not abolish exploitation and oppression. It can, however, be a useful tool in the struggle against exploitation and oppression. Action is always related to events. If there is no knowledge about oppressive practices because they are hidden from the public, then reactions to it are unlikely. Watching the powerful does not necessarily result in struggles, but it can make struggles more likely. This also requires that watchdog organizations do not present examples of corporate irresponsibility as exceptions from the rule and bad practices, but rather as necessary irresponsibilities and necessary bad practices that are caused by the systemic logic of corporate irresponsibility that is inherent to capitalism.

Also WikiLeaks is an online watchdog platform that tries to make power transparent by leaking secret documents about political and economic power. Watchdog organizations (just like alternative media in general; see Fuchs 2010a; Sandoval and Fuchs 2010) try to exert counter-power. But they are facing resource asymmetries that result in an antagonism between resource precariousness and political autonomy. They are facing three serious limits in capitalism:

a) They are frequently based on precarious, self-exploitative labour.

b) They often lack resources.

c) Resource provision by politics or the economy may threaten their political autonomy and make them vulnerable to corporate or political filtering of their contents.

Curbing these limits requires affirmative action politics that tries to overcome the economic censorship (lack of attention, lack of money, lack of resources) of alternative media by providing guaranteed funding to these media. Thereby, the problem of potential pressures by the state on alternative media is posed, and this can only be overcome by installing socialist governments that acknowledge the importance of civil society for democracy and social transformation.

Alternative Internet Platforms

Other attempts to resist corporate domination of the Internet are non-commercial, non-profit Internet platforms. It is not impossible to create successful non-profit Internet platforms, as the example of Wikipedia, which is advertising-free, provides free access and is financed by donations, shows. The most well-known alternative social networking site-project is Diaspora*, which tries to develop an open source alternative to Facebook. The four New York University students Dan Grippi, Maxwell Salzberg, Raphael Sofaer and Ilya Zhitomirskiy created Diaspora* in 2010. The social networking site kaioo is not only non-commercial; the users can also discuss and edit its terms of use and privacy terms in a wiki.

These projects are facing the same dilemma as all alternative media in capitalism: the contradiction between alternative demands and the reality of resource precariousness and precarious labour. The demand to produce non-commercial and non-profit media is crucial for advancing a democratic media landscape, but the problem is at the same time that money is needed for organizing media within capitalism. Also, organizing media against capitalism needs to start within capitalism. Alternative media projects frequently operate with the help of precarious voluntary labour and face a lack of funds. They are confronted with a permanent threat of commercialization. State funding, donation models and subscription models can help, but have their own limitations. Donations and subscriptions are unstable and state funding can create political pressure that functions indirectly as censorship by way of economic means.

11.3. Towards a Truly Social Media and a New Society

The contradictions of the corporate Internet can only be resolved in a framework of society that overcomes inequalities. An alternative Internet requires, together with alternative design principles, an alternative societal setting: a solidary, co-operative information society – a participatory democracy. Calls for the strengthening of privacy in the light of corporate Internet domination are short-sighted and superficial because privacy is intended to protect humans from harm, not to overcome those conditions and structures that cause harms. Slavoj Žižek (2001, 256) suggests in this context not to "retreat into islands of privacy, but an ever stronger socialization of cyberspace" (Žižek

2001, 256). Privacy is a contradictory value, it is proclaimed in liberal ideology, but at the same time constantly undermined by corporate and state surveillance. Privacy as liberal value protects the rich and powerful from public
accountability, which can help to increase and legitimatize inequality. Torbjörn
Tännsjö (2010) stresses that liberal privacy concepts imply "that one can not
only own oneself and personal things, but also the means of production" and
that the consequence is "a very closed society, clogged because of the idea
of business secret, bank privacy, etc." (Tännsjö 2010, 186; translation from
Swedish by the author).

The questions in discussions about privacy should therefore be: Who should
be protected through privacy rights in order to be safe from harm? Whose privacy
rights should be limited in order not to damage the public good? Privacy contradictions can never be resolved in capitalism. The Swedish socialist philosopher
Torbjörn Tännsjö (2010) calls for the establishment of an "open society" that is
based on equality and democracy instead of the strengthening of privacy rights.
Tännsjö's use of the term "open society" is unfortunate because Karl Popper
(1962a, 1962b) employed the same notion for defending the liberal ideology that
Tännsjö criticizes. What Tännsjö actually means by an open society is a participatory democracy.

Facebook and Google are only the two most well-known examples for a more
general contemporary economy that appropriates, expropriates and exploits the
common goods (communication, education, knowledge, care, welfare, nature,
culture, technology, public transport, housing, etc.) that humans create and need
in order to survive. In the area of the Internet, a socialist strategy can try to resist
the commodification of the Internet and the exploitation of users by trying to
claim the common and participatory character of the Internet with the help
of protests, legal measures, alternative projects based on the ideas of free access/
content/software and creative commons, wage campaigns, unionization of social
media prosumers, boycotts, hacktivism, the creation of public service- and
commons-based social media, etc.

The exploitation of digital labour on the Internet is, however, a topic that
is connected to the broader political economy of capitalism, which means that
those who are critical of what social media companies like Facebook do with
their data ought to be also critical of what contemporary capitalism is doing
to humans throughout the world in different forms. If we manage to establish
a participatory democracy, then a truly open society (Tännsjö 2010) might
become possible that requires no surveillance, no protection from surveillance
and no exploitation. A commons-based Internet requires commons-based
design principles and a commons-oriented society (Fuchs 2011b, chapters 8
and 9). It can give a new meaning to the sociality of society and the media.
Humans are essentially social and societal beings. They need to collaborate in
order to exist. A collaborative society requires participatory democracy and
collective ownership and control of the means of production. Collaboration
and co-operation are the fundamental meanings of the terms "social" and "society". Discussions about social media remind us of the need to think and act in

respect of the question about what sociality, what society, and what kind of media we want to have.

Truly public, social and common media require as one of their preconditions not only alternative design priniciples, at also a society that realizes the meaning of the terms "public", "social" and "common" – the public sphere and participatory democracy. Another Internet is possible. Social media are possible.

References

Acquisti, Alessandro and Ralph Gross. 2006. Imagined communities: Awareness, information sharing, and privacy on the Facebook. In *Proceedings of 6th Workshop on Privacy Enhancing Technologies*, ed. Phillipe Golle and George Danezis, 36–58. Cambridge: Robinson College.

Adorno, Theodor W. 2000. *The Adorno reader*. Malden, MA: Blackwell.

Adorno, Theodor W. 2002. *Introduction to sociology*. Cambridge: Polity Press.

Adorno, Theodor W. 1951, 2003. Cultural criticism and society. In *Can one live after Auschwitz? A philosophical reader*, ed. Rolf Tiedemann, 146–162. Stanford, CA: Stanford University Press.

Agger, Ben. 2006. *Critical social theories: An introduction* (2nd edition). Boulder, CO: Paradigm.

Allan, Stuart. 2010. Introduction: Recrafting news and journalism. In *The Routledge companion to news and journalism*, ed. Stuart Allan, xxiii–xliv. Abingdon: Routledge.

Allen, Matthew. 2012. What was web 2.0? Versions and the politics of Internet history. *New Media & Society* 15 (2): 260–275.

Allmer, Thomas. 2012. *Towards a critical theory of surveillance in informational capitalism.* Frankfurt am Main: Peter Lang.

Andrejevic, Mark. 2007. *iSpy: Surveillance and power in the interactive era*. Lawrence, KS: University Press of Kansas.

Andrejevic, Mark. 2012. Exploitation in the data mine. In *Internet and surveillance: The challenges of web 2.0 and social media*, ed. Christian Fuchs, Kees Boersma, Anders Albrechtslund and Marisol Sandoval, 71–88. New York: Routledge.

Aouragh, Miriyam. 2012. Social media, mediation and the Arab revolutions. *tripleC: Communication, Capitalism & Critique: Journal for a Global Sustainable Information Society* 10 (2): 518–536.

Arendt, Hannah. 1958. *The human condition* (2nd edition). Chicago, IL: University of Chicago Press.

Arvidsson, Adam and Elanor Colleoni. 2012. Value in informational capitalism and on the Internet. *The Information Society* 28 (3): 135–150.

Assange, Julian and Slavoj Žižek. 2013. Amy Goodman in conversation with Julian Assange and Slavoj Žižek. In *Beyond WikiLeaks: Implications for the future of communications, journalism and society*, ed. Benedetta Brevini, Arne Hintz and Patrick McCurdy, 254–271. Basingstoke: Palgrave Macmillan.

Atton, Chris. 2004. *An alternative Internet*. Edinburgh: Edinburgh University Press.

Atton, Chris. 2009. Alternative and citizen journalism. In *The handbook of journalism studies*, ed. Karin Wahl-Jorgensen and Thomas Hanitzsch, 265–278. New York: Routledge.

Atton, Chris. 2010 Alternative journalism. In *The Routledge companion to news and journalism*, ed. Stuart Allan, 169–178. Abingdon: Routledge.

Auletta, Ken. 2010. *Googled: The end of the world as we know it*. London: Virgin.

Auray Nicolas, Celine Poudat and Pascal Pons. 2007. Democratizing scientific vulgarisation: The balance between co-operation and conflict in French Wikipedia. *Observatorio Journal* 3: 185–199.

Badiou, Alain. 2008. The communist hypothesis. *New Left Review* 49 (1): 29–42.

Badiou, Alain. 2012. *The rebirth of history: Times of riots and uprisings*. London: Verso.

Ball, Kirstie and Frank Webster. 2003. The intensification of surveillance. In *The intensification of surveillance: Crime, terrorism, and warfare in the information era*, ed. Kirstie Ball and Frank Webster, 1–15. London: Pluto Press.

Barker, Rodney. 1991. Socialism. In *The Blackwell encyclopaedia of political thought*, ed. David Miller and Janet Coleman, 485–489. Malden, MA: Blackwell.

Barnes, Susan. 2006. A privacy paradox: Social networking in the United States. *First Monday* 11 (9).

Barnett, Steven. 2011. *The rise and fall of television journalism: Just wires and lights in a box?* London: Bloomsbury.

Bauwens, Michael. 2003. Peer-to-peer and human evolution. http://economia.unipv.it/novita/seminario/P2PandHumanEvolV2.pdf

Baym, Nancy and danah boyd. 2012. Socially mediated publicness: An introduction. *Journal of Broadcasting & Electronic Media* 56 (3): 320–329.

Beck, Ulrich. 1997. Subpolitics: Ecology and the disintegration of institutional power. *Organization & Environment* 10 (1): 52–65.

Bellman, Steven, Eric J. Johnson, Stephen J. Kobrin and Gerald L. Lohse. 2004. International differences in information privacy concerns: A global survey of consumers. *The Information Society* 20 (5): 313–324.

Benkler, Yochai. 2006. *The wealth of networks*. New Haven, CT: Yale University Press.

Benkler, Yochai. 2011. Networks of power, degrees of freedom. *International Journal of Communication* 5: 721–755.

Benkler, Yochai. 2013. WikiLeaks and the networked fourth estate. In *Beyond WikiLeaks: Implications for the future of communications, journalism and society*, ed. Benedetta Brevini, Arne Hintz and Patrick McCurdy, 11–34. Basingstoke: Palgrave Macmillan.

Bennett, Colin and Charles Raab. 2006. *The governance of privacy*. Cambridge, MA: MIT Press.

Bermejo, Fernando. 2009. Audience manufacture in historical perspective: From broadcasting to Google. *New Media & Society* 11 (1/2): 133–154.

Björklund, Per. 2011. *Arvet efter Mubarak: Egyptens kamp för frihet.* Stockholm: Verbal.

Black, Edwin. 2001. *IBM and the Holocaust: The strategic alliance between Nazi Germany and America's most powerful corporation.* New York: Crown.

Bloustein, Edward J. 1964/1984. Privacy as an aspect of human dignity. In *Philosophical dimensions of privacy*, ed. Ferdinand David Schoeman, 156–202. Cambridge, MA: Cambridge University Press.

Bogard, William. 2006. Surveillance assemblage and lines of flight. In *Theorizing surveillance*, ed. David Lyon, 97–122. Devon: Willan.

Bolin, Göran. 2011. *Value and the media: Cultural production and consumption in digital markets.* Farnham, UK: Ashgate.

Boltanski, Luc and Éve Chiapello. 2005. *The new spirit of capitalism.* London: Verso.

Bourdieu, Pierre. 1986a. *Distinction: A social critique of the judgement of taste.* London: Routledge.

Bourdieu, Pierre. 1986b. The (three) forms of capital. In *Handbook of theory and research in the sociology of education*, ed. John G. Richardson, 241–258. New York: Greenwood Press.

boyd, danah. 2009. "Social media is here to stay . . . Now what?" *Microsoft Research Tech Fest*, Redmond, Washington, DC, February 26. www.danah.org/papers/talks/MSRTechFest2009.html

boyd, danah. 2010. Social network sites as networked publics: Affordances, dynamics, and implications. In *A networked self: Identity, community, and culture on social network sites*, ed. Zizi Papacharissi, 39–58. New York: Routledge.

Brecht, Bertolt. 1932/2000. The radio as an apparatus of communications. In *Brecht on Film & Radio*, ed. Marc Silberman, 41–46. London: Methuen.

Brevini, Benedetta and Graham Murdock. 2013. Following the money: WikiLeaks and the political economy of disclosure. In *Beyond WikiLeaks: Implications for the future of communications, journalism and society*, ed. Benedetta Brevini, Arne Hintz and Patrick McCurdy, 35–55. Basingstoke: Palgrave Macmillan.

Bruns, Axel. 2008. *Blogs, Wikipedia, Second Life, and beyond: From production to produsage.* New York: Peter Lang.

Bunz, Mercedes. 2013. As you like it: Critique in the era of affirmative discourse. In *"Unlike us" reader: Social media monopolies and their alternatives*, ed. Geert Lovink and Miriam Rasch, 137–145. Amsterdam: Institute of Network Cultures.

Burston, Jonathan, Nick Dyer-Witheford and Alison Hearn, eds. 2010. Digital labour. Special issue. *Ephemera* 10 (3/4): 214–539.

Buzby, Anry Lynn. 2010. Socialism. In *Encyclopaedia of political theory*, ed. Mark Bevir, 1295–1301. London: SAGE.

Cabello, Florencio, Marta G. Franco and Alexandra Haché. 2013. Towards a free feder-ated social web: Lorea takes the networks! In *"Unlike us" reader: Social media monop-olies and their alternatives*, ed. Geert Lovink and Miriam Rasch, 338–346. Amsterdam: Institute of Network Cultures.

Calabrese, Andrew and Colin Sparks, eds. 2004. *Toward a political economy of culture*. Lanham, MD: Rowman & Littlefield.

Calhoun, Craig, ed. 1992a. *Habermas and the public sphere*. Cambridge, MA: MIT Press.

Calhoun, Craig. 1992b. Introduction: Habermas and the public sphere. In *Habermas and the public sphere*, ed. Craig Calhoun, 1–48. Cambridge, MA: MIT Press.

Calhoun, Craig. 1995. *Critical social theory*. Cambridge, MA: Blackwell.

Calhoun, Craig, Joseph Gertes, James Moody, Steven Pfaff and Indermohan Virk. 2007. General introduction. In *Classical sociological theory*, ed. Craig Calhoun, Jo-seph Gertes, James Moody, Steven Pfaff and Indermohan Virk, 1–16. Malden, MA: Blackwell.

Cammaerts, Bart. 2008. Critiques on the participatory potentials of web 2.0. *Commu-nication, Culture & Critique* 1 (4): 358–377.

Carpentier, Nico. 2011. *Media and participation. A site of ideological-democratic struggle*. Bristol: Intellect.

Carpentier, Nico and Benjamin de Cleen. 2008. Introduction: Blurring participations and convergences. In *Participation and media production*, ed. Nico Carpentier and Benjamin de Cleen, 1–12. Newcastle: Cambridge Scholars.

Carr, Nicholas. 2009. *The big switch: Rewiring the world, from Edison to Google*. New York: W.W. Norton & Company.

Castells, Manuel. 2000. *End of millennium*. The information age: Economy, society and culture, Volume III (2nd edition). Malden, MA: Blackwell.

Castells, Manuel. 2004. *The power of identity*. The information age: Economy, society and culture, Volume II (2nd edition). Malden, MA: Blackwell.

Castells, Manuel. 2009. *Communication power*. Oxford: Oxford University Press.

Castells, Manuel. 2010a. ¿Quién teme a Wikileaks? *La Vanguardia*, October 30. http://www.lavanguardia.es/internacional/20101030/54062523022/quien-teme-a-wikileaks.html (accessed on August 20, 2011).

Castells, Manuel. 2010b. *The rise of the network society*. The information age: Econ-omy, society and culture, Volume I (2nd edition with a new preface). Malden, MA: Wiley-Blackwell.

Castells, Manuel. 2012. *Networks of outrage and hope: Social movements in the Internet age*. Cambridge: Polity Press.

Castoriadis, Cornelius. 1991. *Philosophy, politics, autonomy*. Oxford: Oxford University Press.

Castoriadis, Cornelius. 1998. *The imaginary institution of society*. Cambridge, MA: MIT Press.

Christensen, Christian. 2011. Discourses of technology and liberation: State aid to net activists in an era of "Twitter revolutions". *The Communication Review* 14 (3): 233–253.

Cleaver, Harry. 1992. The inversion of class perspective in Marxian Theory: From valorisation to self-valorisation. In *Open Marxism* (Vol. 2), ed. Werner Bonefeld, Richard Gunn and Kosmos Psychopedis, 106–144. London: Pluto Press.

Compaine, Benjamin. 2001. Declare the war won. In *The digital divide: Facing a crisis or creating a myth?*, ed. Benjamin Compaine, 315–336. Cambridge, MA: MIT Press.

Couldry, Nick. 2002. *The place of media power.* London: Routledge.

Curran, James. 2002. *Media and power.* London: Routledge.

Curran, James. 2012. Rethinking internet history. In *Misunderstanding the Internet*, ed. James Curran, Natalie Fenton and Des Freedman, 34–65. London: Routledge.

Curran, James and Myung-Jin Park, eds. 2000. *De-westernizing media studies.* Abingdon: Routledge.

Dahlberg, Lincoln. 2001. The Habermasian public sphere encounters cyber-reality. *Javnost (The Public)* 8 (3): 83–96.

Dahlberg, Lincoln. 2004. Net-public sphere research: Beyond the "first phase". *Javnost* 11 (1): 27–44.

Dahlgren, Peter. 2005. The Internet, public spheres, and political communication. *Political Communication* 22 (2): 147–162.

Dahlgren, Peter. 2009. *Media and political engagement.* Cambridge: Cambridge University Press.

Dandeker, Christopher. 1990. *Surveillance, power and modernity: Bureaucracy and discipline from 1700 to present day.* Cambridge: Polity Press.

Dandeker, Christopher. 2006. Surveillance and military transformation: Organizational trends in twenty-first-century armed services. In *Surveillance and visibility*, ed. Kevin Haggerty and Richard Ericson, 225–249. Toronto: University of Toronto Press.

Dean, Jodi. 2005. Communicative capitalism: Circulation and the foreclosure of politics. *Cultural Politics* 1 (1): 51–74.

Dean, Jodi. 2010. *Blog politics.* Cambridge: Polity Press.

Dean, Jodi. 2012. *The communist horizon.* London: Verso.

Deleuze, Gilles. 1995. Postscript on the societies of control. In *Negotiations*, 177–182. New York: Columbia University Press.

Derrida, Jacques. 1994. *Specters of Marx.* New York: Routledge.

Deuze, Mark. 2003. The web and its journalisms. *New Media & Society* 5 (2): 203–230.

Deuze, Mark. 2005. What is journalism? *Journalism* 6 (4): 442–464.

Deuze, Mark. 2007. *Media work.* Cambridge: Polity Press.

Deuze, Mark. 2008. Corporate appropriation of participatory culture. In *Participation and media production*, ed. Nico Carpentier and Benjamin de Cleen, 27–40. Newcastle: Cambridge Scholars.

Deuze, Mark. 2010. Journalism and convergence culture. In *The Routledge companion to news and journalism*, ed. Stuart Allan, 267–276. Abingdon: Routledge.

Donsbach, Wolfgang. 2010. Journalists and their professional identities. In *The Routledge companion to news and journalism*, ed. Stuart Allan, 38–48, xxiii–xliv. Abingdon: Routledge.

Durkheim, Émile. 1982. *Rules of sociological method*. New York: Free Press.

Dwyer, Catherine. 2007. Digital relationships in the "MySpace" generation: Results from a qualitative study. In *Proceedings of the 40th Hawaii International Conference on System Sciences*. Los Alamitos, CA: IEEE Press.

Dwyer, Catherine, Starr Roxanne Hiltz and Katia Passerini. 2007. Trust and privacy concern within social networking sites: A comparison of Facebook and MySpace. In *Proceedings of the 13th Americas Conference on Information Systems*. Redhook, NY: Curran.

Dyer-Witheford, Nick. 1999. *Cyber-Marx: Cycles and circuits of struggle in high-technology capitalism*. Urbana, IL: Universiy of Illinois Press.

Dyer-Witheford, Nick. 2007. Commonism. *Turbulence* 1. http://turbulence.org.uk/turbulence-1/commonism/, accessed on July 3, 2013.

Dyer-Witheford, Nick. 2009. *The circulation of the common*. http://www.globalproject.info/it/in_movimento/nick-dyer-witheford-the-circulation-of-the-common/4797, accessed on July 3, 2013.

Dyer-Witheford, Nick. 2010. Digital labour, species-becoming and the global worker. *Ephemera* 10 (3/4): 484–503.

Eagleton, Terry. 2011. *Why Marx was right*. London and New Haven, CT: Yale University Press.

Eley, Geoff. 1992. Nations, public and political cultures: Placing Habermas in the nineteenth century. In *Habermas and the public sphere*, ed. Craig Calhoun, 289–339. Cambridge, MA: MIT Press.

Elliott, Anthony. 2009. *Contemporary social theory*. London: Routledge.

Engels, Friedrich. 1843/1844. Outlines of a critique of political economy. In *Economic and philosophic manuscripts of 1844 and the Communist Manifesto*, 171–202. Amherst, MA: Prometheus.

Engels, Friedrich. 1886. *Dialectics of nature*. New York: International Publishers.

Enyedy, Edgar and Nataniel Tkacz. 2011. "Good luck with your wikiPAIDia": Reflections on the 2002 Fork of the Spanish Wikipedia. An interview with Edgar Enyedy. In *Critical point of view: A Wikipedia reader*, ed. Geert Lovink and Nathaniel Tkacz, 110–118. Amsterdam: Institute of Network Cultures.

Enzensberger, Hans Magnus. 1970/1997. Baukasten zu einer Theorie der Medien. In *Baukasten zu einer Theorie der Medien. Kritische Diskurse zur Pressefreiheit*, 97–132. München: Fischer.

Ess, Charles. 2009. *Digital media ethics*. Cambridge: Polity Press.

Etzioni, Amitai. 1999. *The limits of privacy*. New York: Basic Books.

Fairclough, Norman. 1995. *Critical discourse analysis: The critical study of language*. London: Longman.

Federal Trade Commission. 2000. *Privacy online: Fair information practices in the electronic marketplace*. www.ftc.gov/reports/privacy2000/privacy2000.pdf, accessed on July 3, 2013.

Feenberg, Andrew. 2002. *Transforming technology: A critical theory revisited*. Oxford: Oxford University Press.

Ferguson, Marjorie and Peter Golding, eds. 1997. *Cultural studies in question*. London: Sage.

Findahl, Olle. 2012. *Swedes and the Internet*. Stockholm: SE.

Fisher, Eran. 2010a. Contemporary technology discourse and the legitimation of capitalism. *European Journal of Social Theory* 13 (2): 229–252.

Fisher, Eran. 2010b. *Media and new capitalism in the digital age: The spirit of networks*. Basingstoke: Palgrave Macmillan.

Fiske, John. 1996. *Media matters*. Minneapolis, MN: University of Minnesota Press.

Fogel, Joshua and Elham Nehmad. 2009. Internet social network communities: Risk taking, trust, and privacy concerns. *Computers in Human Behavior* 25 (1): 153–160.

Foglia, Marc. 2008. *Wikipedia, média de la connaissance démocratique?* Limoges: FYP.

Foster, John Bellamy and Fred Magdoff. 2009. *The great financial crisis: Causes and consequences*. New York: Monthly Review Press.

Foucault, Michel. 1977. *Discipline and punish*. New York: Vintage.

Foucault, Michel. 1980. *Power/knowledge: Selected interviews and other writings, 1972–77*. Brighton: Harvester.

Foucault, Michel. 1994. *Power*. New York: New Press.

Fraser, Nancy. 1992. Rethinking the public sphere. In *Habermas and the public sphere*, ed. Craig Calhoun, 109–142. Cambridge, MA: MIT Press.

Freedman, Des. 2012. Web 2.0 and the death of the blockbuster economy. In *Misunderstanding the Internet*, ed. James Curran, Natalie Fenton and Des Freedman, 69–94. London: Routledge.

Fuchs, Christian. 2003. Structuration theory and self-organization. *Systemic Practice and Action Research* 16 (2): 133–167.

Fuchs, Christian. 2008a. *Internet and society: Social theory in the information age*. New York: Routledge.

Fuchs, Christian. 2008b. Review essay of "Wikinomics: How mass collaboration changes everything", by Don Tapscott and Anthony D. Williams. *International Journal of Communication* 2, Review Section: 1–11.

Fuchs, Christian. 2009a. Information and communication technologies and society: A contribution to the critique of the political economy of the Internet. *European Journal of Communication* 24 (1): 69–87.

Fuchs, Christian. 2009b. *Social networking sites and the surveillance society: A critical case study of the usage of studiVZ, Facebook, and MySpace by students in Salzburg in the context of electronic surveillance.* Salzburg/Vienna: Research Group UTI.

Fuchs, Christian. 2010a. Alternative media as critical media. *European Journal of Social Theory* 13 (2): 173–192.

Fuchs, Christian. 2010b. Grounding critical communication studies: An inquiry into the communication theory of Karl Marx. *Journal of Communication Inquiry* 34 (1): 15–41.

Fuchs, Christian. 2010c. Labor in informational capitalism and on the Internet. *The Information Society* 26 (3): 179–196.

Fuchs, Christian. 2010d. Social networking sites and complex technology assessment. *International Journal of E-Politics* 1 (3): 19–38.

Fuchs, Christian. 2010e. studiVZ: Social networking sites in the surveillance society. *Ethics and Information Technology* 12 (2): 171–185.

Fuchs, Christian. 2011a. Critique of the political economy of web 2.0 surveillance. In *Internet and surveillance: The challenges of web 2.0 and social media*, ed. Christian Fuchs, Kees Boersma, Anders Albrechtslund and Marisol Sandoval, 31–70. New York: Routledge.

Fuchs, Christian. 2011b. *Foundations of critical media and information studies.* New York: Routledge.

Fuchs, Christian. 2011c. How can surveillance be defined? *MATRIZes* 5 (1): 109–133.

Fuchs, Christian. 2012a. Dallas Smythe today – the audience commodity, the digital labour debate, Marxist Political Economy and Critical Theory: Prolegomena to a digital labour theory of value. *tripleC: Communication, Capitalism & Critique: Journal for a Global Sustainable Information Society* 10 (2): 692–740.

Fuchs, Christian. 2012b. Some reflections on Manuel Castells' book *Networks of outrage and hope: Social movements in the Internet age. tripleC: Communication, Capitalism & Critique: Journal for a Global Sustainable Information Society* 10 (2): 775–797.

Fuchs, Christian. 2012c. With or without Marx? With or without capitalism? A rejoinder to Adam Arvidsson and Eleanor Colleoni. *tripleC: Communication, Capitalism & Critique: Journal for a Global Sustainable Information Society* 10 (2): 633–645.

Fuchs, Christian. 2013. *OccupyMedia! The Occupy movement and social media in crisis capitalism.* Alresford: Zero Books.

Fuchs, Christian. 2014. *Digital labour and Karl Marx.* New York: Routledge.

Fuchs, Christian and Wolfgang Hofkirchner. 2005. Self-organization, knowledge, and responsibility. *Kybernetes* 34 (1–2): 241–260.

Fuchs, Christian, Wolfgang Hofkirchner, Matthias Schafranek, Celina Raffl, Marisol Sandoval and Robert Bichler. 2010. Theoretical foundations of the web: Cognition, communication, and co-operation. Towards an understanding of web 1.0, 2.0, 3.0. *Future Internet* 2 (1): 41–59.

Galtung, Johan. 1990. Cultural violence. *Journal of Peace Research* 27 (3): 291–305.

Gandy, Oscar H. 1993. *The panoptic sort: A political economy of personal information.* Boulder, CO: Westview Press.

Gandy, Oscar H. 2009. *Coming to terms with chance: Engaging rational discrimination and cumulative disadvantage.* Farnham, UK: Ashgate.

Gandy, Oscar H. 2011. Consumer protection in cyberspace. *tripleC: Communication, Capitalism & Critique: Journal for a Global Sustainable Information Society* 9 (2): 175–189.

Garnham, Nicholas. 1990. *Capitalism and communication.* London: SAGE.

Garnham, Nicholas. 1992. The media and the public sphere. In *Habermas and the public sphere*, ed. Craig Calhoun, 359–376. Cambridge, MA: MIT Press.

Garnham, Nicholas. 1995/1998. Political Economy and Cultural Studies: Reconciliation or divorce? In *Cultural theory and popular culture*, ed. John Storey, 600–612. Harlow: Pearson.

Garnham, Nicholas. 2000. *Emancipation, the media, and modernity: Arguments about the media and social theory.* Oxford: Oxford University Press.

Garnham, Nicholas. 2011. The political economy of communication revisited. In *The handbook of political economy of communication*, ed. Janet Wasko, Graham Murdock and Helena Sousa, 41–61. Malden, MA: Wiley-Blackwell.

Gauntlett, David. 2011. *Making is connecting: The social meaning of creativity, from DIY and knitting to YouTube and Web 2.0.* Cambridge: Polity Press.

Gaus, Gerald F. 1996. *Justificatory liberalism.* Oxford: Oxford University Press.

Gaus, Gerald and Shane D. Courtland. 2011. Liberalism. In *The Stanford encyclopedia of philosophy (Spring 2011 edition)*, ed. Edward N. Zalta, http://plato.stanford.edu/archives/spr2011/entries/liberalism (accessed on August 20, 2011).

Gerbaudo, Paolo. 2012. *Tweets and the streets: Social media and contemporary activism.* London: Pluto Press.

Ghonim, Wael. 2012. *Revolution 2.0: The power of the people is greater than the people in power. A memoir.* New York: Houghton Mifflin Harcourt.

Giddens, Anthony. 1981. *A contemporary critique of Historical Materialism. Vol. 1: Power, property and the state.* London/Basingstoke: Macmillan.

Giddens, Anthony. 1984. *The constitution of society: Outline of the theory of structuration.* Cambridge: Polity Press.

Giddens, Anthony. 1985. *A contemporary critique of Historical Materialism. Vol. 2: The nation-state and violence.* Cambridge: Polity Press.

Giddens, Anthony. 1987. *Social theory and modern sociology.* Cambridge: Polity Press.

Gillmor, Dan. 2006. *We the media.* Sebastopol, CA: O'Reilly.

Girard, Bernard. 2009. *The Google way: How one company is revolutionizing management as we know it.* San Francisco, CA: No Starch Press.

Gladwell, Malcolm. 2010. Small change: Why the revolution will not be tweeted. *The New Yorker* October: 42–49.

Gladwell, Malcolm and Clay Shirky. 2011. From innovation to revolution: Do social media make protests possible? *Foreign Affairs* 90 (2): 153–154.

Glott, Ruediger, Philipp Schmidt and Rishab Ghosh. 2010. *Wikipedia survey – Overview of results*. www.wikipediastudy.org./docs/Wikipedia_Overview_15March2010-FINAL.pdf, accessed on July 3, 2013.

Golding, Peter and Graham Murdock. 1978. Theories of communication and theories of society. *Communication Research* 5 (3): 339–356.

Golding, Peter and Graham Murdock. 1997a. Introduction: Communication and capitalism. In *The political economy of the media I*, ed. Peter Golding and Graham Murdock, xiii–xviii. Cheltenham: Edward Elgar.

Golding, Peter and Graham Murdock, eds. 1997b. *The political economy of the media*. Cheltenham: Edward Elgar.

Goodwin, Jeff. 2001. *No other way out: States and revolutionary movements, 1945–1991*. Cambridge: Cambridge University Press.

Green, Joshua and Henry Jenkins. 2009. The moral economy of web 2.0. Audience research and convergence culture. In *Media industries: History, theory, and method*, ed. Jennifer Holt and Alisa Perren, 213–225. Malden, MA: Wiley-Blackwell.

Gross, Ralph and Alessandro Acquisti. 2005. Information revelation and privacy in online social networks. In *Proceedings of the 2005 ACM workshop on privacy in the electronic society*, 71–80. New York: ACM Press.

Grossberg, Lawrence. 1995/1998. Cultural Studies vs. Political Economy: Is anybody else bored with this debate? In *Cultural theory and popular culture*, ed. John Storey, 613–624. Harlow: Pearson.

Guattari, Félix and Antonio Negri. 1990. *Comunists like us*. New York: Semiotext(e).

Habermas, Jürgen. 1971. *Knowledge and human interest*. Boston, MA: Beacon Press.

Habermas, Jürgen. 1984. *Theory of communicative action* (Vol. 1). Boston, MA: Beacon Press.

Habermas, Jürgen. 1987. *Theory of communicative action* (Vol. 2). Boston, MA: Beacon Press.

Habermas, Jürgen. 1989a. The horrors of autonomy: Carl Schmitt in English. In *The new conservatism: Cultural criticism and the historians' debate*, 128–139. Cambridge, MA: MIT Press.

Habermas, Jürgen. 1989b. The public sphere: An encyclopedia article. In *Critical theory and society: A reader*, ed. Stephen E. Bronner and Douglas Kellner, 136–142. New York: Routledge.

Habermas, Jürgen. 1989c. *The structural transformation of the public sphere*. Cambridge, MA: MIT Press.

Habermas, Jürgen. 1992. Further reflections on the public sphere and concluding remarks. In *Habermas and the public sphere*, ed. Craig Calhoun, 421–479. Cambridge, MA: MIT Press.

Habermas, Jürgen. 1996. *Between facts and norms*. Cambridge, MA: MIT Press.

Habermas, Jürgen. 2006. Political communication in media society: Does democracy still enjoy an epistemic dimension? The impact of normative theory on empirical research. *Communication Theory* 16 (4): 411–426.

Haggerty Kevin. 2006. Tear down the walls: On demolishing the panopticon. In *Theorizing surveillance*, ed. David Lyon, 23–45. Devon: Willan.

Haggerty, Kevin and Richard Ericson. 2006. The new politics of surveillance and visibility. In *Surveillance and visibility*, ed. Kevin Haggerty and Richard Ericson, 3–33. Toronto: University of Toronto Press.

Hall, Stuart, Chas Critcher, Tony Jefferson, John Clarke and Brian Roberts. 1978. *Policing the crisis: Mugging, the state and law and order*. London: Macmillan.

Hanitzsch, Thomas. 2007. Deconstructing journalism culture. *Communication Theory* 17 (4): 367–385.

Harcup, Tony. 2009. *Journalism: Principles & practice* (2nd edition). London: SAGE.

Hardt, Michael and Antonio Negri. 2000. *Empire*. Cambridge, MA: Harvard University Press.

Hardt, Michael and Antonio Negri. 2009. *Commonwealth*. Cambridge, MA: Belknap Press.

Hardy, Jonathan. 2010. The contribution of critical political economy. In *Media and society*, ed. James Curran, 186–209. London: Bloomsbury.

Hars, Alexander and Shaosong Ou. 2002. Working for free? Motivations for participating in open-source projects. *International Journal of Electronic Commerce* 6 (3): 25–39.

Harvey, David. 2005a. *Spaces of neoliberalization: Towards a theory of uneven geographical development*. Heidelberg: Franz Steiner Verlag.

Harvey, David. 2005b. *The new imperialism*. Oxford: Oxford University Press.

Harvey, David. 2007. *A brief history of neoliberalism*. Oxford: Oxford University Press.

Harvey, David. 2010a. *A companion to Marx's Capital*. London: Verso.

Harvey, David. 2010b. *The enigma of capital*. London: Profile Books.

Harvey, David. 2012. *Rebel cities: From the right to the city to the urban revolution*. London: Verso.

Hayek, Friedrich August. 1948. *Individualism and economic order*. Chicago, IL: University of Chicago Press.

Hayek, Friedrich August. 1988. *The fatal conceit: The errors of socialism*. London: Routledge.

Hegel, Georg Willhelm Friedrich. 1991. *The encyclopaedia logic*. Indianapolis, IN: Hackett.

Held, David. 1980. *Introduction to critical theory*. Berkeley, CA: University of California Press.

Held, David. 2006. *Models of democracy* (3rd edition). Cambridge: Polity Press.

Hier, Sean P. and Josh Greenberg, eds. 2007. *The surveilance studies reader.* Maidenhead: Open University Press.

Hodge, Matthew J. 2006. The Fourth Amendment and privacy issues on the "new" Internet: Facebook.com and MySpace.com. *Southern Illinois University Law Journal* 31: 95–122.

Hofkirchner, Wolfgang. 2002. *Projekt Eine Welt: Kognition – Kommunikation – Kooperation: Versuch über die Selbstorganisation der Informationsgesellschaft.* Münster: LIT.

Hofkirchner, Wolfgang. 2013. *Emergent information: A unified theory of information framework.* Singapore: World Scientific.

Holzer, Horst. 1973. *Kommunikationssoziologie.* Reinbek: Rowohlt.

Holzer, Horst. 1994. *Medienkommunikation.* Opladen: Westdeutscher Verlag.

Hong, Yu. 2011. *Labor, class formation, and China's informationalized policy of economic development.* Lanham, MD: Lexington Books.

Horkheimer, Max. 1947. *Eclipse of reason.* New York: Continuum.

Horkheimer, Max. 2002. *Critical theory.* New York: Continuum.

Horkheimer, Max and Theodor W. Adorno. 2002. *Dialectic of enlightenment.* Stanford, CA: Stanford University Press.

Howe, Jeff. 2008. *Crowdsourcing: Why the power of the crowd is driving the future of business.* New York: Three Rivers Press.

Huws, Ursula. 2003. *The making of a cybertariat: Virtual work in a real world.* New York: Monthly Review Press.

International Monetary Fund. 1997. *Good governance: The IMF's role.* www.imf.org/external/pubs/ft/exrp/govern/govindex.htm (accessed on April 25, 2011).

Jakobsson, Peter and Fredrik Stiernstedt. 2010. Pirates of Silicon Valley: State of exception and dispossession in web 2.0. *First Monday* 15 (7).

Jameson, Frederic. 1988. On Negt and Kluge. *October* 46: 151–177.

Jenkins, Henry. 1992. *Textual poachers: Television fans and participatory culture.* New York: Routledge.

Jenkins, Henry. 2006. *Fans, bloggers, and gamers.* New York: New York University Press.

Jenkins, Henry. 2008. *Convergence culture.* New York: New York University Press.

Jenkins, Henry. 2009. What happened before YouTube? In *YouTube*, ed. Jean Burgess and Joshua Green, 109–125. Cambridge: Polity Press.

Jenkins, Henry, Sam Ford and Joshua Green. 2013. *Spreadable media: Creating value and meaning in a networked culture.* New York: New York University Press.

Jenkins, Henry, Xiaochang Li, Ana Domb Krauskopf and Joshua Green. 2009. *If it doesn't spread, it's dead: Eight parts.* www.henryjenkins.org/2009/02/if_it_doesnt_spread_its_dead_p.html (accessed on August 1, 2011).

Jenkins, Henry, Ravi Purushotma, Margaret Weigel, Katie Clinton and Alice J. Robison. 2009. *Confronting the challenges of participatory culture*. Chicago, IL: MacArthur Foundation.

Jessop, Bob. 2002. *The future of the capitalist state*. Cambridge: Polity Press.

Jessop, Bob. 2008. *State power: A strategic-relational approach*. Cambridge: Polity Press.

Jhally, Sut. 1987. *The codes of advertising*. New York: Routledge.

Jhally, Sut. 2006. *The spectacle of accumulation*. New York: Peter Lang.

John, Nicholas A. 2013. Sharing and web 2.0: The emergence of a keyword. *New Media & Society* 15 (2): 167–182.

Johnson, Deborah G. and Kent A. Wayland. 2010. Surveillance and transparency as sociotechnical systems of accountability. In *Surveillance and democracy*, ed. Kevin D. Haggerty and Minas Samatas, 19–33. New York: Routledge.

Jónsdóttir, Birgitta. 2013. Foreword. In *Beyond WikiLeaks: Implications for the future of communications, journalism and society*, ed. Benedetta Brevini, Arne Hintz and Patrick McCurdy, xi–xvii. Basingstoke: Palgrave Macmillan.

Jullien, Nicolas. 2011. *Mais qui sont les Wikipédiens? Résultats d'études*. http://blog.wikimedia.fr/qui-sont-les-wikipediens-2961 (accessed July 3, 2013)

Juris, Jeffrey S. 2012. Reflections on #occupy everywhere: Social media, public space, and emerging logics of aggregation. *American Ethnologist* 39 (2): 259–279.

Kang, Hyunjin and Matthew P. McAllister. 2011. Selling you and your clicks: Examining the audience commodification of Google. *tripleC: Communication, Capitalism & Critique: Journal for a Global Sustainable Information Society* 9 (2): 141–153.

Kant, Immanuel. 2002. *Groundwork for the metaphysics of morals*. New Haven, CT: Yale University Press.

Karatani, Kojin. 2005. *Transcritique*. Cambridge, MA: MIT Press.

Kellner, Douglas. 1989. *Critical theory, Marxism and modernity*. Baltimore, MD: Johns Hopkins University Press.

Kellner Douglas. 1995 *Media culture: Cultural studies, identity and politics between the modern and the postmodern*. London: Routledge.

Kellner, Douglas. 2009. Toward a critical media/cultural studies. In *Media/cultural studies: Critical approaches*, ed. Rhonda Hammer and Douglas Kellner, 5–24. New York: Peter Lang.

Kinsey, Marie. 2005. Journalism. In *Key concepts in journalism studies*, ed. Bob Franklin, Martin Hamer, Mark Hanna, Marie Kinsey and John E. Richardson, 124–125. London: SAGE.

Knoche, Manfred. 2005. Kommunikationswissenschaftliche Medienökonomie als Kritik der Politischen Ökonomie der Medien. In *Internationale partizipatorische Kommunikationspolitik*, ed. Petra Ahrweiler and Barbara Thomaß, 101–109. Münster: LIT.

Laclau, Ernesto and Chantalle Mouffe. 1985. *Hegemony and socialist strategy*. London: Verso.

Lee, Micky. 2011. Google ads and the blindspot debate. *Media, Culture & Society* 33 (3): 433–447.

Lévy, Pierre. 1997. *Collective intelligence*. New York: Plenum.

Lewis, Kevin, Jason Kaufman and Nicholas Christakis. 2008. The taste for privacy: An analysis of college student privacy settings in an online social network. *Journal of Computer-Mediated Communication* 14 (1): 79–100.

Lindgren, Simon and Ragnar Lundström. 2011. Pirate culture and hacktivist mobilization: The cultural and social protocols of #WikiLeaks on Twitter. *New Media & Society* 13 (6): 999–1018.

Lipietz, Alain. 1995. The post-fordist world: Labour relations, international hierarchy and global ecology. *Review of International Political Economy* 4 (1): 1–41.

Livant, Bill. 1979. The audience commodity: On the "blindspot" debate. *Canadian Journal of Political and Social Theory* 3 (1): 91–106.

Livingstone, Sonia. 2008. Taking risky opportunities in youthful content creation: Teenagers' use of social networking sites for intimacy, privacy and self-expression. *New Media & Society* 10 (3): 393–411.

Lotan, Gilad, Erhardt Graeff, Mike Ananny, Devin Gaffney, Ian Pearce and danah boyd. 2011. The Arab Spring! The revolutions were tweeted: Information flows during the 2011 Tunisian and Egyptian revolutions. *International Journal of Communication* 5: 1375–1405.

Lovink, Geert. 2008. *Zero comments: Blogging and critical internet culture*. New York: Routledge.

Lovink, Geert. 2011. *Networks without a cause: A critique of social media*. Cambridge: Polity Press.

Luhmann, Niklas. 1998. *Die Gesellschaft der Gesellschaft*. Frankfurt/Main: Suhrkamp.

Luhmann, Niklas. 2000. *Die Politik der Gesellschaft*. Frankfurt/Main: Suhrkamp.

Lukács, Georg. 1923/1972. *History and class consciousness*. Cambridge, MA: MIT Press.

Lynd, Staughton. 1965. The new radicals and "participatory democracy". *Dissent* 12 (3): 324–333.

Lyon, David. 1994. *The electronic eye: The rize of surveillance society*. Cambridge: Polity Press.

Macpherson, Crawford Brough. 1973. *Democratic theory*. Oxford: Oxford University Press.

Mandiberg, Michael. 2012. Introduction. In *The social media reader*, ed. Michael Mandiberg, 1–10. New York: New York University Press.

Marcuse, Herbert. 1941. *Reason and revolution: Hegel and the rise of social theory* (2nd edition). London: Routledge.

Marcuse, Herbert. 1941/1998. Some social implications of modern technology. In *Technology, war and fascism*, ed. Douglas Kellner, 39–65. London: Routledge.

Marcuse, Herbert. 1964. *One-dimensional man*. Boston, MA: Beacon Press.

Marcuse, Herbert. 1988. *Negations: Essays in critical theory*. London: Free Association Books.

Marx, Gary T. 2007. Surveillance. In *Encyclopedia of privacy*, ed. William G. Staples, 535–544. Westport, CN: Greenwood Press.

Marx, Karl. 1843a. Critique of Hegel's doctrine of the state. In *Early writings*, 57–198. London: Penguin.

Marx, Karl. 1843b. *Letter to Arnold Ruge*. www.marxists.org/archive/marx/works/1843/letters/43_09-alt.htm

Marx, Karl. 1843c. On the Jewish question. In *Writings of the young Marx on philosophy and society*, 216–248. Indianapolis, IN: Hackett.

Marx, Karl. 1844. *Economic and philosophic manuscripts of 1844*. Mineola, NY: Dover.

Marx, Karl. 1857/1858. *Grundrisse: Foundations of the critique of political economy*. Harmondsworth: Penguin.

Marx, Karl. 1859. A contribution to the critique of the political economy. In *Marx Engels Collected Works (MECW), Volume 29*, 257–417. New York: International Publishers.

Marx, Karl. 1867. *Capital. Volume I*. London: Penguin.

Marx, Karl. 1871. The civil war in France. In *Selected works in one volume*, 237–295. London: Lawrence & Wishart.

Marx, Karl. 1875. Critique of the Gotha programme. In *Selected works in one volume*, 297–317. London: Lawrence & Wishart.

Marx, Karl. 1885. *Capital. Volume II*. London: Penguin.

Marx, Karl 1894. *Capital. Volume III*. London: Penguin.

Marx, Karl. 1997. *Writings of the young Marx on philosophy and society*. Indianapolis, IN: Hackett.

Marx, Karl and Friedrich Engels. 1846. *The German ideology*. Amherst, NY: Prometheus Books.

Marx, Karl and Friedrich Engels. 1848. The communist manifesto. In *Economic and philosophic manuscripts of 1844*, 203–243. Amherst, NY: Prometheus Books.

Marx, Karl and Friedrich Engels. 1968. *Selected works in one volume*. London: Lawrence & Wishart.

Maurer, Hermann, Tilo Balke, Frank Kappe, Narayanan Kulathuramaiyer, Stefan Weber and Bilal Zaka. 2007. *Report on dangers and opportunities posed by large search engines, particularly Google*. Retrieved July 3, 2013 (http://www.iicm.tugraz.at/iicm_papers/dangers_google.pdf).

Maxwell, Richard. 1991. The image is gold: Value, the audience commodity, and fetishism. *Journal of Film and Video* 43 (1/2): 29–45.

Maxwell, Richard and Toby Miller. 2012. *Greening the media*. Oxford: Oxford University Press.

McChesney, Robert. 2008. *The political economy of media*. New York: Monthly Review Press.

McLuhan, Marshall. 2001. *Understanding media*. New York: Routledge.

McQuail, Denis. 2000. *McQuail's mass communication theory* (4th edition). London: SAGE.

McQuail, Denis. 2010. *McQuail's mass communication theory* (6th edition). London: SAGE.

MECW. 1975 et seq. *Marx-Engels-Collected Works*. New York: International Publishers.

Meehan, Eileen. 1984. Ratings and the institutional approach. A third answer to the commodity question. *Critical Studies in Mass Communication* 1 (2): 216–225.

MEGA. 1975 et seq. *Marx-Engels-Gesamtausgabe*. Berlin: Dietz.

Meikle, Graham and Sherman Young. 2012. *Media convergence: Networked digital media in everyday life*. Basingstoke: Palgrave Macmillan.

MEW. 1962 et seq. *Marx-Engels-Werke*. Berlin: Dietz.

Mill, John Stuart. 1965. *Principles of political economy* (2 volumes). London: University of Toronto Press.

Mill, John Stuart. 2002. *On liberty*. Mineola, NY: Dover.

Miller, Toby. 2008. "Step away from the croissant". Media Studies 3.0. In *The media and social theory*, ed. David Hesmondhalgh and Jason Toynbee, 213–230. London: Routledge.

Mills, Charles Wright. 2000. *The power elite*. Oxford: Oxford University Press.

Moglen, Eben. 2003. *The dotCommunist manifesto*. http://emoglen.law.columbia.edu/my_pubs/dcm.html#tex2html2 (accessed July 3, 2013).

Moor, James H. 2000. Toward a theory of privacy in the information age. In *Cyberethics*, ed. Robert M. Baird, Reagan Ramsower and Stuart E. Rosenbaum, 200–212. Amherst, NY: Prometheus Books.

Moore, Barrington. 1984. *Privacy: Studies in social and cultural history*. Armonk, NY: M.E. Sharpe.

Morozov, Evgeny. 2009. The brave new world of slacktivism. http://neteffect.foreignpolicy.com/posts/2009/05/19/the_brave_new_world_of_slacktivism (accessed July 3, 2013).

Morozov, Evgeny. 2010. *The net delusion: How not to liberate the world*. London: Allen Lane.

Morozov, Evgeny. 2013. *To save everything, click here: Technology, solutionism and the urge to fix problems that don't exist*. London: Allen Lane.

Mosco, Vincent. 2004. *The digital sublime*. Cambridge, MA: MIT Press.

Mosco, Vincent. 2009. The *political economy of communication* (2nd edition). London: SAGE.

Mosco, Vincent and Janet Wasko, eds. 1988. *The political economy of information*. Madison, WI: University of Wisconsin Press.

Murdock, Graham. 1978. Blindspots about Western Marxism: A reply to Dallas Smythe. In *The political economy of the media I*, ed. Peter Golding and Graham Murdock, 465–474. Cheltenham: Edward Elgar.

Murdock, Graham and Peter Golding. 1974. For a political economy of mass communications. In *The political economy of the media I*, ed. Peter Golding and Graham Murdock, 3–32. Cheltenham: Edward Elgar.

Murdock, Graham and Peter Golding. 2005. Culture, communications and political economy. In *Mass media and society* (4th edition), ed. James Curran and Michael Gurevitch, 60–83. London: Hodder.

Murthy, Dhiraj. 2013. *Twitter: Social communication in the Twitter age*. Cambridge: Polity Press.

Negri, Antonio. 1991. *Marx beyond Marx: Lessons on the Grundrisse*. London: Pluto Press.

Negt, Oskar and Alexander Kluge. 1972. *Öffentlichkeit und Erfahrung: Zur Organisationsanalyse von bürgerlicher und proletarischer Öffentlichkeit*. Frankfurt/Main: Suhrkamp.

Nissenbaum, Helen. 2010. *Privacy in context*. Stanford, CA: Stanford University Press.

Norris, Clive and Gary Armstrong. 1999. *The maximum surveillance sociey. The rise of CCTV*. Oxford: Berg.

O'Reilly, Tim. 2005a. *What is web 2.0?* www.oreillynet.com/pub/a/oreilly/tim/news/2005/09/30/what-is-web-20.html?page=1 (accessed on February 26, 2013).

O'Reilly, Tim. 2005b. *Web 2.0: Compact definition*. http://radar.oreilly.com/archives/2005/10/web_20_compact_definition.html (accessed on February 26, 2013).

O'Reilly, Tim and John Battelle. 2009. *Web squared: Web 2.0 five years on*. Special report. http://assets.en.oreilly.com/1/event/28/web2009_websquared-whitepaper.pdf (accessed on February 26, 2013).

Orwell, George. 1945. *Animal farm*. Harlow: Heinemann.

Papacharissi, Zizi. 2002. The virtual sphere: The Internet as a public sphere. *New Media & Society* 4 (1): 9–27.

Papacharissi, Zizi. 2009. The virtual sphere 2.0: The Internet, the public shpere, and beyond. In *Routledge handbook of Internet politics*, ed. Andrew Chadwick and Philip N. Howard, 230–245. New York: Routledge.

Papacharissi, Zizi A. 2010. *A private sphere: Democracy in a digital age*. Cambridge: Polity.

Pasquinelli, Matteo. 2009. Google's PageRank algorithm: A diagram of cognitive capitalism and the rentier of the common intellect. In *Deep search: The politics of search beyond Google*, ed. Konrad Becker and Felix Stalder, 152–162. Innsbruck: StudienVerlag.

Pateman, Carole. 1970. *Participation and democratic theory*. Cambridge: Cambridge University Press.

Petersen, Søren Mørk. 2008. Loser generated content: From participation to exploita-tion. *First Monday* 13 (3).

Popper, Karl. 1962a. *The open society and its enemies. Volume 2: Hegel and Marx.* Princeton, NJ: Princeton University Press.

Popper, Karl R. 1962b. Zur Logik der Sozialwissenschaften. *Kölner Zeitschrift für Soziologie und Sozialpsychologie* 14 (2): 233–248.

Qiu, Jack Linchuan. 2009. *Working-class network society. Communication technology and the information have-less in China.* Cambridge, MA: MIT Press.

Quinn, Michael. 2006. *Ethics for the information age.* Boston, MA: Pearson.

Ritzer, George and Nathan Jurgenson. 2010. Production, consumption, prosumption. *Journal of Consumer Culture* 10 (1): 13–36.

Roberts, John Michael and Nick Crossley, eds. 2004a. *After Habermas: New perspec-tives on the public sphere.* Malden, MA: Blackwell.

Roberts, John Michael and Nick Crossley. 2004b. Introduction. In *After Habermas: New perspectives on the public sphere*, ed. Nick Crossley and John Michael Roberts, 1–27. Malden, MA: Blackwell.

Robins, Kevin and Frank Webster. 1999. *Times of the technoculture.* New York: Routledge.

Rule, James B. 2007. *Privacy in peril.* Oxford: Oxford University Press.

Rushkoff, Douglas. 2010. *Program or be programmed: Ten commands for a digital age.* New York: OR Books. Kindle version.

Rushkoff, Douglas. 2013. Unlike – Why I'm leaving Facebook. www.rushkoff.com/blog/2013/2/25/cnn-unlike-why-im-leaving-facebook.html

Ryker, Randy, Elizabeth Lafleur, Chris Cox and Bruce Mcmanis. 2002. Online privacy policies: An assessment of the fortune E-50. *Journal of Computer Information Systems* 42 (4): 15–20.

Sandoval, Marisol. 2009. A critical contribution to the foundations of alternative me-dia studies. *Kurgu-Online International Journal of Communication Studies* 1, www.kurgu.anadolu.edu.tr/dosyalar/6.pdf (accessed on August 20, 2011).

Sandoval, Marisol. 2013. Foxconned labour as the dark side of the information age. Working conditions at Apple's contract manufacturers in China. *tripleC: Communica-tion, Capitalism & Critique* 11 (2): 318–347.

Sandoval, Marisol. 2014. *From corporate to social media? Critical perspectives on cor-porate social responsibility in media and communication industries.* London: Routledge.

Sandoval, Marisol and Christian Fuchs. 2010. Towards a critical theory of alternative media. *Telematics and Informatics* 27 (2): 141–150.

Schmitt, Carl. 1996. *The concept of the political.* Chicago, IL: Chicago University Press.

Schoeman, Ferdinand David, ed. 1984a. *Philosophical dimensions of privacy.* Cambridge, MA: Cambridge University Press.

Schoeman, Ferdinand David. 1984b. Privacy: Philosophical dimensions of the literature. In *Philosophical dimensions of privacy*, ed. Ferdinand David Schoeman, 1–33. Cambridge, MA: Cambridge University Press.

Scholz, Trebor. 2008. Market ideology and the myths of web 2.0. *First Monday* 13 (3).

Scholz, Trebor, ed. 2013. *Digital labor: The Internet as playground and factory*. New York: Routledge.

Sevignani, Sebastian. 2012. The problem of privacy in capitalism and the alternative social networking site Diaspora*. *tripleC: Communication, Capitalism & Critique: Journal for a Global Sustainable Information Society* 10 (2): 600–617.

Sevignani, Sebastian. 2013. Facebook vs. Diaspora: A critical study. In *"Unlike us" reader: Social media monopolies and their alternatives*, ed. Geert Lovink and Miriam Rasch, 323–337. Amsterdam: Institute of Network Cultures.

Shirky, Clay. 2008. *Here comes everybody*. London: Penguin.

Shirky, Clay. 2011a. *Cognitive surplus: How technology makes consumers into collaborators*. London: Penguin.

Shirky, Clay. 2011b. The political power of social media. *Foreign Affairs* 90 (1): 28–41.

Smythe, Dallas W. 1977. Communications: Blindspot of Western Marxism. *Canadian Journal of Political and Social Theory* 1 (3): 1–27.

Smythe, Dallas W. 1981. *Dependency road*. Norwood, NJ: Ablex.

Smythe, Dallas W. 1981/2006. On the audience commodity and its work. In *Media and cultural studies*, ed. Meenakshi G. Durham and Douglas M. Kellner, 230–256. Malden, MA: Blackwell.

Smythe, Dallas W. 1994. *Counterclockwise*. Boulder, CO: Westview Press.

Solove, Daniel J. 2008. *Understanding privacy*. Cambridge, MA: Harvard University Press.

Sparks, Colin. 2001. The Internet and the global public sphere. In *Mediated politics: Communication in the future of society*, ed. W. Lance Bennett and Robert M. Entman, 75–95. New York: Cambridge University Press.

Stanyer, James. 2009. Web 2.0 and the transformation of news and journalism. In *Routledge handbook of Internet politics*, ed. Andrew Chadwick and Philip N. Howard, 201–213. New York: Routledge.

Starke-Meyerring, Doreen and Laura Gurak. 2007. Internet. In *Encyclopedia of privacy*, ed. William G. Staples, 297–310. Westport, CN: Greenwood Press.

Stross, Randall. 2008. *Planet Google*. New York: Free Press.

Stutzman, Frederic. 2006. An evaluation of identity-sharing behavior in social network communities. *iDMAa Journal* 3 (1).

Sullivan, Andrew. 2009. The revolution will be twittered. *The Atlantic*. www.theatlantic.com/daily-dish/archive/2009/06/the-revolution-will-be-twittered/200478/ (accessed July 3, 2013).

Tännsjö, Torbjörn. 2010. *Privatliv*. Lidingö: Fri Tanke.

Tapscott, Don and Anthony D. Williams. 2007. *Wikinomics: How mass collaboration changes everything*. New York: Penguin.

Tavani, Herman T. 2008. Informational privacy: Concepts, theories, and controversies. In *The handbook of information and computer ethics*, ed. Kenneth Einar Himma and Herman T. Tavani, 131–164. Hoboken, NJ: Wiley.

Tavani, Herman T. 2010. *Ethics and technolog: Controversies, questions and strategies for ethical computing*. Hoboken, NJ: Wiley.

Terranova, Tiziana. 2004. *Network culture*. London: Pluto.

Terranova, Tiziana and Joan Donovan. 2013. Occupy social networks: The paradoxes of corporate social media for networked social movements. In *"Unlike us" reader: Social media monopolies and their alternatives*, ed. Geert Lovink and Miriam Rasch, 296–311. Amsterdam: Institute of Network Cultures.

Thompson, Edward P. 1957. Socialist humanism. *The New Reasoner* 1: 105–143. www.marxists.org/archive/thompson-ep/1957/sochum.htm (accessed on August 20, 2011).

Thompson, John B. 1995. *The media and modernity: A social theory of the media*. Cambridge: Polity Press.

Thussu, Daya. 2009. Why internationalize media studies and how? In *Internationalizing media studies*, ed. Daya Thussu, 13–31. Abingdon: Routledge.

Toffler, Alvin. 1980. *The third wave*. New York: Bantam.

Tönnies, Ferdinand. 1988. *Community & society*. New Brunswick, NJ: Transaction Books.

Tufekci, Zeynep. 2008. Can you see me now? Audience and disclosure regulation in online social network sites. *Bulletin of Science, Technology and Society* 28 (1): 20–36.

Turow, Joseph. 2006. *Niche envy: Marketing discrimination in the digital age*. Cambridge, MA: MIT Press.

Vaidhyanathan, Siva. 2011. *The Googlization of everything (and why we should worry)*. Berkeley, CA: University of California Press.

van Dijck, José. 2009. Users like you? Theorizing agency in user-generated content. *Media, Culture & Society* 31 (1): 41–58.

van Dijck, José. 2013. *The culture of connectivity: A critical history of social media*. Oxford: Oxford University Press.

van Dijck, José and David Nieborg. 2009. Wikinomics and its discontents: a critical analysis of web 2.0 business manifestors. *New Media & Society* 11 (5): 855–874.

van Dijk, Teun A. 1993. Principles of critical discourse analysis. *Discourse & Society* 4 (2): 249–283.

van Dijk, Teun A. 1997. The study of discourse. In *Discourse as structure and process*, ed. Teun A. van Dijk, 1–34. London: SAGE.

van Dijk, Teun A. 2011. Discourse and ideology. In *Discourse studies*, ed. Teun van Dijk, 379–407. London: SAGE.

Vise, David A. 2005. *The Google story*. London: Macmillan.

Wacks, Raymond. 2010. *Privacy: A very short introduction*. Oxford: Oxford University Press.

Wall, David S. 2007. *Cybercrime*. Cambridge: Polity Press.

Warren, Samuel and Louis Brandeis. 1890. The right to privacy. *Harvard Law Review* 4 (5): 193–220.

Wasko, Janet. 2004. The political economy of communications. In *The SAGE handbook of media studies*, ed. John Downing, Denis McQuail, Philip Schlesinger and Ellen Wartella, 309–329. Thousand Oaks, CA: SAGE.

Wasko, Janet and Mary Erickson. 2009. The political economy of YouTube. In *The YouTube reader*, ed. Pelle Snickars and Patrick Vonderau, 372–386. Stockholm: National Library of Sweden.

Wasko, Janet, Graham Murdock and Helena Sousa, eds. 2011. *The handbook of political economy of communication*. Malden, MA: Wiley-Blackwell.

Weber, Max. 1978. *Economy and society*. Berkeley, CA: University of California Press.

Westin, Alan. 1967. *Privacy and freedom*. New York: Altheneum.

Wiggershaus, Rolf. 1995. *The Frankfurt school: Its history, theories and political significance*. Cambridge, MA: MIT Press.

WikiLeaks. 2010. *WikiLeaks: About*. www.wikileaks.ch/wiki/WikiLeaks:About (accessed on March 4, 2013).

WikiLeaks. 2011. *What is WikiLeaks?* www.wikileaks.ch/About.html (accessed on March 4, 2013).

Wikimedia Foundation. 2010. *Wikimedia Foundation annual report 2009–2010*. http://upload.wikimedia.org/wikipedia/commons/9/9f/AR_web_all-spreads_24mar11_72_FINAL.pdf (accessed July 3, 2013).

Williams, Raymond. 1983. *Keywords*. New York: Oxford University Press.

Wilson, Christopher and Alexandra Dunn. 2011. Digital media in the Egyptian revolution: Descriptive analysis from the Tahrir data sets. *International Journal of Communication* 5: 1248–1272.

Winner, Langdon. 1980/1999. Do artifacts have politics? In *The social shaping of technology*, ed. Donald MacKenzie and Judy Wajcman, 28–40. Maidenhead: Open University Press.

Winseck, Dwayne. 2011. The political economies of media and the transformation of the global media industries: An introductory essay. In *The political economies of media*, ed. Dwayne Winseck and Dal Yong Jin, 3–48. London: Bloomsbury Academic.

Winseck, Dwayne and Robert M. Pike. 2007. *Communication and empire*. Durham, NC: Duke University Press.

Wright, Erik Olin. 2010. *Envisioning real utopias*. London: Verso.

Zhao, Yuezhi. 2008. *Communication in China*. Lanham, MD: Rowman & Littlefield.

Žižek, Slavoj. 2001. *Did somebody say totalitarianism?* London: Verso.

Žižek Slavoj. 2008. *In defense of lost causes*. London: Verso.

Žižek, Slavoj. 2010. How to begin from the beginning. In *The idea of communism*, ed. Slavoj Žižek and Costas Douzinas, 209–226. London: Verso.

Žižek, Slavoj. 2011. Good manners in the age of WikiLeaks. *London Review of Books* 33 (3). www.lrb.co.uk/v33/n02/slavoj-zizek/good-manners-in-the-age-of-wikileaks#fn-ref-asterisk (accessed on August 20, 2011).

Žižek, Slavoj. 2012a. The revolt of the salaried bourgeoisie. *London Review of Books* 34 (2): 9–10.

Žižek, Slavoj. 2012b. *The year of dreaming dangerously*. London: Verso.

Žižek, Slavoj and Costas Douzinas, eds. 2010. *The idea of communism*. London: Verso.

Zureik, Elia. 2003. Theorizing surveillance. The case of the workplace. In *Surveillance as social sorting*, ed. David Lyon, 31–56. New York: Routledge.

Zureik, Elia. 2010. Cross-cultural study of surveillance and privacy: Theoretical and empirical observations. In *Surveillance, privacy and the globalization of personal information*, ed. Elia Zureik, Lynda Harling Stalker, Emily Smith, David Lyon and Yolane E. Chan, 348–359. Montreal: McGill-Queen's University Press.

Zureik, Elia and L. Lynda Harling Stalker. 2010. The cross-cultural study of privacy. In *Surveillance, privacy and the globalization of personal information*, ed. Elia Zureik, Lynda Harling Stalker, Emily Smith, David Lyon and Yolane E. Chan, 8–30. Montreal: McGill-Queen's University Press.

Index